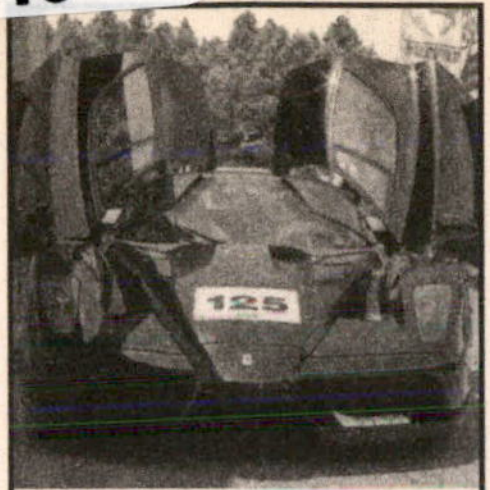

武井宏之

Normal is boring. It's easy to be normal. You just round off your edges and blend like one pebble among the millions on the bank of a stream. But life as a nondescript pebble lacks pizzazz. So who needs normal? These were the thoughts that went through my mind when I saw Enzo Ferrari's sports car.

—*Hiroyuki Takei*

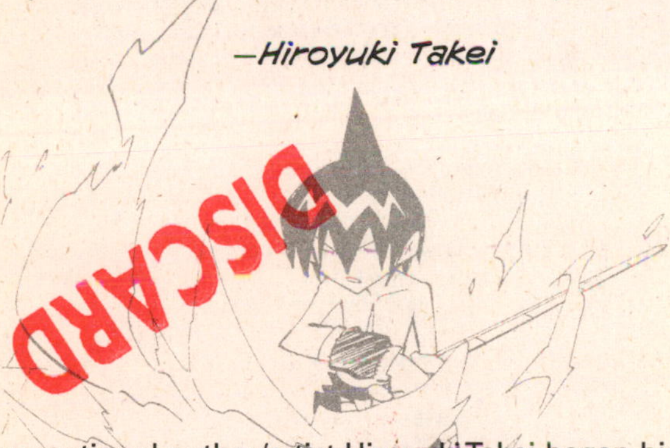

Unconventional author/artist Hiroyuki Takei began his career by winning the coveted Hop Step Award (for new manga artists) and the Osamu Tezuka Award (named after the famous artist of the same name). After working as an assistant to famed artist Nobuhiro Watsuki, Takei debuted in **Weekly Shonen Jump** in 1997 with **Butsu Zone**, an action series based on Buddhist mythology. His multicultural adventure manga **Shaman King**, which debuted in 1998, became a hit and was adapted into an anime TV series. Takei lists Osamu Tezuka, American comics and robot anime among his many influences.

SHAMAN KING VOL. 26
SHONEN JUMP Manga Edition

STORY AND ART BY
HIROYUKI TAKEI

English Adaptation/Lance Caselman
Translation/Lillian Olsen
Touch-up Art & Lettering/John Hunt
Design/Nozomi Akashi
Editor/Eric Searleman

VP, Production/Alvin Lu
VP, Publishing Licensing/Rika Inouye
VP, Sales & Product Marketing/Gonzalo Ferreyra
VP, Creative/Linda Espinosa
Publisher/Hyoe Narita

SHAMAN KING © 1998 by Hiroyuki Takei. All rights reserved.
First published in Japan in 1998 by SHUEISHA Inc., Tokyo.
English translation rights arranged by SHUEISHA Inc.

The rights of the author(s) of the work(s) in this publication
to be so identified have been asserted in accordance with the
copyright, Designs and Patents Act 1988. A CIP catalogue record
for this book is available from the British Library.

The stories, characters and incidents mentioned in this
publication are entirely fictional.

No portion of this book may be reproduced or transmitted
in any form or by any means without written permission
from the copyright holders.

Printed in the U.S.A.

Published by VIZ Media, LLC
P.O. Box 77010
San Francisco, CA 94107

10 9 8 7 6 5 4 3 2 1
First printing, January 2010

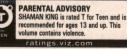

PARENTAL ADVISORY
SHAMAN KING is rated T for Teen and is
recommended for ages 13 and up. This
volume contains violence.
ratings.viz.com

www.viz.com

THE WORLD'S
MOST POPULAR MANGA

www.shonenjump.com

SHONEN JUMP MANGA

Shaman King

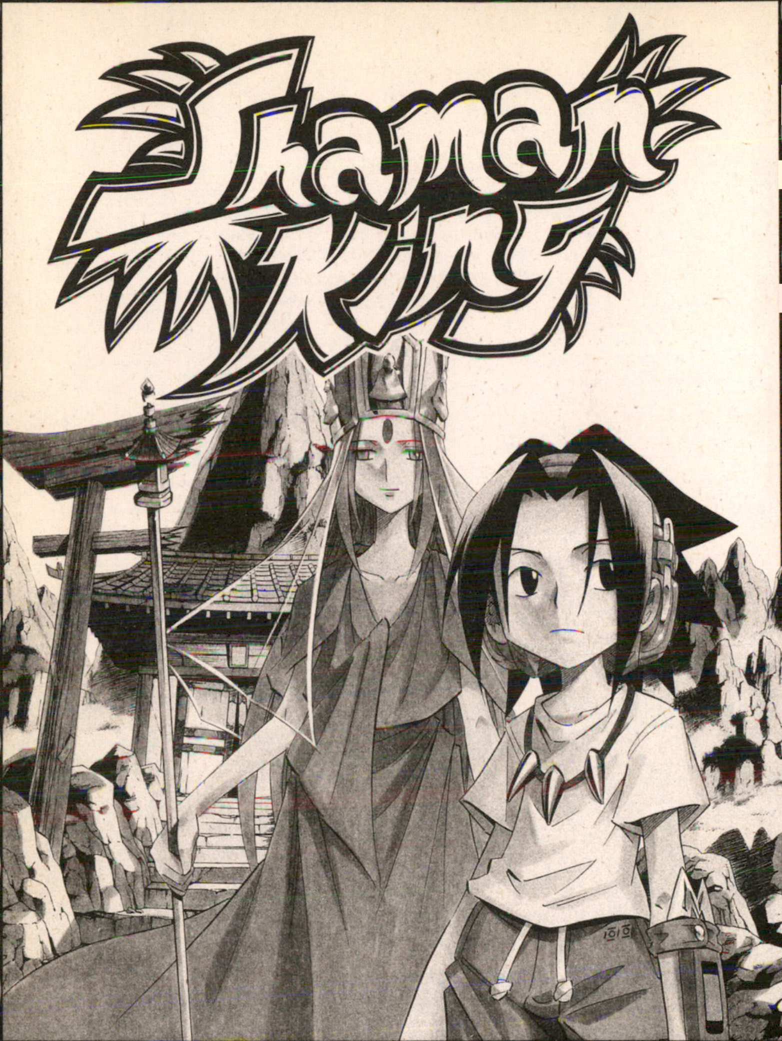

VOL. 26
THE BROTHER'S NOSE

STORY AND ART BY
HIROYUKI TAKEI

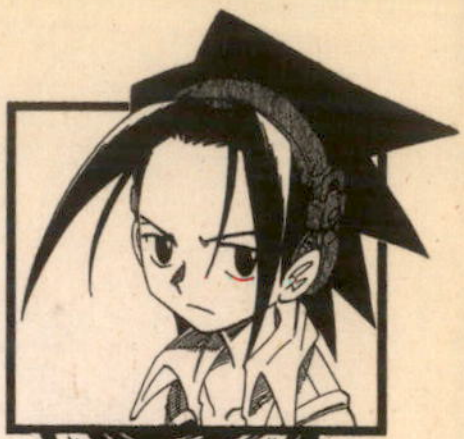

Yoh Asakura
Outwardly carefree and easygoing, Yoh bears a great responsibility as heir to a long line of Japanese shamans.

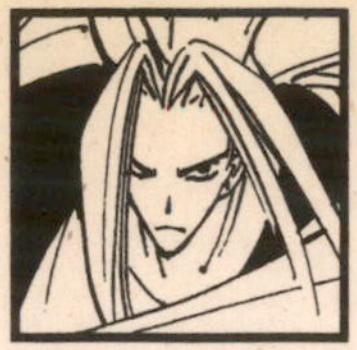

Amidamaru
"The Fiend"
Amidamaru was, in life, a samurai of such skill and ferocity that he was a veritable one-man army. Now he is Yoh's loyal, and formidable, spirit ally.

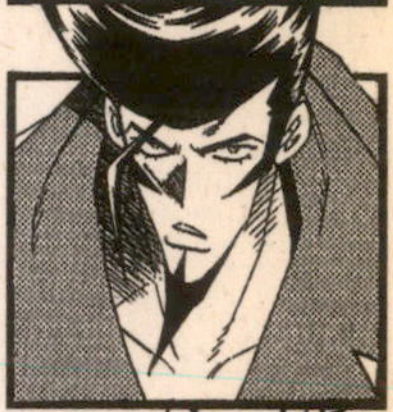

"Wooden Sword" Ryu
On a quest to find his Happy Place. Along the way, he became a shaman.

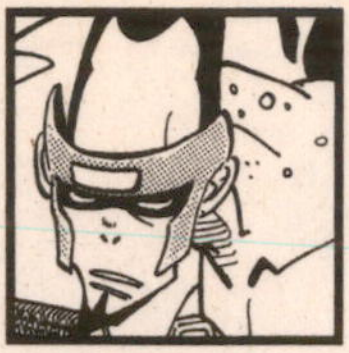

Tokagero
The ghost of a bandit slain by Amidamaru. He is now Ryu's spirit ally.

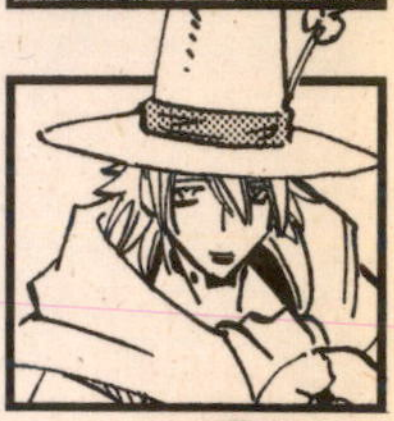

Faust VIII
A creepy German doctor and necromancer who is now Yoh's ally.

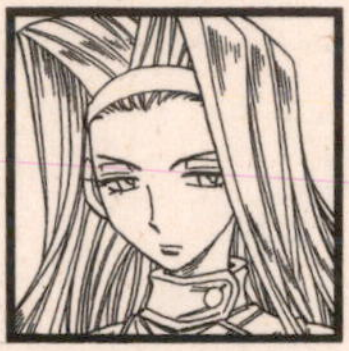

Eliza
Faust's late wife.

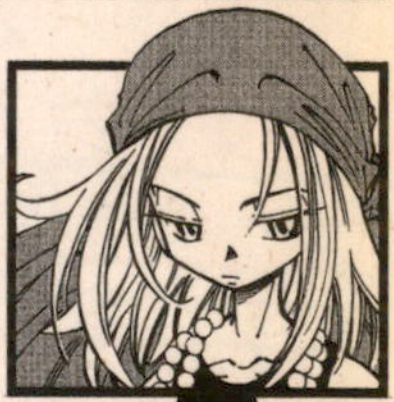

Anna Kyoyama
Yoh's butt-kicking fiancée. Anna is an itako, a traditional Japanese village shaman.

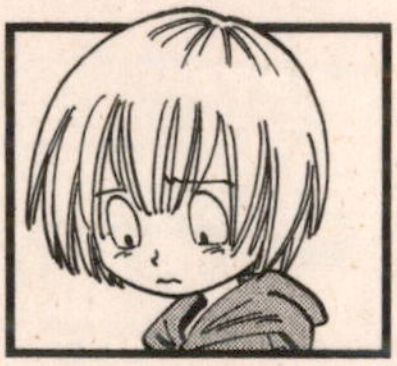

Manta Oyamada
A high-strung boy with a huge dictionary. He has enough sixth sense to see ghosts, but not enough to control them.

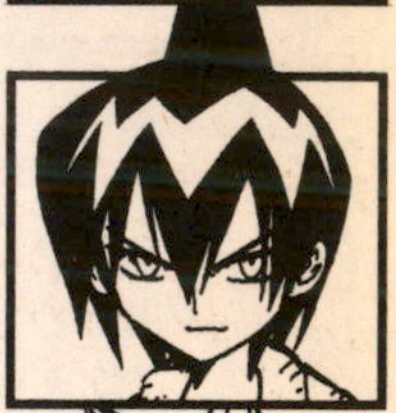

Tao Ren
A powerful shaman and the scion of the ruthless Tao Family.

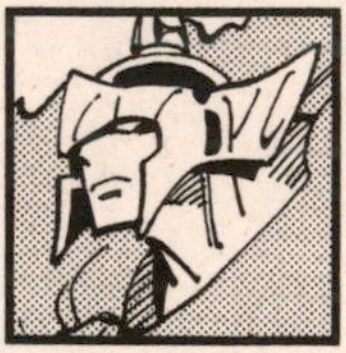

Bason
Ren's spirit ally is the ghost of a fearsome warlord from ancient China.

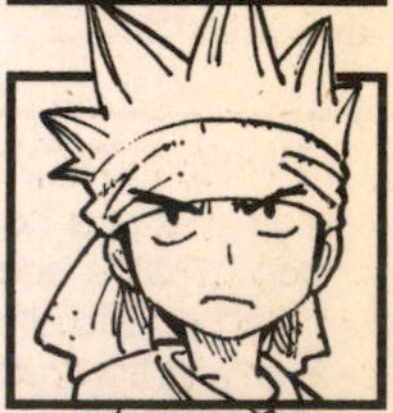

Horohoro
An Ainu shaman whose Over Soul looks like a snowboard.

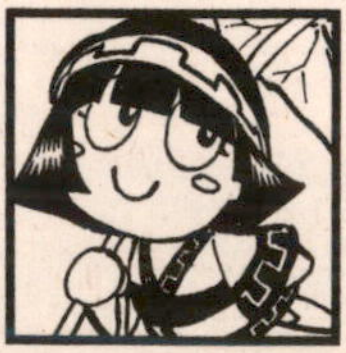

Kororo
Horohoro's spirit ally is one of the little nature spirits that the Ainu call Koropokkur.

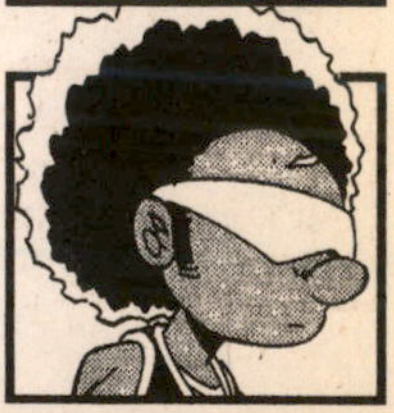

Joco
A shaman who uses humor as a weapon. Or tries to.

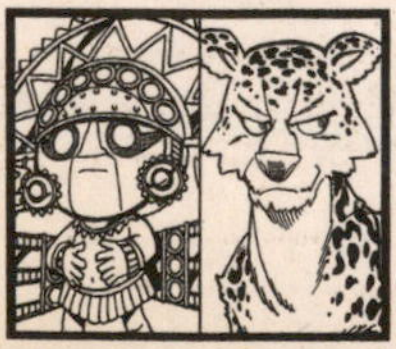

Mic & Pascual Abaj
Joco's jaguar spirit ally and the ghost of an Indio shaman.

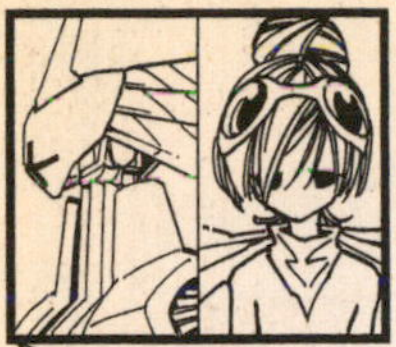

Morphea & Zeruel
Lyserg's poppy fairy and his new Angel.

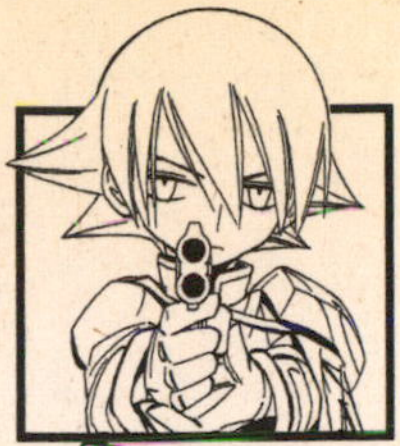

Lyserg
A young shaman with a vendetta against Hao.

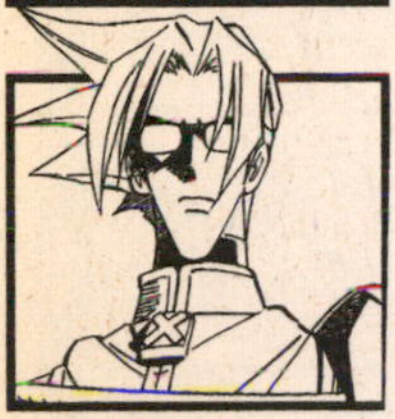

Marco
A former leader of the X-LAWS.

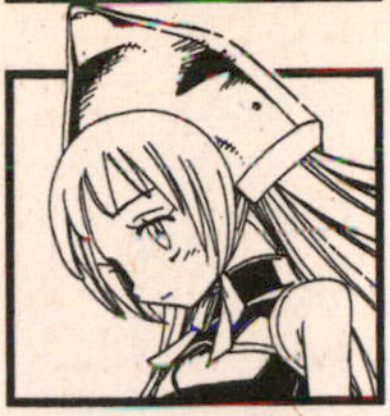

Jeanne, the Iron Maiden
The nominal leader of the X-LAWS. Spends most of her time in a medieval torture cabinet.

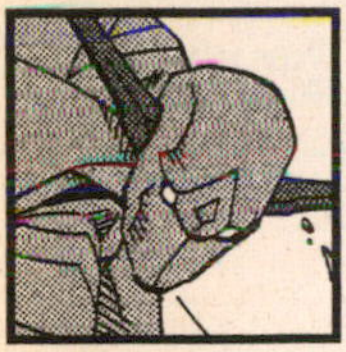

Spirit of Fire
One of the five High Spirits, and Hao's spirit ally.

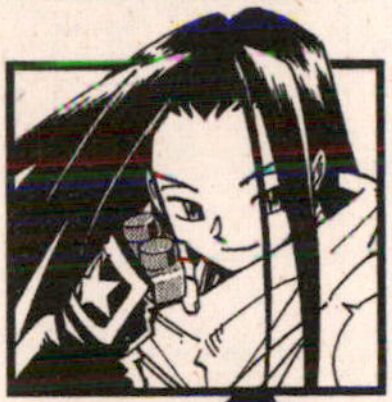

Hao
An enigmatic figure who calls himself the "Future King."

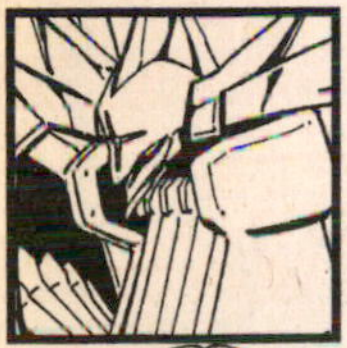

Lucifer
The first Angel, controlled by Luchist.

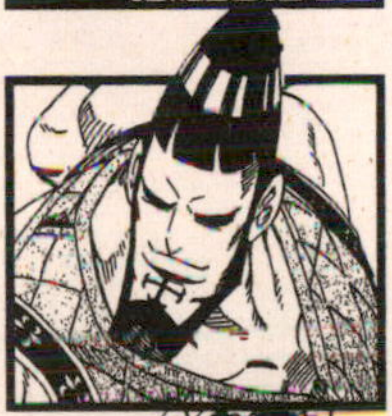

Luchist
The founder of the X-LAWS who now wants to destroy them for his master, Hao.

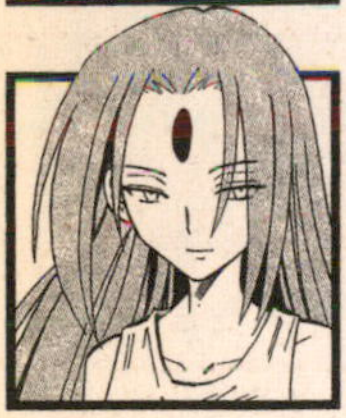

Sati
The leader of Gandala, who brought Ryu and Joco back from death.

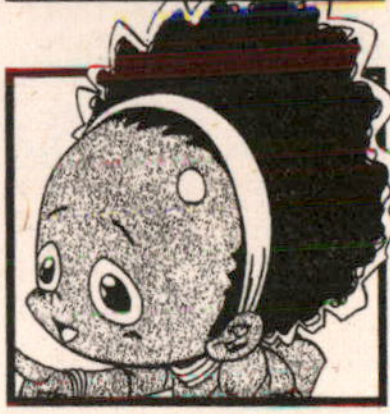

Opacho
One of Hao's most faithful minions, Opacho has the ability to see the future.

THE STORY THUS FAR

Yoh Asakura not only sees dead people, he talks and fights with them, too. That's because Yoh is a shaman, a traditional holy man able to interact with the spirit world. Yoh is now a competitor in the Shaman Fight, a tournament held every 500 years to decide who will become the Shaman King and shape humanity's future.

Luchist, one of Hao's minions, tries to destroy the X-LAWS, who only survive thanks to Lyserg's quick thinking. Now the tournament resumes with Team Ren facing god-wielding Gandala. And when Ren and Joco are beaten, Horohoro is left to fight alone! But there is more to the cocky young Ainu than meets the eye.

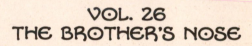

SHAMAN KING 26

「兄の鼻」

目 次

VOL. 26
THE BROTHER'S NOSE

CONTENTS

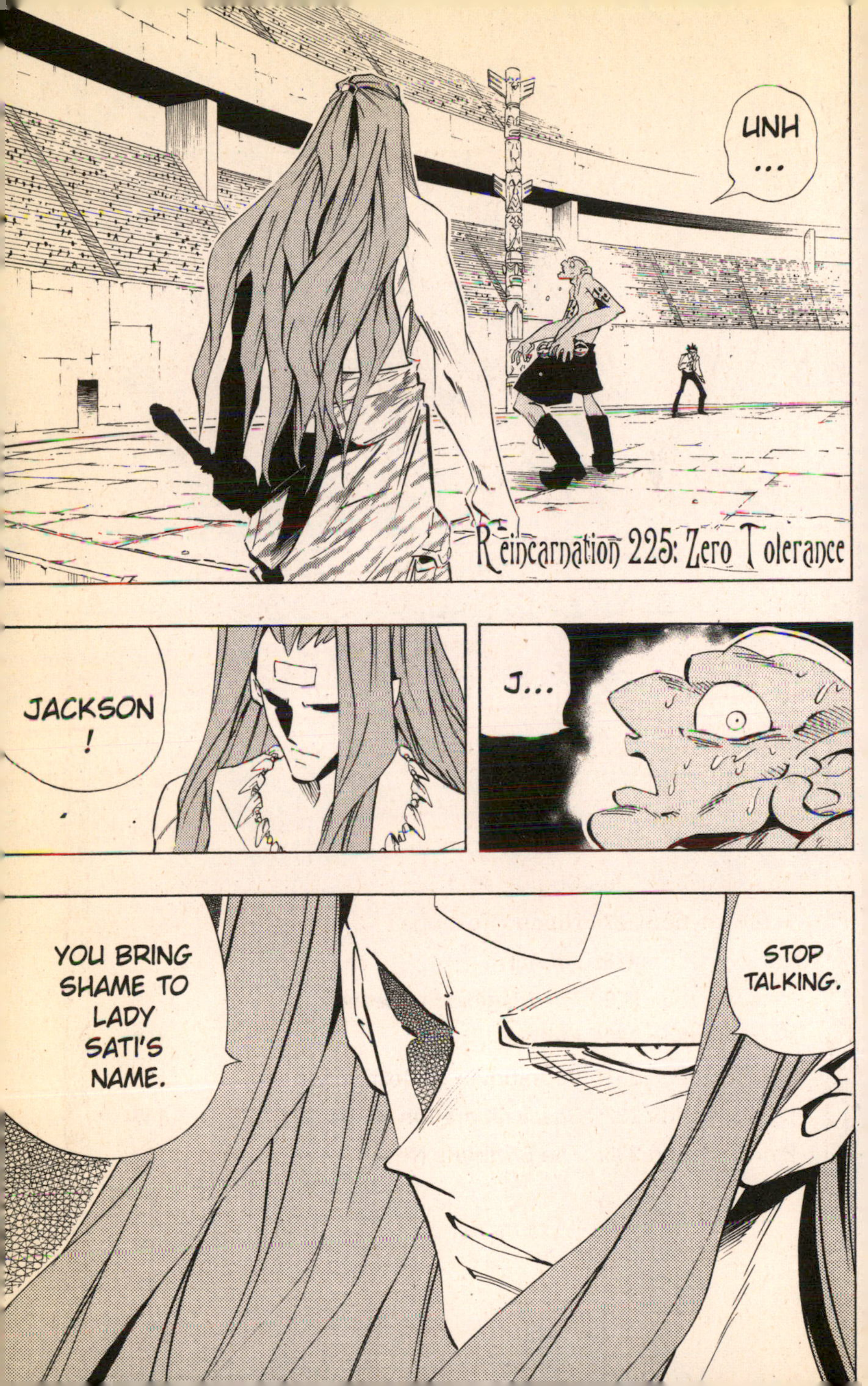
UNH ...
Reincarnation 225: Zero Tolerance
J...
JACKSON!
STOP TALKING.
YOU BRING SHAME TO LADY SATI'S NAME.

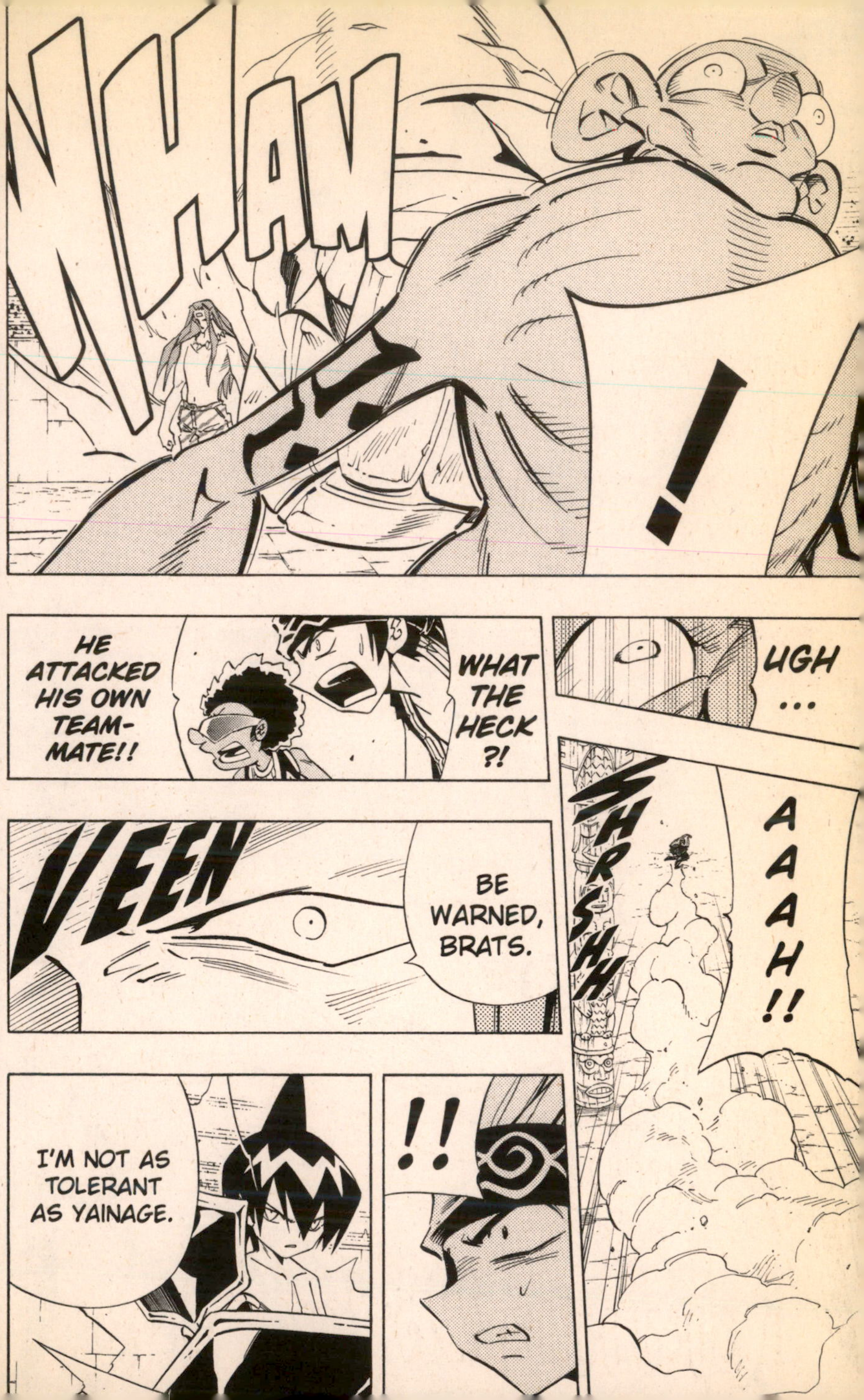
WHAM
!
UGH...
SHRSHH
AAAAH!!
WHAT THE HECK?!
HE ATTACKED HIS OWN TEAM-MATE!!
VEEN
BE WARNED, BRATS.
!!
I'M NOT AS TOLERANT AS YAINAGE.

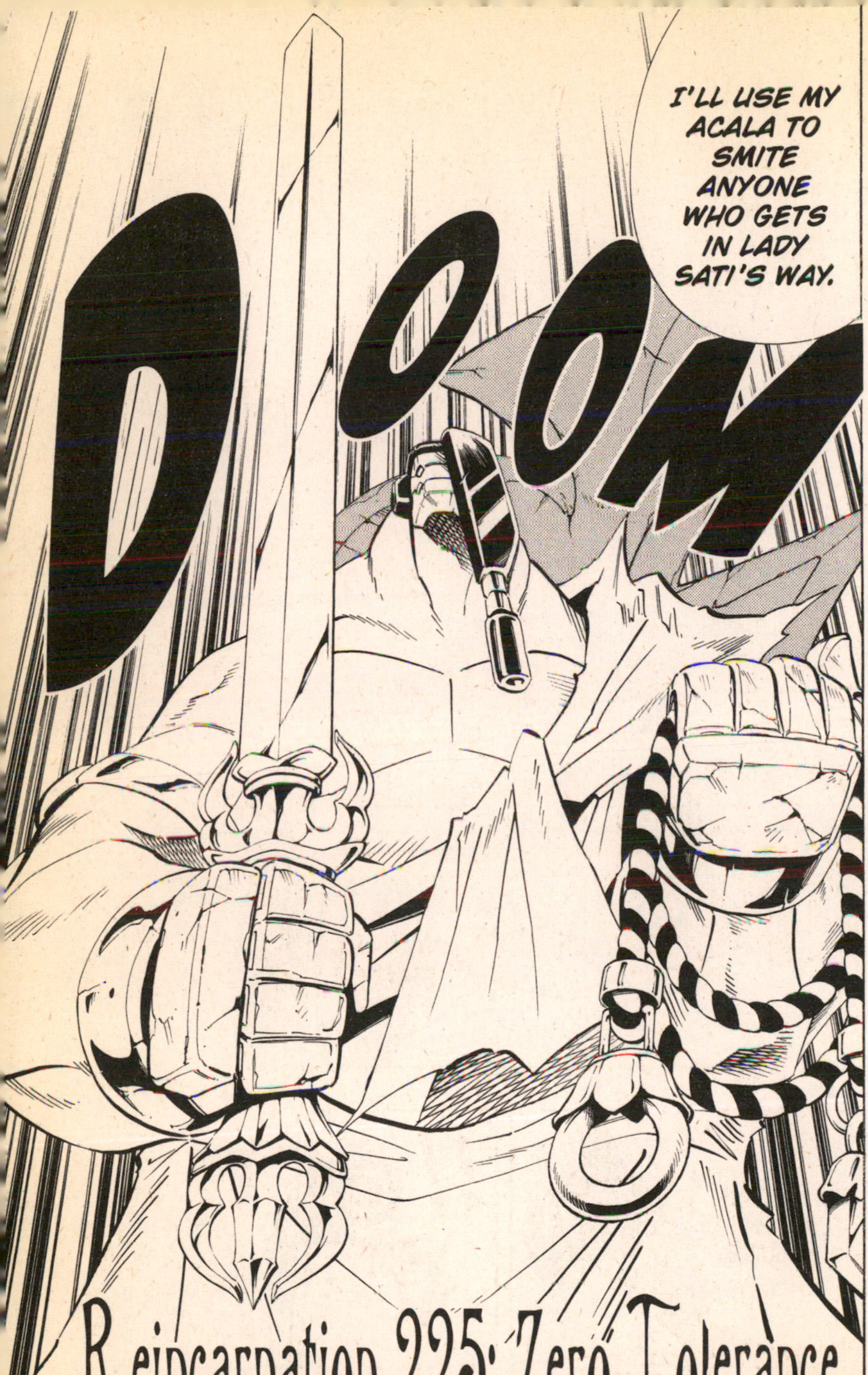
DOOM
I'LL USE MY ACALA TO SMITE ANYONE WHO GETS IN LADY SATI'S WAY.

Reincarnation 225: Zero Tolerance

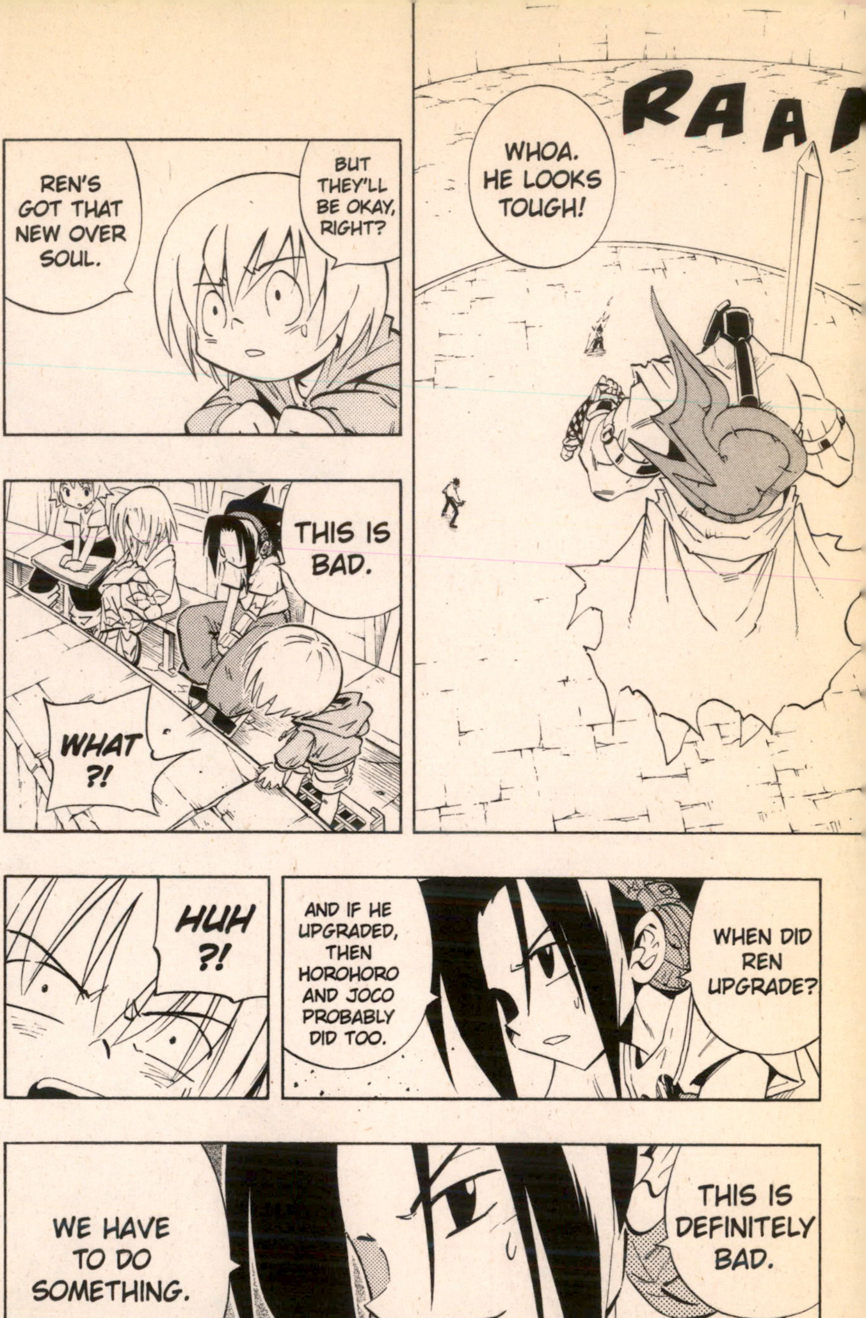
RAA
WHOA. HE LOOKS TOUGH!
BUT THEY'LL BE OKAY, RIGHT?
REN'S GOT THAT NEW OVER SOUL.
THIS IS BAD.
WHAT ?!
WHEN DID REN UPGRADE?
AND IF HE UPGRADED, THEN HOROHORO AND JOCO PROBABLY DID TOO.
HUH ?!
THIS IS DEFINITELY BAD.
WE HAVE TO DO SOMETHING.

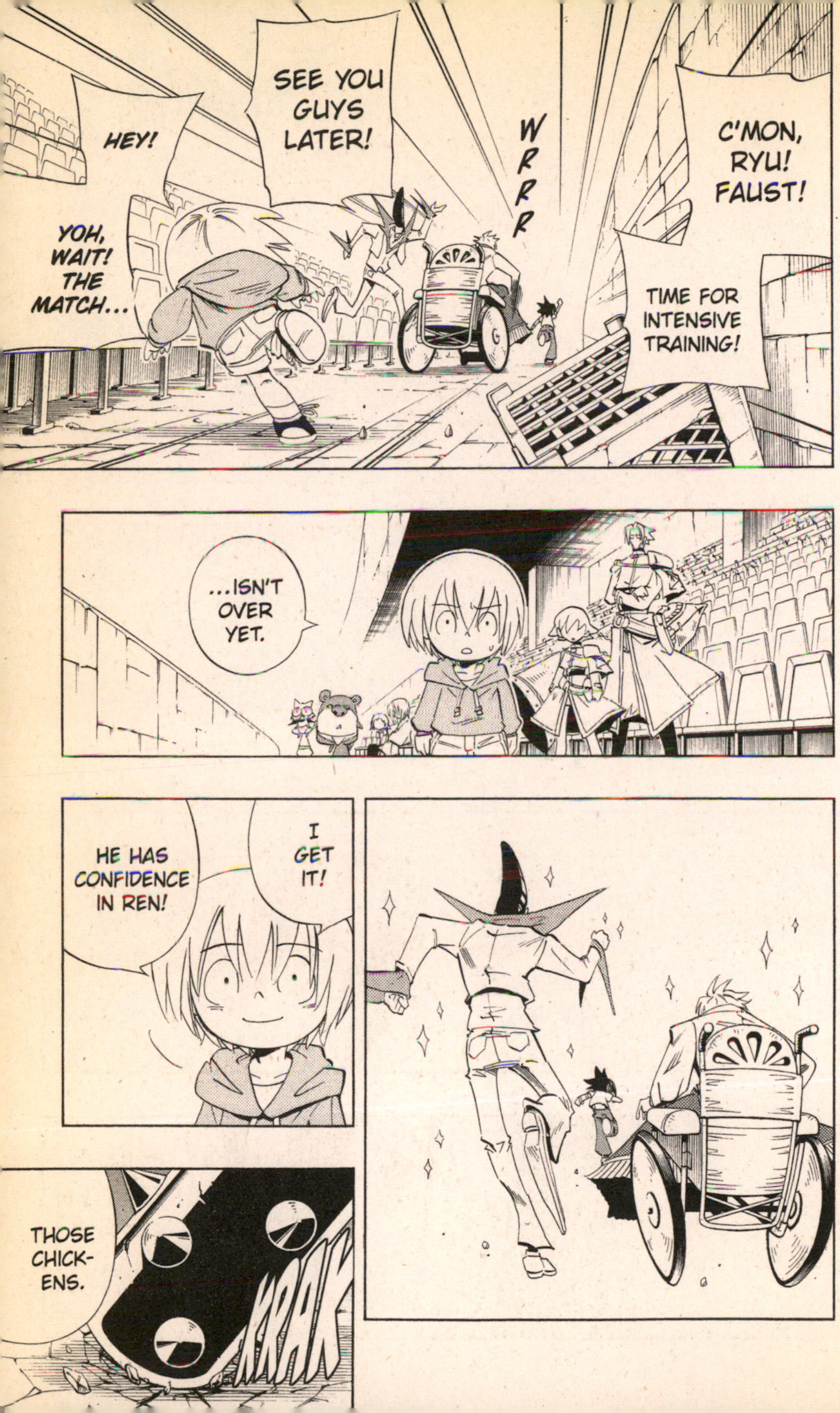
C'MON, RYU! FAUST!
TIME FOR INTENSIVE TRAINING!
WRRR
SEE YOU GUYS LATER!
HEY!
YOH, WAIT! THE MATCH...
...ISN'T OVER YET.
I GET IT!
HE HAS CONFIDENCE IN REN!
THOSE CHICK- ENS.
KRAK

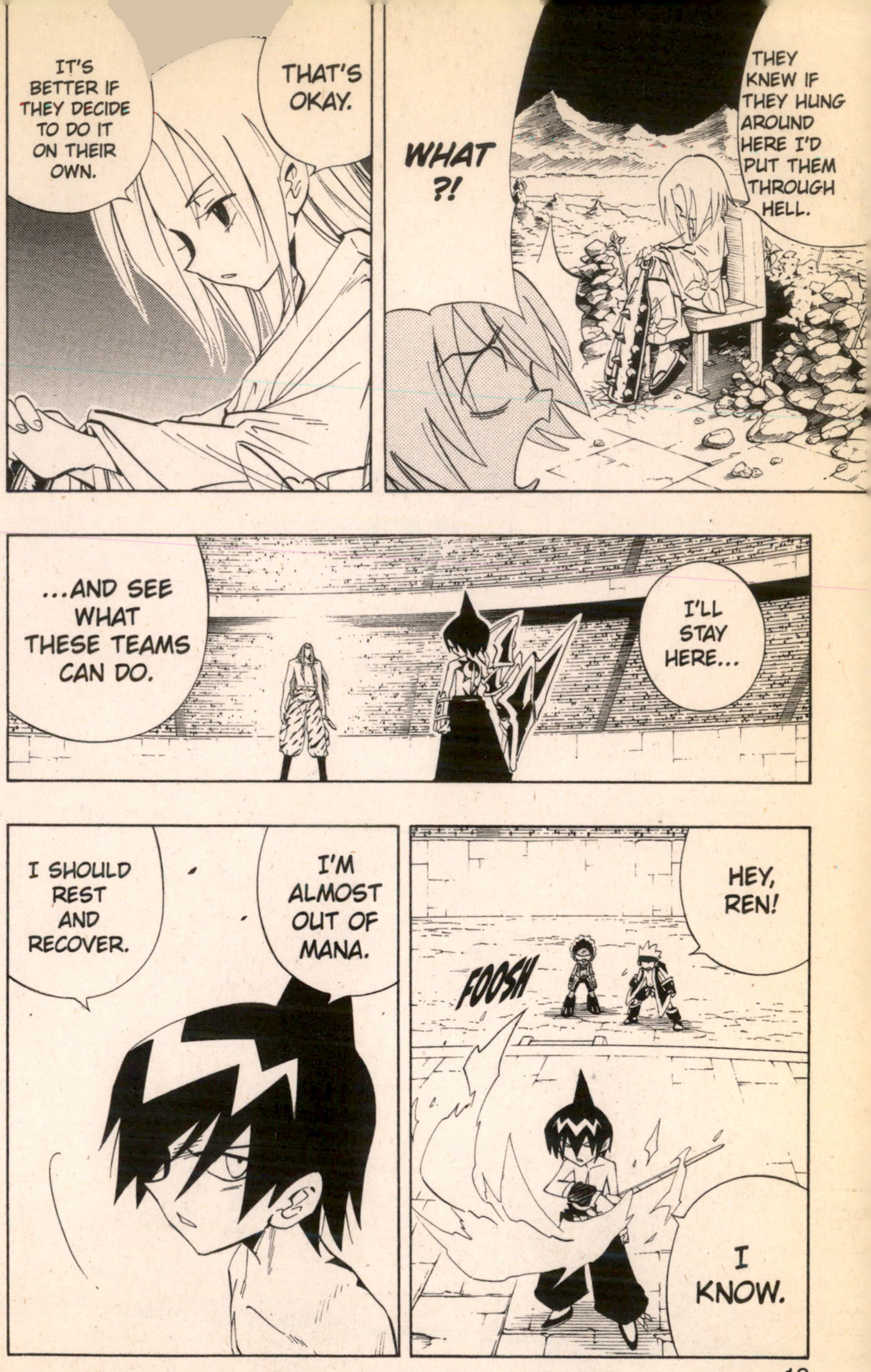
THEY KNEW IF THEY HUNG AROUND HERE I'D PUT THEM THROUGH HELL.
WHAT?!
THAT'S OKAY.
IT'S BETTER IF THEY DECIDE TO DO IT ON THEIR OWN.
I'LL STAY HERE...
...AND SEE WHAT THESE TEAMS CAN DO.
HEY, REN!
FOOSH
I KNOW.
I'M ALMOST OUT OF MANA.
I SHOULD REST AND RECOVER.

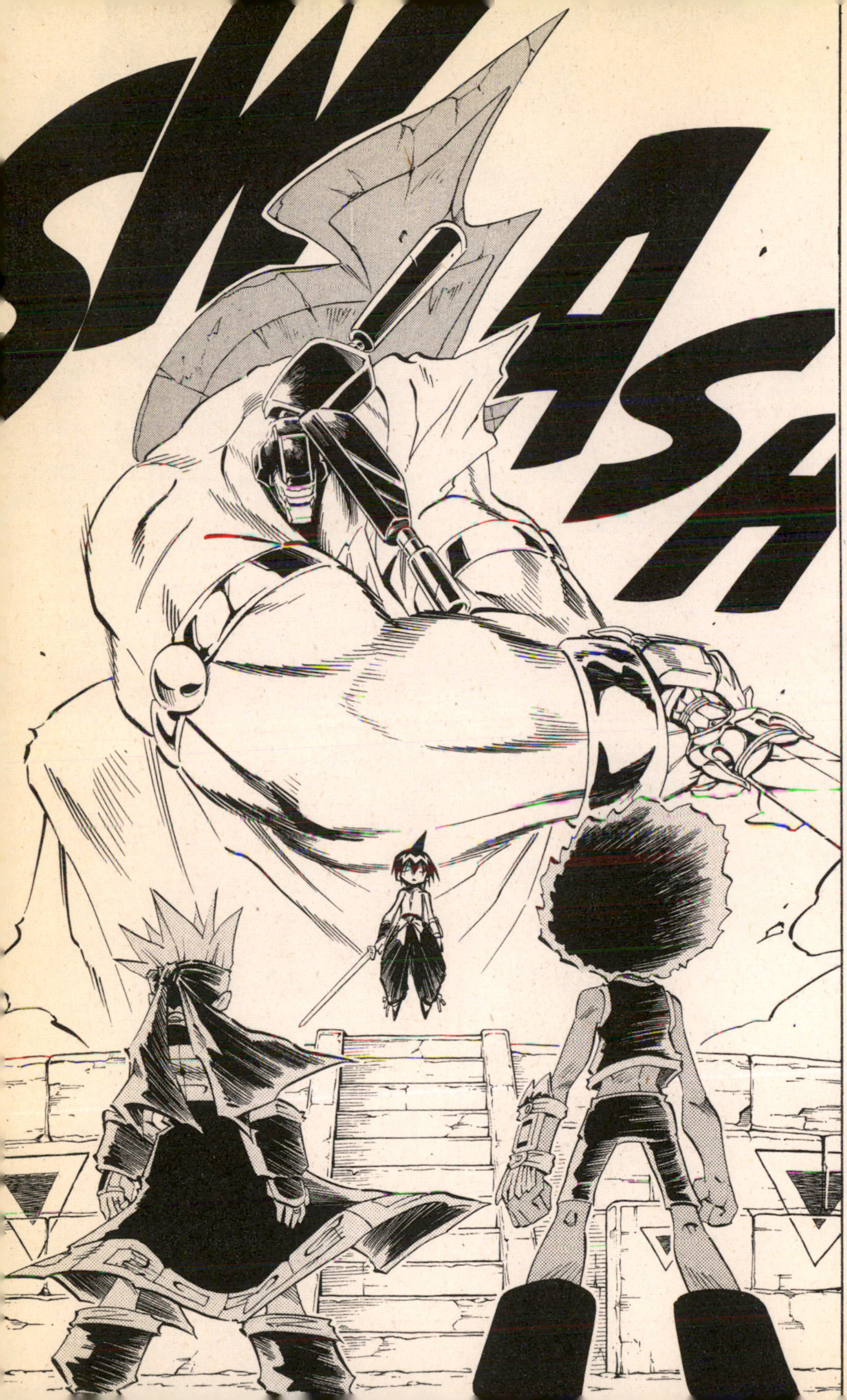
SWASH

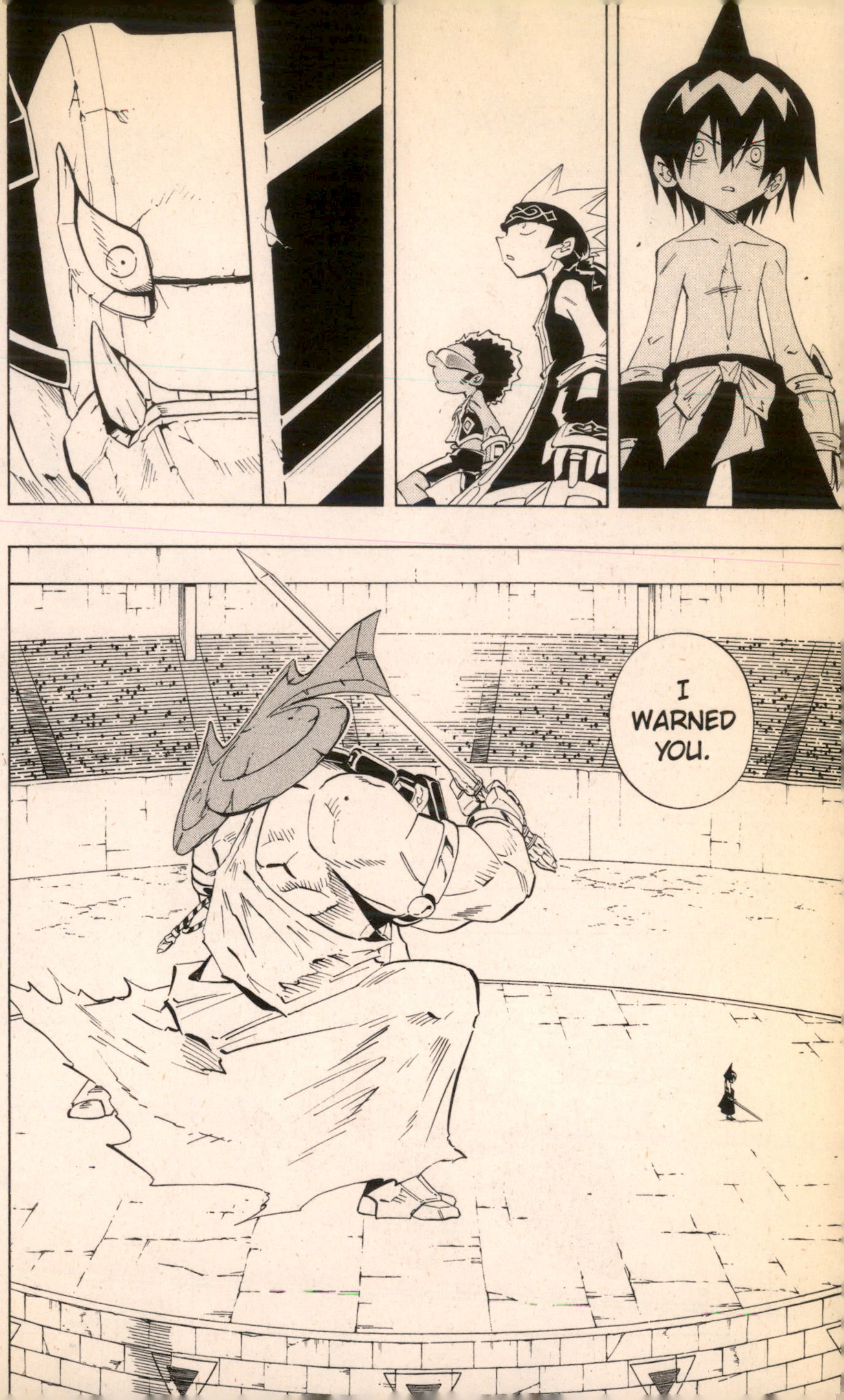
I WARNED YOU.

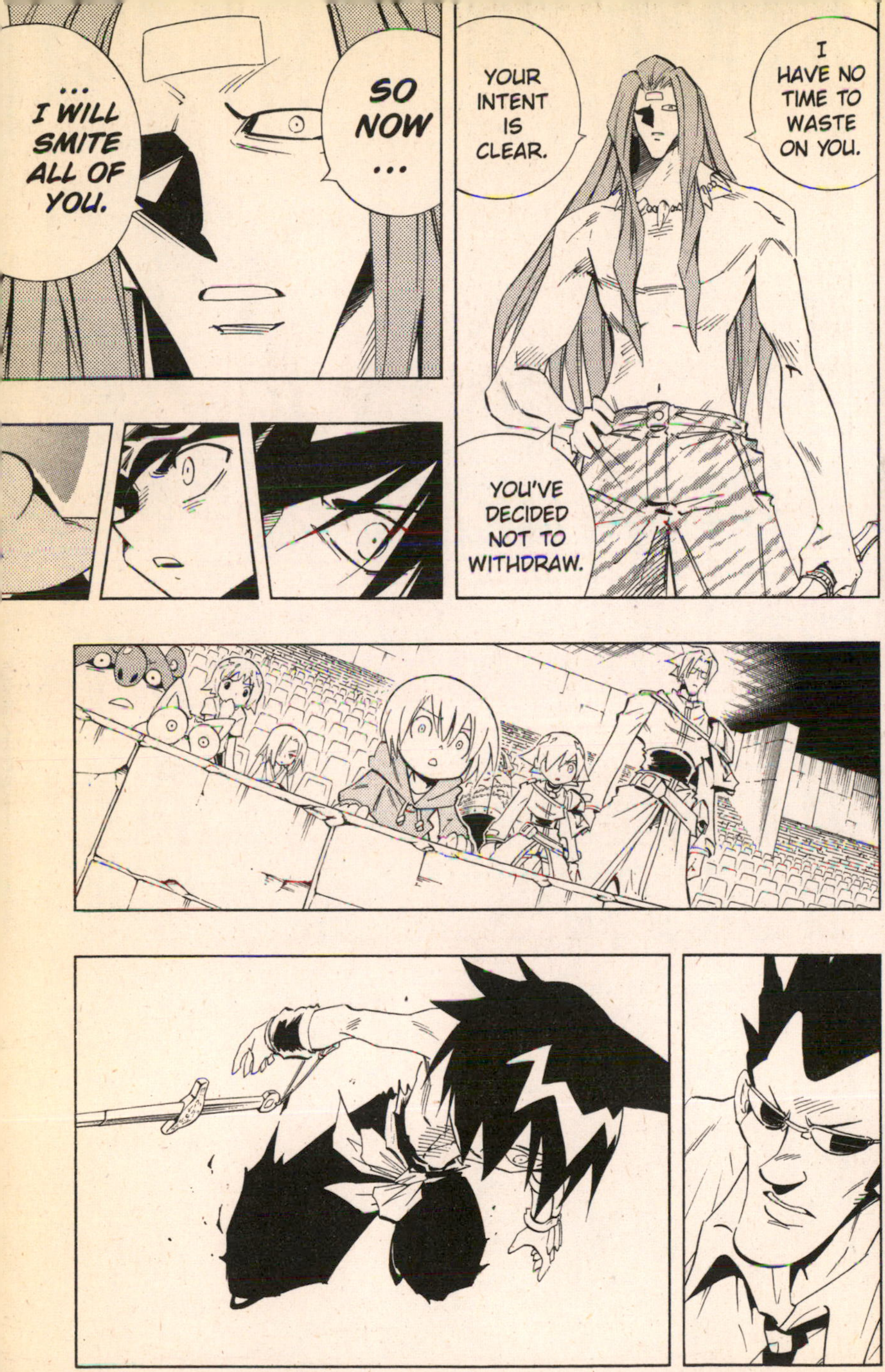
I HAVE NO TIME TO WASTE ON YOU.
YOUR INTENT IS CLEAR.
YOU'VE DECIDED NOT TO WITHDRAW.
SO NOW...
... I WILL SMITE ALL OF YOU.

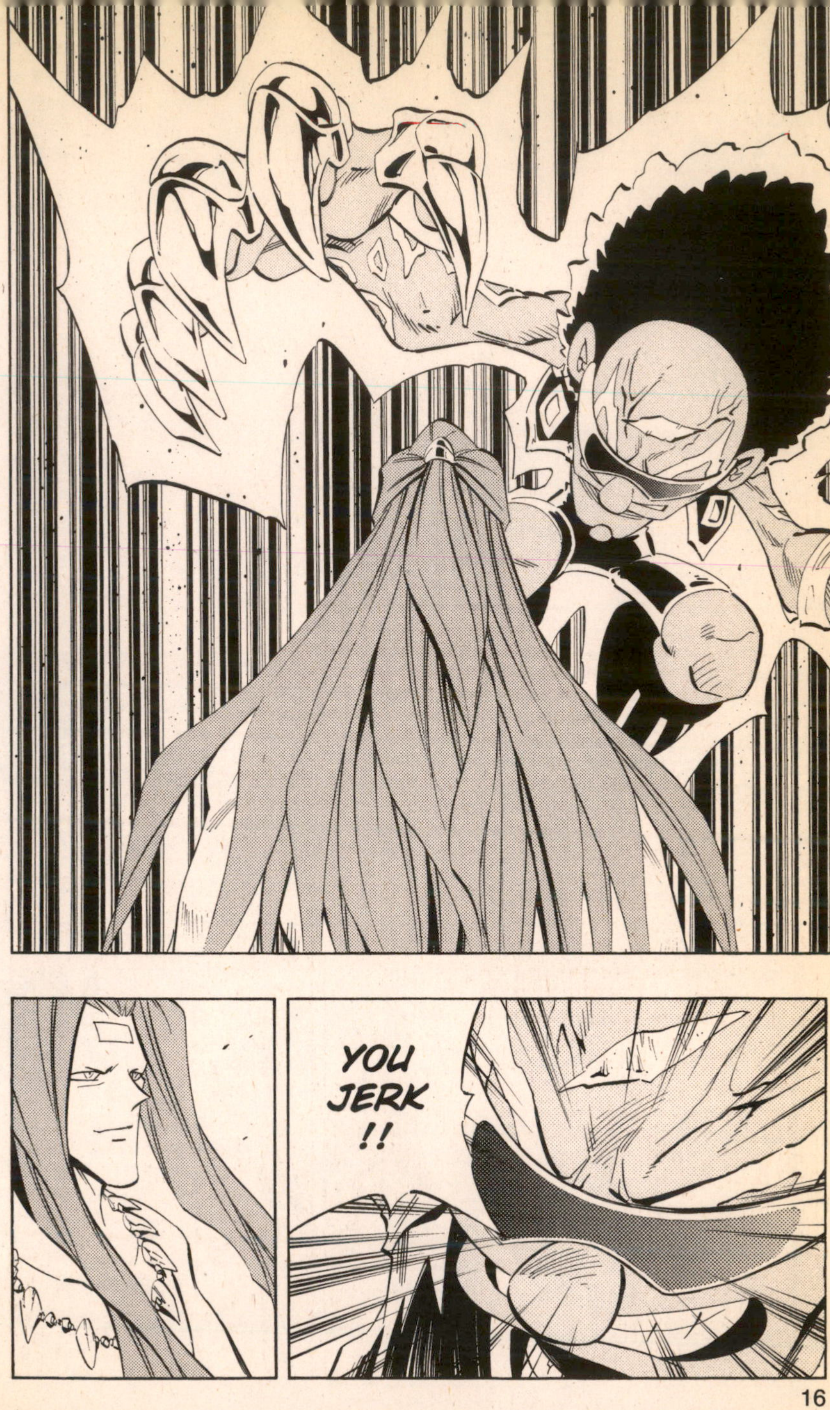
YOU JERK !!

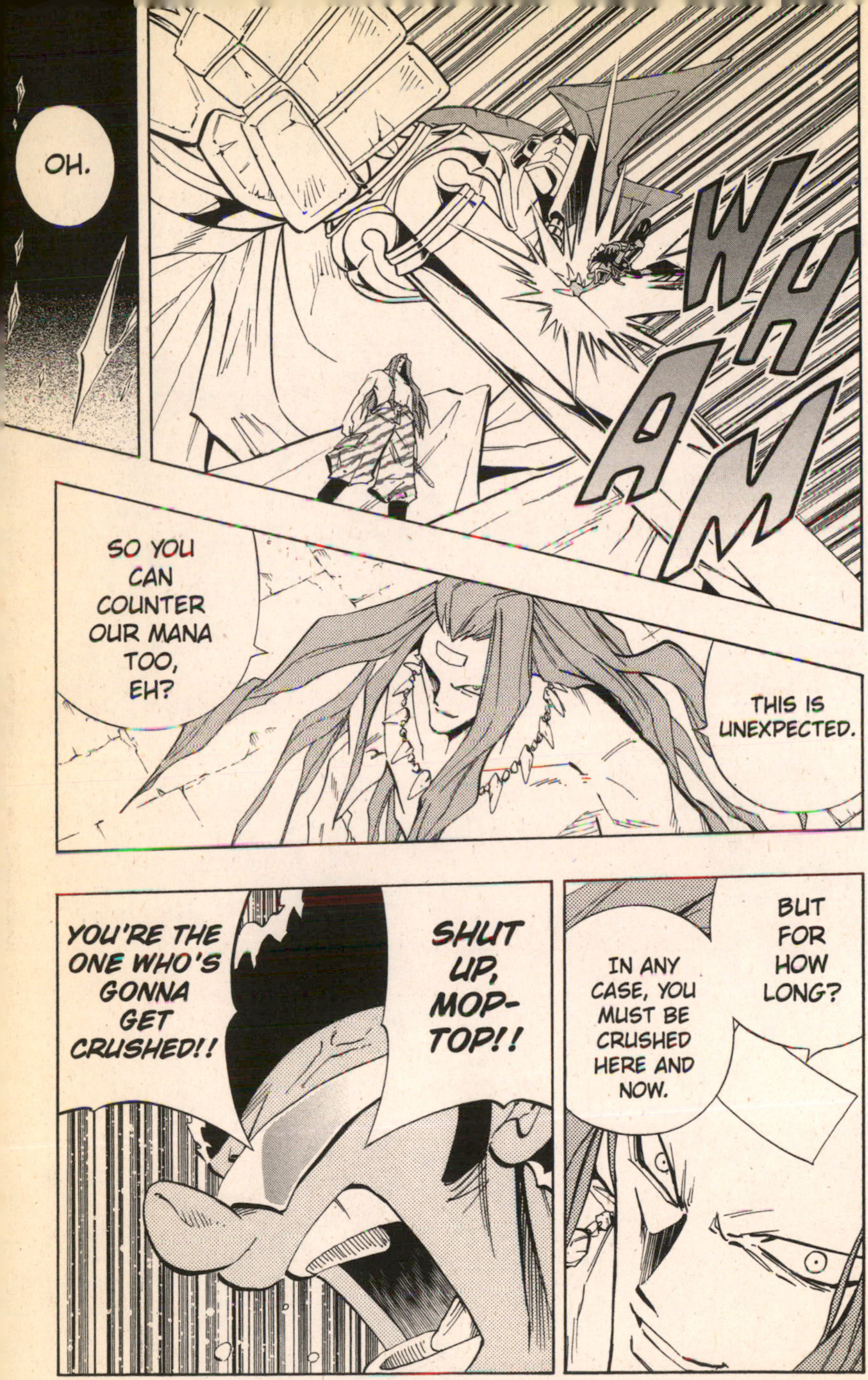
WHAM
OH.
SO YOU CAN COUNTER OUR MANA TOO, EH?
THIS IS UNEXPECTED.
BUT FOR HOW LONG?
IN ANY CASE, YOU MUST BE CRUSHED HERE AND NOW.
SHUT UP, MOP-TOP!!
YOU'RE THE ONE WHO'S GONNA GET CRUSHED!!

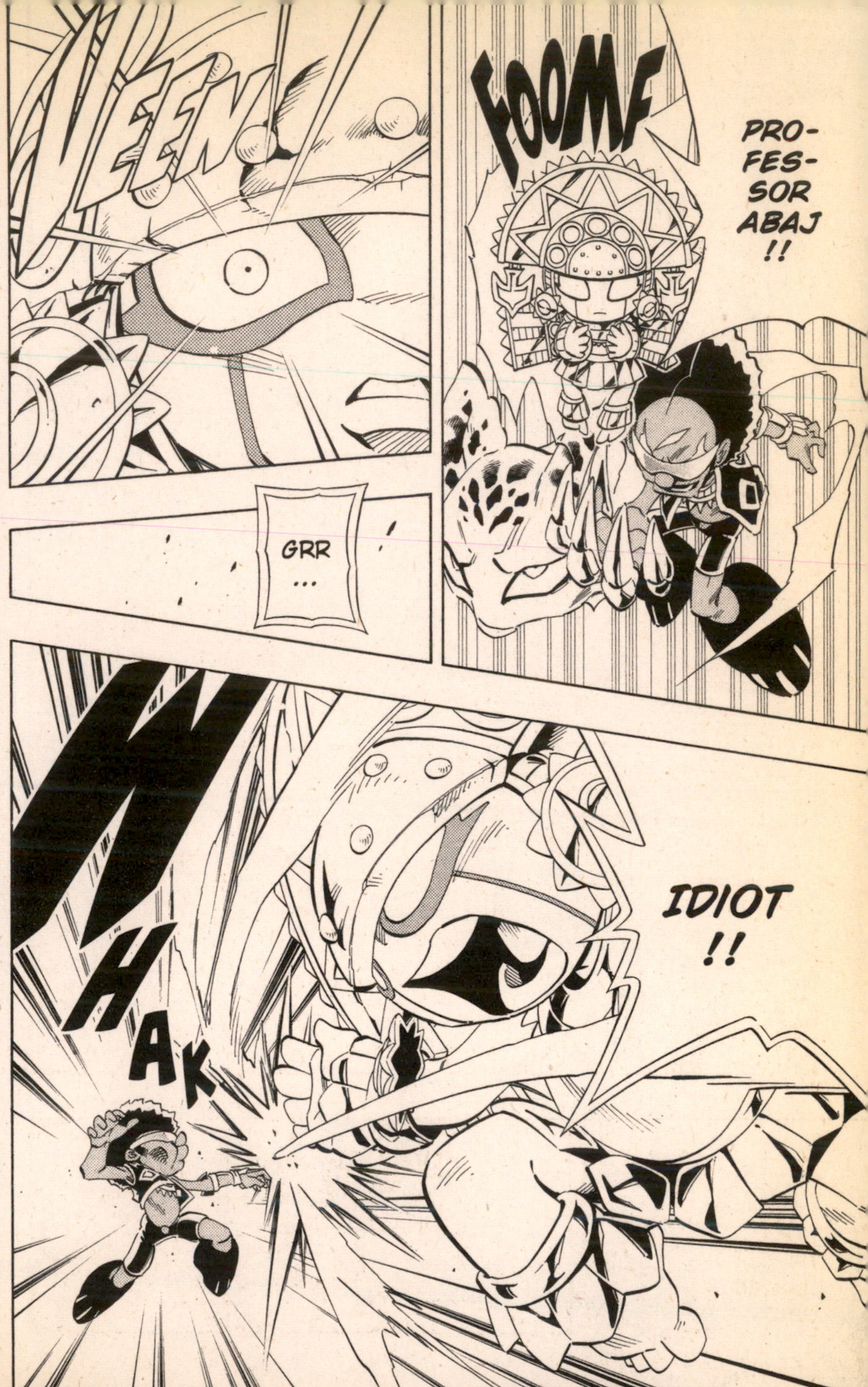

FOOMF
PRO-FES-SOR ABAJ !!
VEEN
GRR ...
IDIOT !!
WHAK

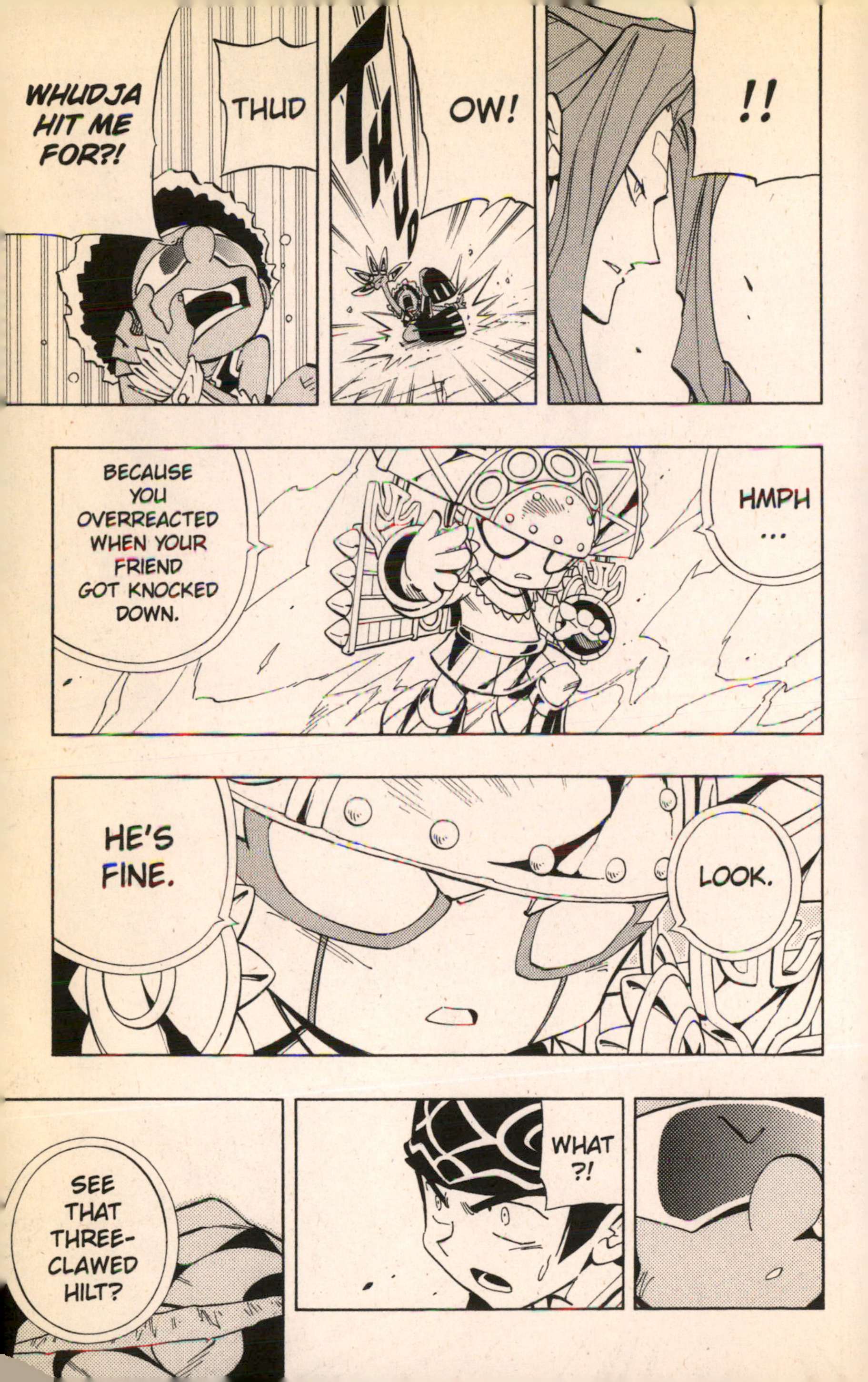
!!
OW!
THUD
THUD
WHUDJA HIT ME FOR?!
HMPH ...
BECAUSE YOU OVERREACTED WHEN YOUR FRIEND GOT KNOCKED DOWN.
LOOK.
HE'S FINE.
WHAT ?!
SEE THAT THREE-CLAWED HILT?

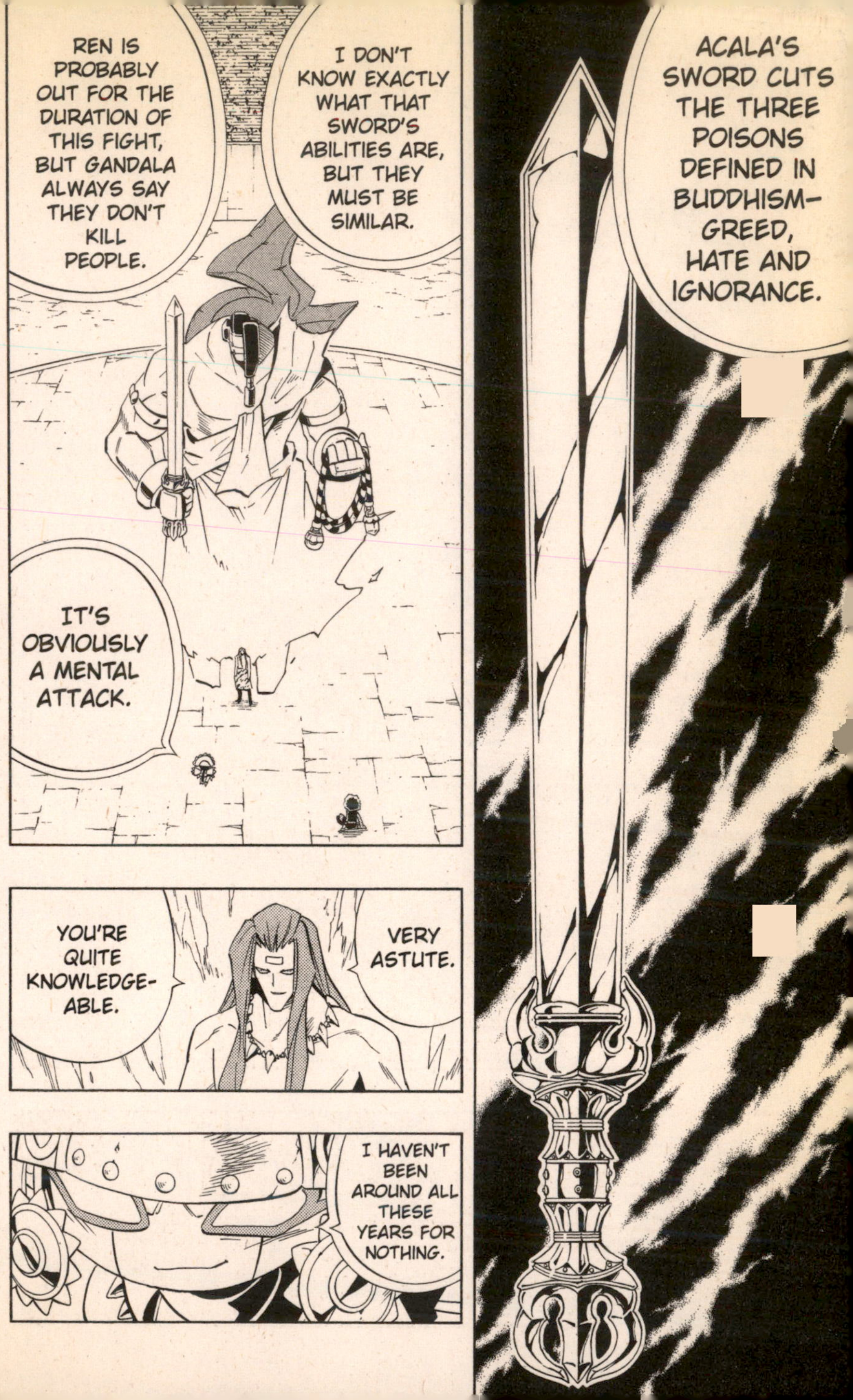
ACALA'S SWORD CUTS THE THREE POISONS DEFINED IN BUDDHISM-GREED, HATE AND IGNORANCE.
I DON'T KNOW EXACTLY WHAT THAT SWORD'S ABILITIES ARE, BUT THEY MUST BE SIMILAR.
REN IS PROBABLY OUT FOR THE DURATION OF THIS FIGHT, BUT GANDALA ALWAYS SAY THEY DON'T KILL PEOPLE.
IT'S OBVIOUSLY A MENTAL ATTACK.
VERY ASTUTE.
YOU'RE QUITE KNOWLEDGE-ABLE.
I HAVEN'T BEEN AROUND ALL THESE YEARS FOR NOTHING.

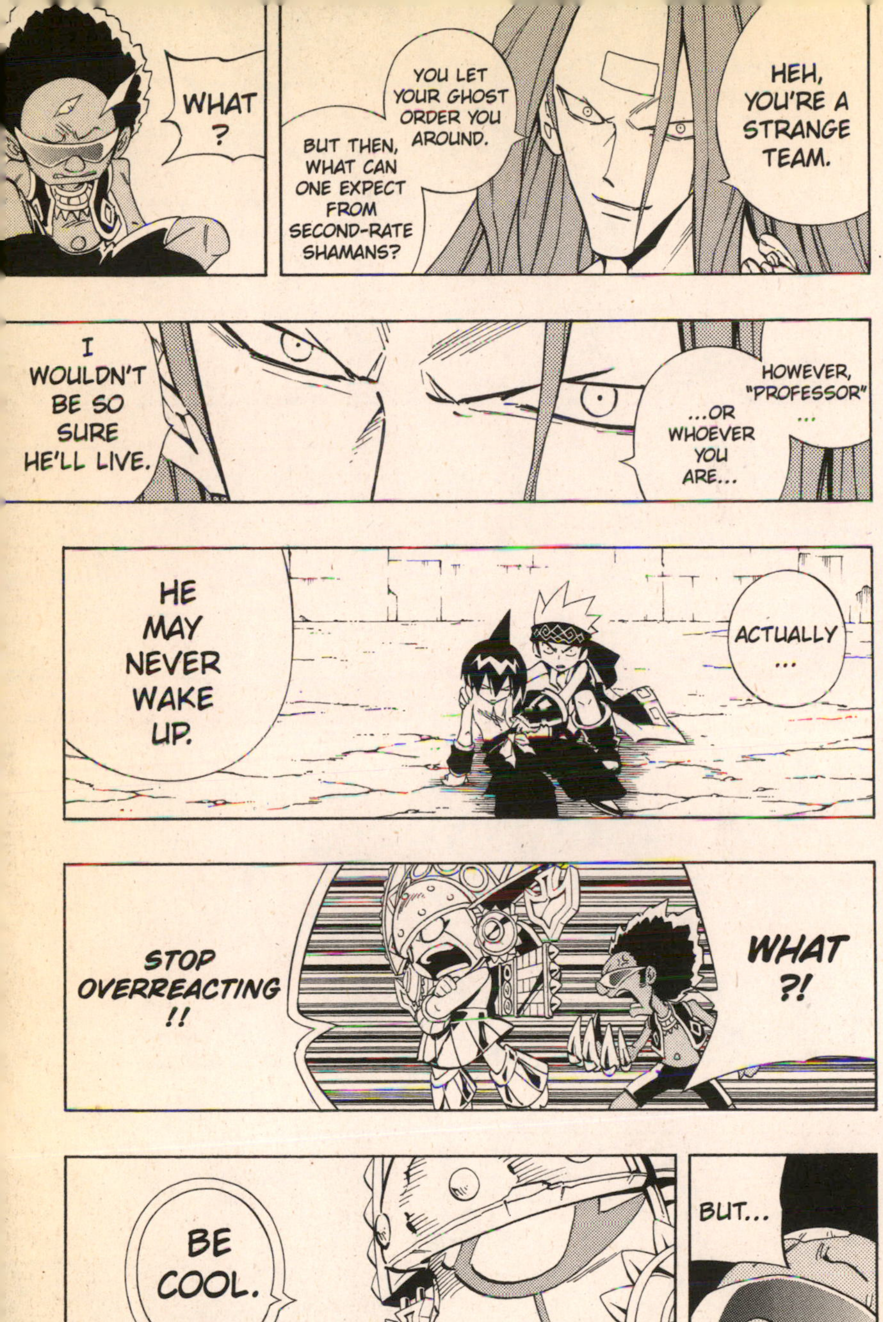
HEH, YOU'RE A STRANGE TEAM.
YOU LET YOUR GHOST ORDER YOU AROUND.
BUT THEN, WHAT CAN ONE EXPECT FROM SECOND-RATE SHAMANS?
WHAT?
HOWEVER, "PROFESSOR"...
...OR WHOEVER YOU ARE...
I WOULDN'T BE SO SURE HE'LL LIVE.
ACTUALLY...
HE MAY NEVER WAKE UP.
WHAT?!
STOP OVERREACTING!!
BUT...
BE COOL.

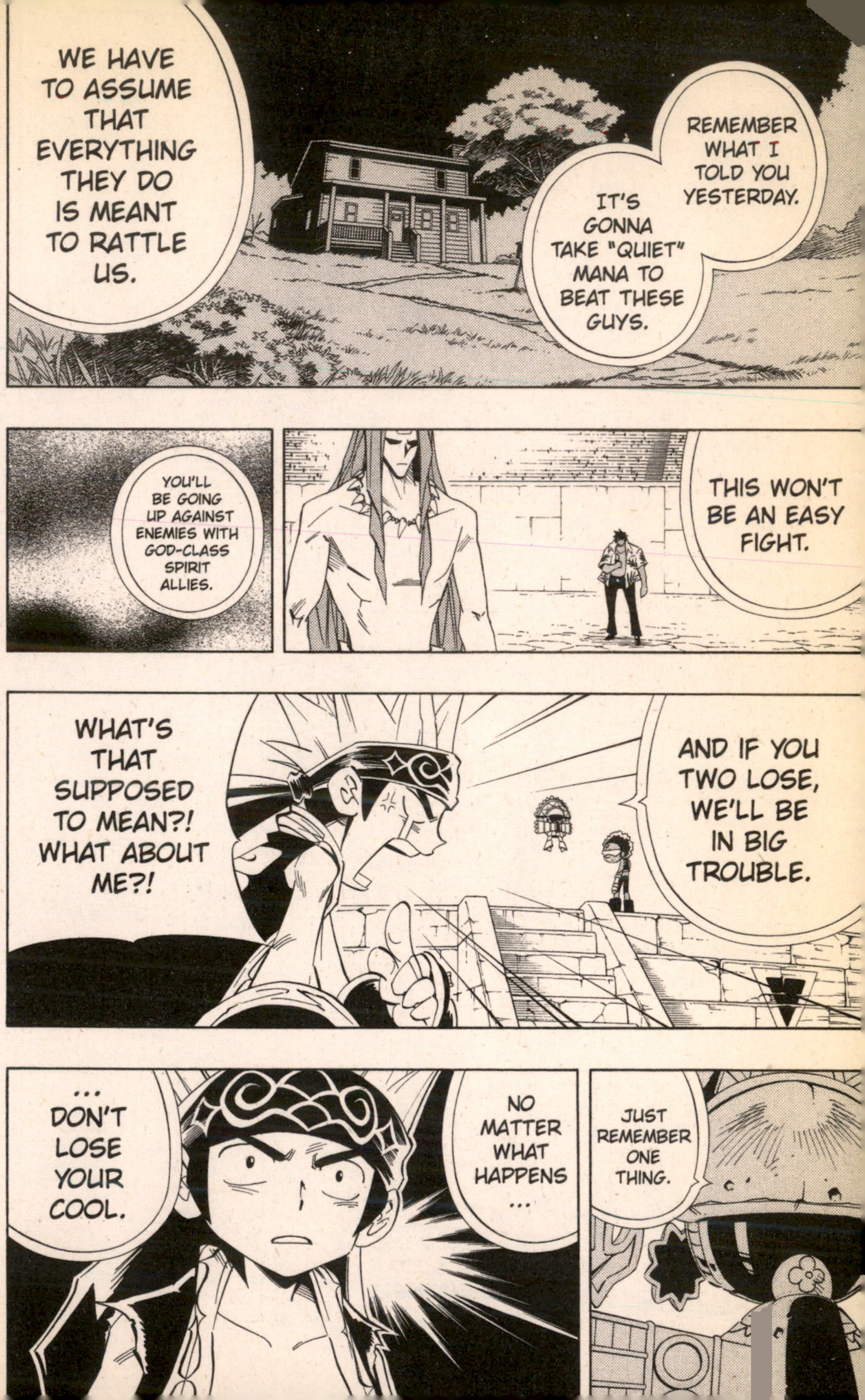
REMEMBER WHAT I TOLD YOU YESTERDAY.
IT'S GONNA TAKE "QUIET" MANA TO BEAT THESE GUYS.
WE HAVE TO ASSUME THAT EVERYTHING THEY DO IS MEANT TO RATTLE US.
THIS WON'T BE AN EASY FIGHT.
YOU'LL BE GOING UP AGAINST ENEMIES WITH GOD-CLASS SPIRIT ALLIES.
AND IF YOU TWO LOSE, WE'LL BE IN BIG TROUBLE.
WHAT'S THAT SUPPOSED TO MEAN?! WHAT ABOUT ME?!
JUST REMEMBER ONE THING.
NO MATTER WHAT HAPPENS ...
... DON'T LOSE YOUR COOL.

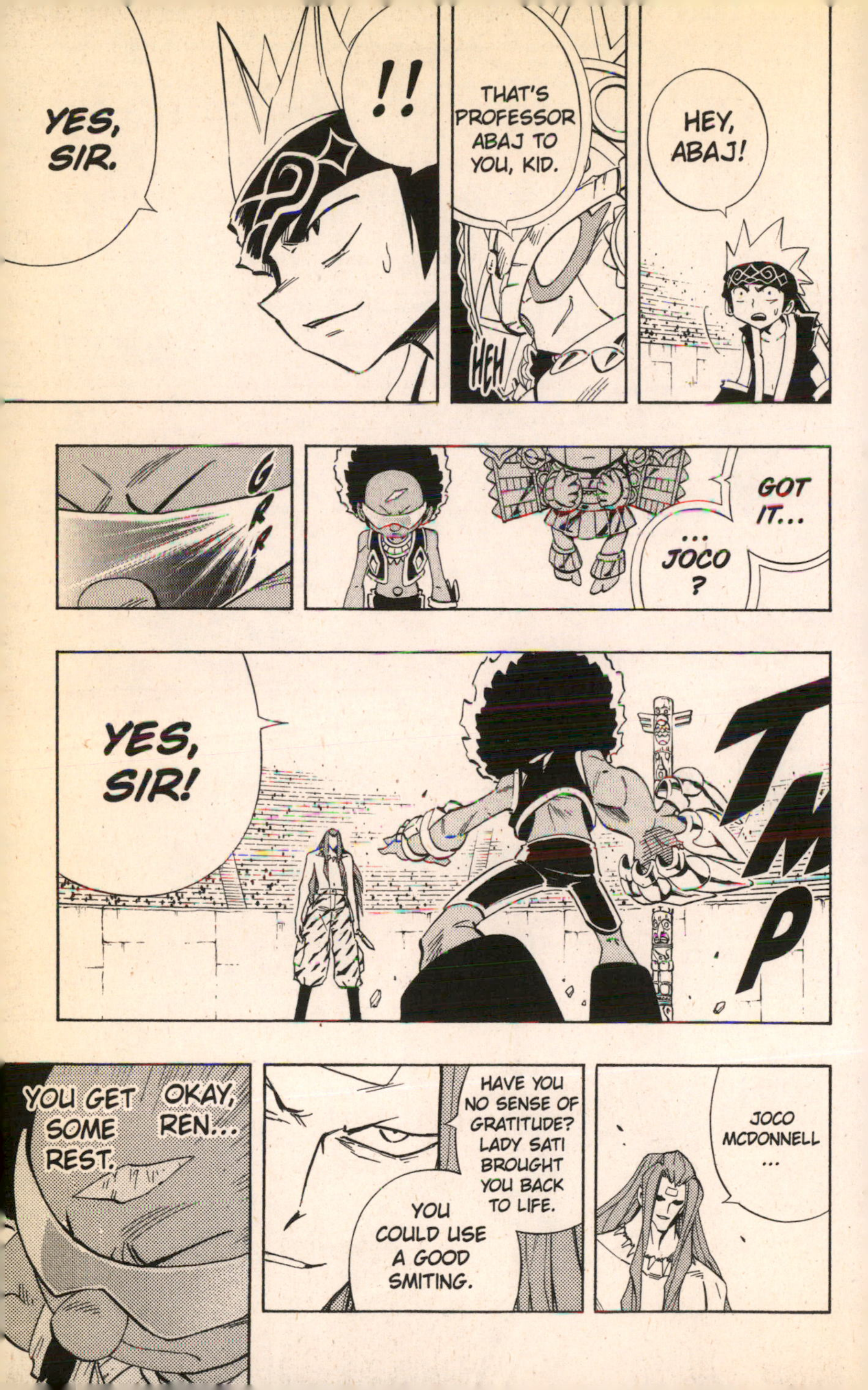
HEY, ABAJ!
THAT'S PROFESSOR ABAJ TO YOU, KID.
HEH
!!
YES, SIR.
GOT IT...
... JOCO?
GRR
YES, SIR!
TMP
JOCO MCDONNELL ...
HAVE YOU NO SENSE OF GRATITUDE? LADY SATI BROUGHT YOU BACK TO LIFE.
YOU COULD USE A GOOD SMITING.
OKAY, REN...
YOU GET SOME REST.

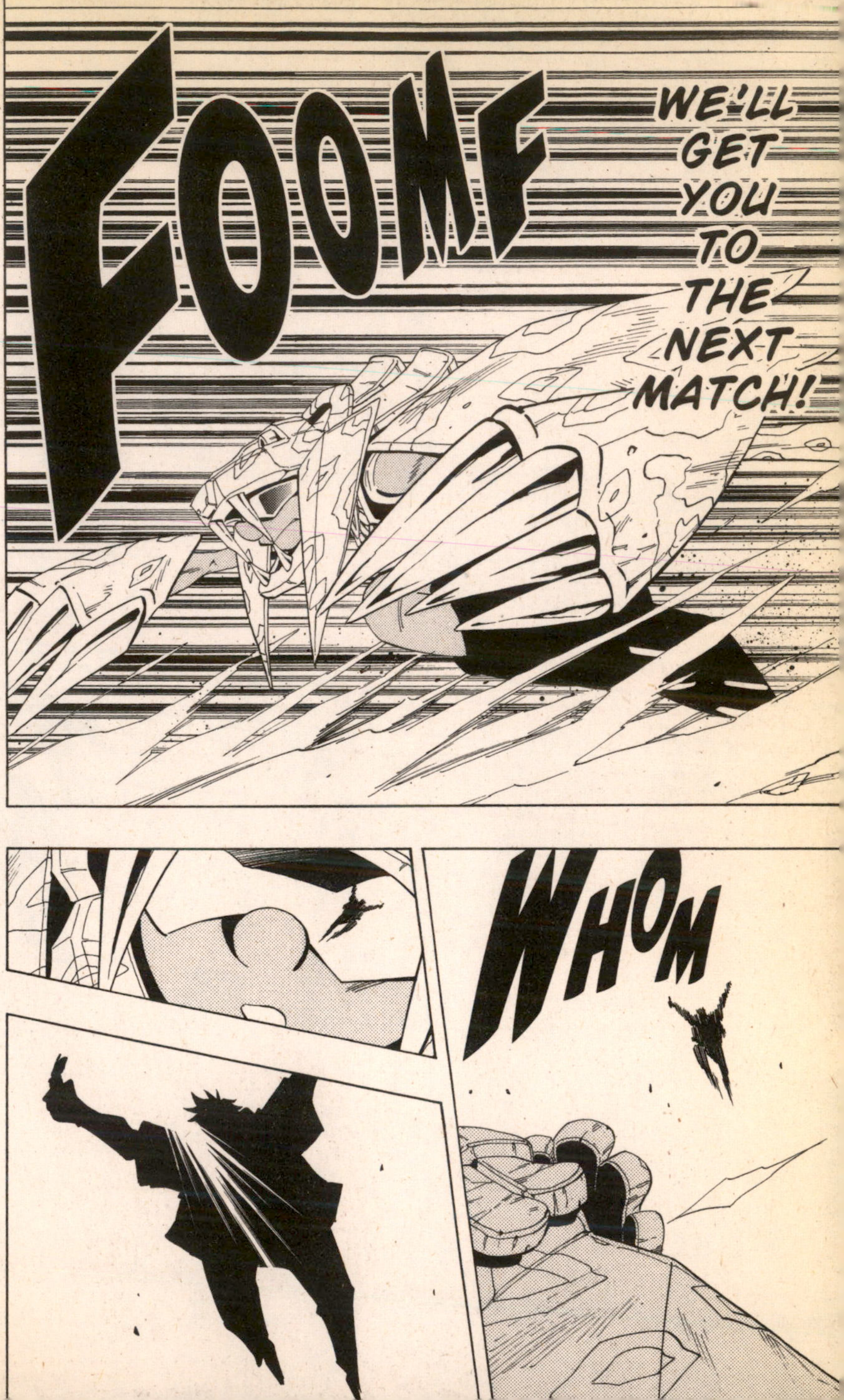
WE'LL GET YOU TO THE NEXT MATCH!
FOOMF
WHOM

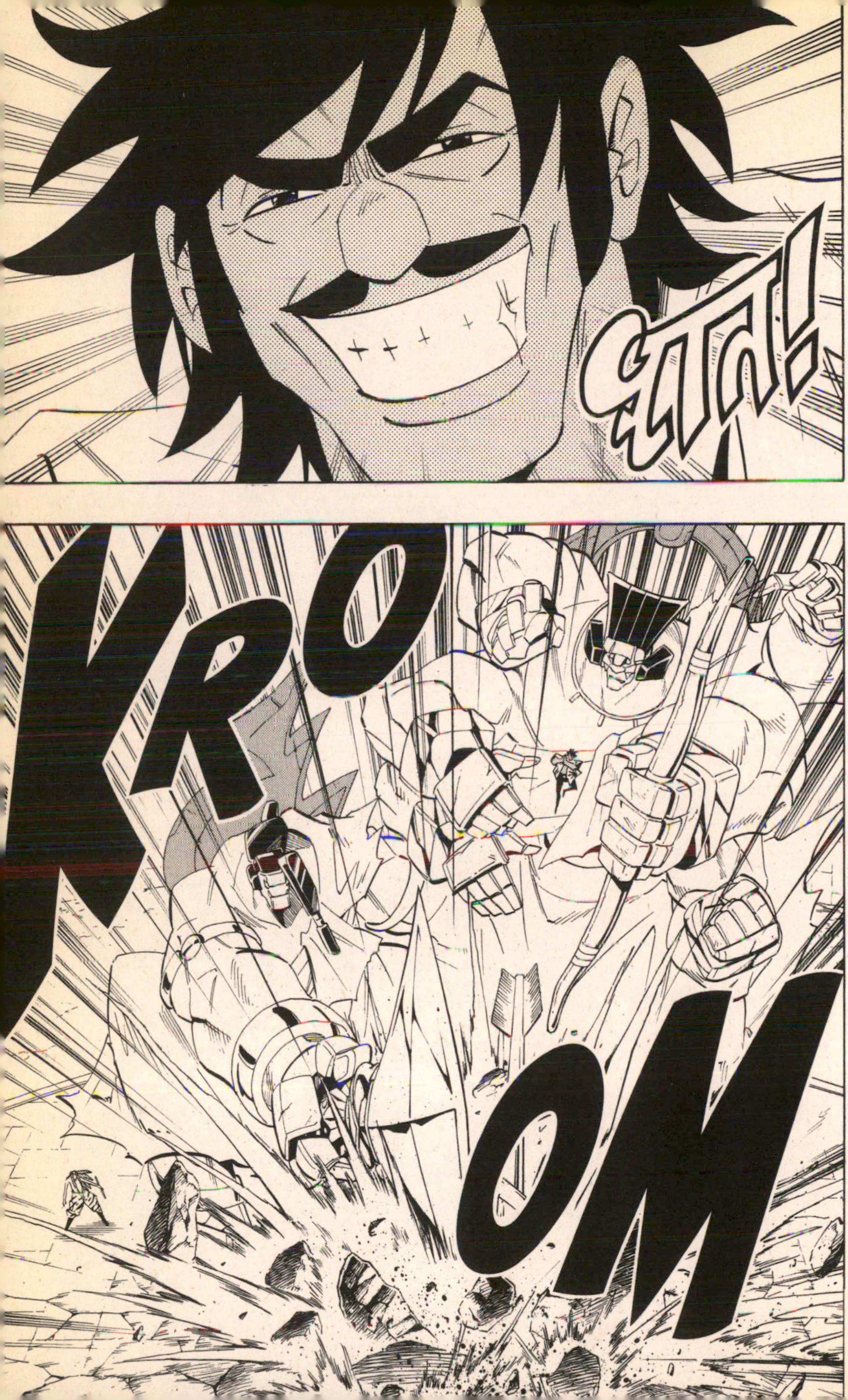
GRIN!
KROOM

SHAMAN KING CHARACTER FILE No.130

ヤイナゲ

YAINAGE

2001
(JAN)

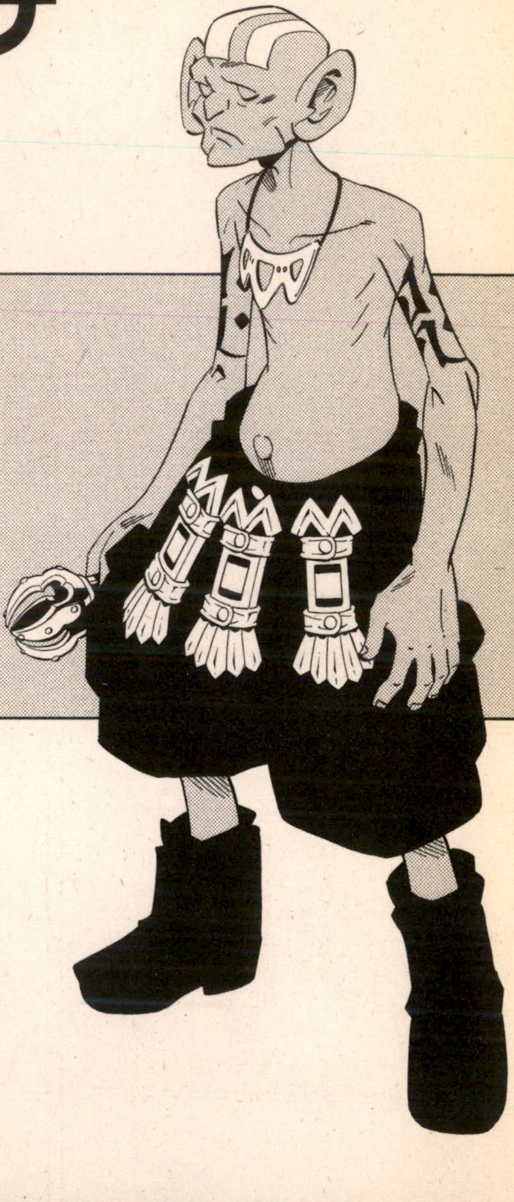

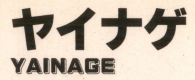

BIRTHDAY:
OCTOBER 29, 1963
ASTROLOGICAL SIGN:
SCORPIO
BLOOD TYPE: B
37 YEARS OLD

Reincarnation 226: Coordinated Cool

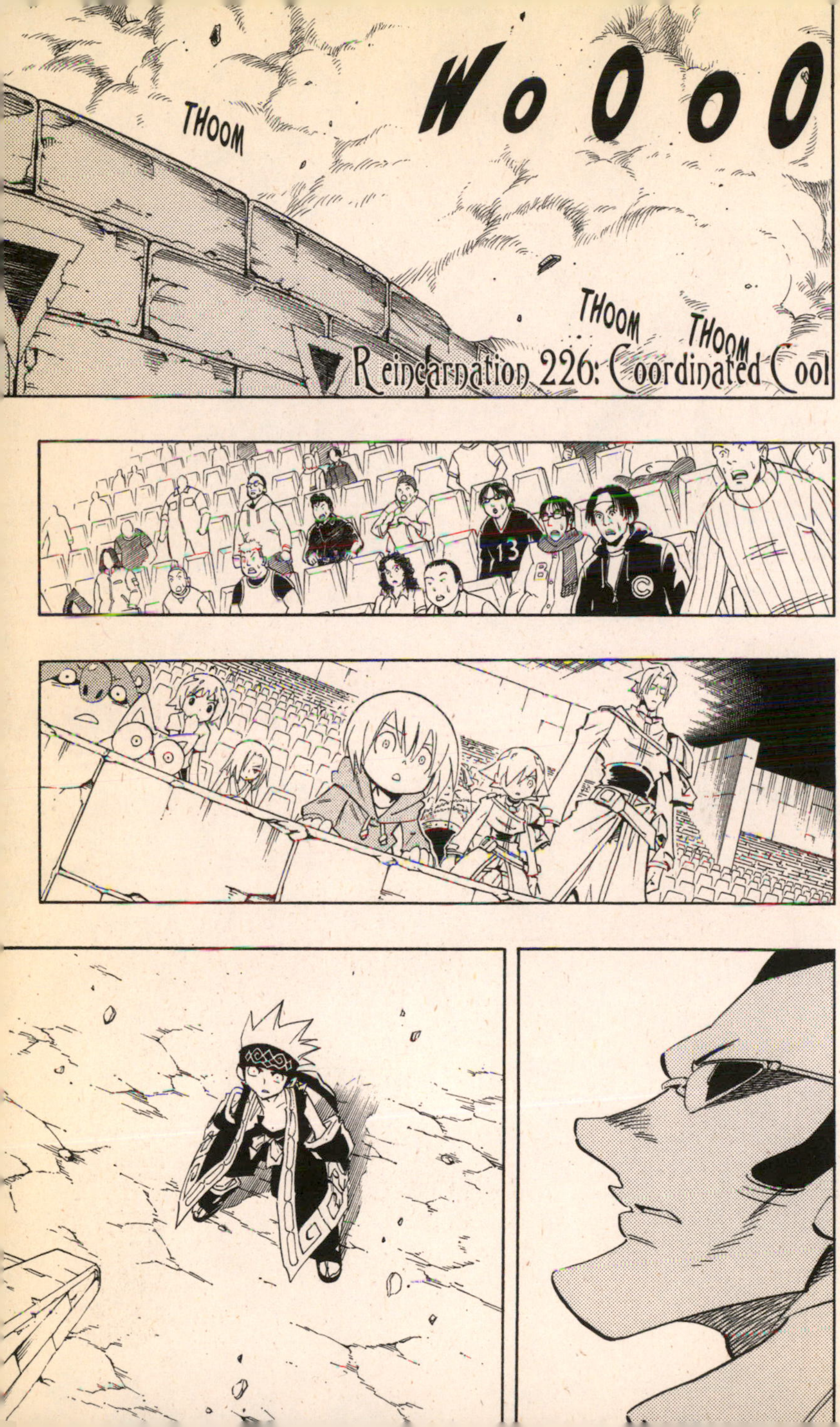
WoOOO
THOOM
THOOM
THOOM

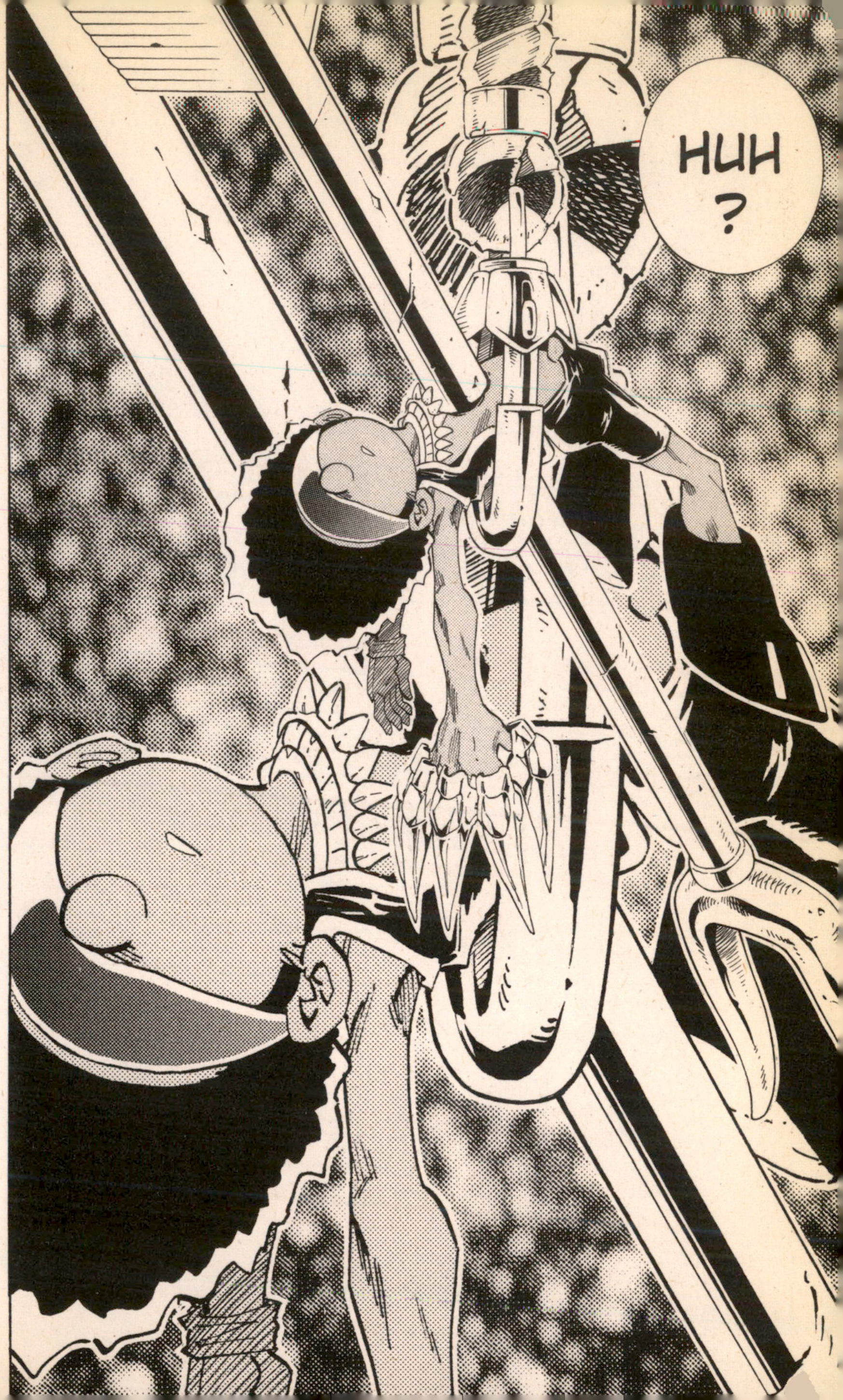
HUH
?

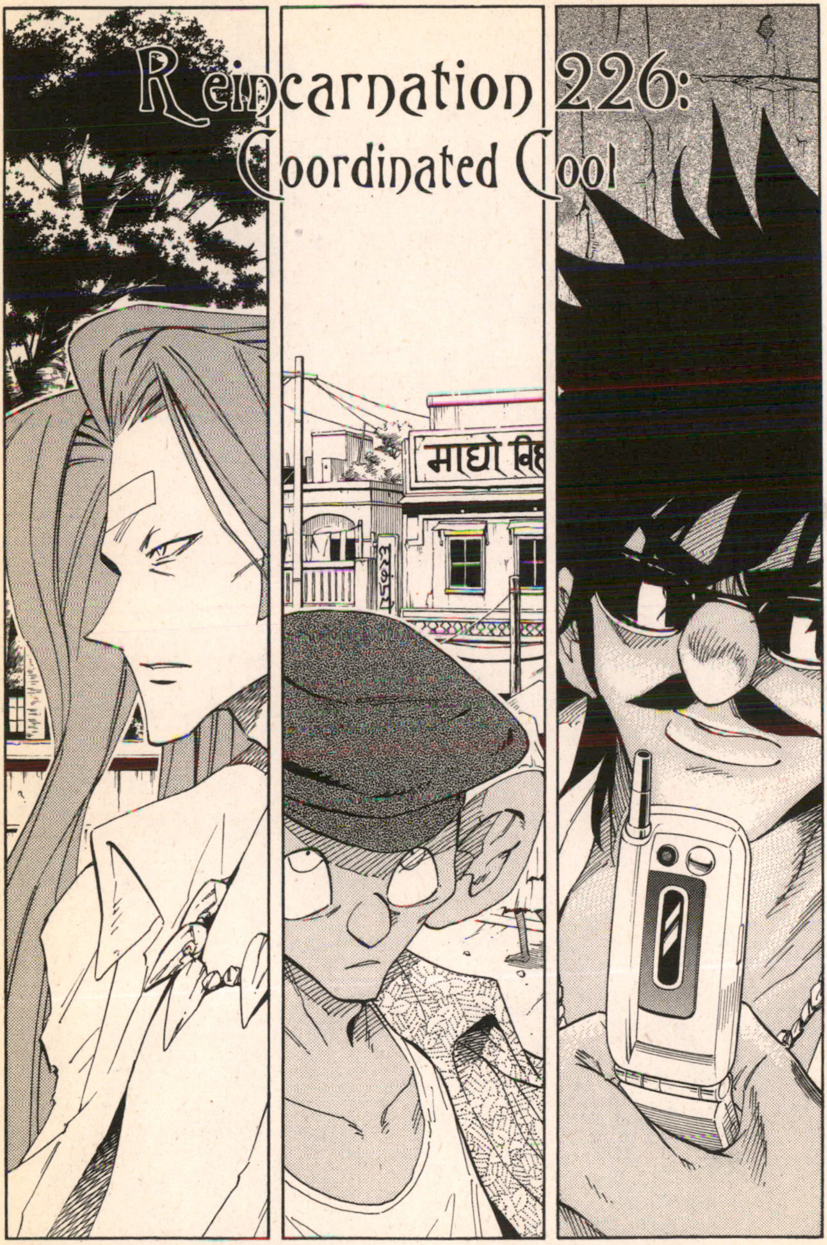
Reincarnation 226:
Coordinated Cool

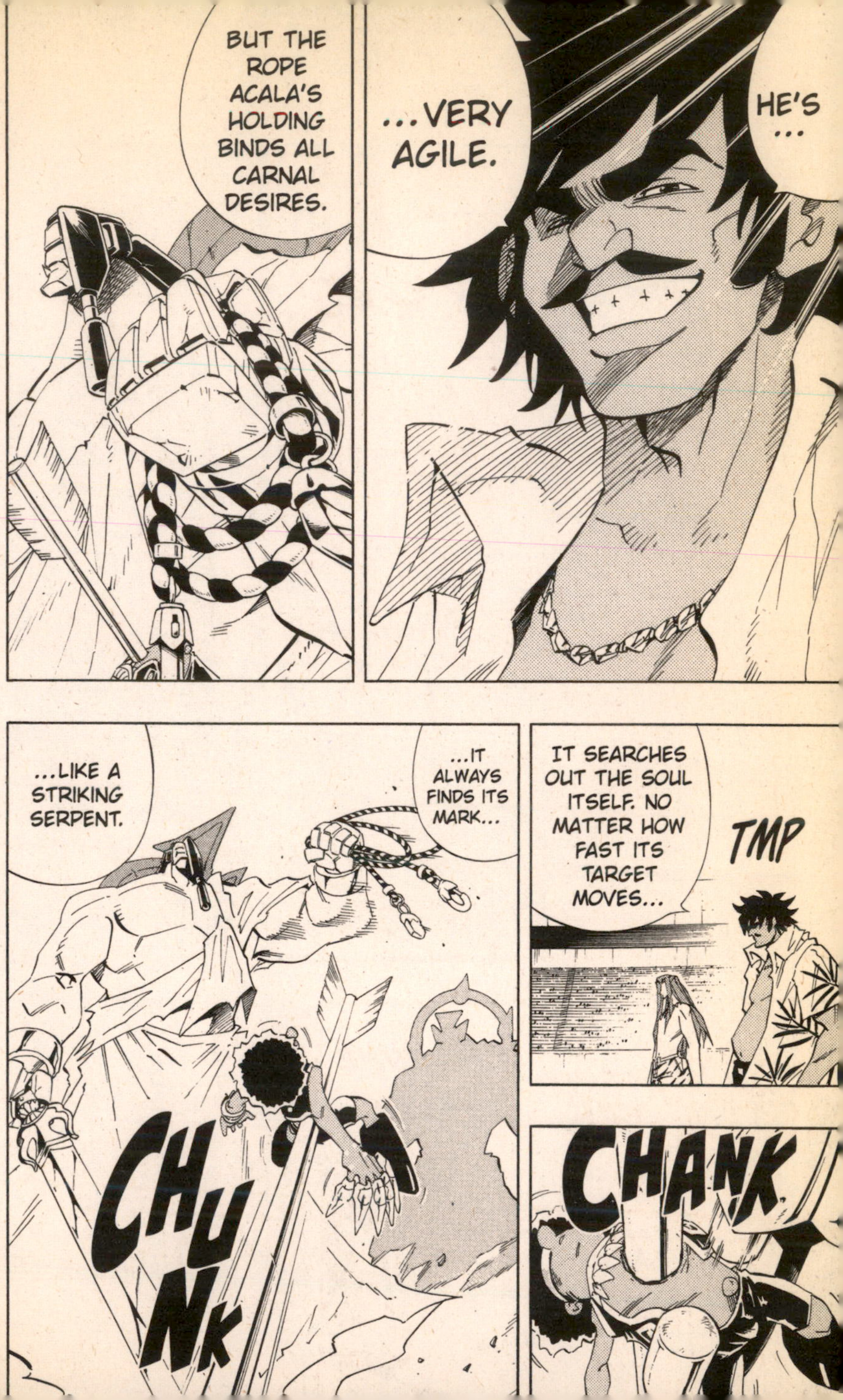
HE'S...
...VERY AGILE.
BUT THE ROPE ACALA'S HOLDING BINDS ALL CARNAL DESIRES.
IT SEARCHES OUT THE SOUL ITSELF. NO MATTER HOW FAST ITS TARGET MOVES...
TMP
CHANK
...IT ALWAYS FINDS ITS MARK...
...LIKE A STRIKING SERPENT.
CHUNK

...MY RAGARAJA'S ARROWS OF LOVE HAVE THAT POWER TOO.

OF COURSE...

KREEK

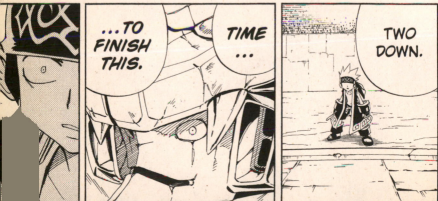

...TO FINISH THIS.

TIME...

TWO DOWN.

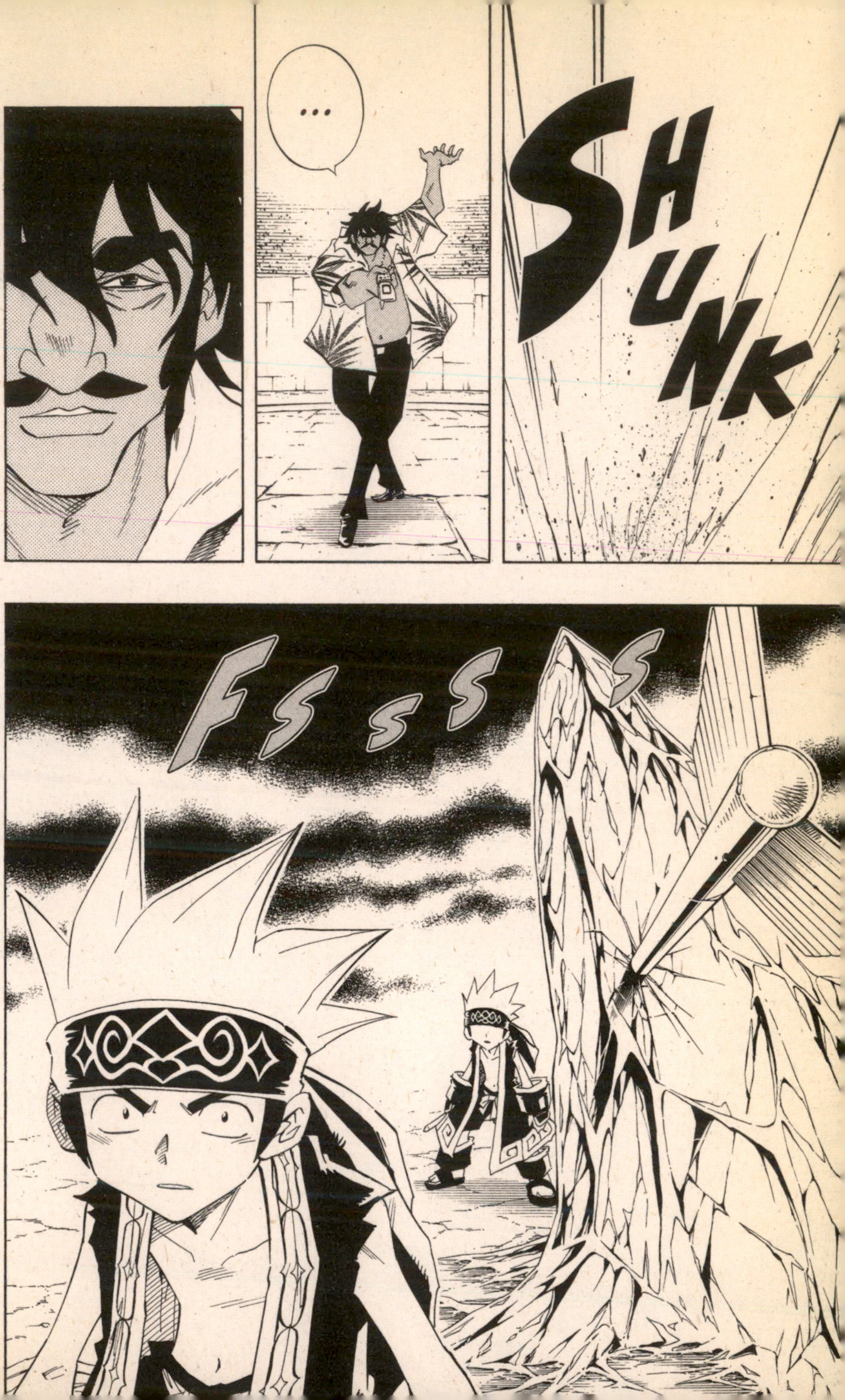
SHUNK
...
FSSSS

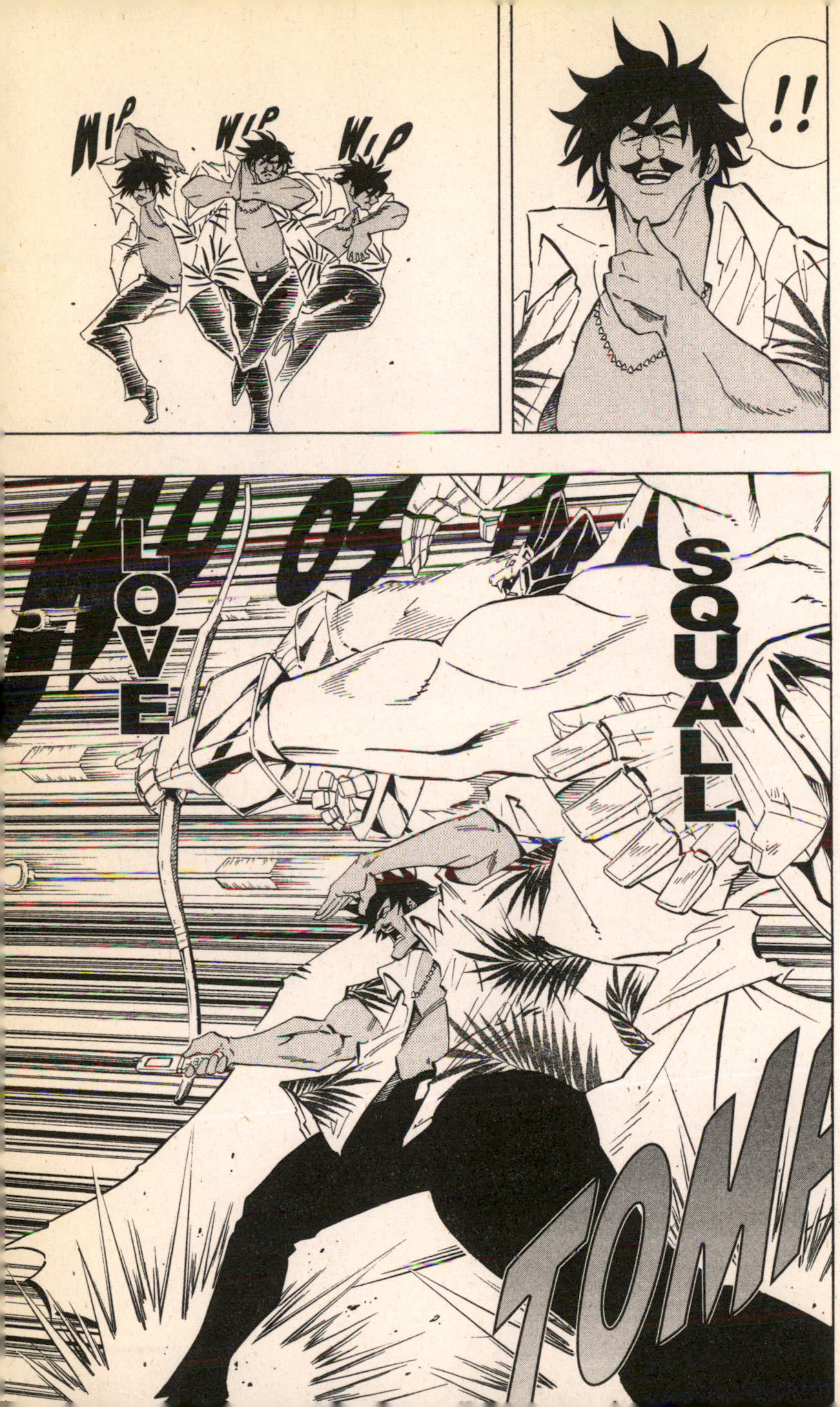

!!
WIP
WIP
WIP
LOVE
SQUALL
TOM

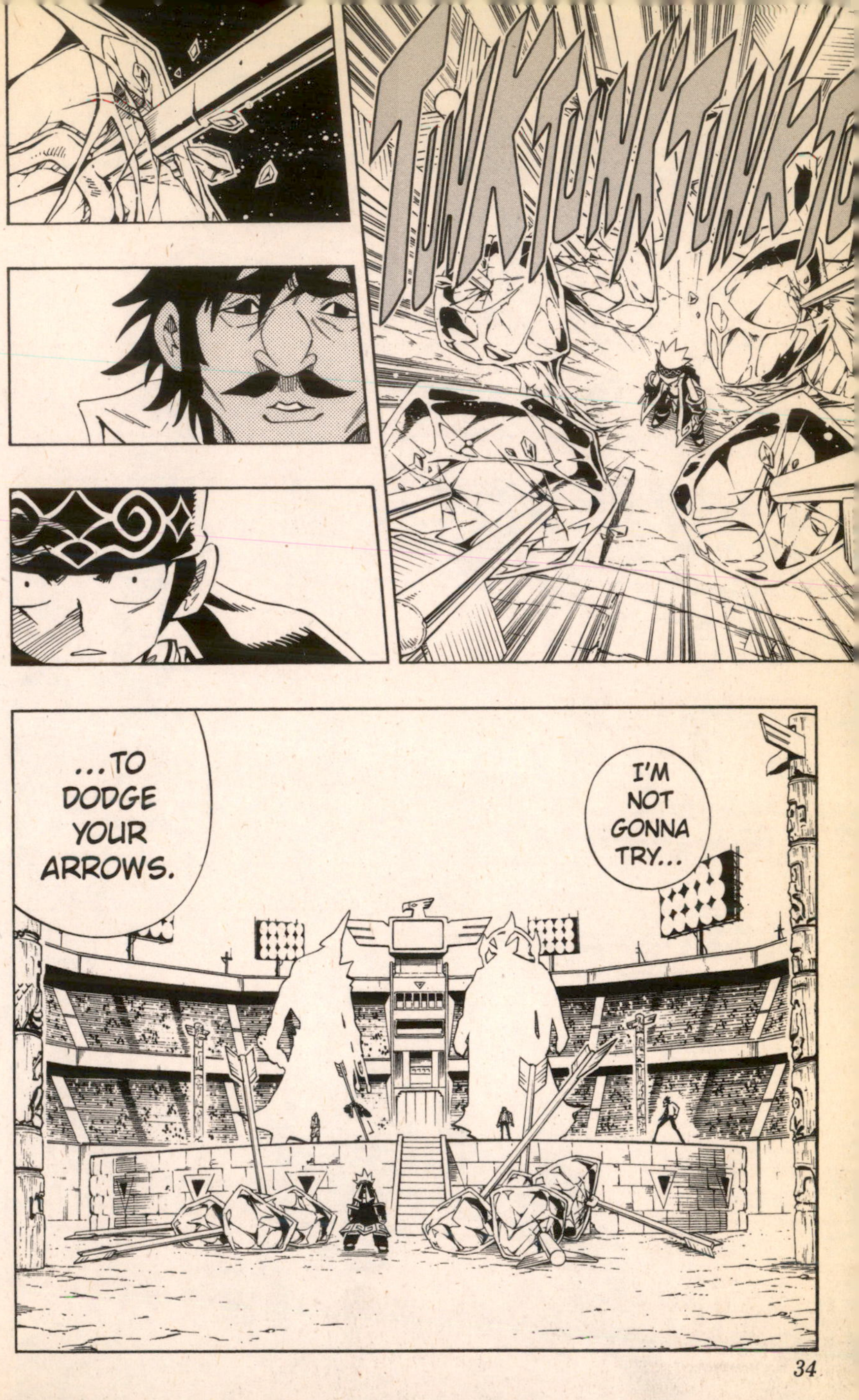
TUNK TUNK TUNK TU
I'M NOT GONNA TRY...
...TO DODGE YOUR ARROWS.

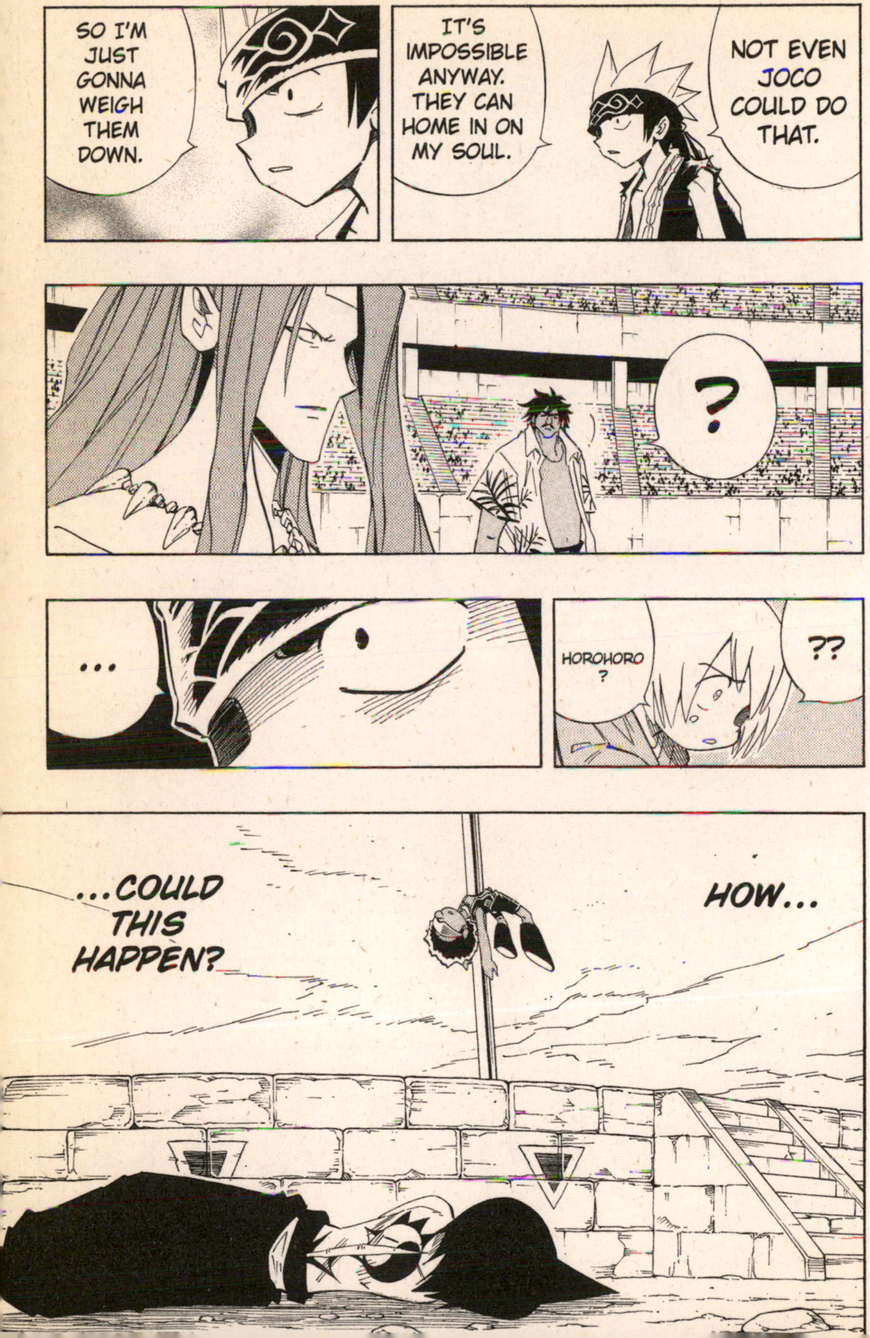
NOT EVEN JOCO COULD DO THAT.
IT'S IMPOSSIBLE ANYWAY. THEY CAN HOME IN ON MY SOUL.
SO I'M JUST GONNA WEIGH THEM DOWN.
?
??
HOROHORO?
...
HOW...
...COULD THIS HAPPEN?

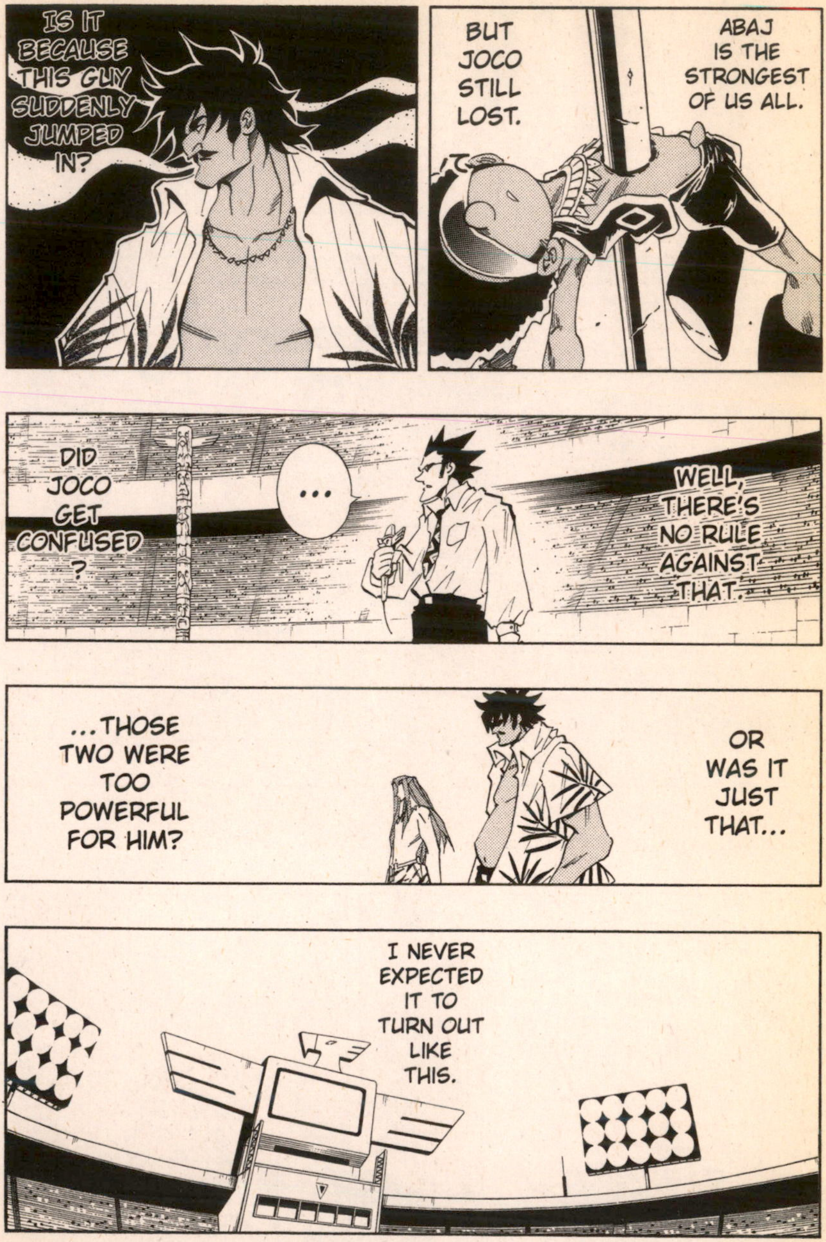
ABAJ IS THE STRONGEST OF US ALL.
BUT JOCO STILL LOST.
IS IT BECAUSE THIS GUY SUDDENLY JUMPED IN?
WELL, THERE'S NO RULE AGAINST THAT.
...
DID JOCO GET CONFUSED?
OR WAS IT JUST THAT...
...THOSE TWO WERE TOO POWERFUL FOR HIM?
I NEVER EXPECTED IT TO TURN OUT LIKE THIS.

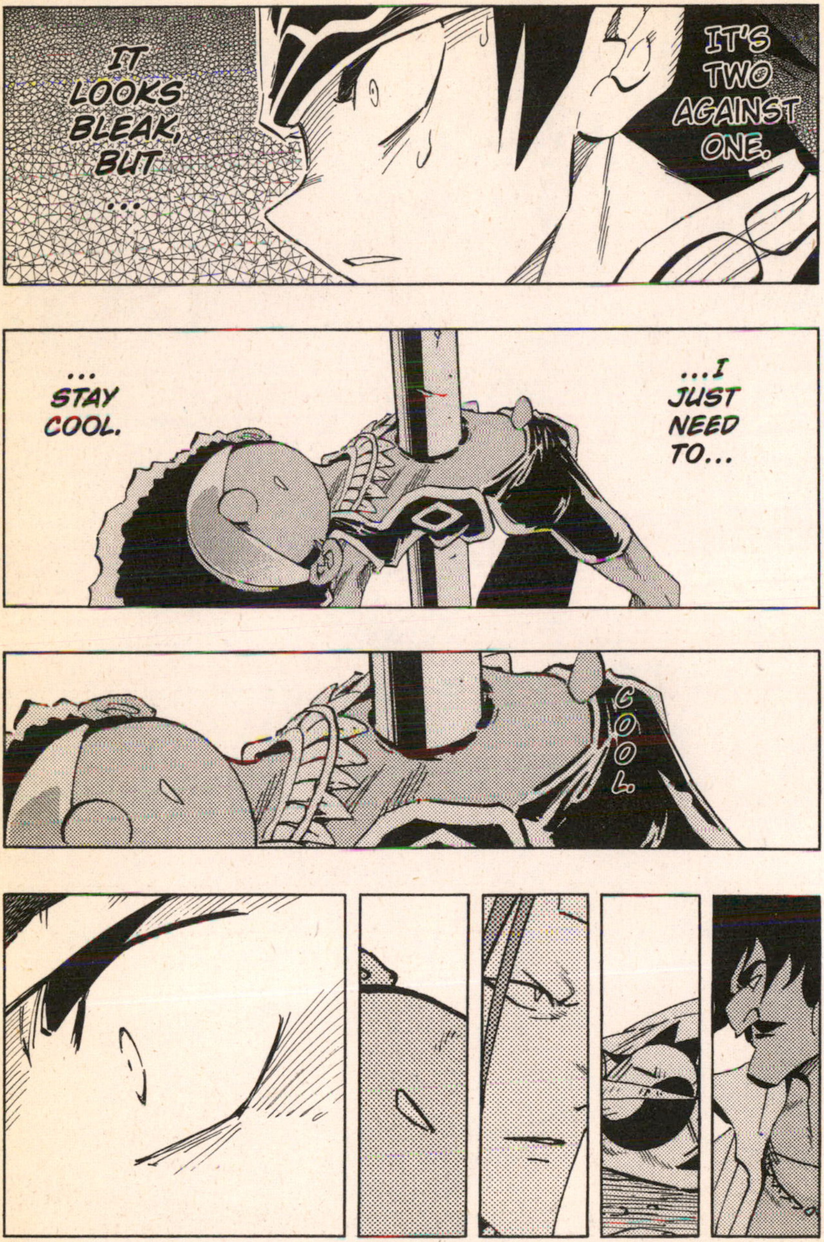
IT'S TWO AGAINST ONE.
IT LOOKS BLEAK, BUT ...
...I JUST NEED TO...
... STAY COOL.
COOL.

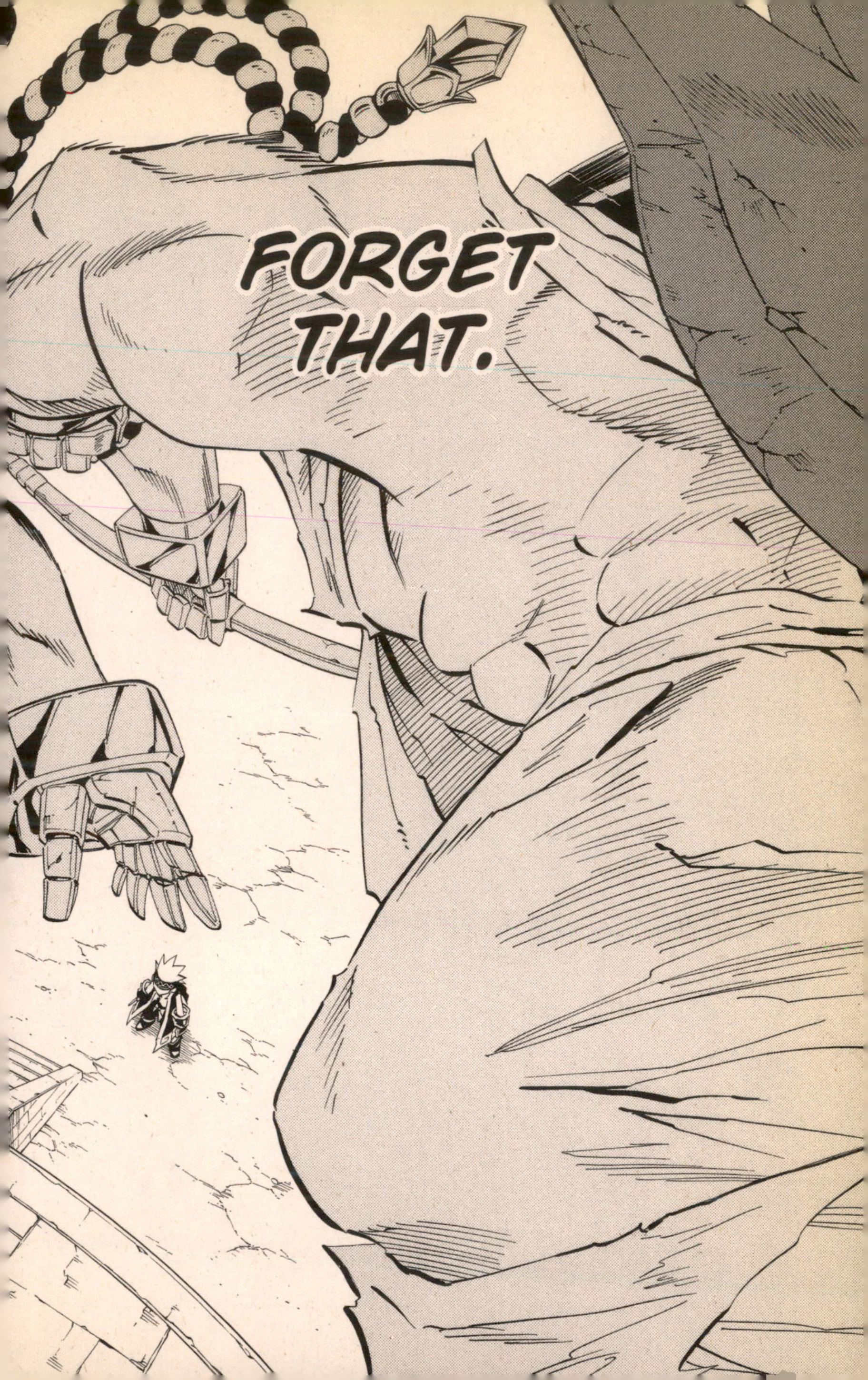
FORGET THAT.

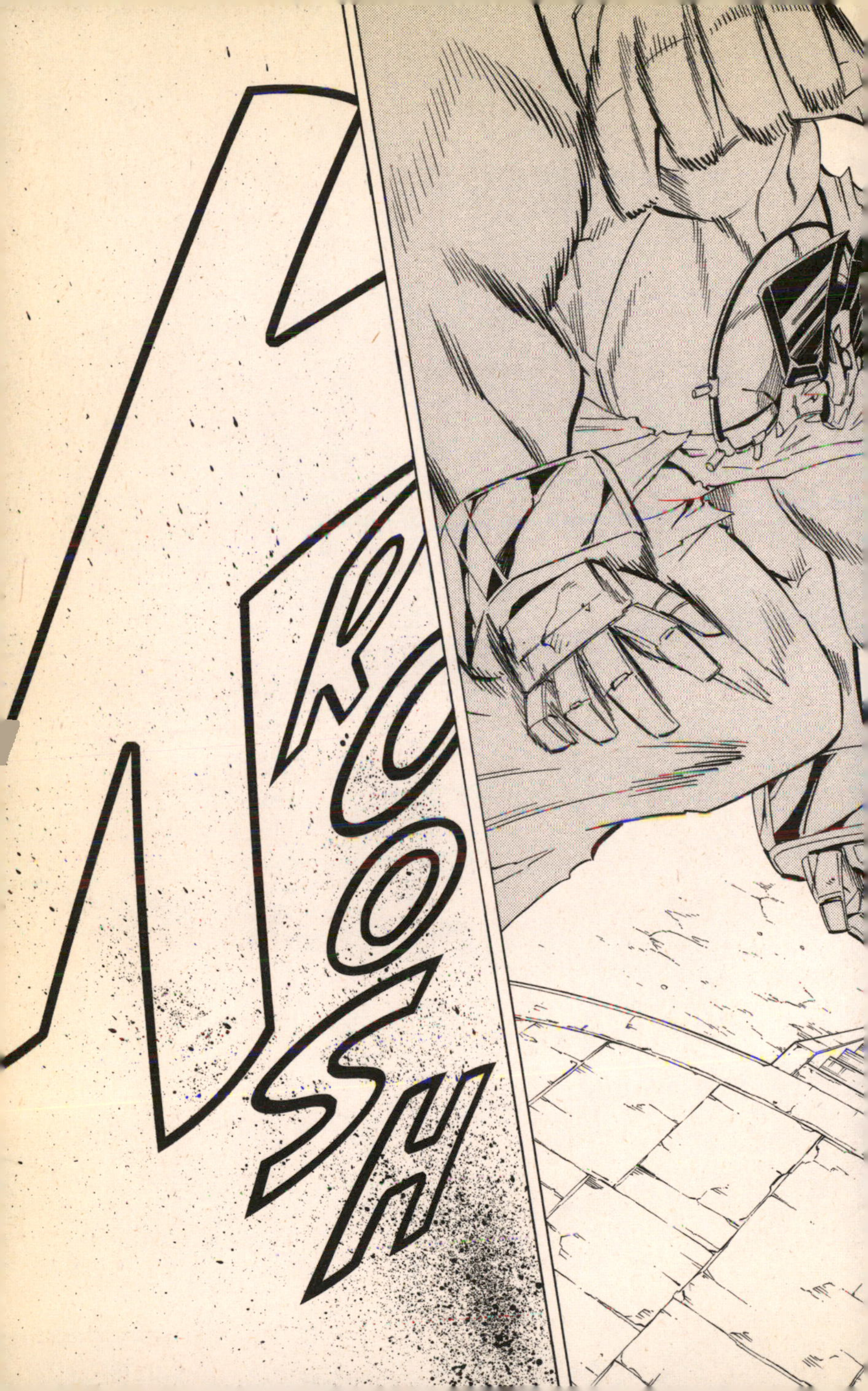
WOOSH

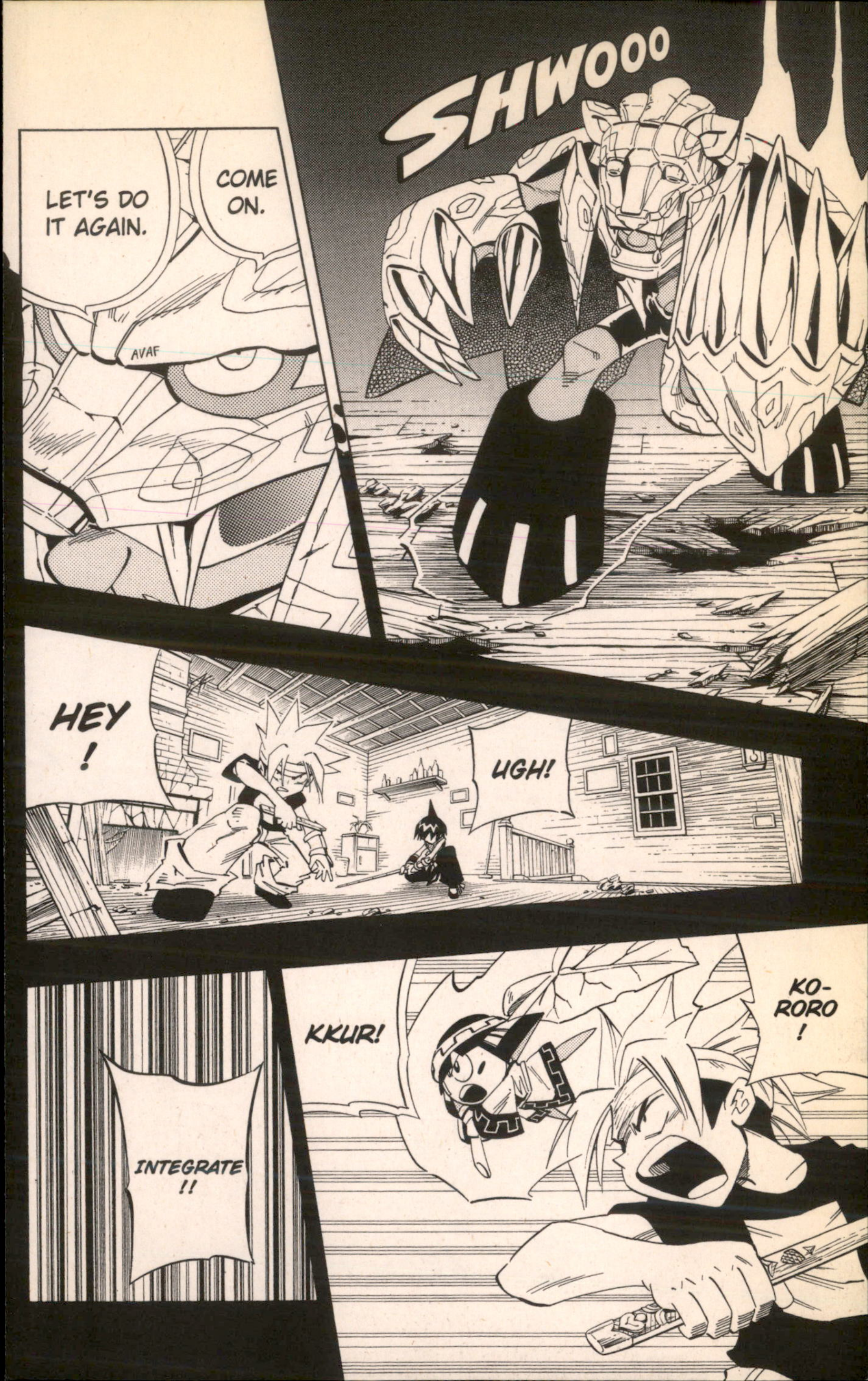
SHWOOO
COME ON.
LET'S DO IT AGAIN.
AVAF
UGH!
HEY !
KO-RORO !
KKUR!
INTEGRATE !!

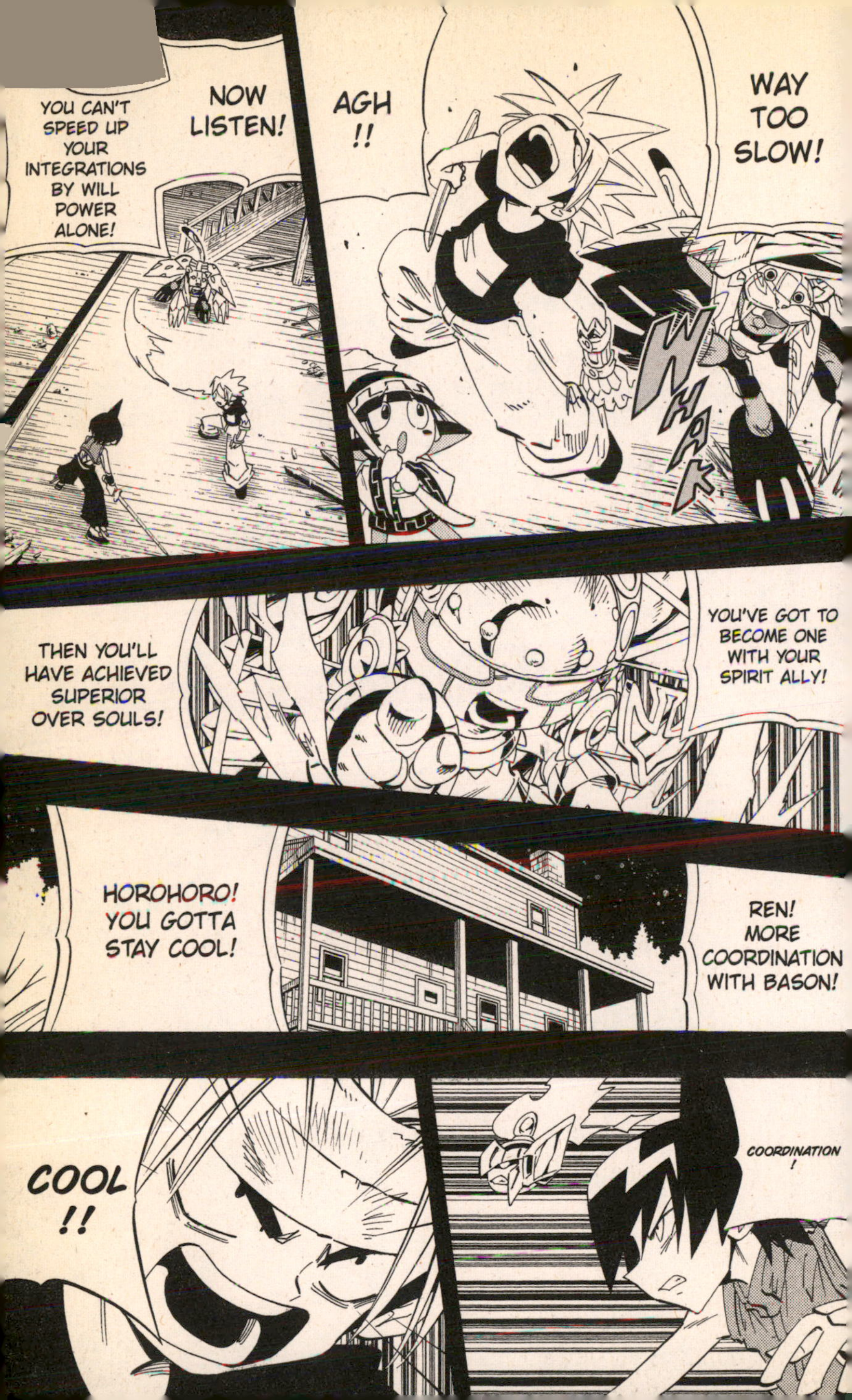
WAY TOO SLOW!
AGH !!
WHAK
NOW LISTEN!
YOU CAN'T SPEED UP YOUR INTEGRATIONS BY WILL POWER ALONE!
YOU'VE GOT TO BECOME ONE WITH YOUR SPIRIT ALLY!
THEN YOU'LL HAVE ACHIEVED SUPERIOR OVER SOULS!
REN! MORE COORDINATION WITH BASON!
HOROHORO! YOU GOTTA STAY COOL!
COORDINATION !
COOL !!

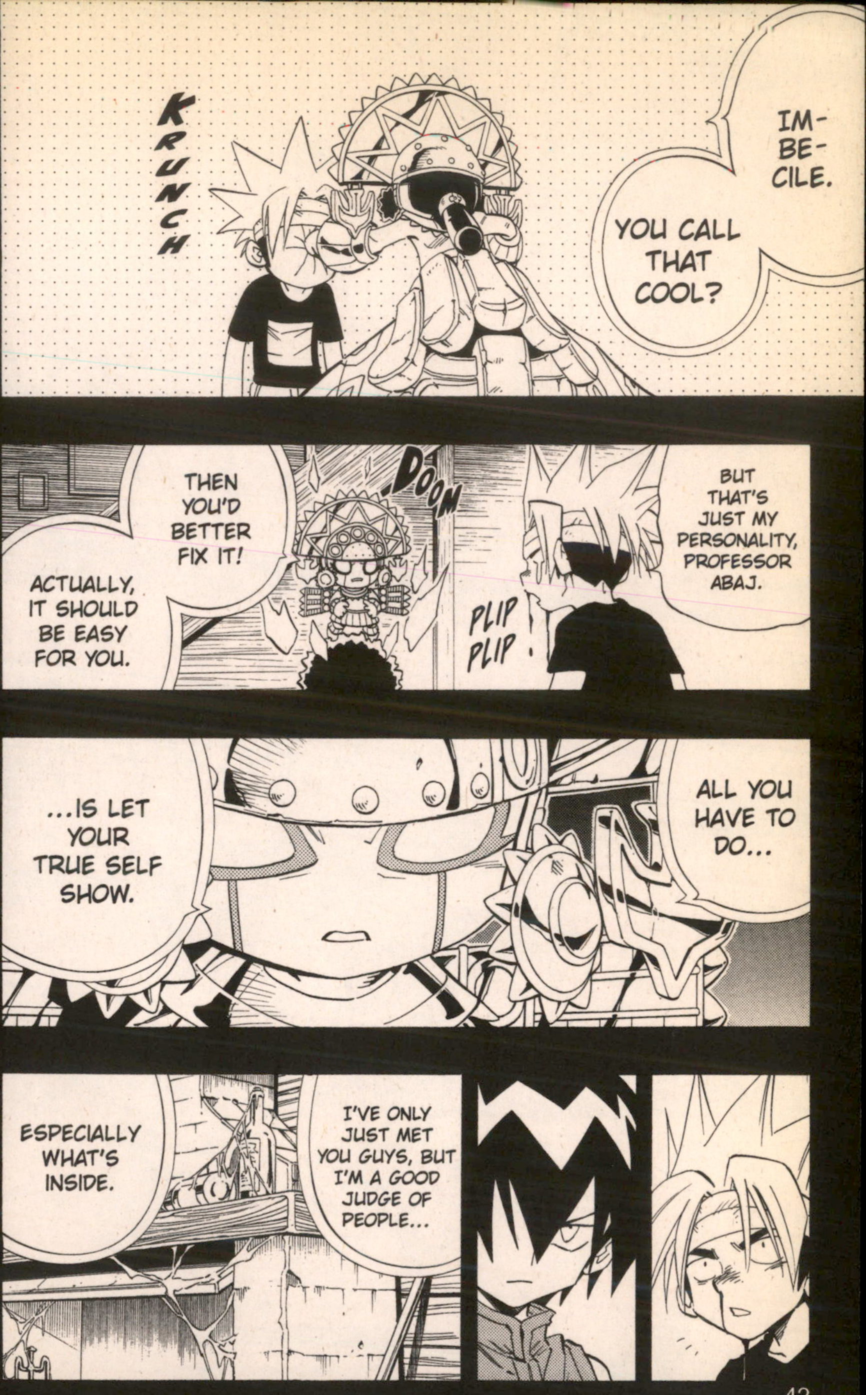
IM-BE-CILE.
YOU CALL THAT COOL?
KRUNCH
BUT THAT'S JUST MY PERSONALITY, PROFESSOR ABAJ.
PLIP PLIP
DOOM
THEN YOU'D BETTER FIX IT!
ACTUALLY, IT SHOULD BE EASY FOR YOU.
ALL YOU HAVE TO DO...
...IS LET YOUR TRUE SELF SHOW.
I'VE ONLY JUST MET YOU GUYS, BUT I'M A GOOD JUDGE OF PEOPLE...
ESPECIALLY WHAT'S INSIDE.

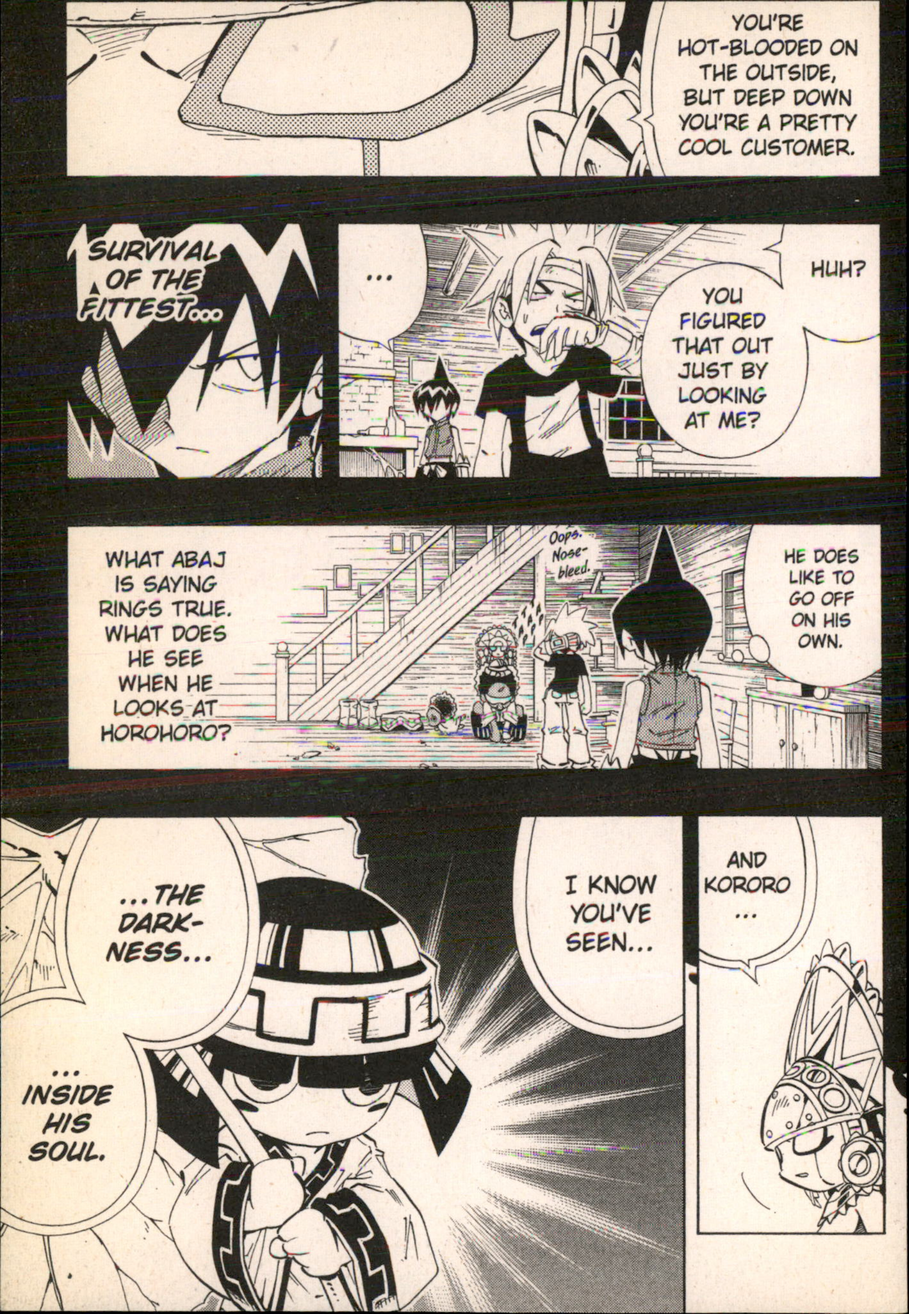
YOU'RE HOT-BLOODED ON THE OUTSIDE, BUT DEEP DOWN YOU'RE A PRETTY COOL CUSTOMER.
HUH?
YOU FIGURED THAT OUT JUST BY LOOKING AT ME?
...
SURVIVAL OF THE FITTEST...
HE DOES LIKE TO GO OFF ON HIS OWN.
Oops. Nose-bleed.
WHAT ABAJ IS SAYING RINGS TRUE. WHAT DOES HE SEE WHEN HE LOOKS AT HOROHORO?
AND KORORO ...
I KNOW YOU'VE SEEN...
...THE DARK-NESS...
... INSIDE HIS SOUL.

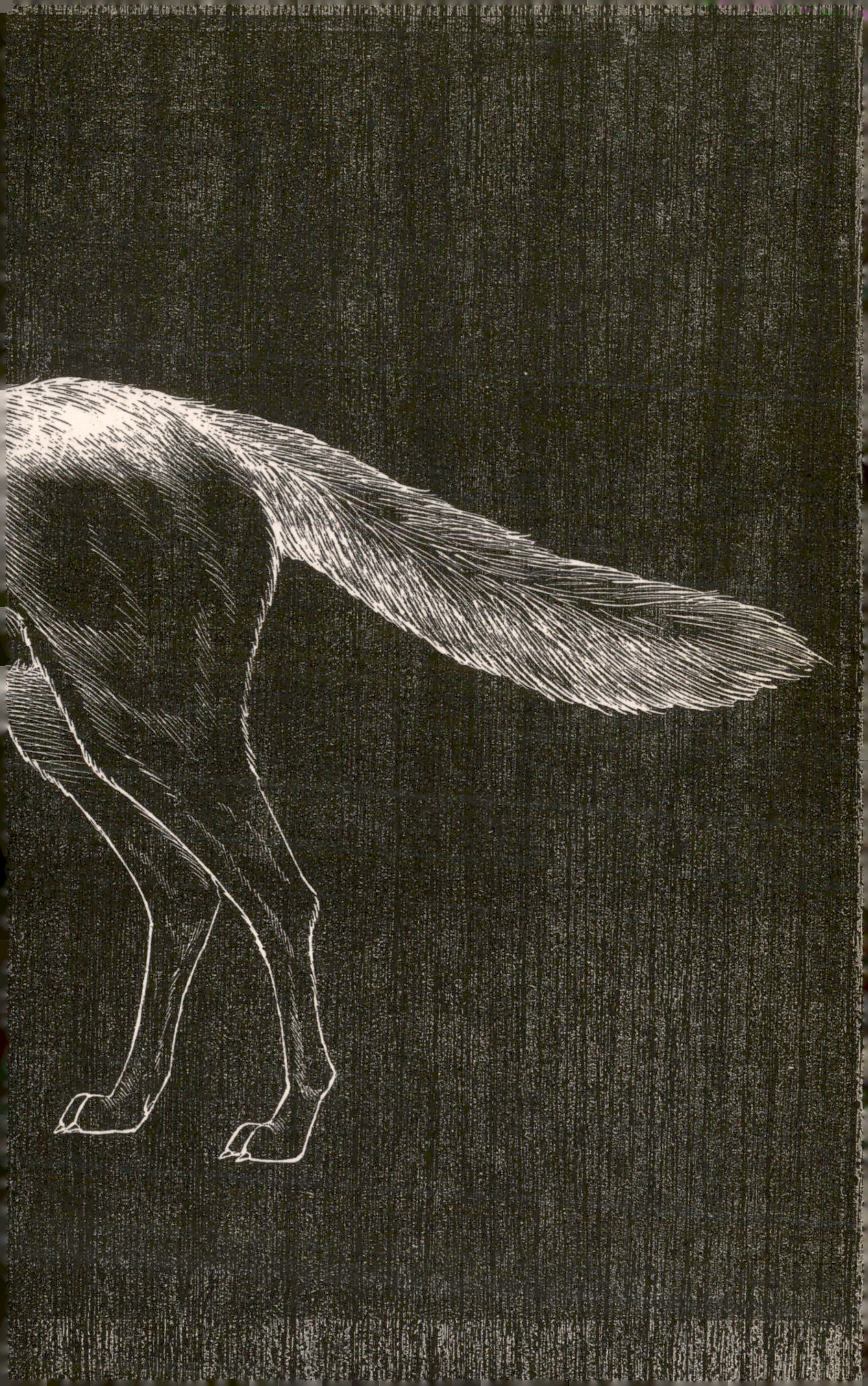

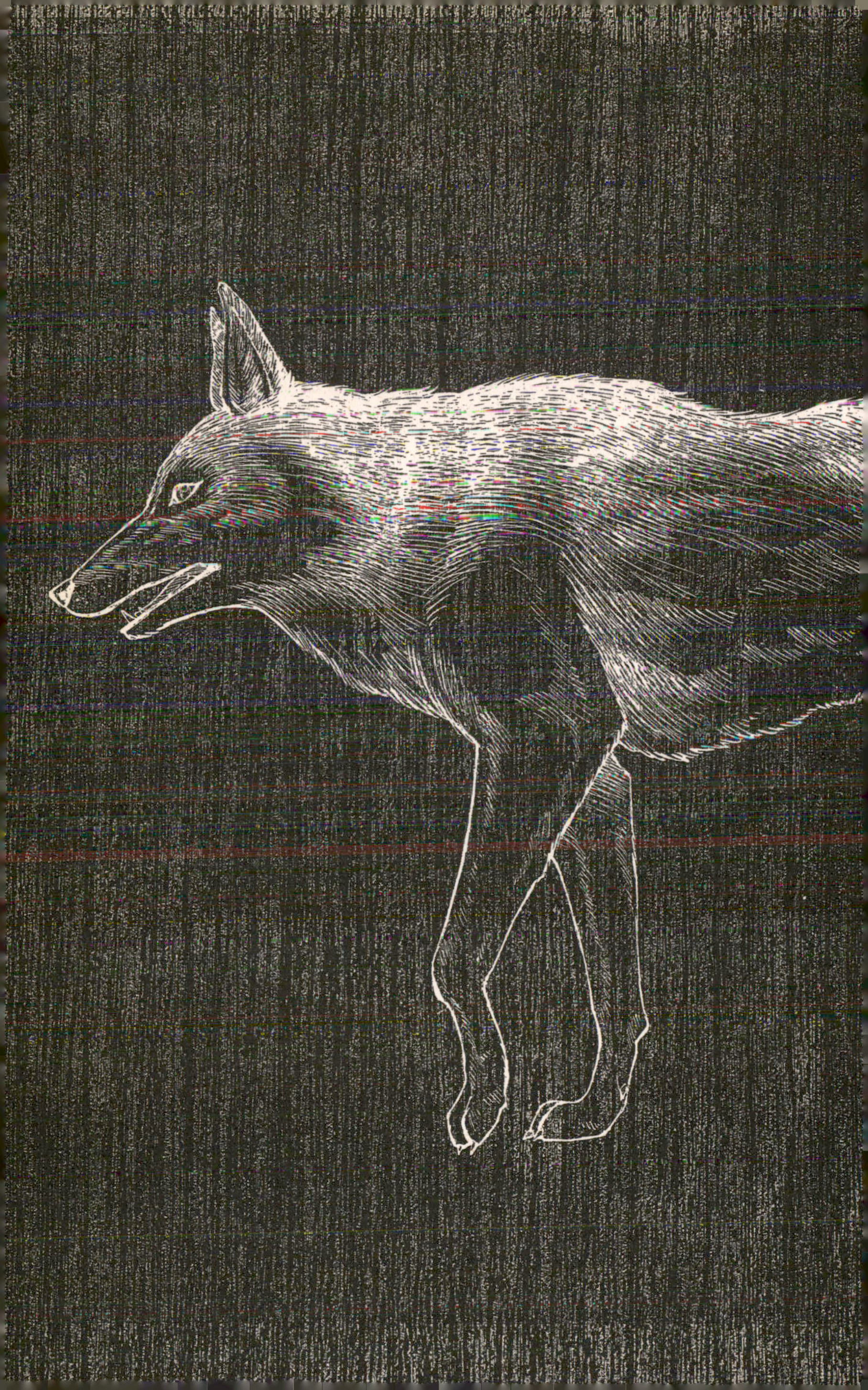

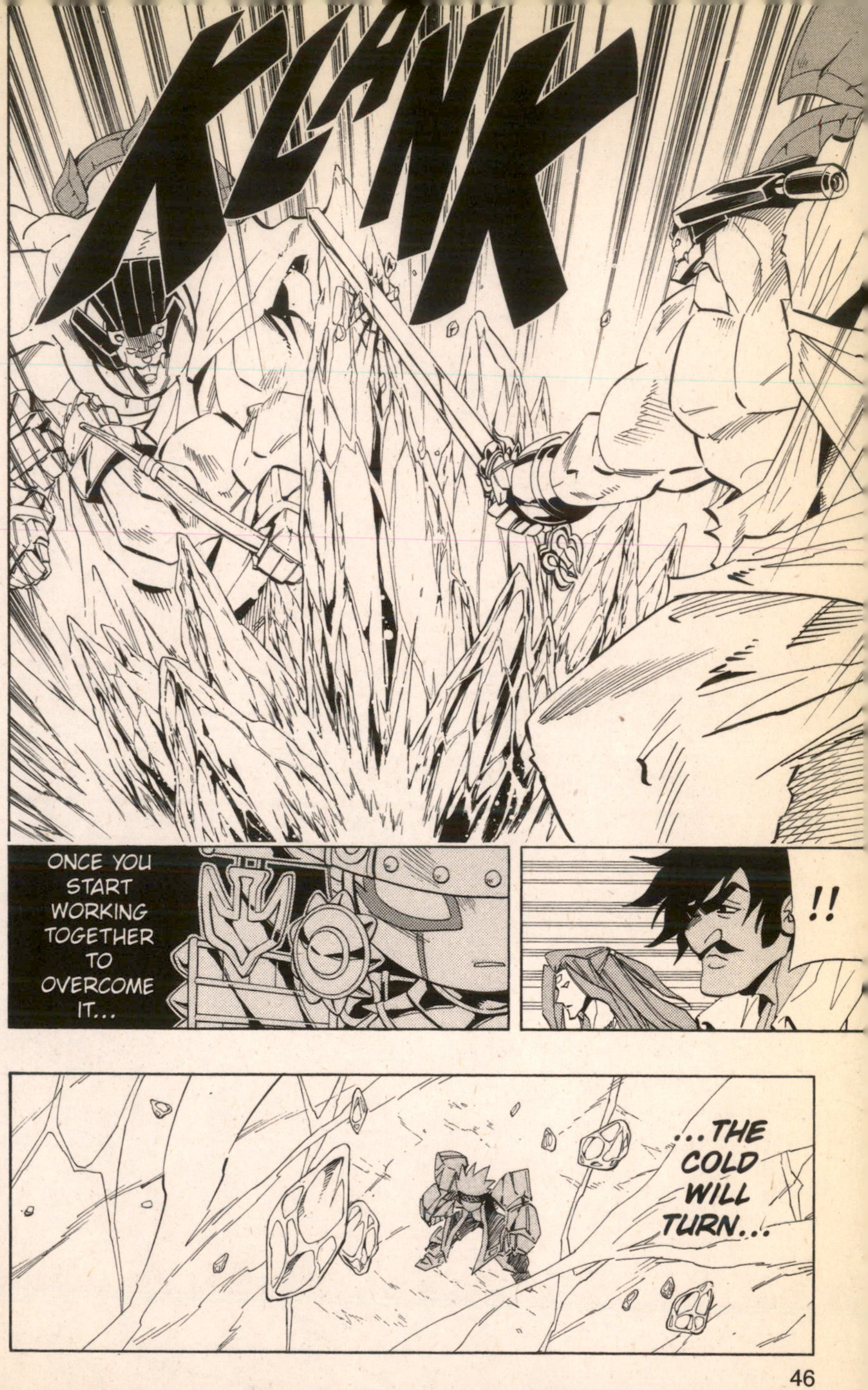
KLANK
!!
ONCE YOU START WORKING TOGETHER TO OVERCOME IT...
...THE COLD WILL TURN...

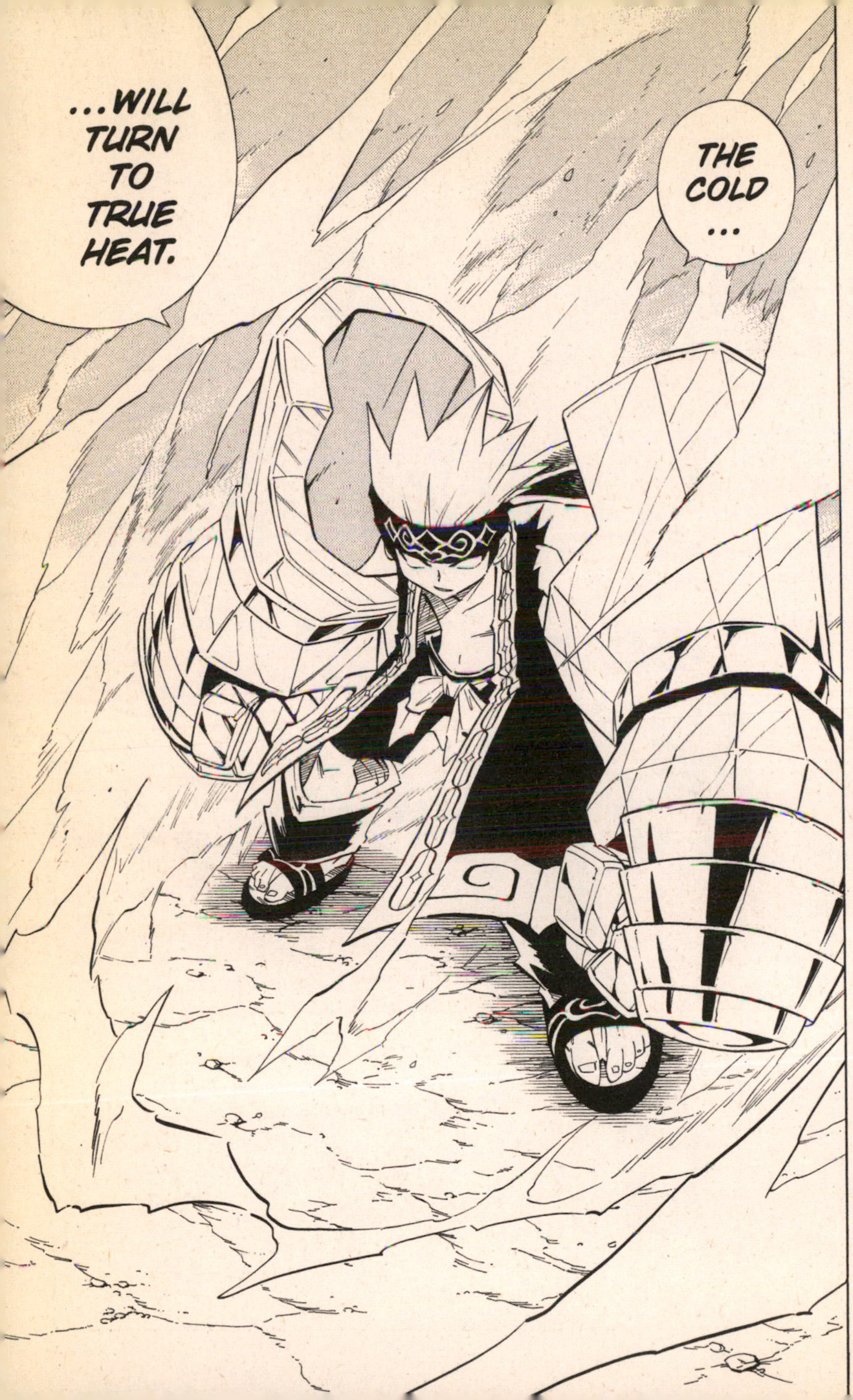
THE COLD ...
...WILL TURN TO TRUE HEAT.

SHAMAN KING CHARACTER FILE No.131

カドゥ

KADU

2001
(JAN)

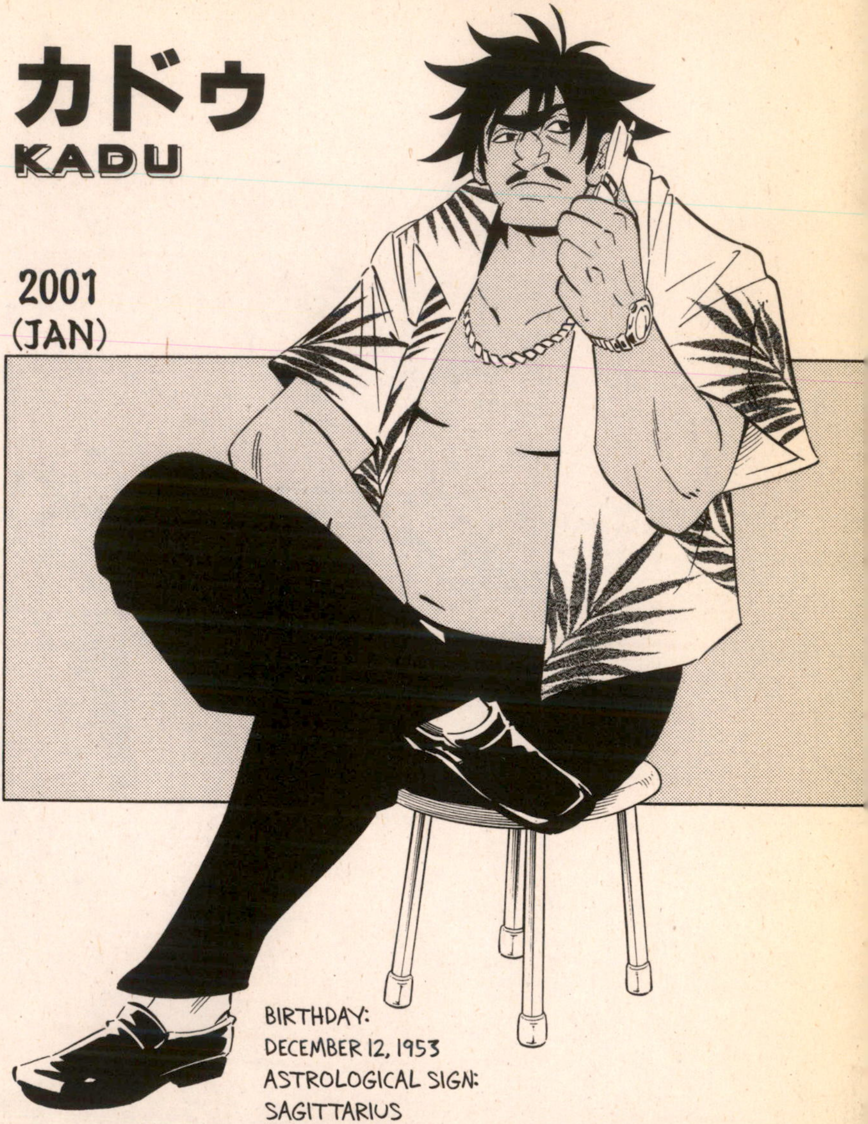

BIRTHDAY:
DECEMBER 12, 1953
ASTROLOGICAL SIGN:
SAGITTARIUS
BLOOD TYPE: B
47 YEARS OLD

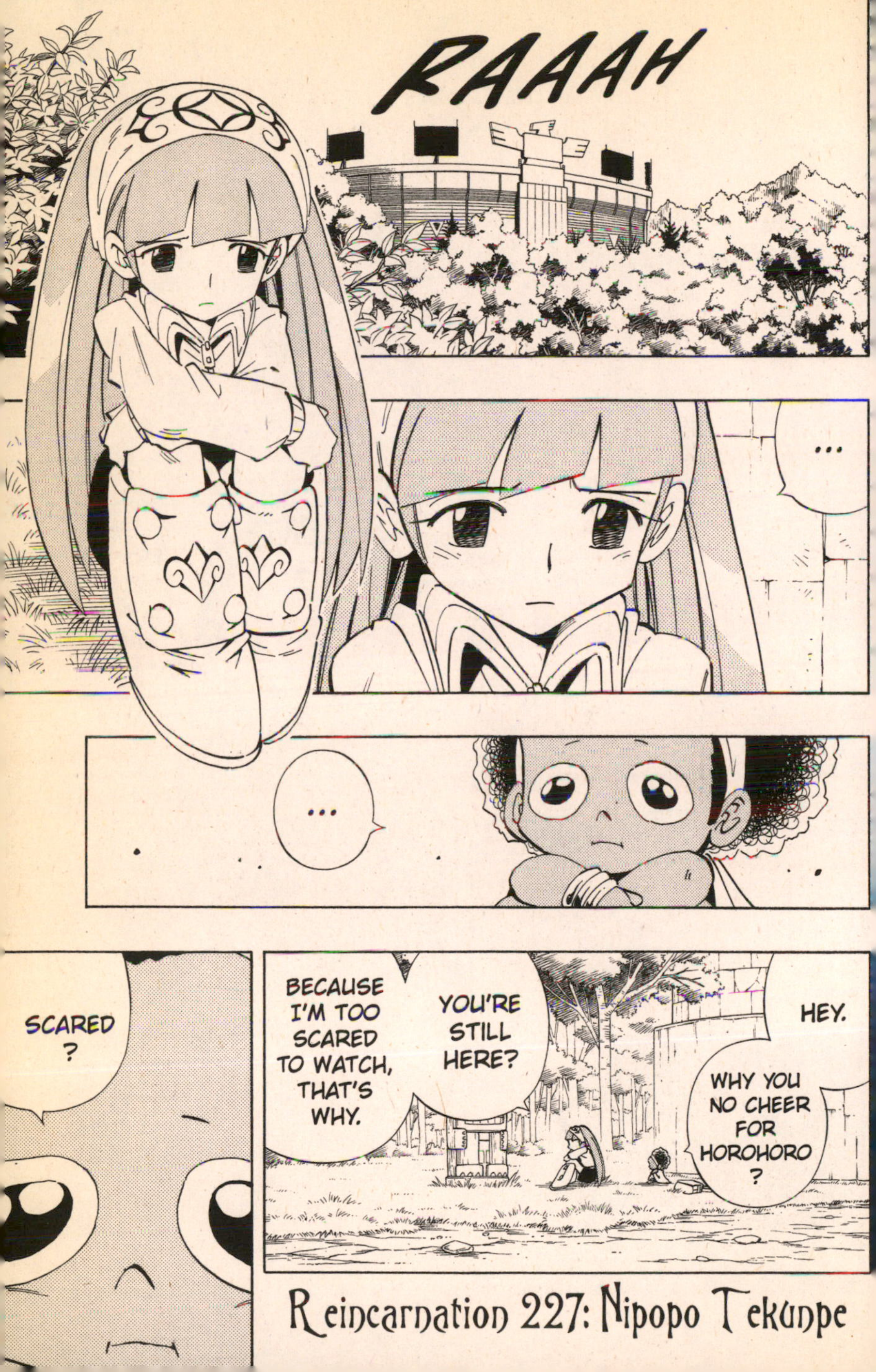
RAAAH
...
...
HEY.
WHY YOU NO CHEER FOR HOROHORO?
YOU'RE STILL HERE?
BECAUSE I'M TOO SCARED TO WATCH, THAT'S WHY.
SCARED?

Reincarnation 227: Nipopo Tekunpe

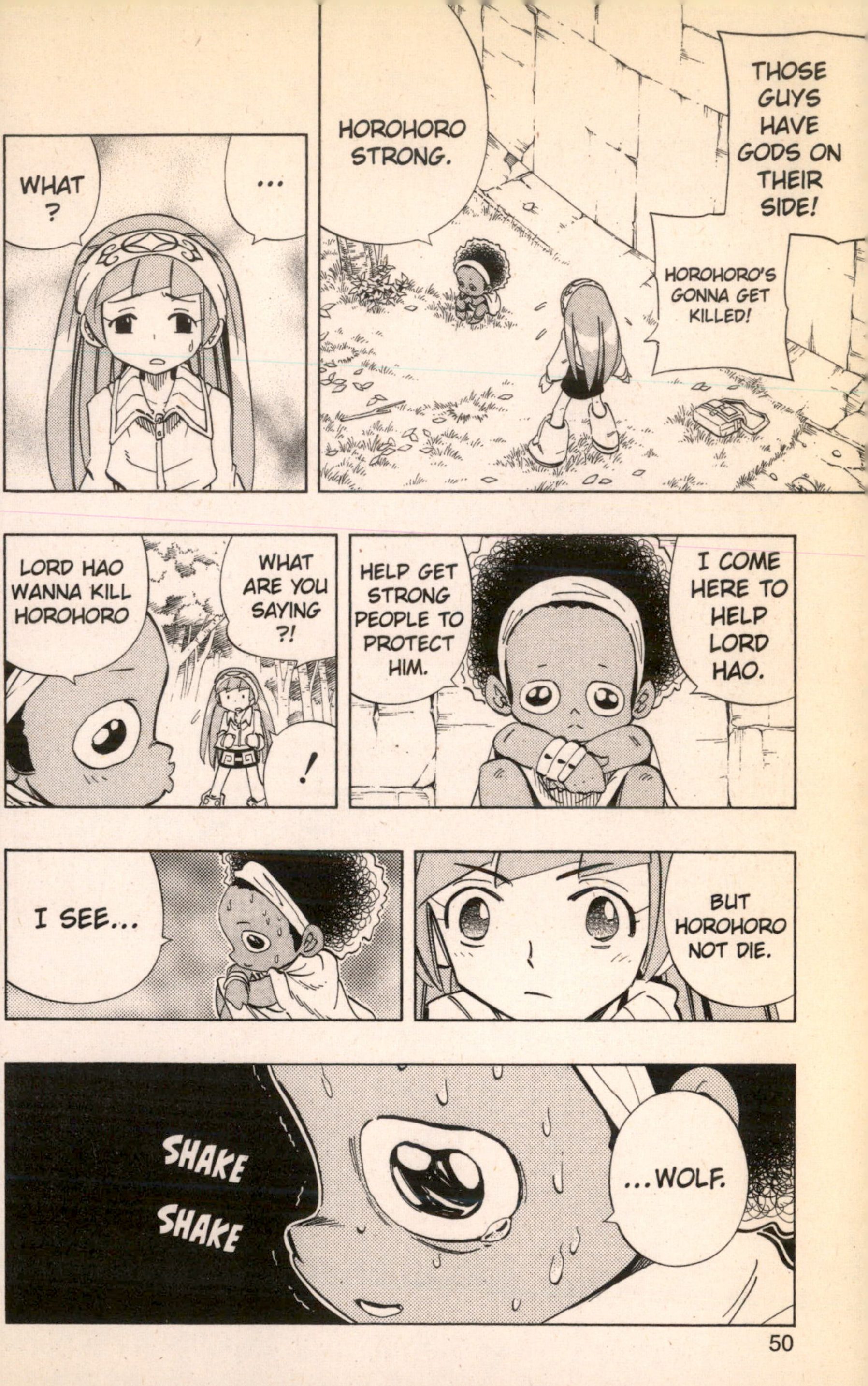
THOSE GUYS HAVE GODS ON THEIR SIDE!
HOROHORO'S GONNA GET KILLED!
HOROHORO STRONG.
...
WHAT ?
I COME HERE TO HELP LORD HAO.
HELP GET STRONG PEOPLE TO PROTECT HIM.
WHAT ARE YOU SAYING ?!
LORD HAO WANNA KILL HOROHORO
!
BUT HOROHORO NOT DIE.
I SEE...
...WOLF.
SHAKE SHAKE

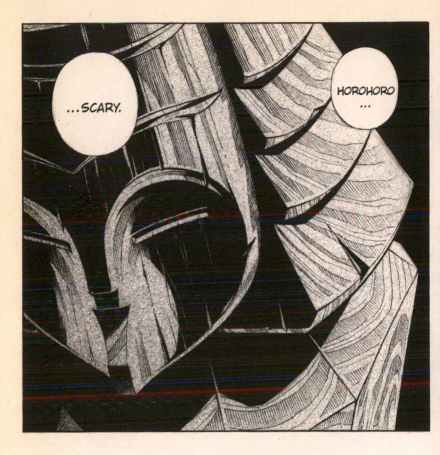

Reincarnation 227: Nipopo Tekunpe

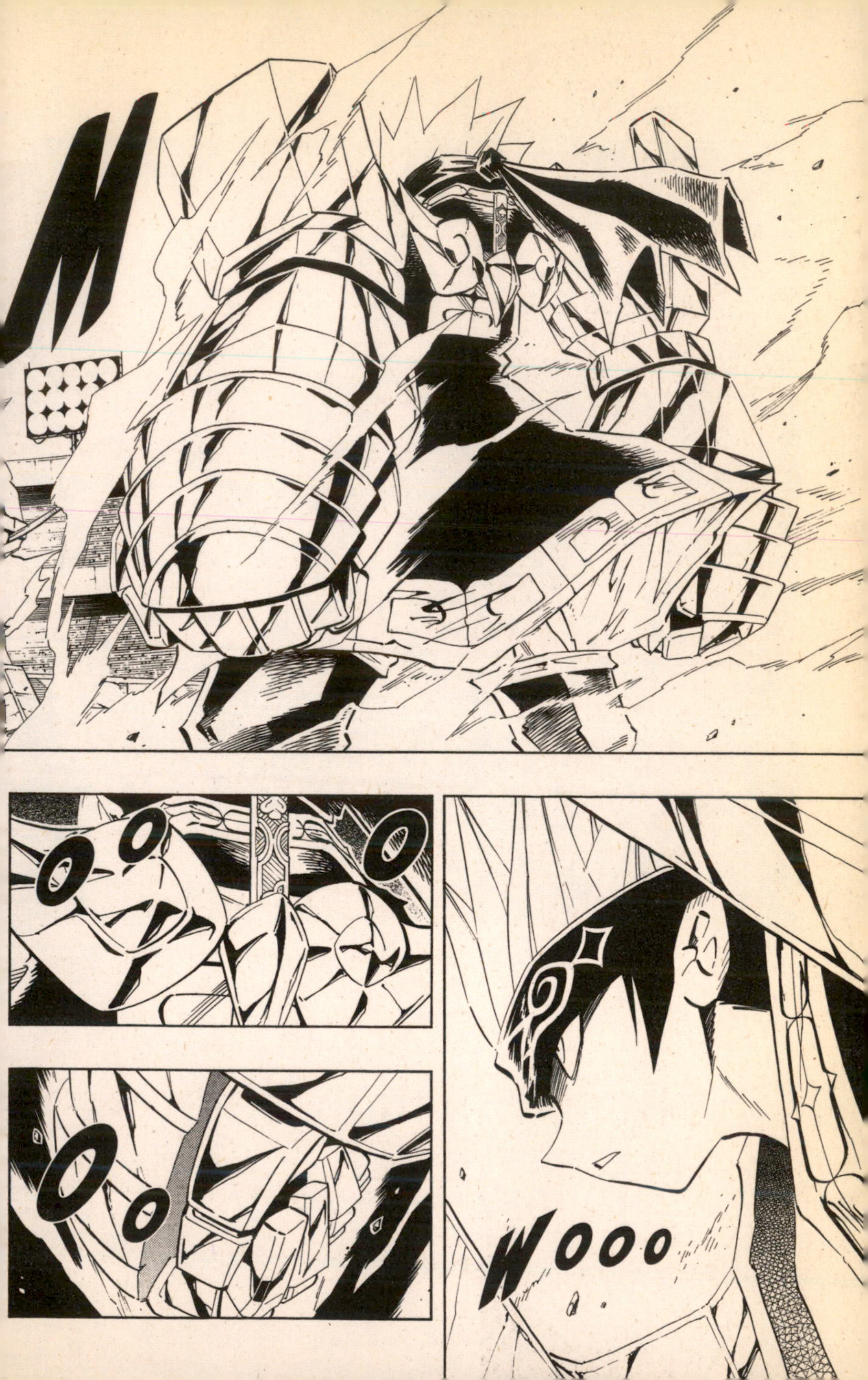
M
WOOO

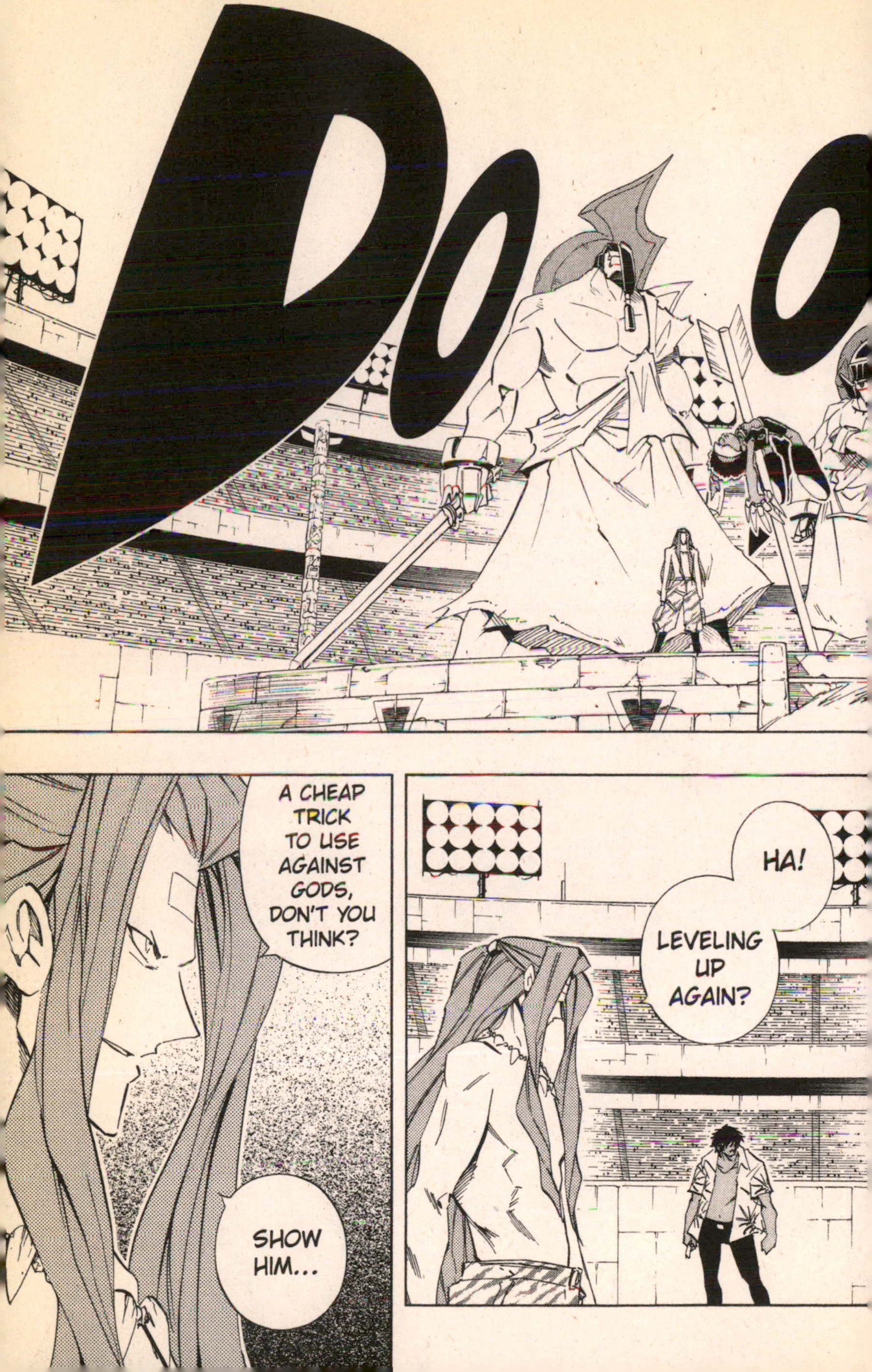
DOO
HA!
LEVELING UP AGAIN?
A CHEAP TRICK TO USE AGAINST GODS, DON'T YOU THINK?
SHOW HIM...

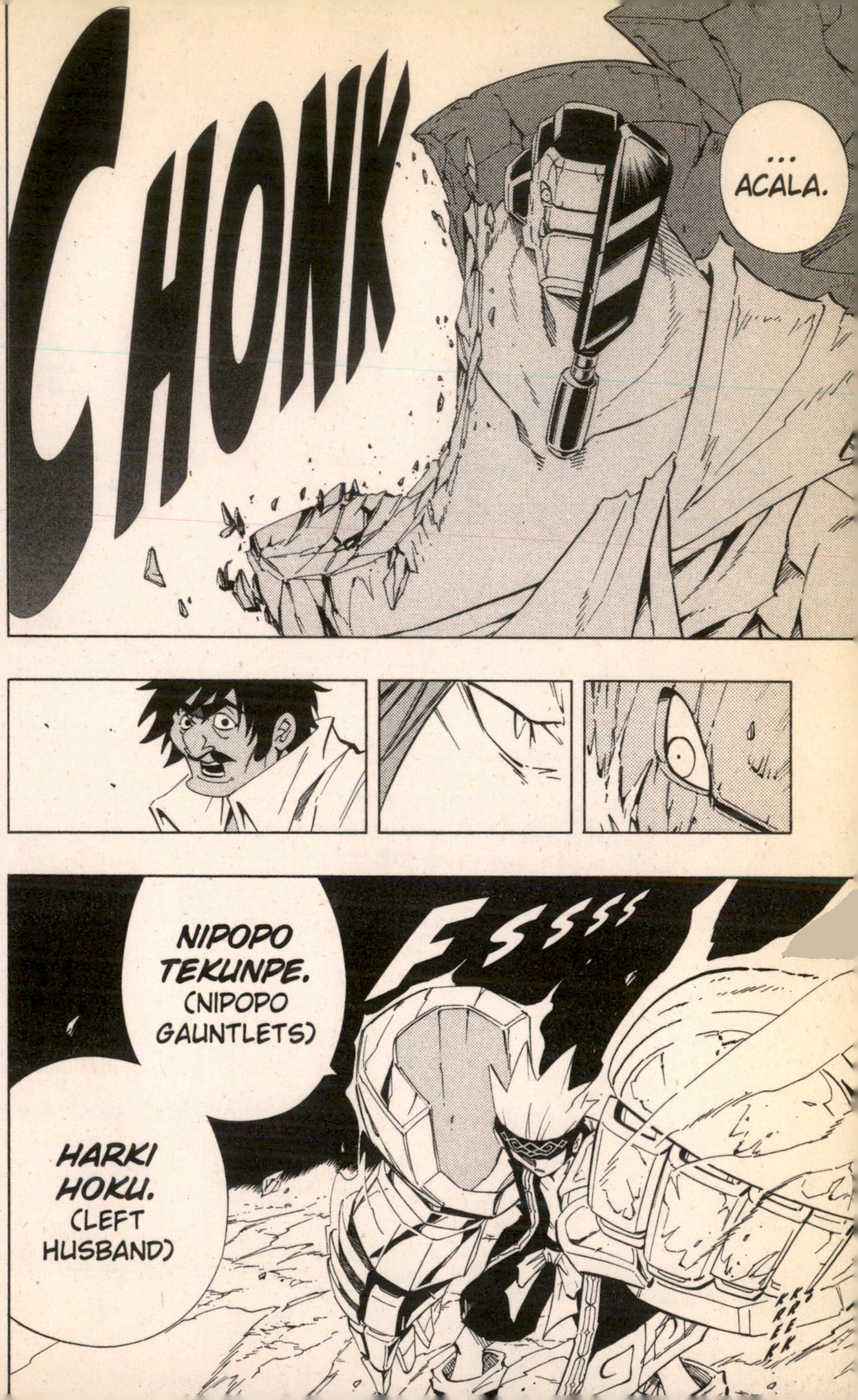
... ACALA.
CHONK
FSSSS
NIPOPO TEKUNPE. (NIPOPO GAUNTLETS)
HARKI HOKU. (LEFT HUSBAND)
KREK KREK

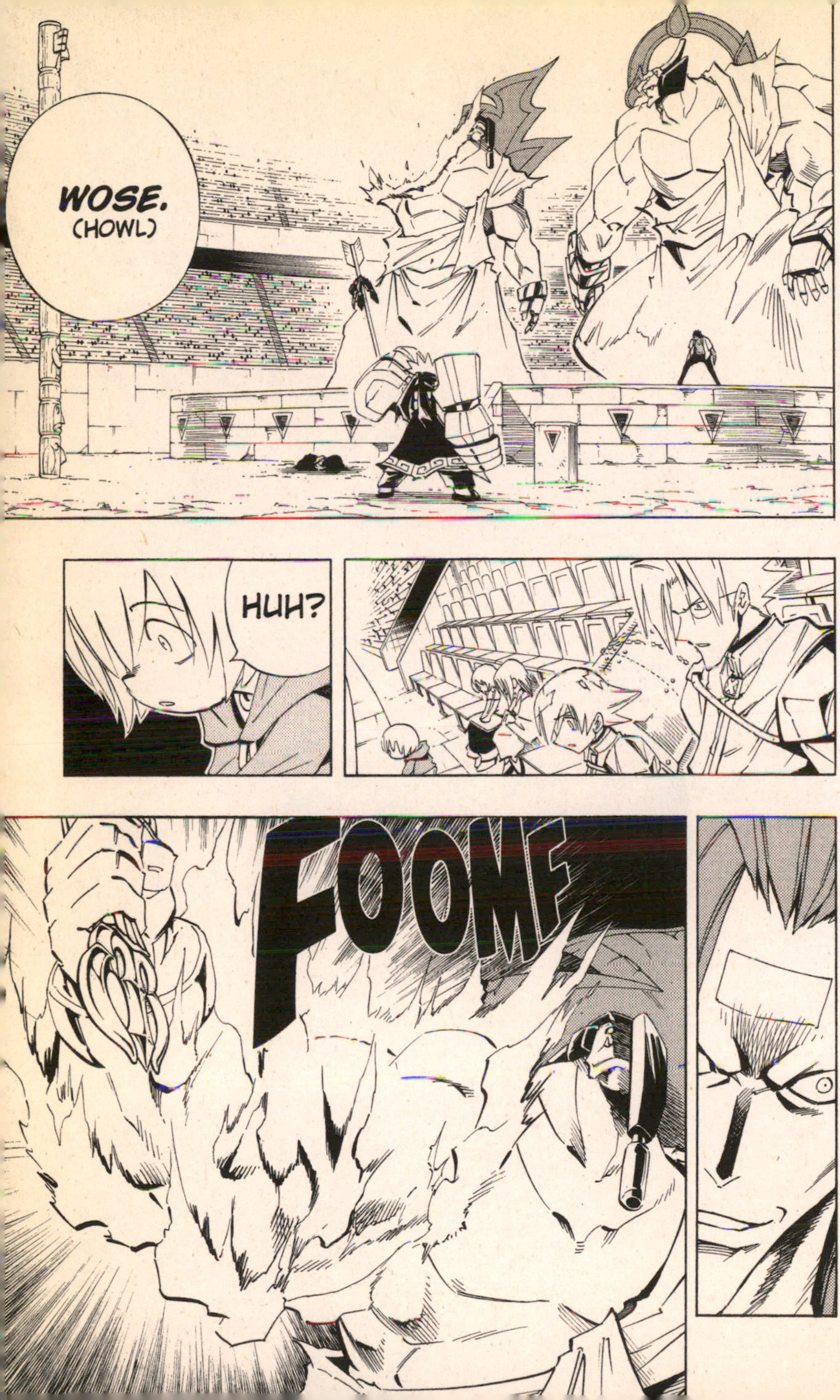
WOSE.
(HOWL)
HUH?
FOOMF

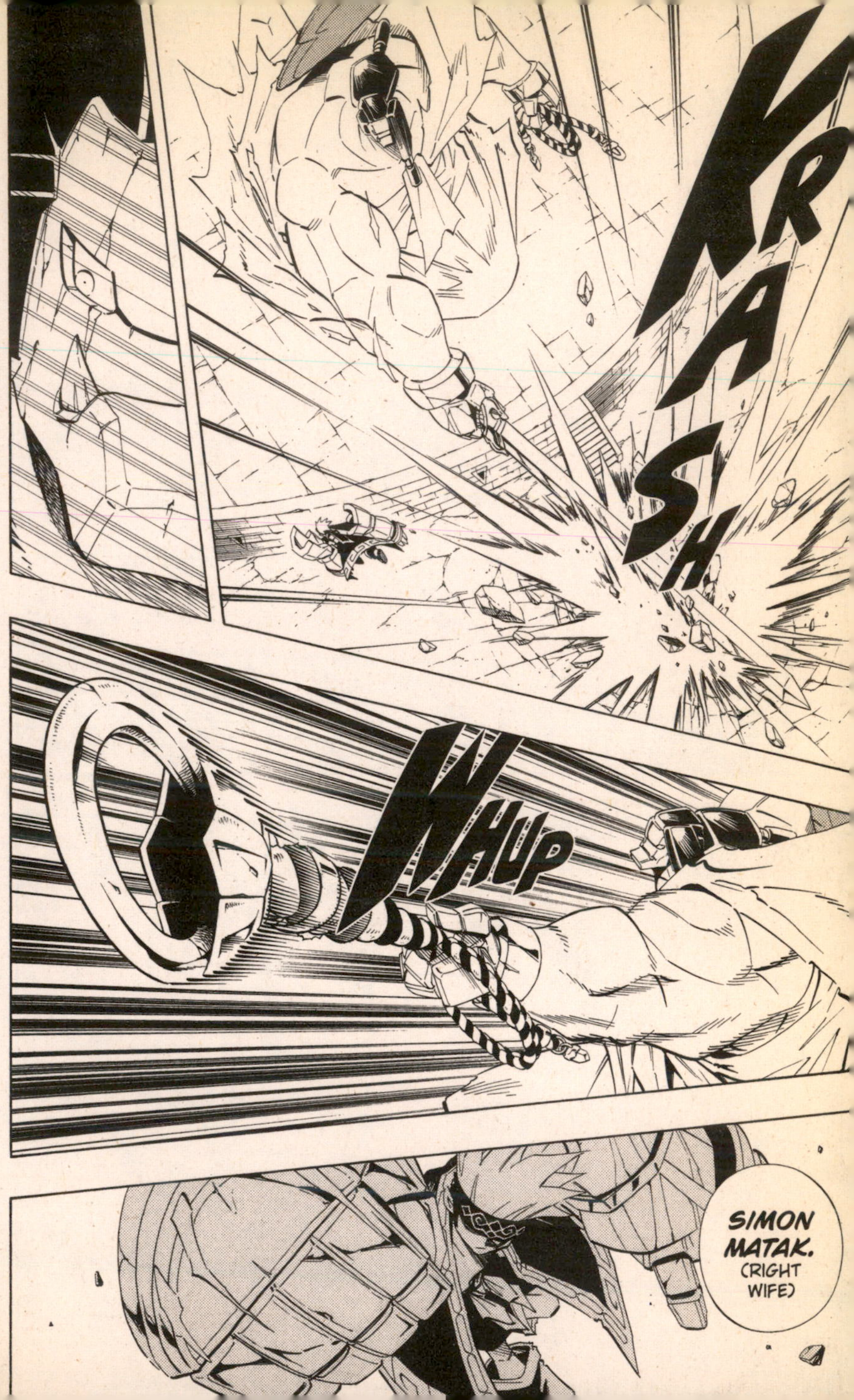
KRASH
WHUP
SIMON MATAK.
(RIGHT WIFE)

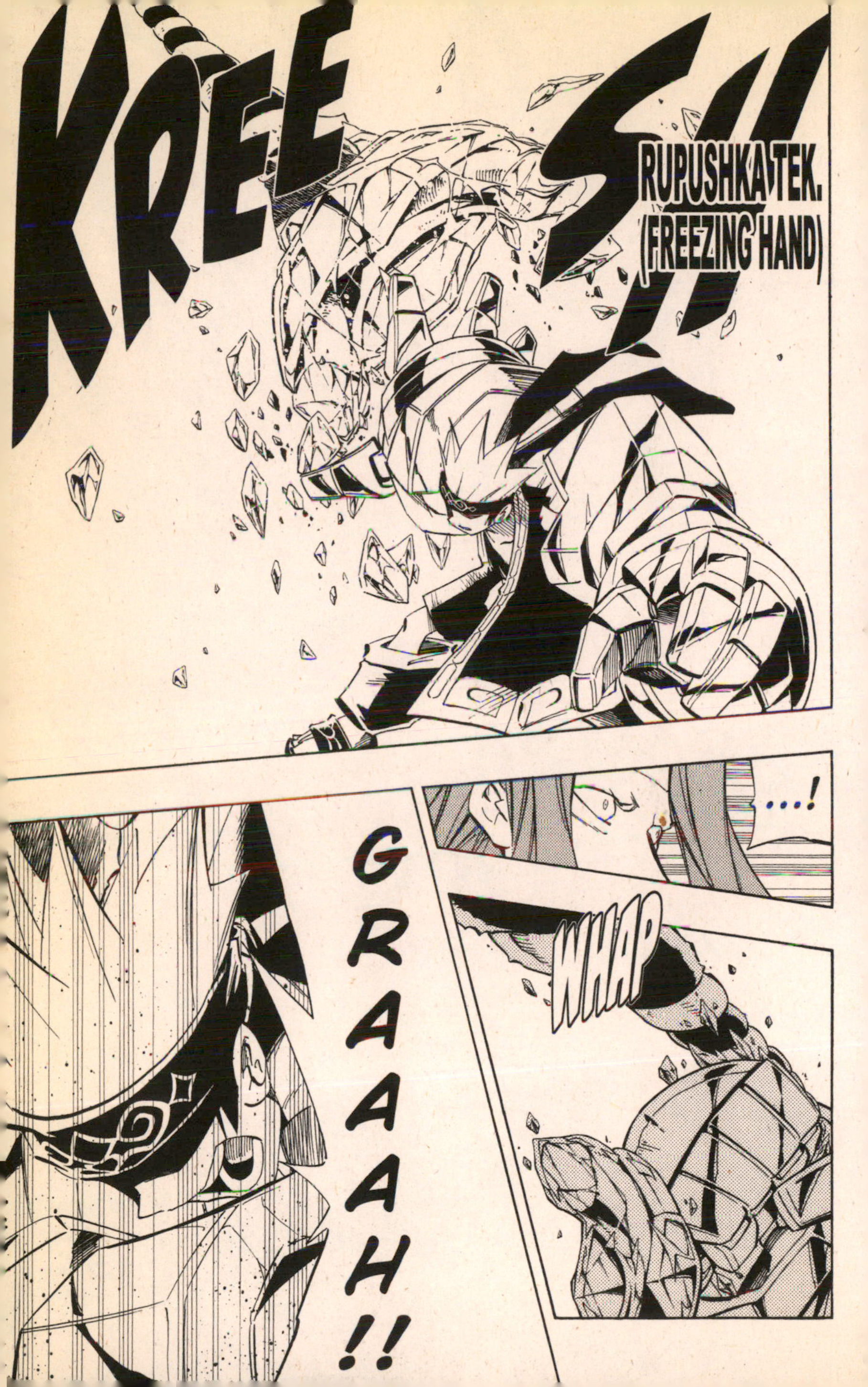
KREESH
RUPUSHKA TEK.
(FREEZING HAND)
...!
WHAP
GRAAAH!!

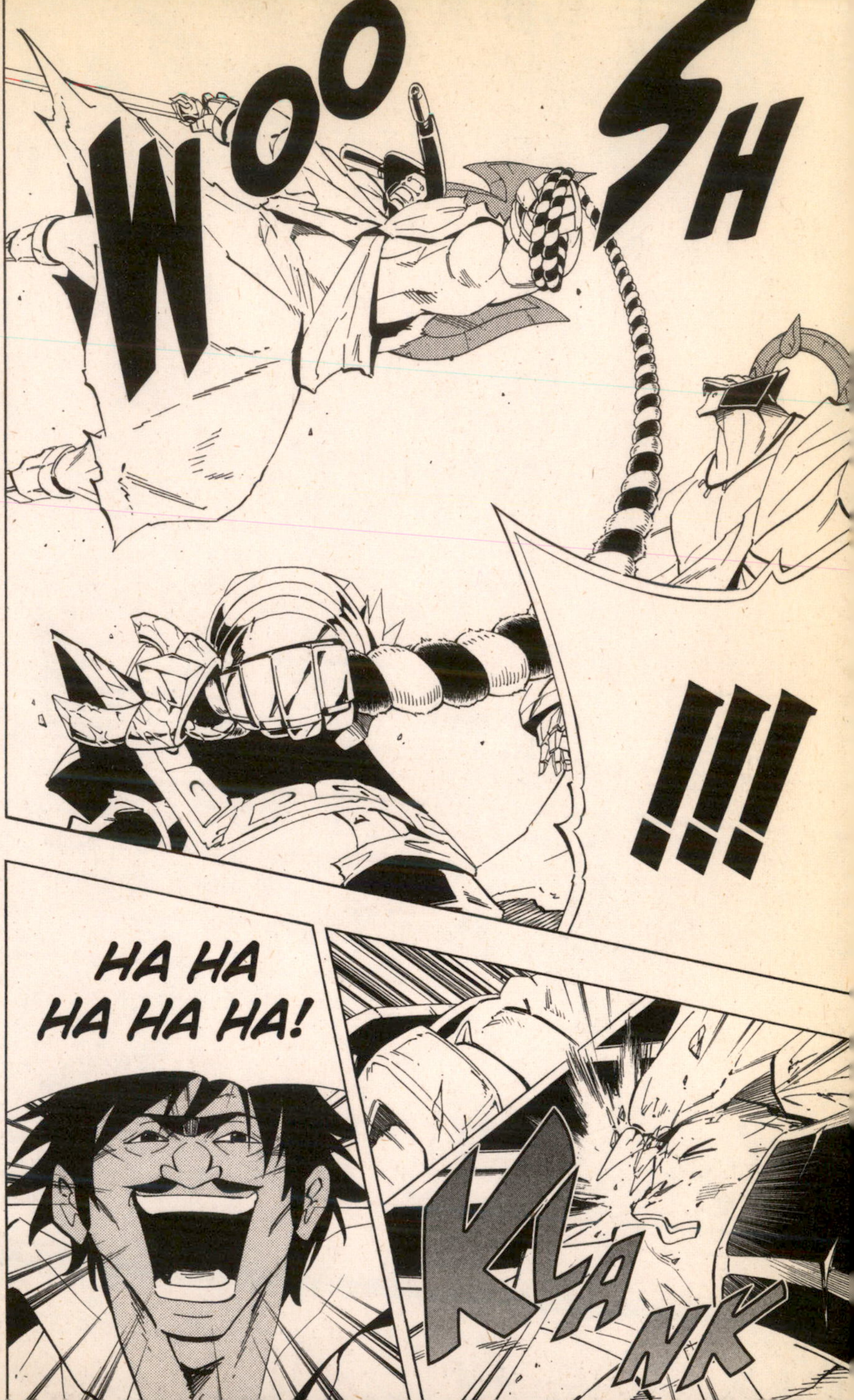
WOOSH
!!!
KLANK
HA HA
HA HA HA!

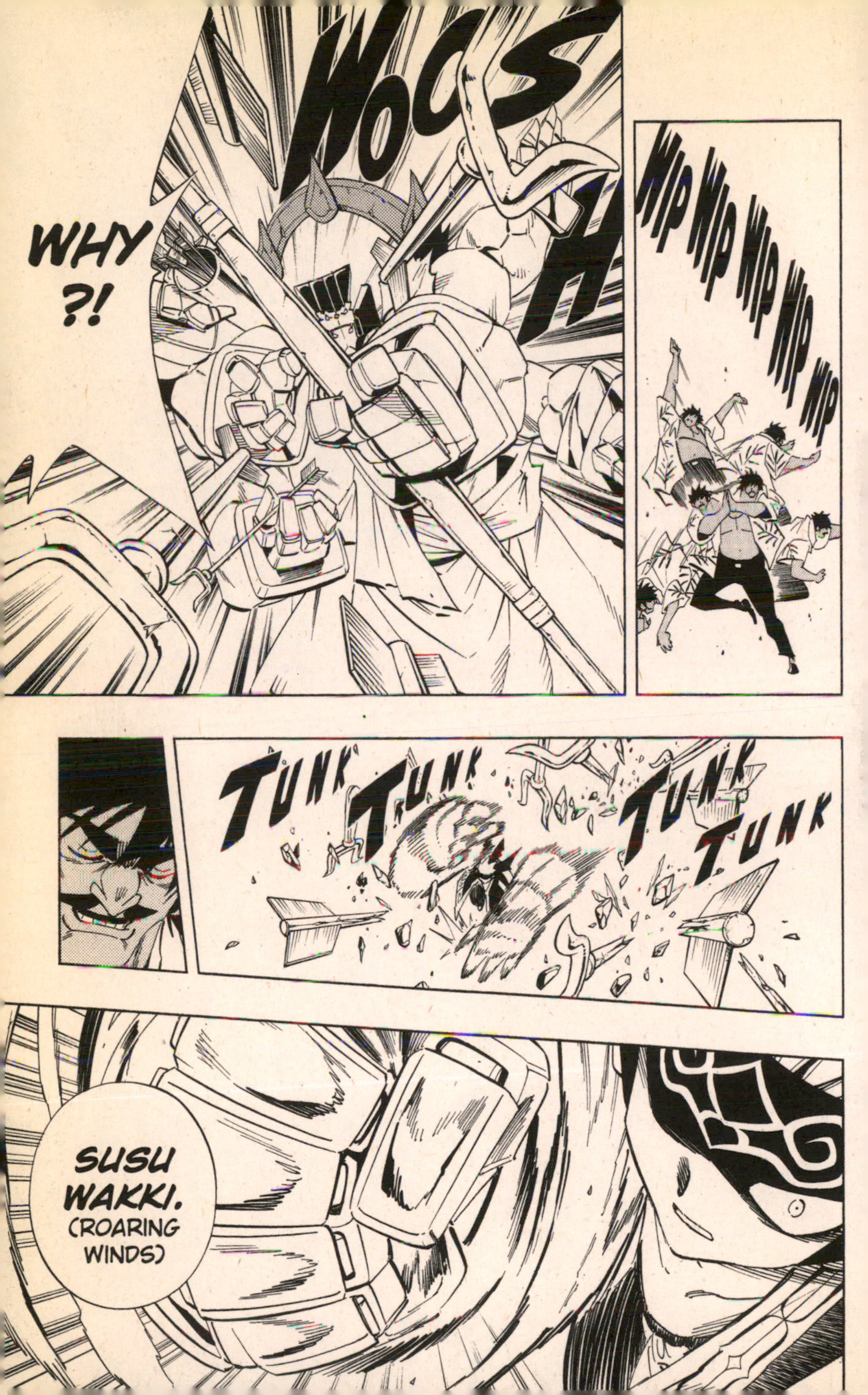
WIP WIP WIP WIP WIP WIP
WHOOSH
WHY ?!
TUNK TUNK TUNK TUNK
SUSU WAKKI. (ROARING WINDS)

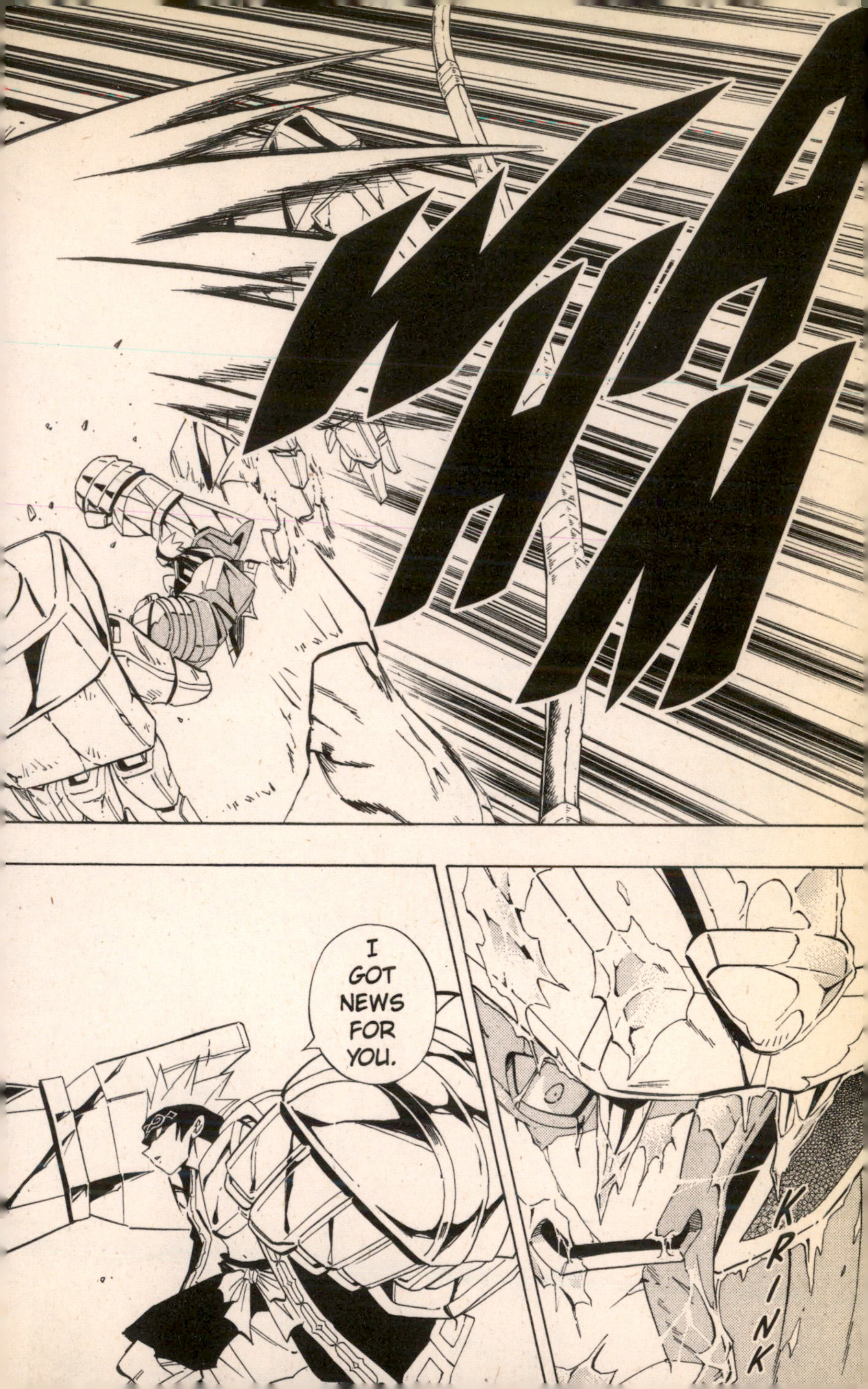
KRINK
I GOT NEWS FOR YOU.

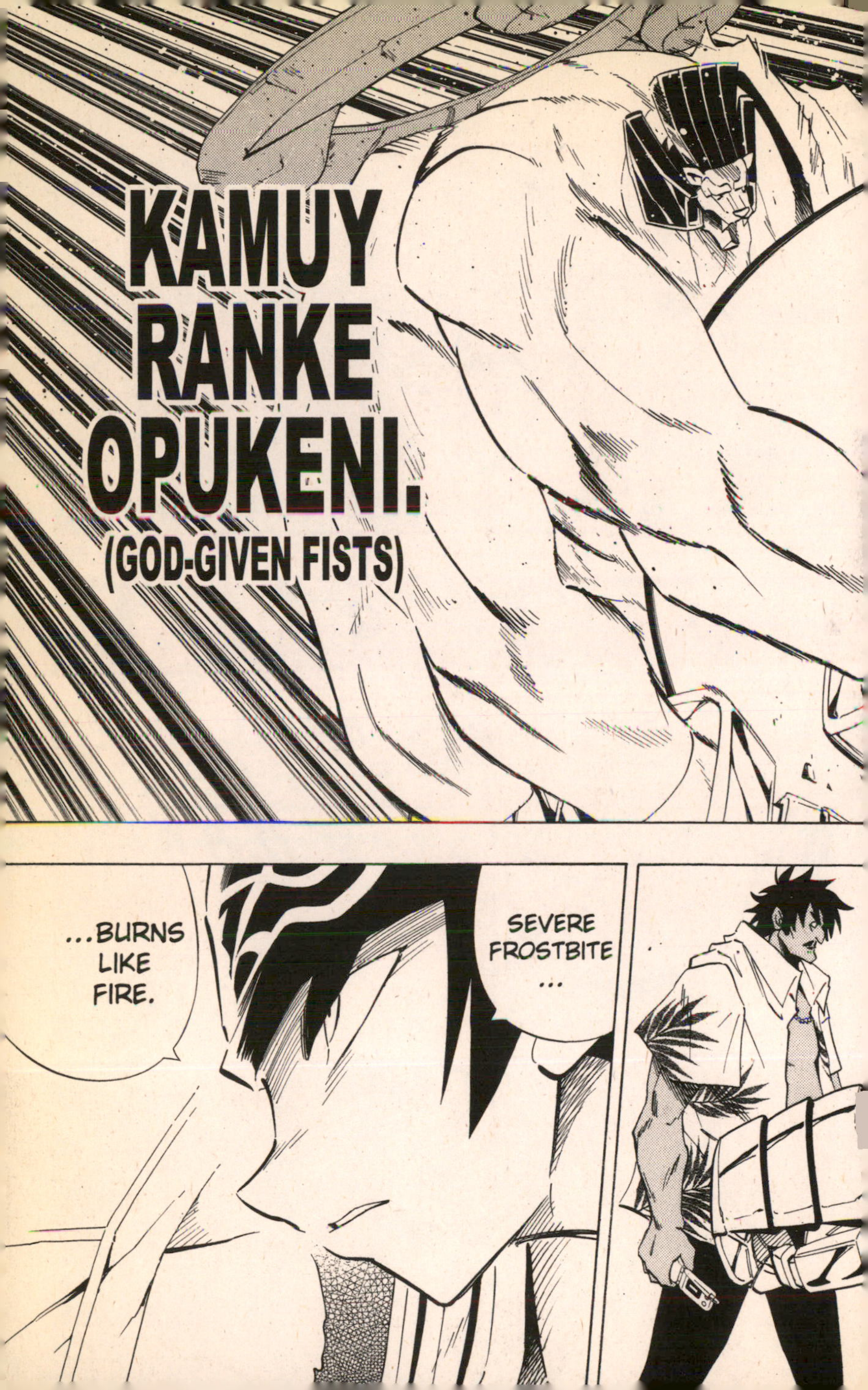
KAMUY RANKE OPUKENI.
(GOD-GIVEN FISTS)
SEVERE FROSTBITE ...
...BURNS LIKE FIRE.

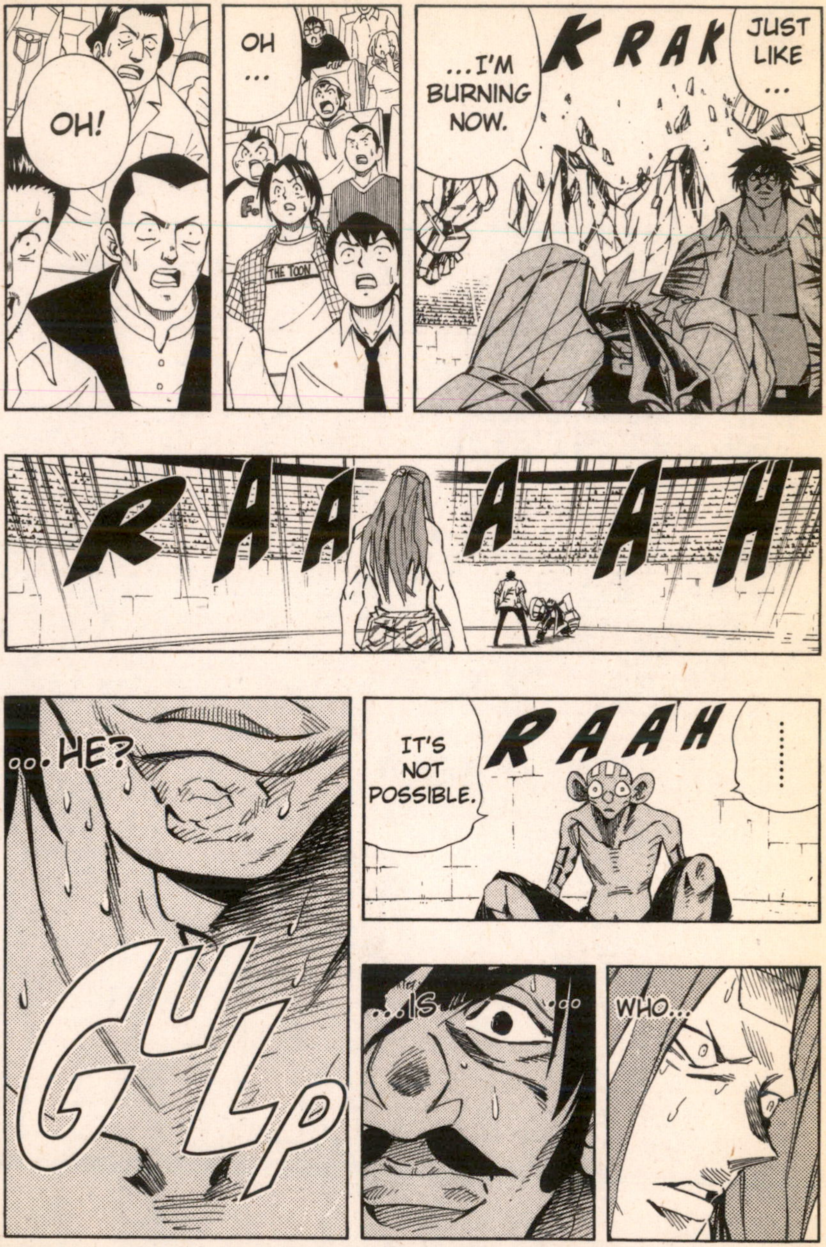
JUST LIKE ...
KRAK
...I'M BURNING NOW.
OH ...
OH!
RAAAAH
......
RAAH
IT'S NOT POSSIBLE.
WHO...
...IS ...
...HE?
GULP

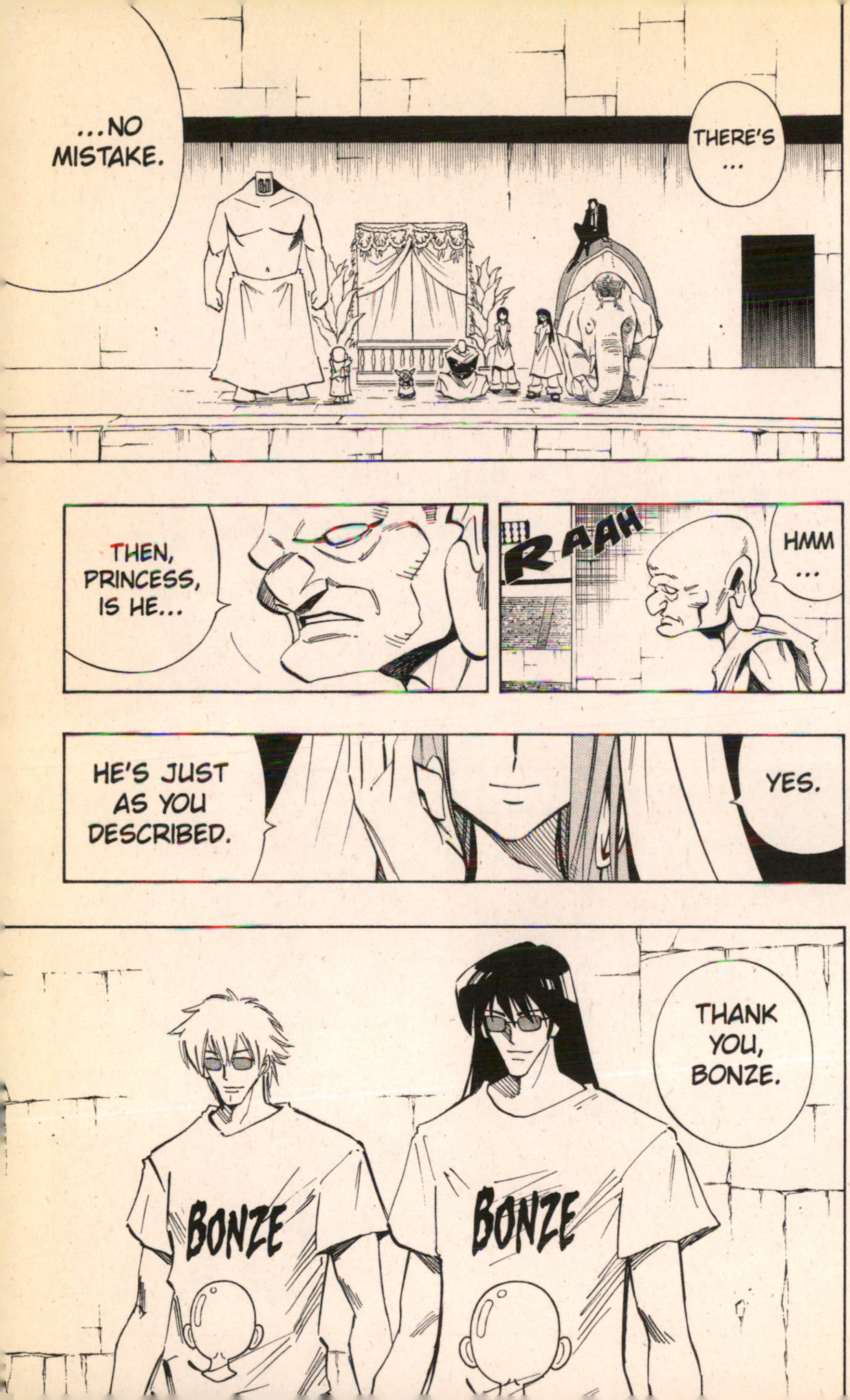
THERE'S ...
...NO MISTAKE.
RAAH
HMM ...
THEN, PRINCESS, IS HE...
YES.
HE'S JUST AS YOU DESCRIBED.
THANK YOU, BONZE.
BONZE
BONZE

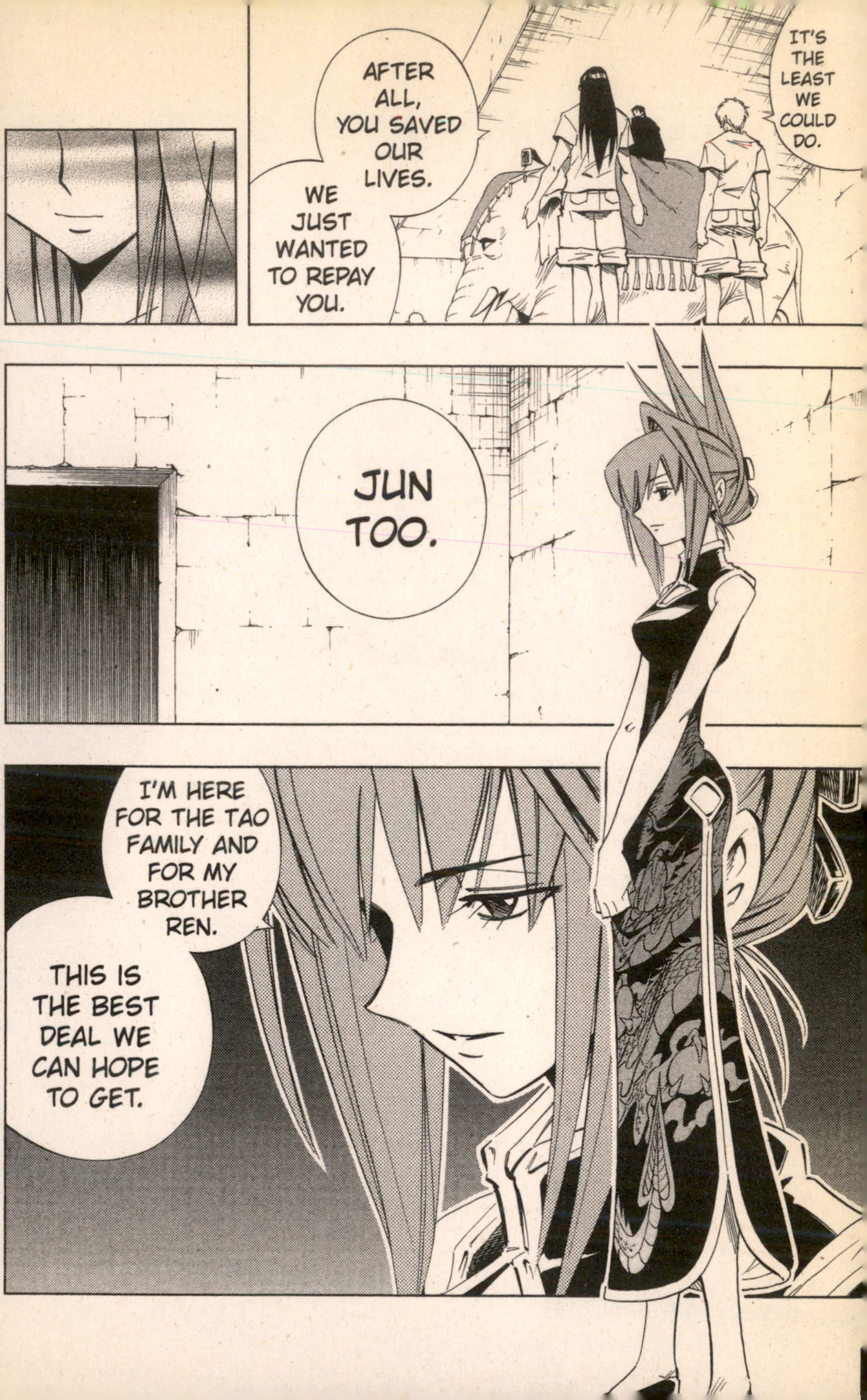
IT'S THE LEAST WE COULD DO.
AFTER ALL, YOU SAVED OUR LIVES.
WE JUST WANTED TO REPAY YOU.
JUN TOO.
I'M HERE FOR THE TAO FAMILY AND FOR MY BROTHER REN.
THIS IS THE BEST DEAL WE CAN HOPE TO GET.

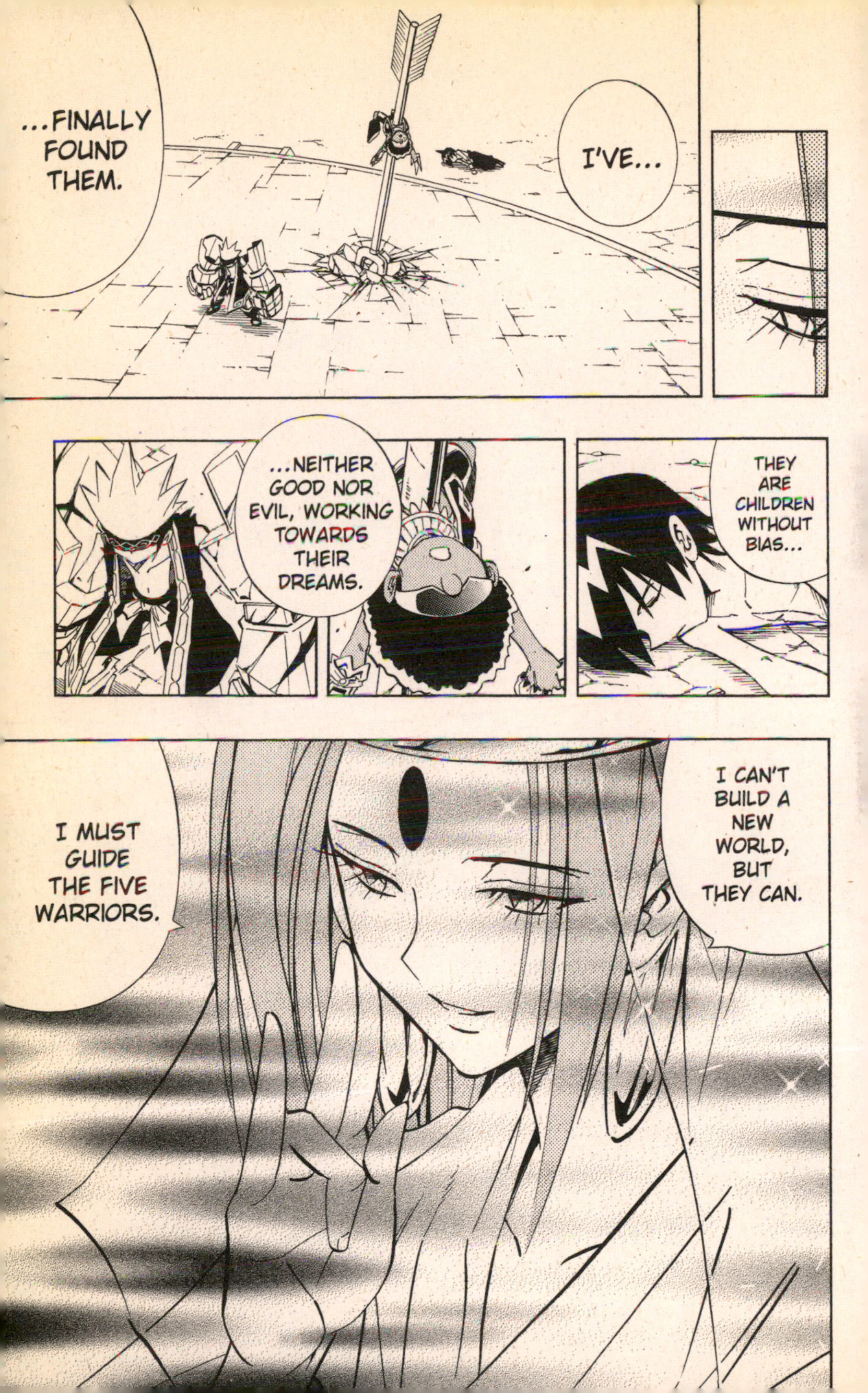
I'VE...
...FINALLY FOUND THEM.
THEY ARE CHILDREN WITHOUT BIAS...
...NEITHER GOOD NOR EVIL, WORKING TOWARDS THEIR DREAMS.
I CAN'T BUILD A NEW WORLD, BUT THEY CAN.
I MUST GUIDE THE FIVE WARRIORS.

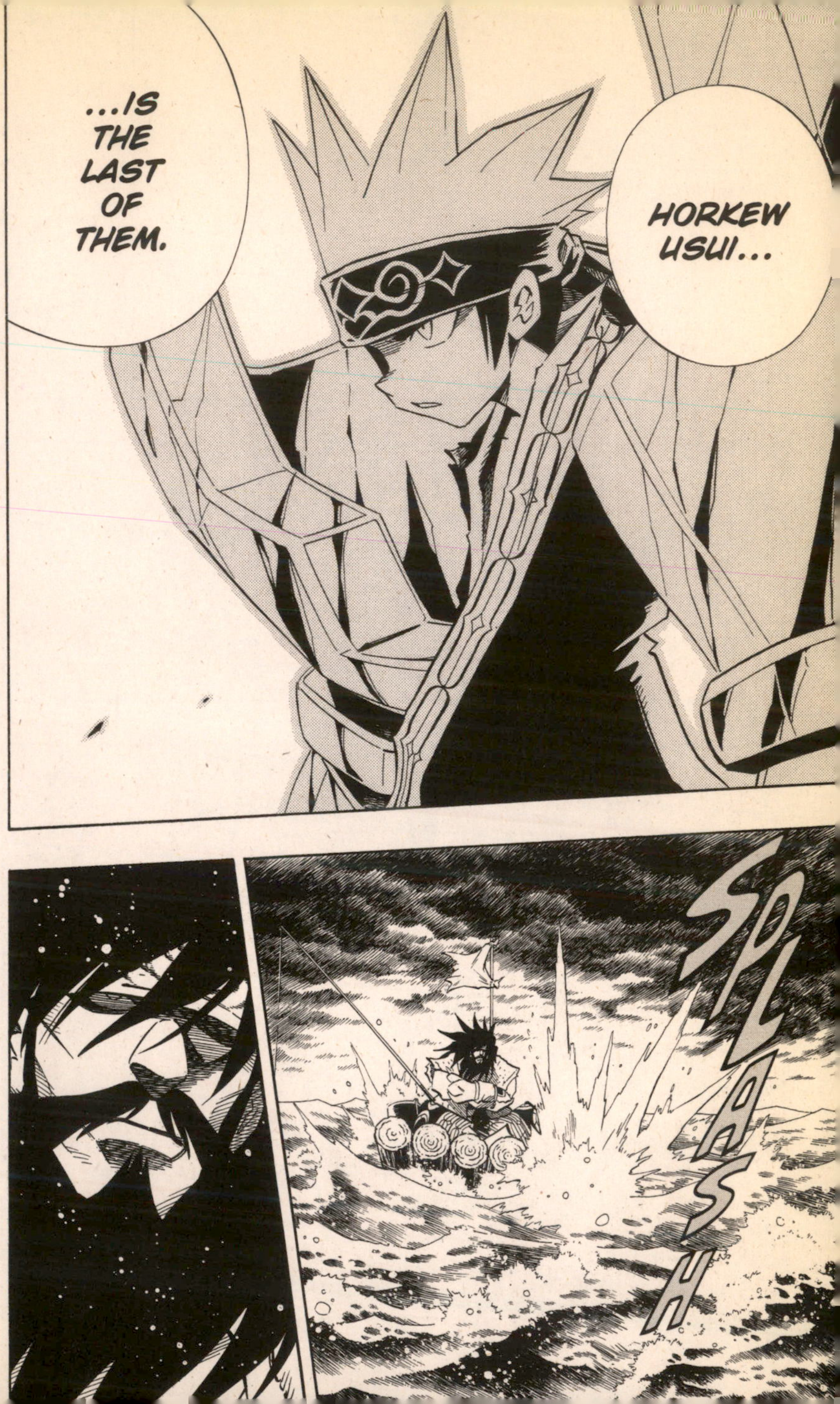
HORKEW USUI...
...IS THE LAST OF THEM.
SPLASH

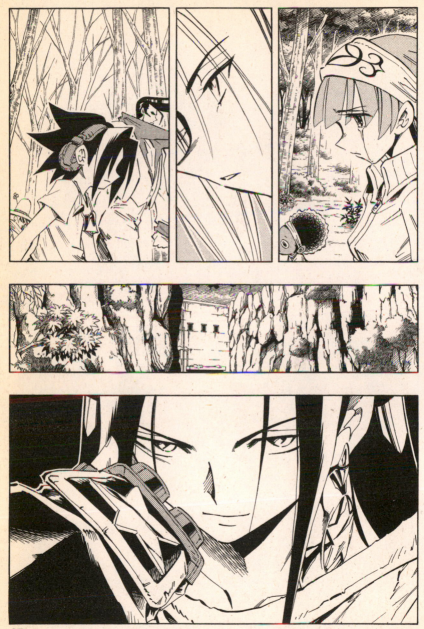

SHAMAN KING CHARACTER FILE No.132

寂尊

JACKSON

2001
(JAN)

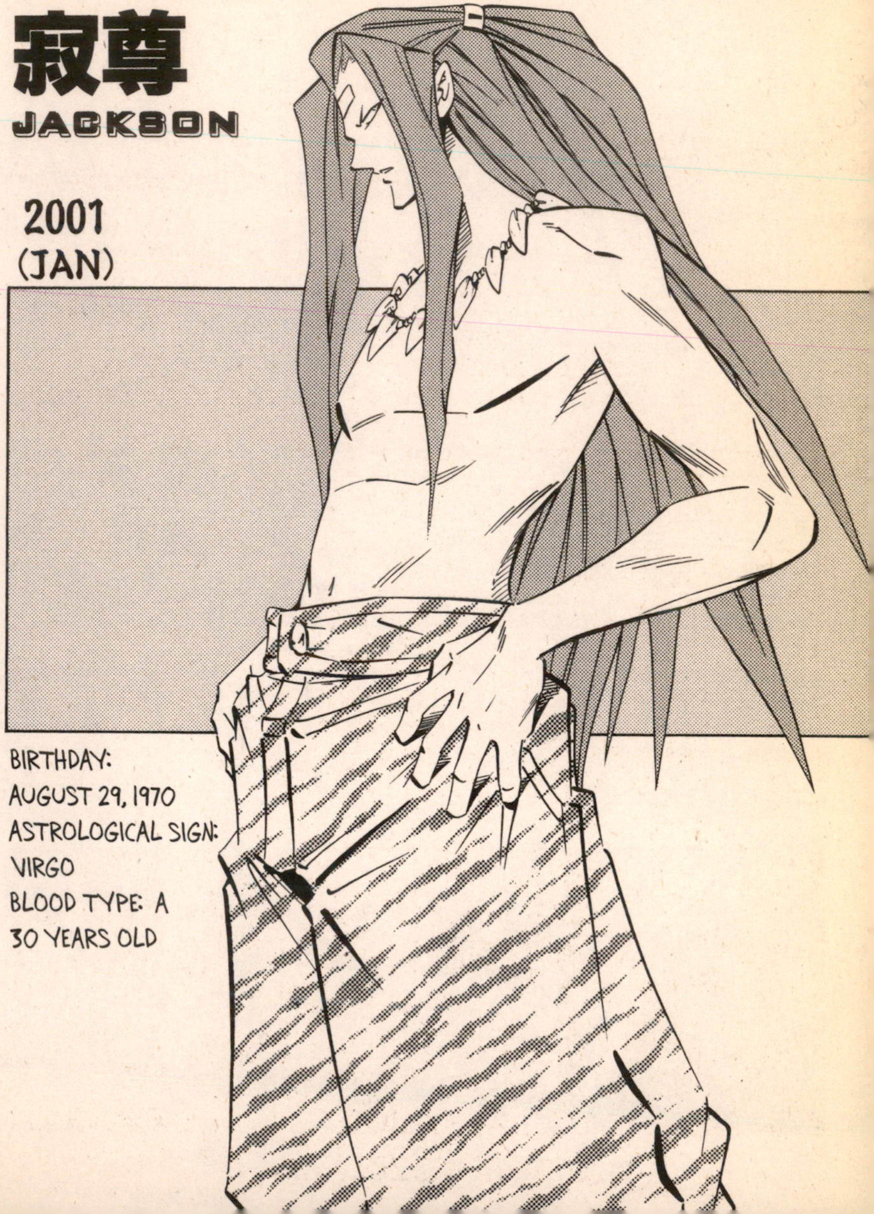

BIRTHDAY:
AUGUST 29, 1970
ASTROLOGICAL SIGN:
VIRGO
BLOOD TYPE: A
30 YEARS OLD

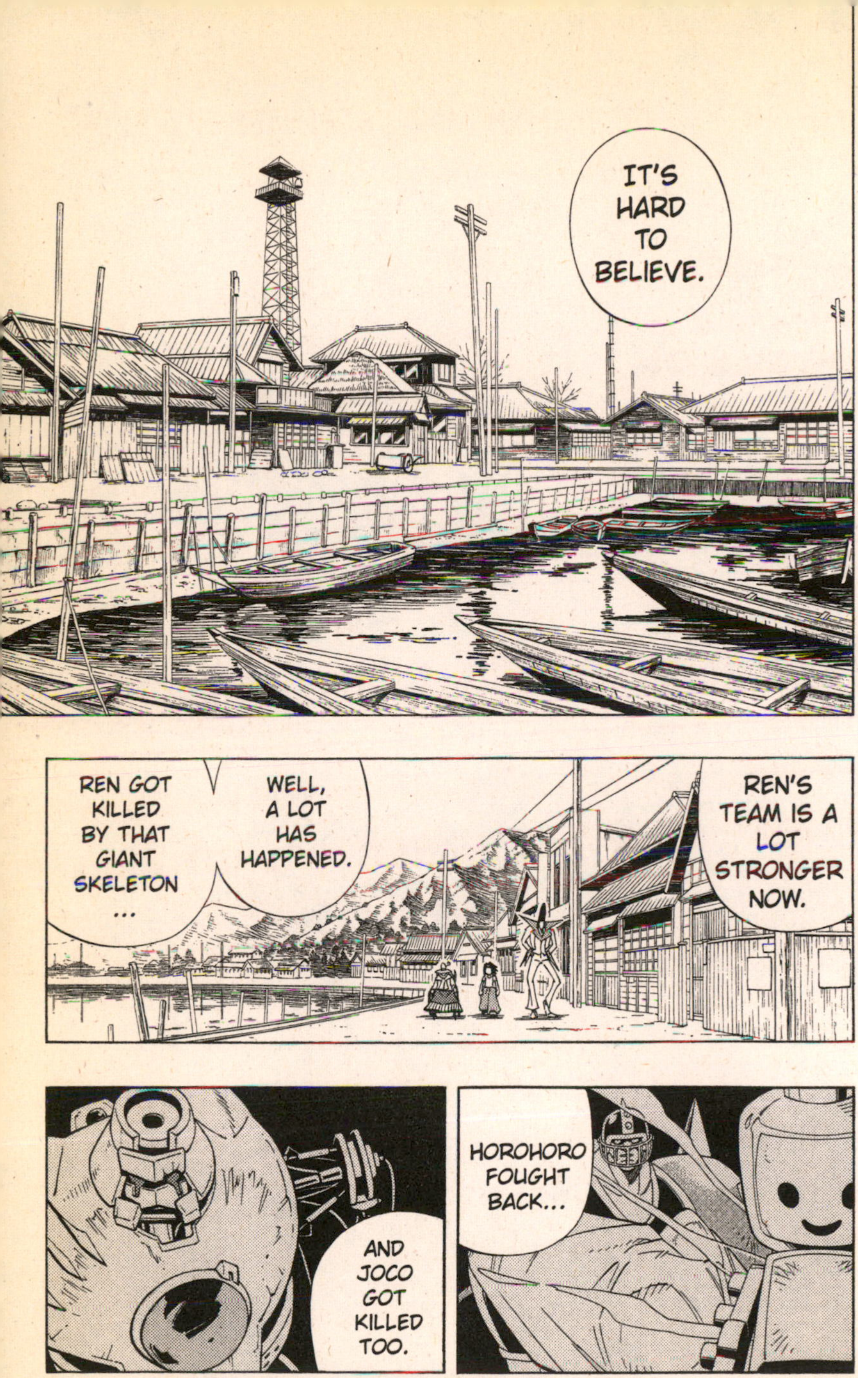
IT'S HARD TO BELIEVE.
REN'S TEAM IS A LOT STRONGER NOW.
WELL, A LOT HAS HAPPENED.
REN GOT KILLED BY THAT GIANT SKELETON ...
HOROHORO FOUGHT BACK...
AND JOCO GOT KILLED TOO.

Reincarnation 228: An Act

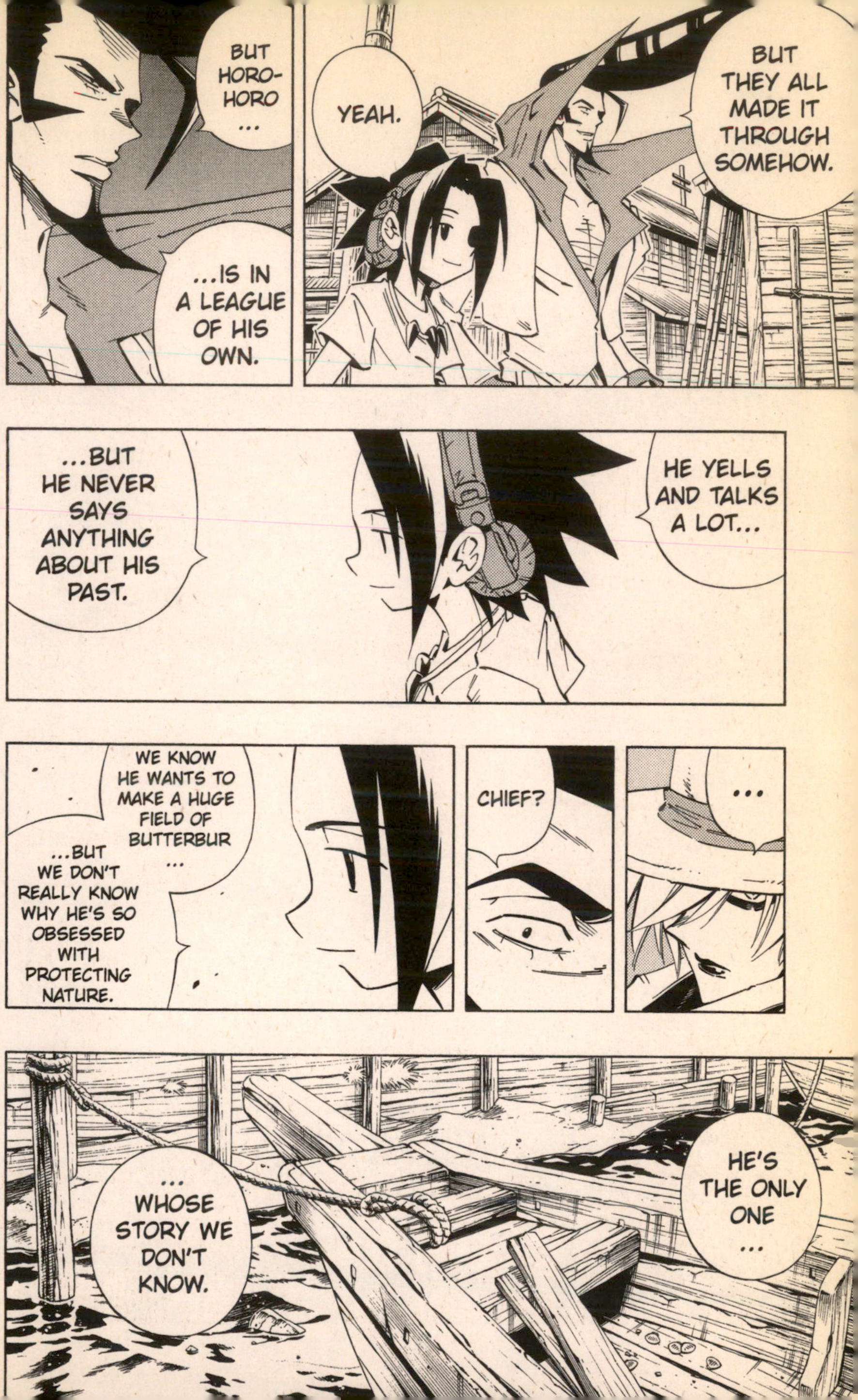
BUT THEY ALL MADE IT THROUGH SOMEHOW.
YEAH.
BUT HORO-HORO ...
...IS IN A LEAGUE OF HIS OWN.
HE YELLS AND TALKS A LOT...
...BUT HE NEVER SAYS ANYTHING ABOUT HIS PAST.
...
CHIEF?
WE KNOW HE WANTS TO MAKE A HUGE FIELD OF BUTTERBUR ...
...BUT WE DON'T REALLY KNOW WHY HE'S SO OBSESSED WITH PROTECTING NATURE.
HE'S THE ONLY ONE ...
... WHOSE STORY WE DON'T KNOW.

Reincarnation 228: An Act

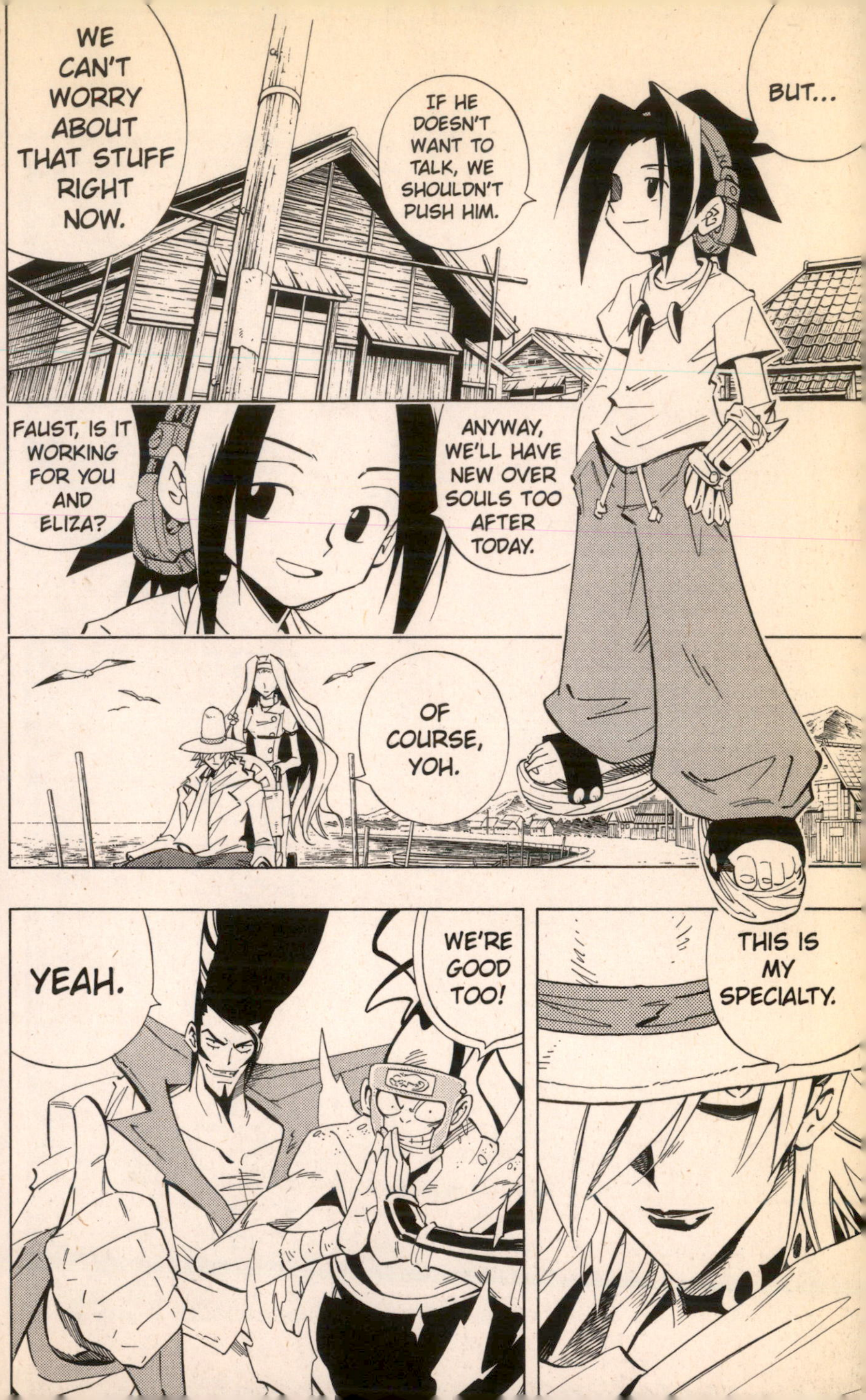
BUT...
IF HE DOESN'T WANT TO TALK, WE SHOULDN'T PUSH HIM.
WE CAN'T WORRY ABOUT THAT STUFF RIGHT NOW.
ANYWAY, WE'LL HAVE NEW OVER SOULS TOO AFTER TODAY.
FAUST, IS IT WORKING FOR YOU AND ELIZA?
OF COURSE, YOH.
THIS IS MY SPECIALTY.
WE'RE GOOD TOO!
YEAH.

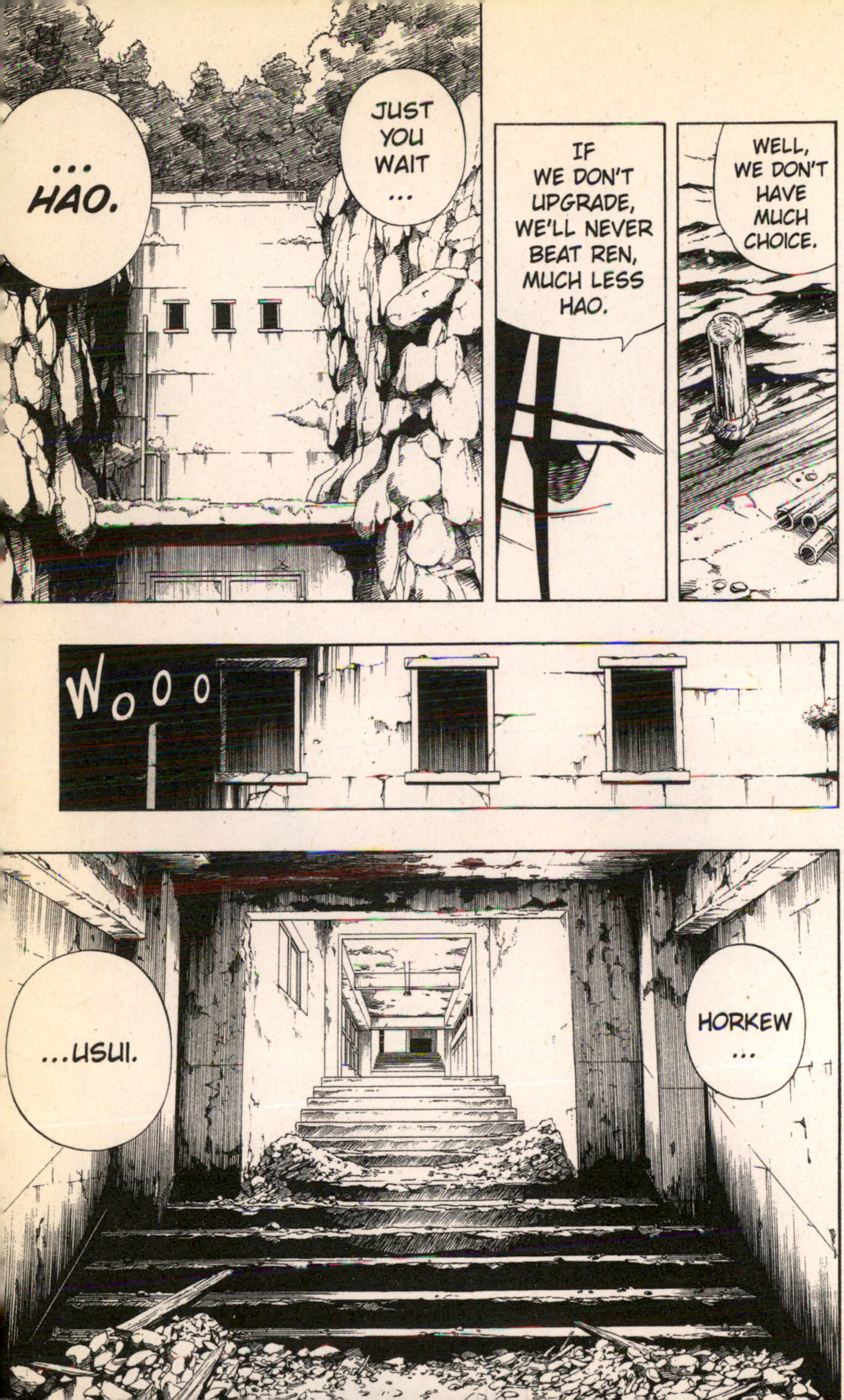
WELL, WE DON'T HAVE MUCH CHOICE.
IF WE DON'T UPGRADE, WE'LL NEVER BEAT REN, MUCH LESS HAO.
JUST YOU WAIT ...
... HAO.
WOOO
HORKEW ...
...USUI.

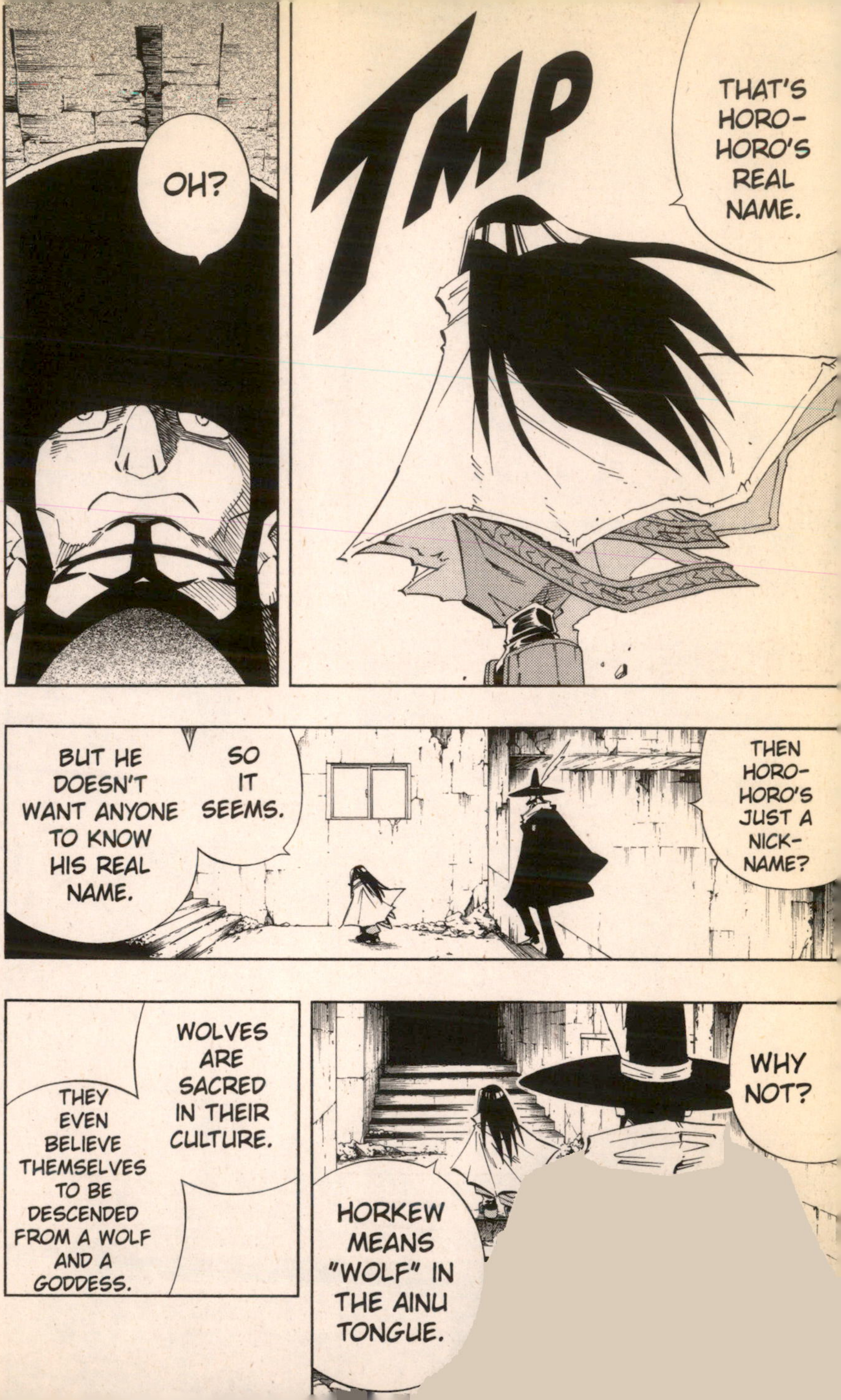
TMP
THAT'S HORO-HORO'S REAL NAME.
OH?
THEN HORO-HORO'S JUST A NICK-NAME?
SO IT SEEMS.
BUT HE DOESN'T WANT ANYONE TO KNOW HIS REAL NAME.
WHY NOT?
HORKEW MEANS "WOLF" IN THE AINU TONGUE.
WOLVES ARE SACRED IN THEIR CULTURE.
THEY EVEN BELIEVE THEMSELVES TO BE DESCENDED FROM A WOLF AND A GODDESS.

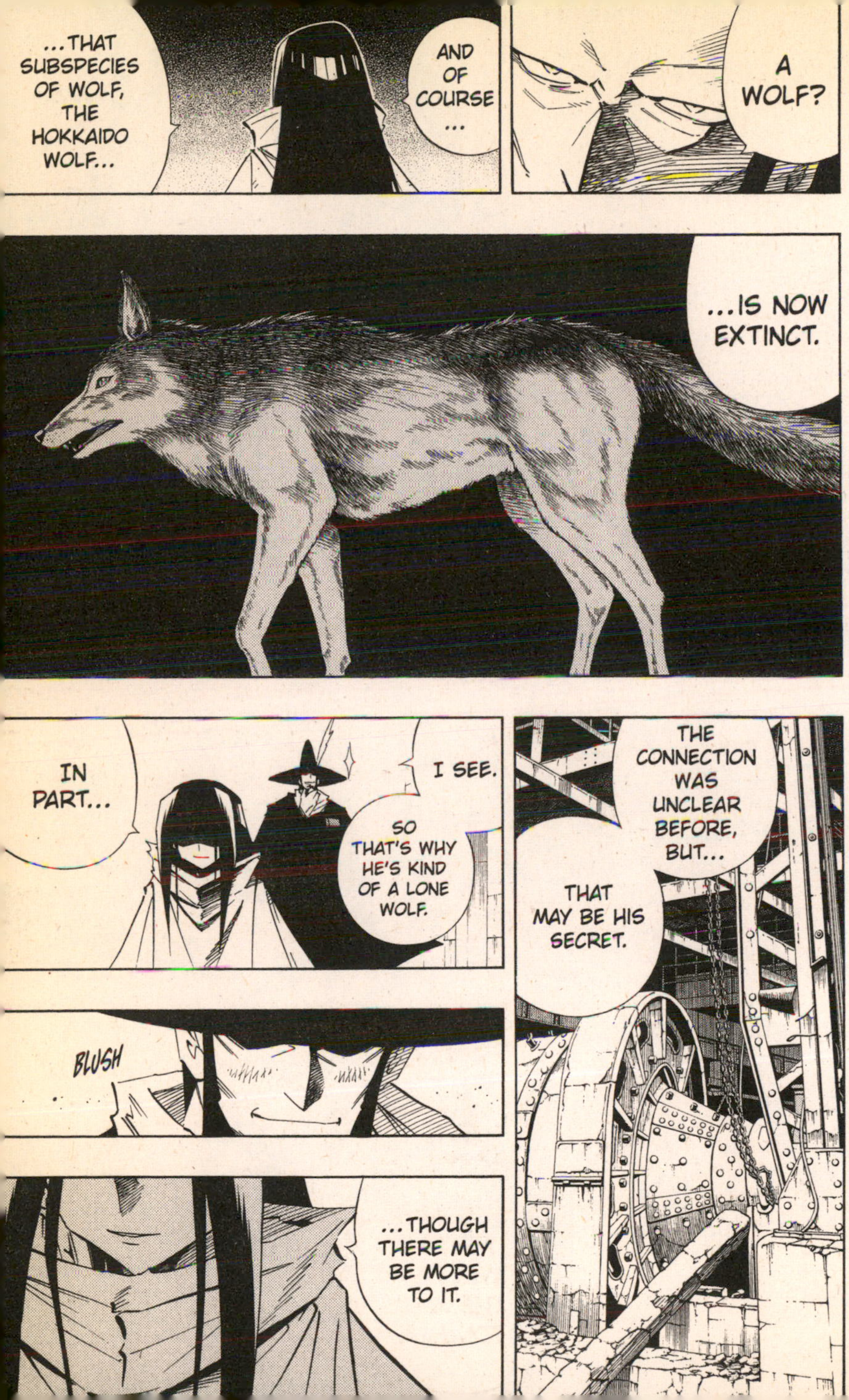
A WOLF?
AND OF COURSE...
...THAT SUBSPECIES OF WOLF, THE HOKKAIDO WOLF...
...IS NOW EXTINCT.
THE CONNECTION WAS UNCLEAR BEFORE, BUT...
THAT MAY BE HIS SECRET.
I SEE.
SO THAT'S WHY HE'S KIND OF A LONE WOLF.
IN PART...
BLUSH
...THOUGH THERE MAY BE MORE TO IT.

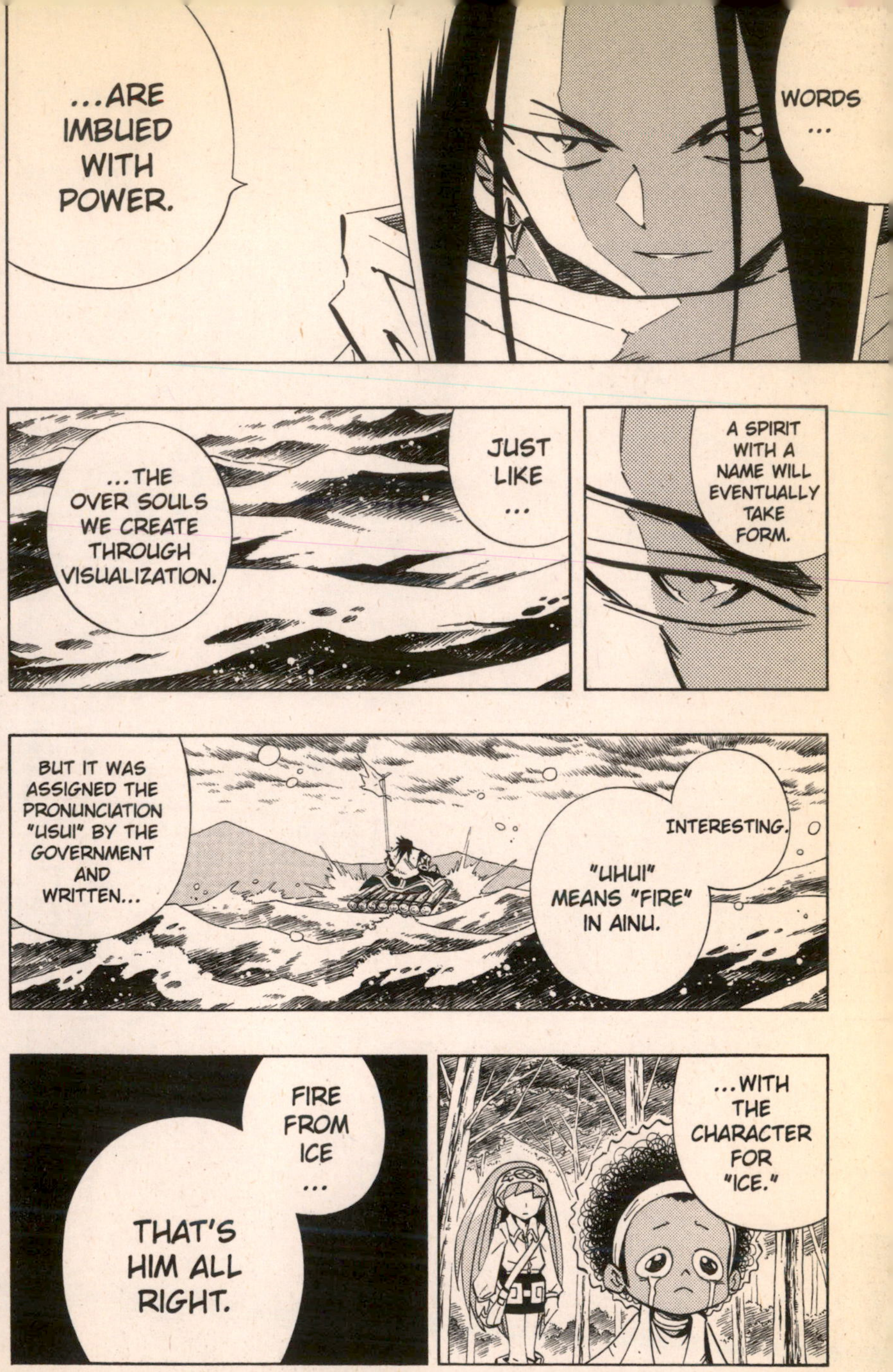
WORDS ...
...ARE IMBUED WITH POWER.
A SPIRIT WITH A NAME WILL EVENTUALLY TAKE FORM.
JUST LIKE ...
...THE OVER SOULS WE CREATE THROUGH VISUALIZATION.
INTERESTING.
"UHUI" MEANS "FIRE" IN AINU.
BUT IT WAS ASSIGNED THE PRONUNCIATION "USUI" BY THE GOVERNMENT AND WRITTEN...
...WITH THE CHARACTER FOR "ICE."
FIRE FROM ICE ...
THAT'S HIM ALL RIGHT.

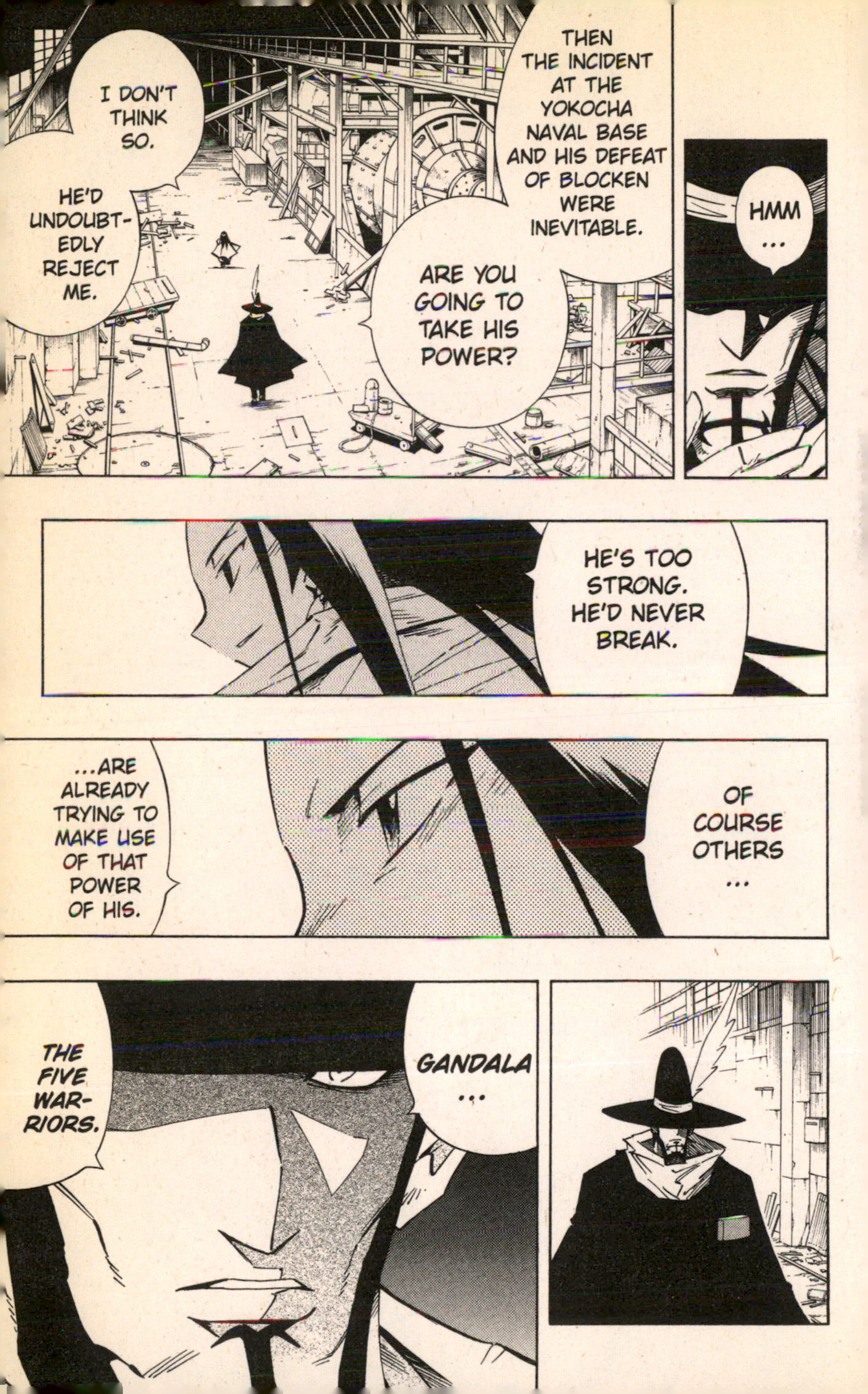
HMM...
THEN THE INCIDENT AT THE YOKOCHA NAVAL BASE AND HIS DEFEAT OF BLOCKEN WERE INEVITABLE.
ARE YOU GOING TO TAKE HIS POWER?
I DON'T THINK SO.
HE'D UNDOUBTEDLY REJECT ME.
HE'S TOO STRONG. HE'D NEVER BREAK.
OF COURSE OTHERS...
...ARE ALREADY TRYING TO MAKE USE OF THAT POWER OF HIS.
GANDALA...
THE FIVE WARRIORS.

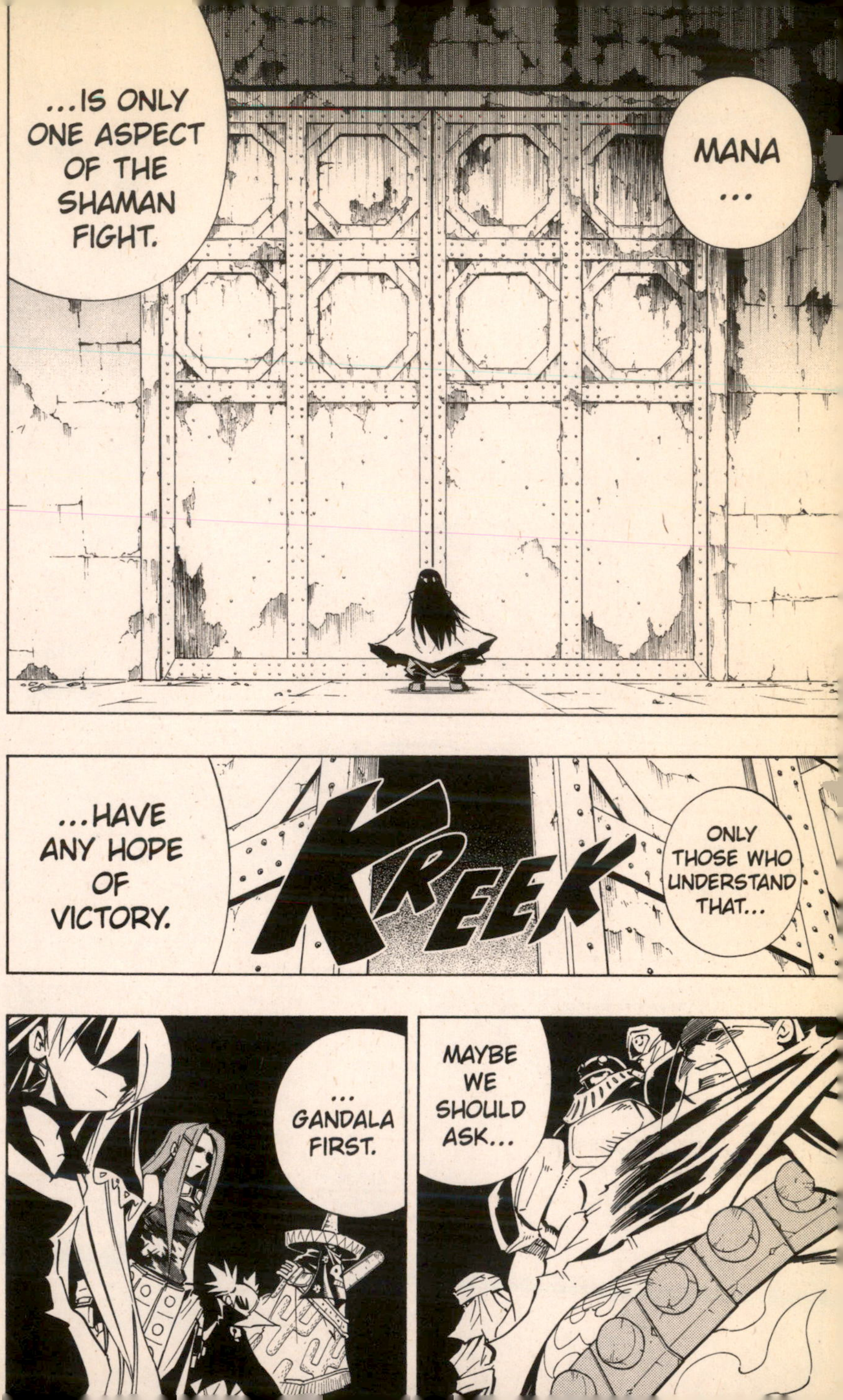
MANA ...
...IS ONLY ONE ASPECT OF THE SHAMAN FIGHT.
ONLY THOSE WHO UNDERSTAND THAT...
KREEK
...HAVE ANY HOPE OF VICTORY.
MAYBE WE SHOULD ASK...
... GANDALA FIRST.

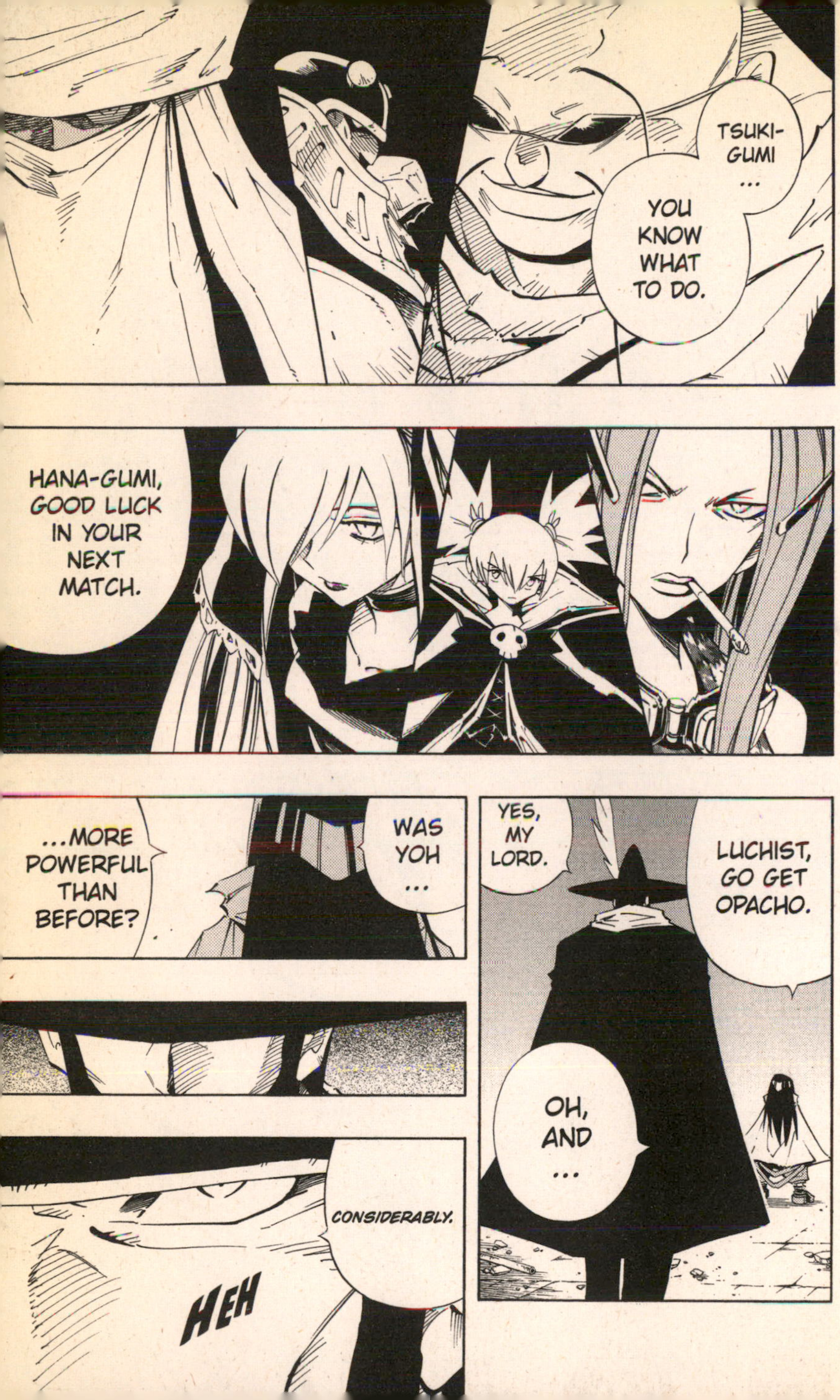
TSUKI-GUMI ...
YOU KNOW WHAT TO DO.
HANA-GUMI, GOOD LUCK IN YOUR NEXT MATCH.
LUCHIST, GO GET OPACHO.
YES, MY LORD.
OH, AND ...
WAS YOH ...
...MORE POWERFUL THAN BEFORE?
CONSIDERABLY.
HEH

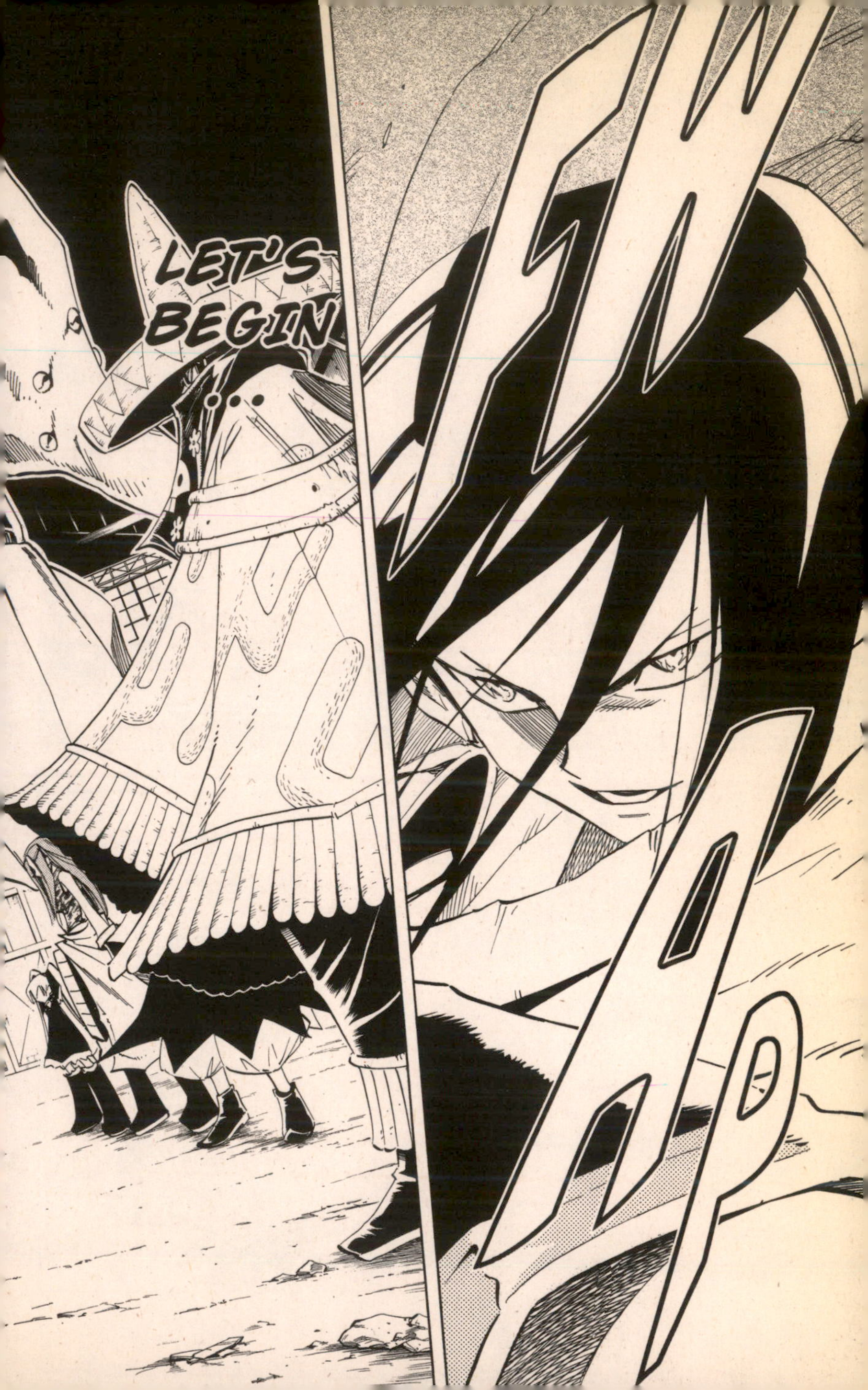
LET'S BEGIN...

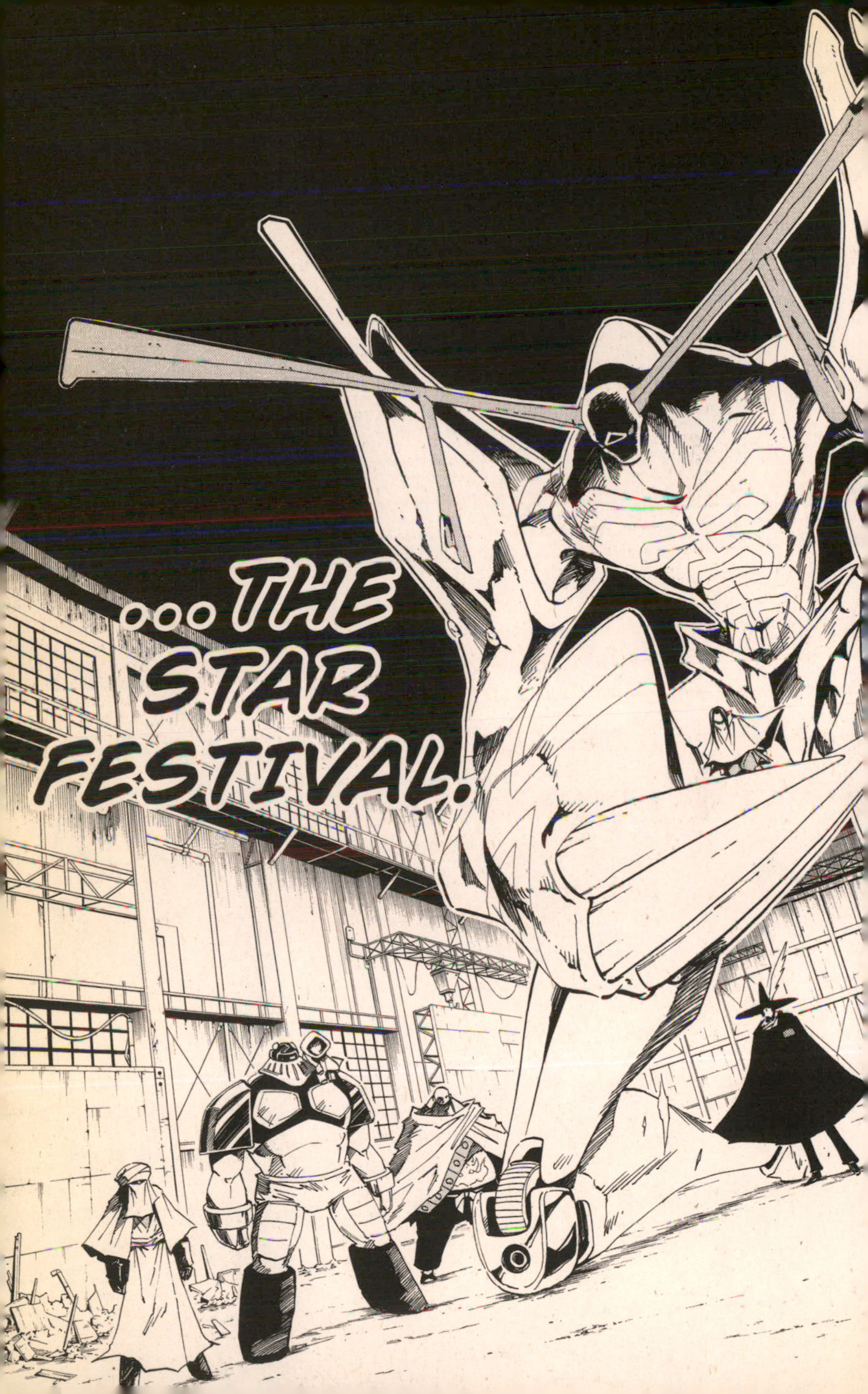
...THE STAR FESTIVAL.

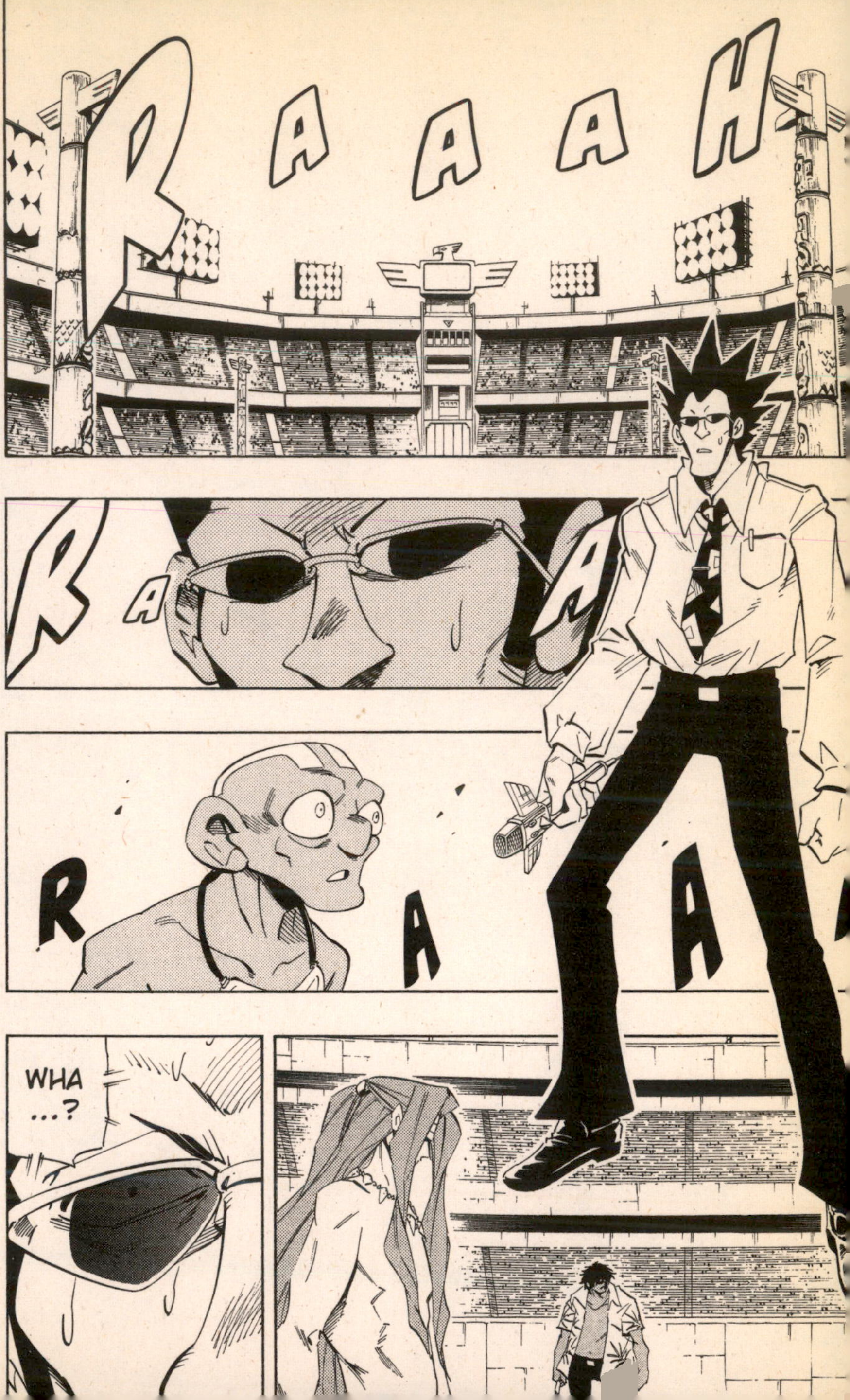
RAAAH
RAA
RAAA
WHA ...?

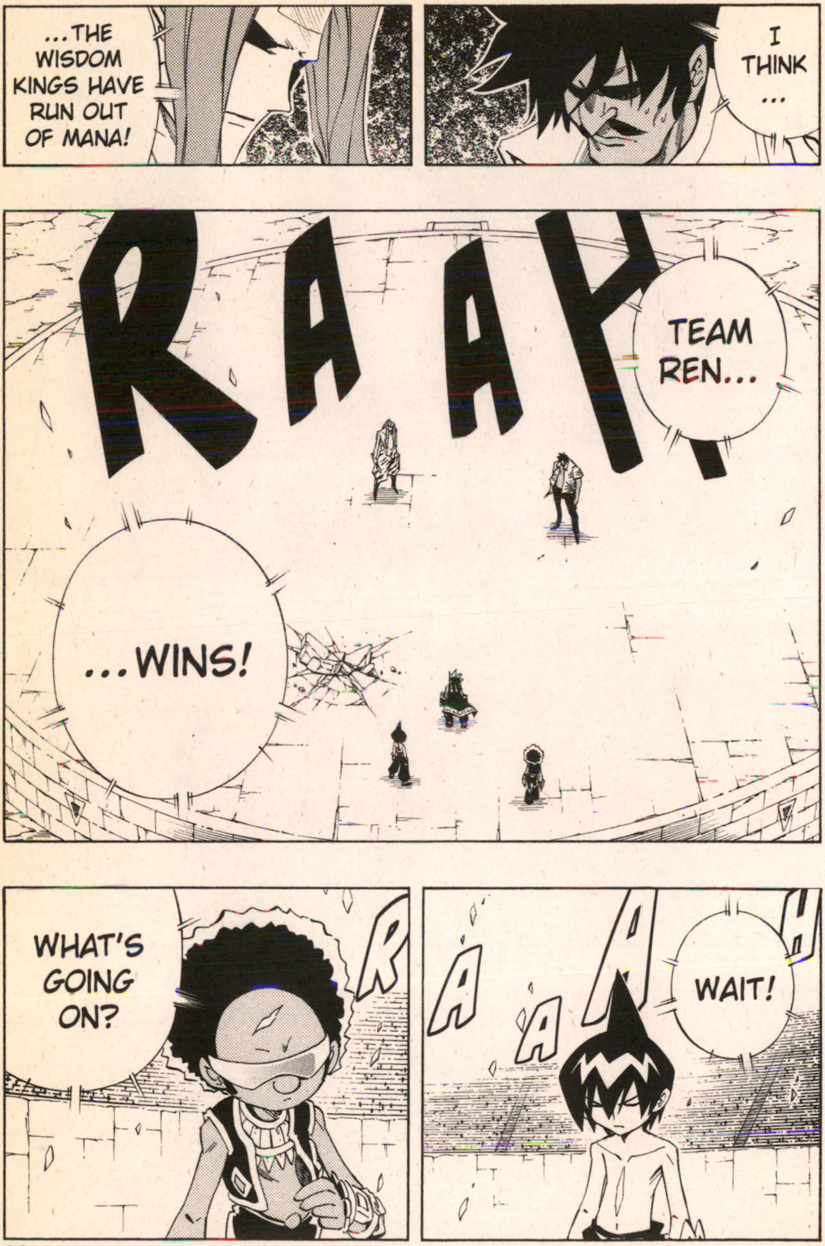
I THINK...
...THE WISDOM KINGS HAVE RUN OUT OF MANA!
RAAAH
TEAM REN...
...WINS!
AAAH
WAIT!
R
WHAT'S GOING ON?

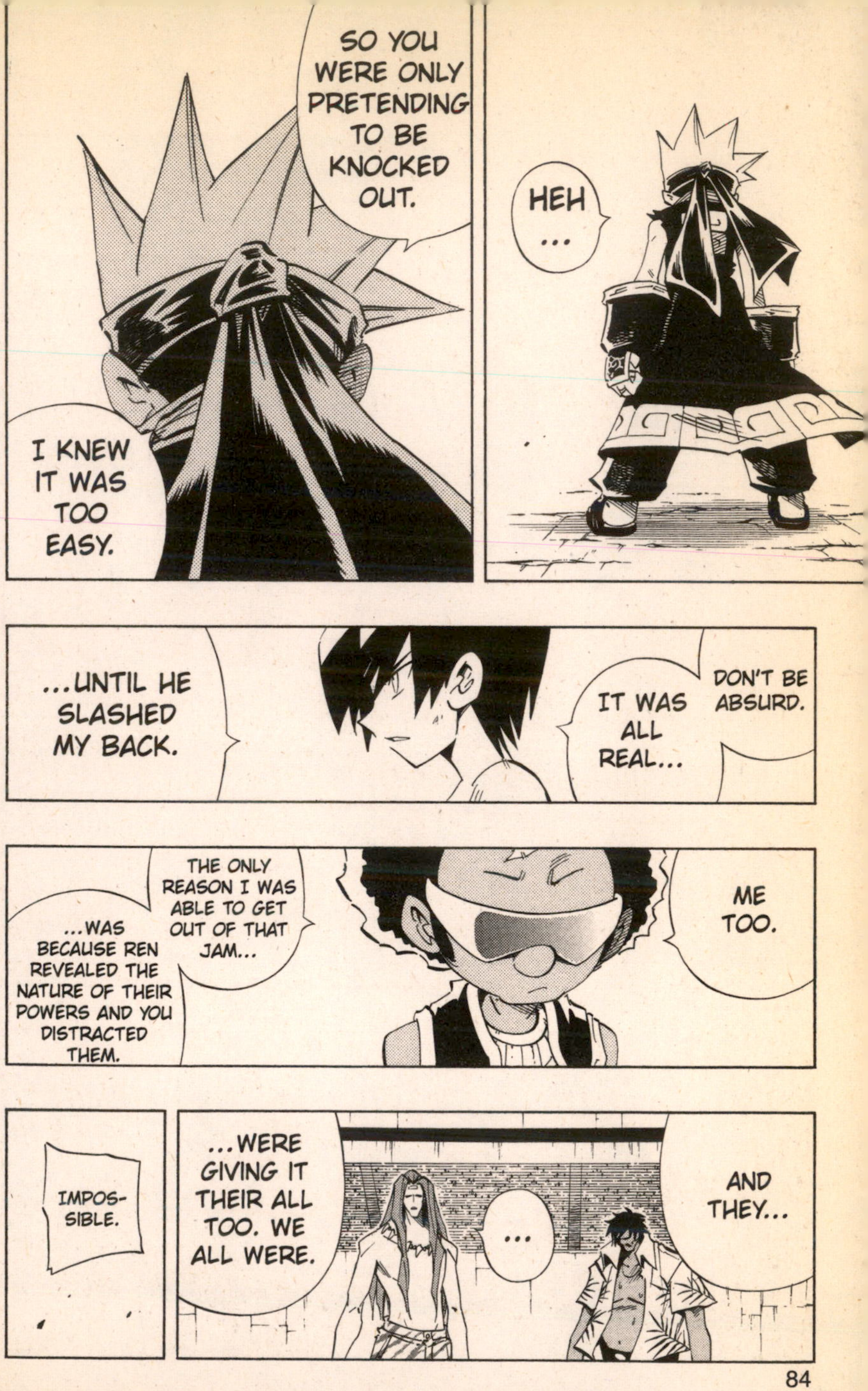
HEH ...
SO YOU WERE ONLY PRETENDING TO BE KNOCKED OUT.
I KNEW IT WAS TOO EASY.
DON'T BE ABSURD.
IT WAS ALL REAL...
...UNTIL HE SLASHED MY BACK.
ME TOO.
THE ONLY REASON I WAS ABLE TO GET OUT OF THAT JAM...
...WAS BECAUSE REN REVEALED THE NATURE OF THEIR POWERS AND YOU DISTRACTED THEM.
AND THEY...
...
...WERE GIVING IT THEIR ALL TOO. WE ALL WERE.
IMPOS-SIBLE.

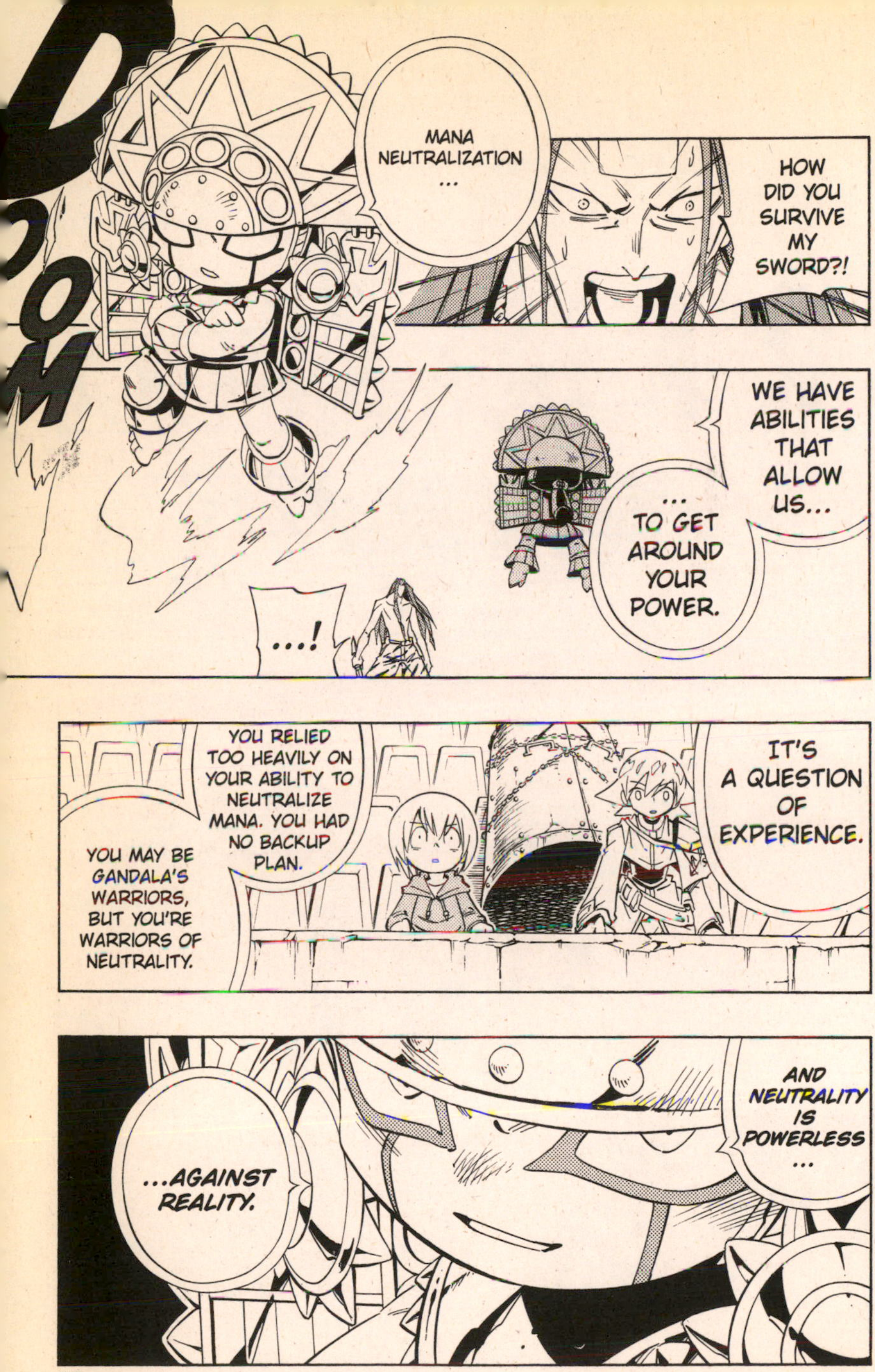
HOW DID YOU SURVIVE MY SWORD?!
MANA NEUTRALIZATION ...
DOOM
WE HAVE ABILITIES THAT ALLOW US...
... TO GET AROUND YOUR POWER.
...!
IT'S A QUESTION OF EXPERIENCE.
YOU RELIED TOO HEAVILY ON YOUR ABILITY TO NEUTRALIZE MANA. YOU HAD NO BACKUP PLAN.
YOU MAY BE GANDALA'S WARRIORS, BUT YOU'RE WARRIORS OF NEUTRALITY.
AND NEUTRALITY IS POWERLESS ...
...AGAINST REALITY.

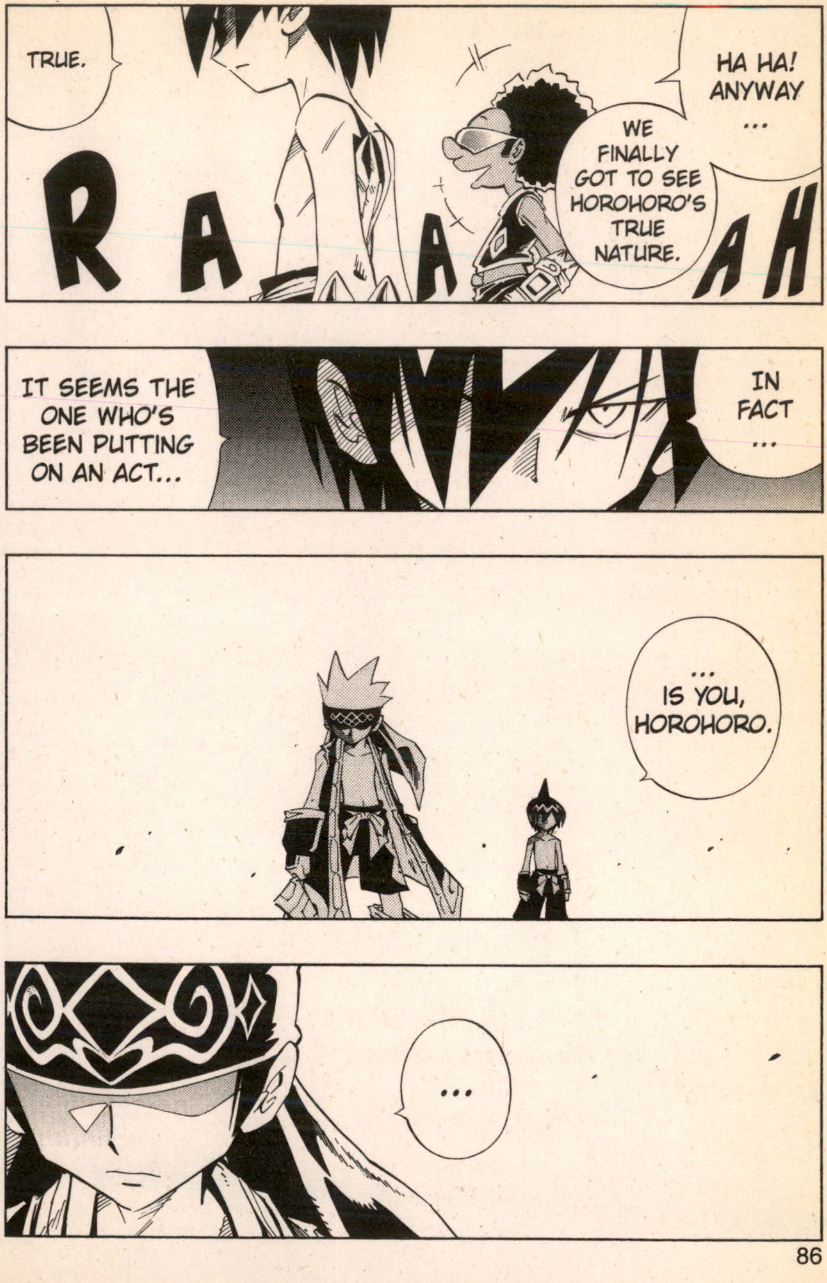
HA HA! ANYWAY ...
WE FINALLY GOT TO SEE HOROHORO'S TRUE NATURE.
TRUE.
RAAAH
IN FACT ...
IT SEEMS THE ONE WHO'S BEEN PUTTING ON AN ACT...
... IS YOU, HOROHORO.
...

HMPH. I'M NOT INTERESTED IN ANY SOB STORIES.

I'LL EXPLAIN...

...SOMEDAY.

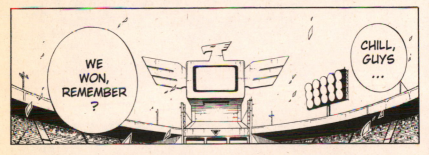

WE WON, REMEMBER?

CHILL, GUYS...

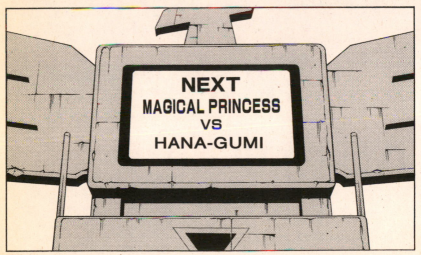

NEXT
MAGICAL PRINCESS
VS
HANA-GUMI

SHAMAN KING CHARACTER FILE No.133

ニポポテクンペ

(ニポポ手甲)

NIPOPO TEKUNPE GAUNTLETS

2001

(JAN)

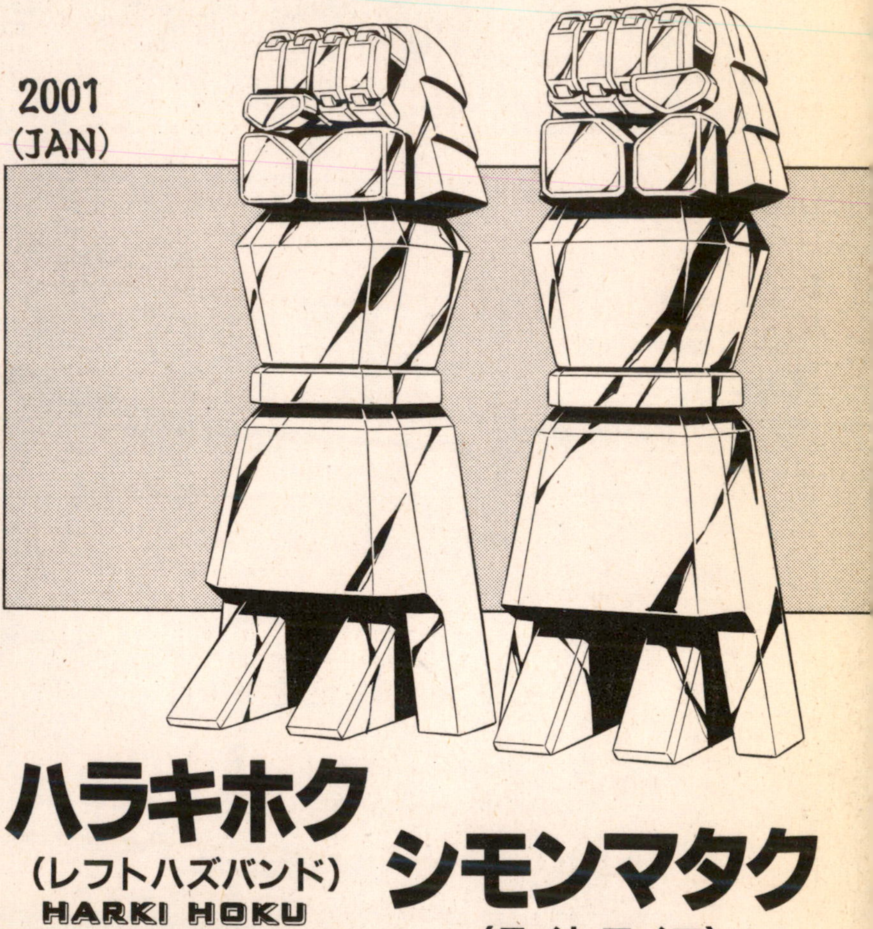

ハラキホク

(レフトハズバンド)

HARKI HOKU

(LEFT HUSBAND)

シモンマタク

(ライトワイフ)

SIMON MATAK

(RIGHT WIFE)

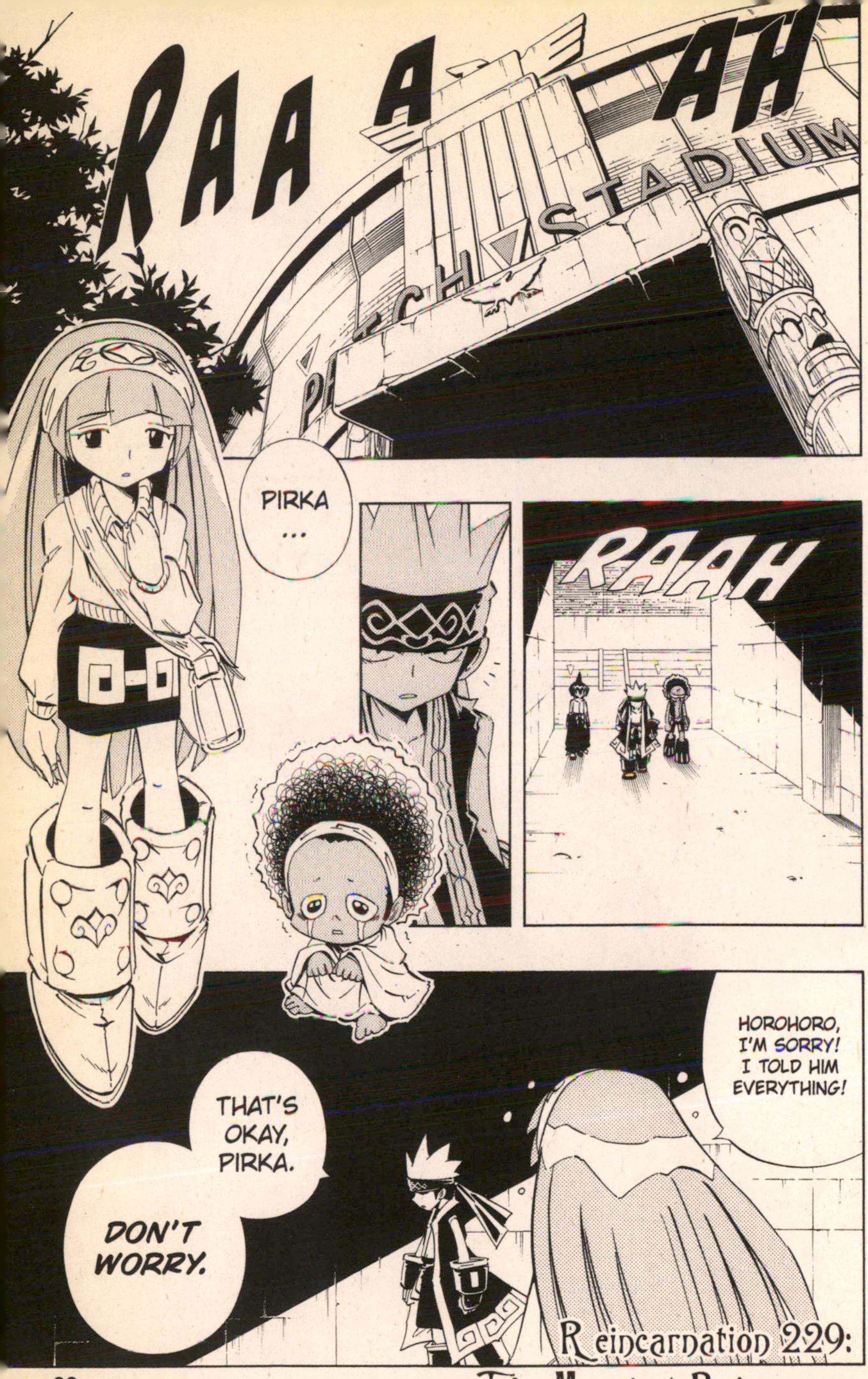
RAA A AH
STADIUM
RAAH
PIRKA ...
HOROHORO, I'M SORRY! I TOLD HIM EVERYTHING!
THAT'S OKAY, PIRKA.
DON'T WORRY.

Reincarnation 229: The Magical Princesses

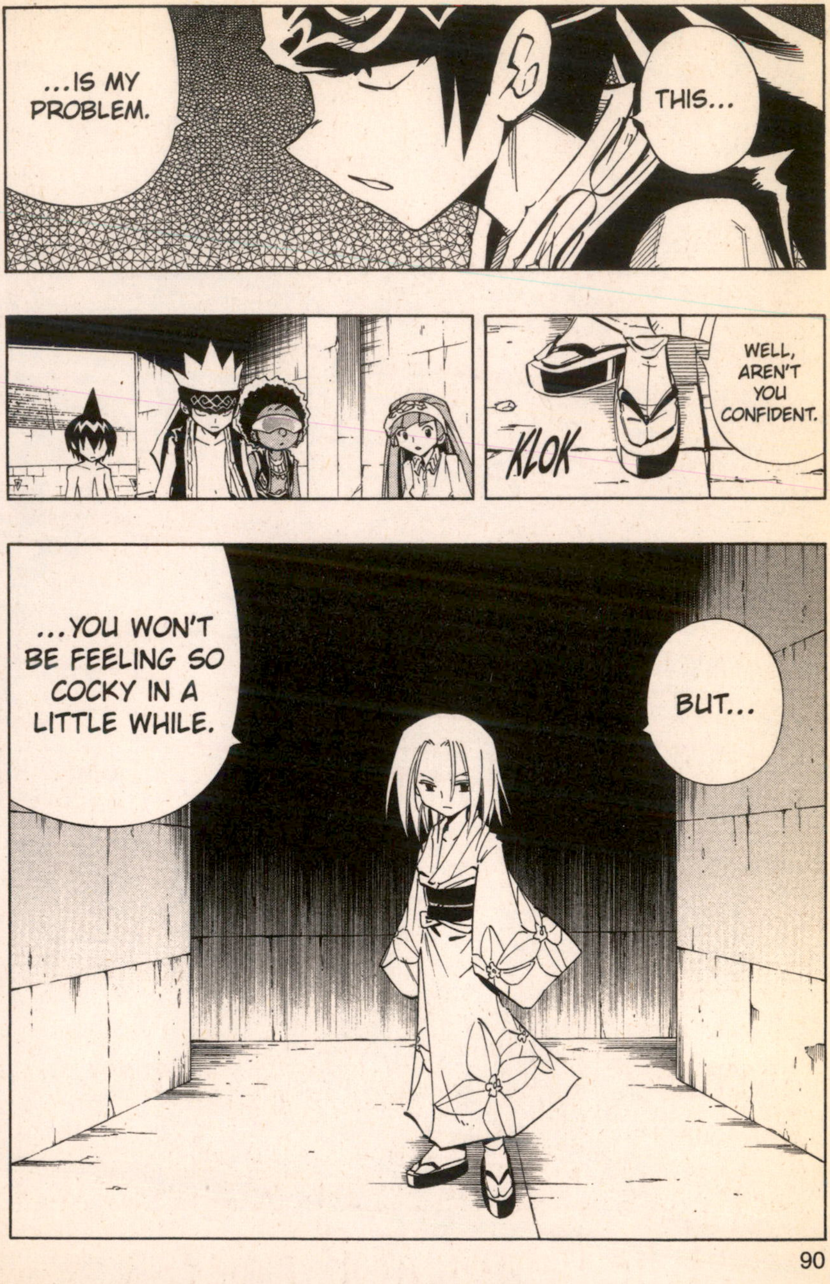
THIS...
...IS MY PROBLEM.
WELL, AREN'T YOU CONFIDENT.
KLOK
BUT...
...YOU WON'T BE FEELING SO COCKY IN A LITTLE WHILE.

Reincarnation 229:

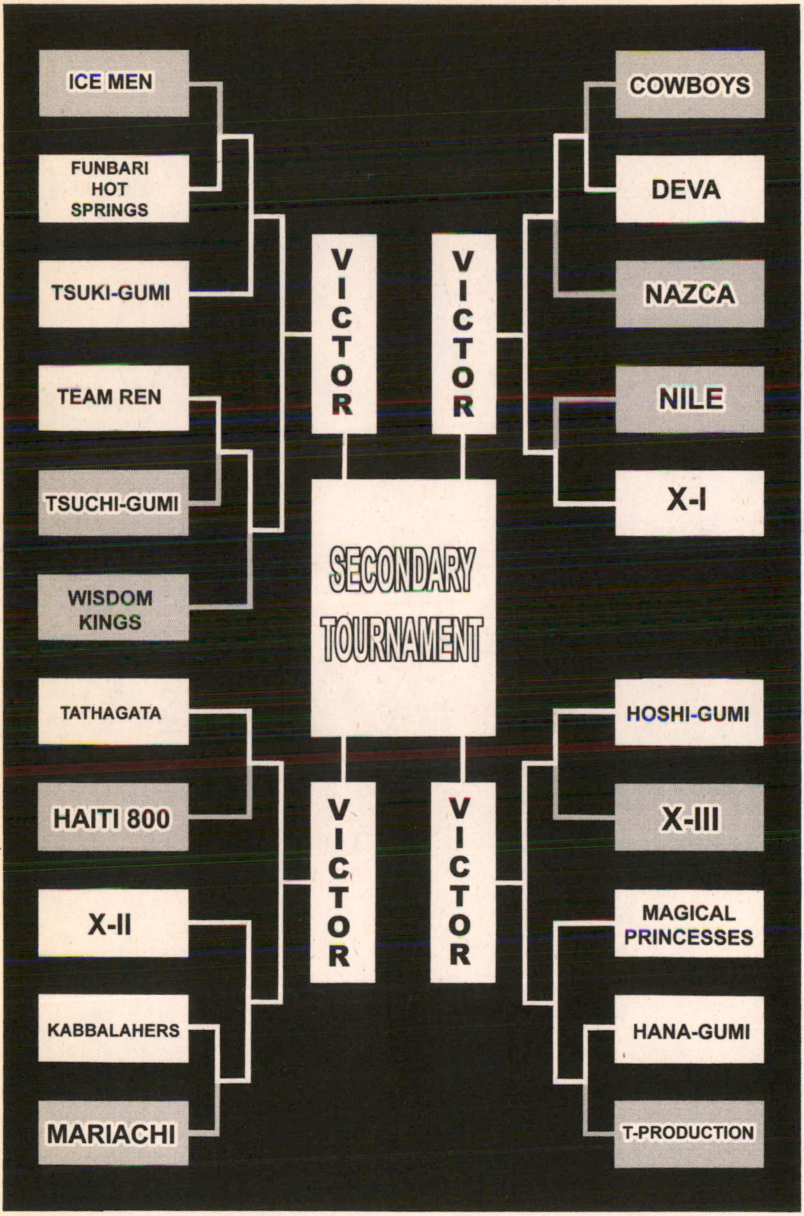
COWBOYS
DEVA
NAZCA
NILE
X-I
HOSHI-GUMI
X-III
MAGICAL PRINCESSES
HANA-GUMI
T-PRODUCTION
VICTOR
VICTOR
SECONDARY TOURNAMENT
VICTOR
VICTOR
ICE MEN
FUNBARI HOT SPRINGS
TSUKI-GUMI
TEAM REN
TSUCHI-GUMI
WISDOM KINGS
TATHAGATA
HAITI 800
X-II
KABBALAHERS
MARIACHI

The Magical Princesses

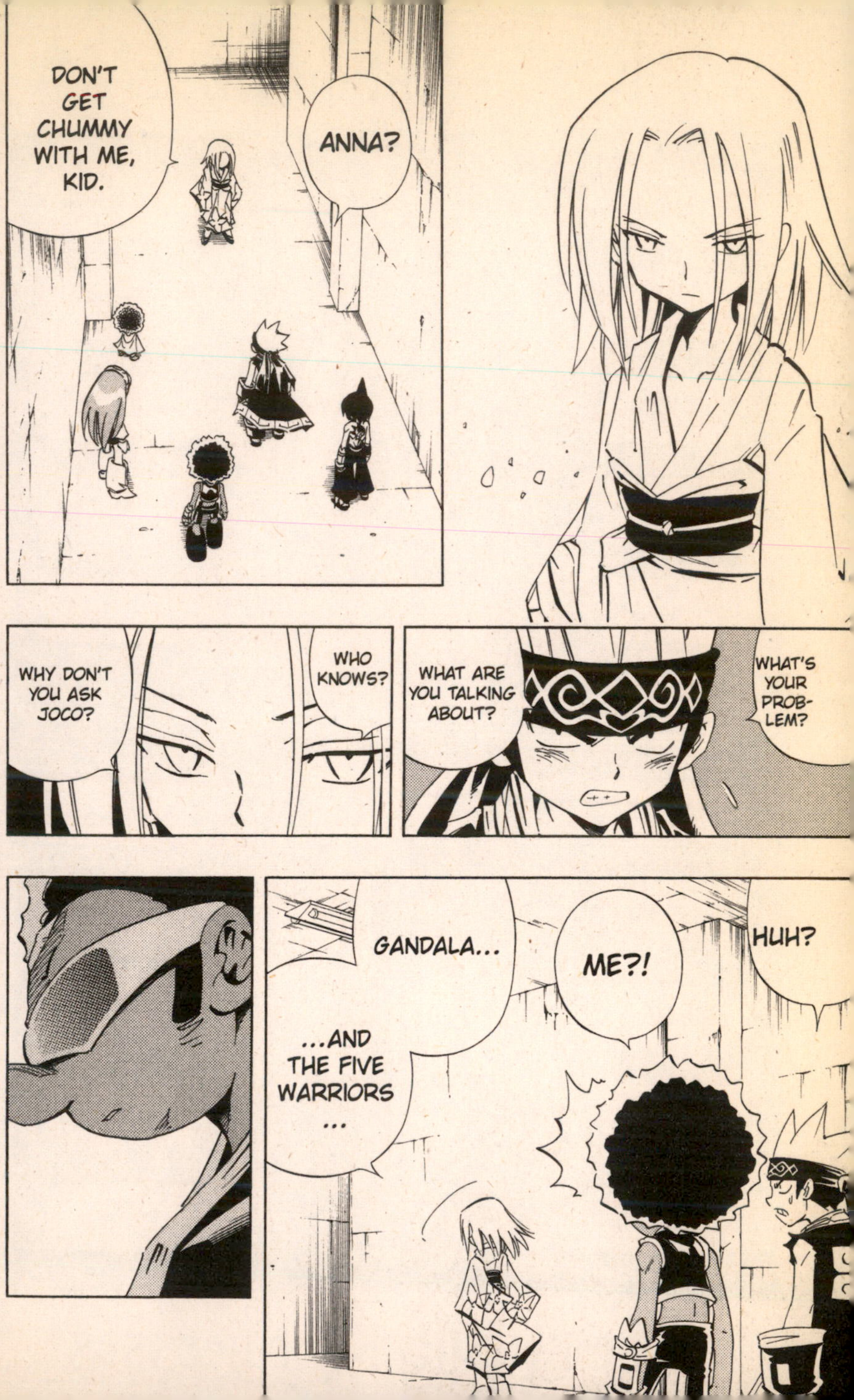
ANNA?
DON'T GET CHUMMY WITH ME, KID.
WHAT'S YOUR PROB-LEM?
WHAT ARE YOU TALKING ABOUT?
WHO KNOWS?
WHY DON'T YOU ASK JOCO?
HUH?
ME?!
GANDALA...
...AND THE FIVE WARRIORS ...

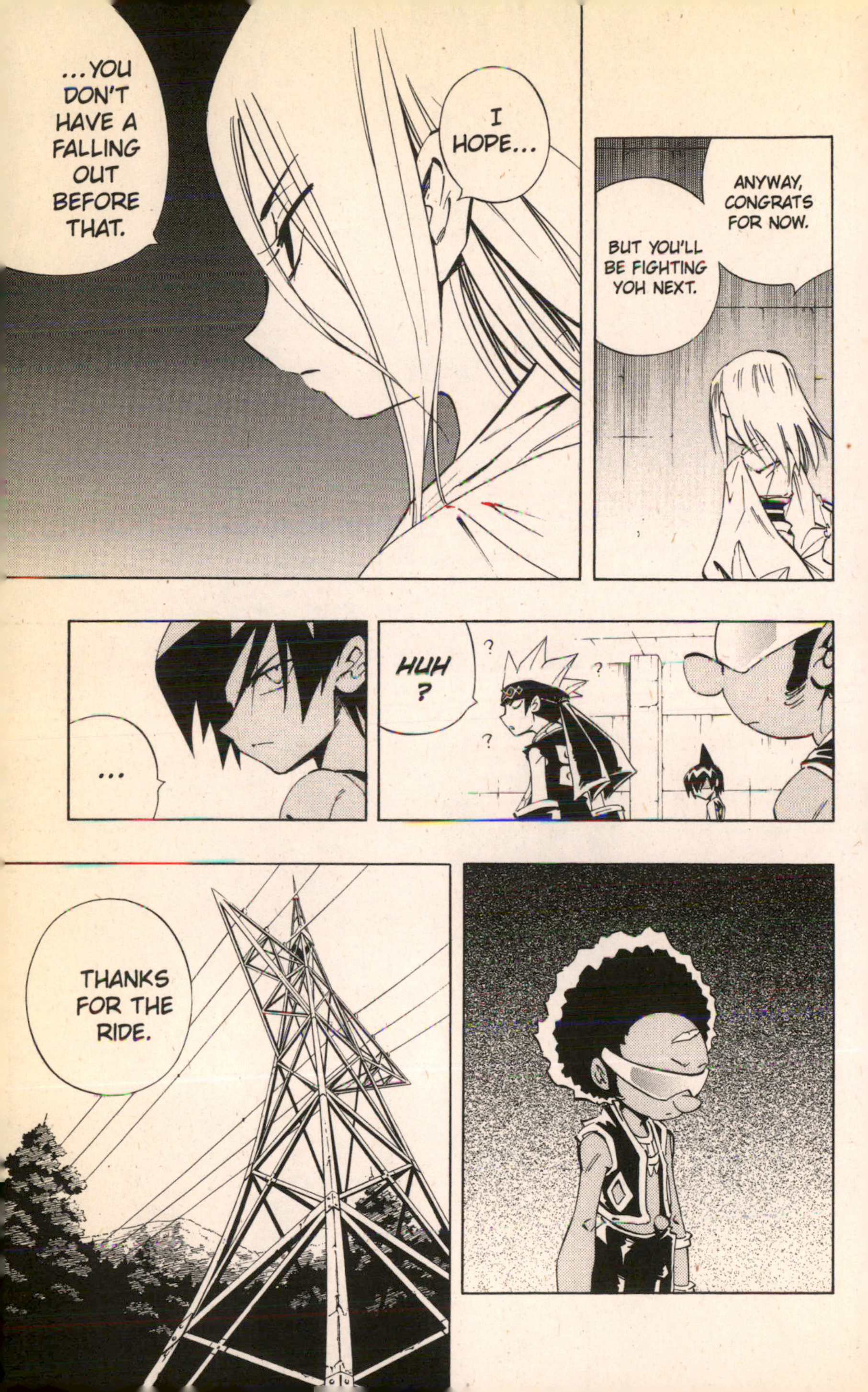
ANYWAY, CONGRATS FOR NOW.
BUT YOU'LL BE FIGHTING YOH NEXT.
I HOPE...
...YOU DON'T HAVE A FALLING OUT BEFORE THAT.
HUH?
...
THANKS FOR THE RIDE.

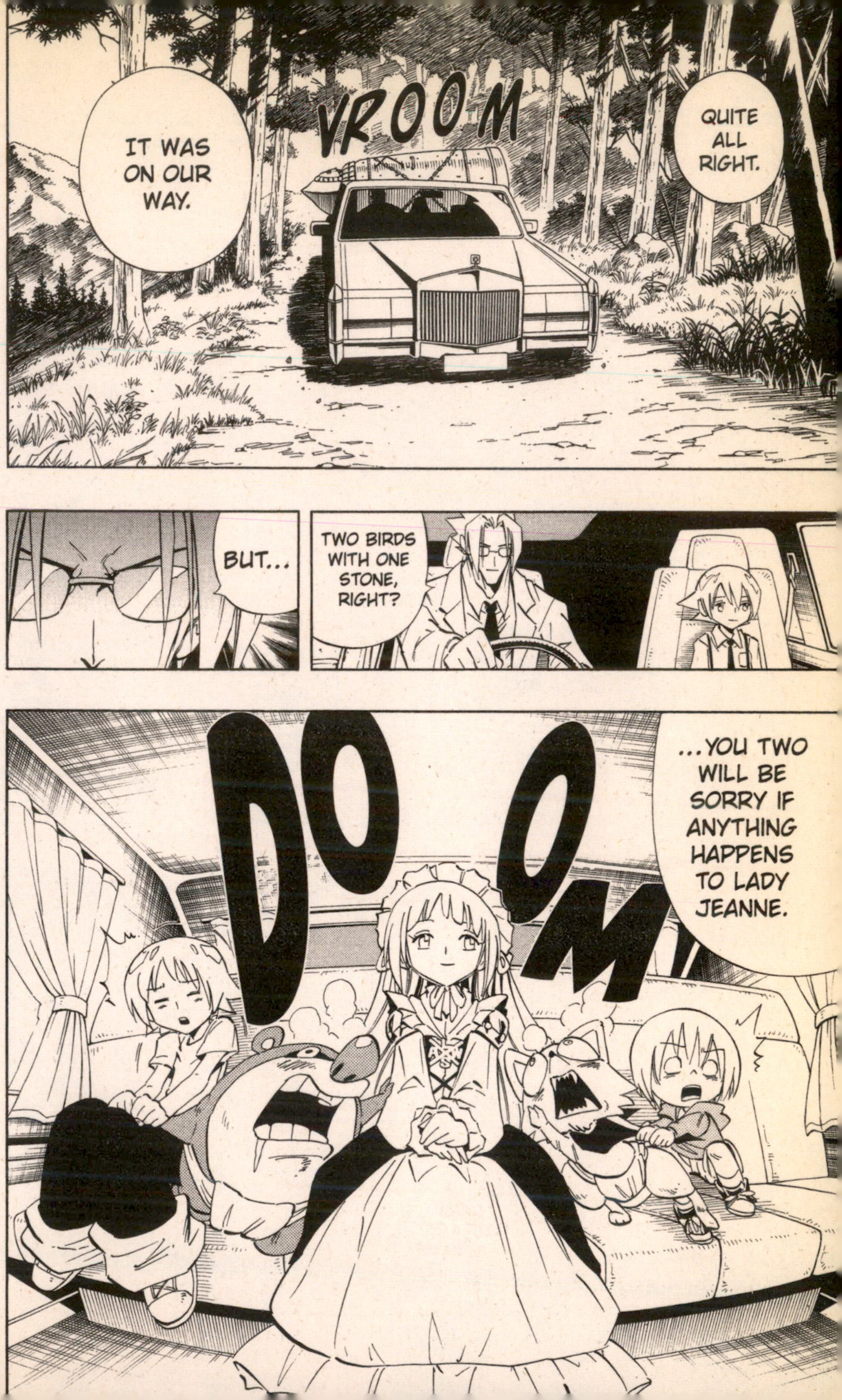
QUITE ALL RIGHT.
VROOM
IT WAS ON OUR WAY.
TWO BIRDS WITH ONE STONE, RIGHT?
BUT...
...YOU TWO WILL BE SORRY IF ANYTHING HAPPENS TO LADY JEANNE.
DOOM

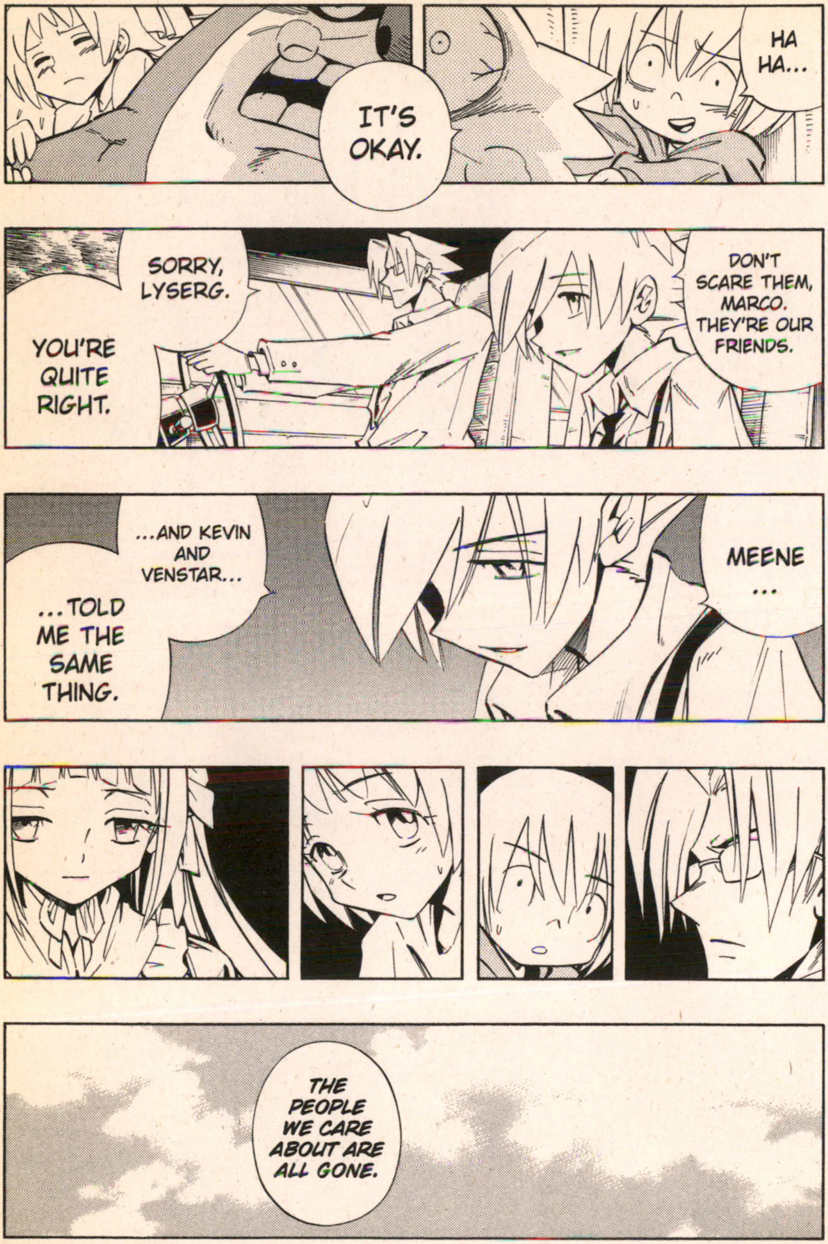
HA HA...
IT'S OKAY.
DON'T SCARE THEM, MARCO. THEY'RE OUR FRIENDS.
SORRY, LYSERG.
YOU'RE QUITE RIGHT.
MEENE ...
...AND KEVIN AND VENSTAR...
...TOLD ME THE SAME THING.
THE PEOPLE WE CARE ABOUT ARE ALL GONE.

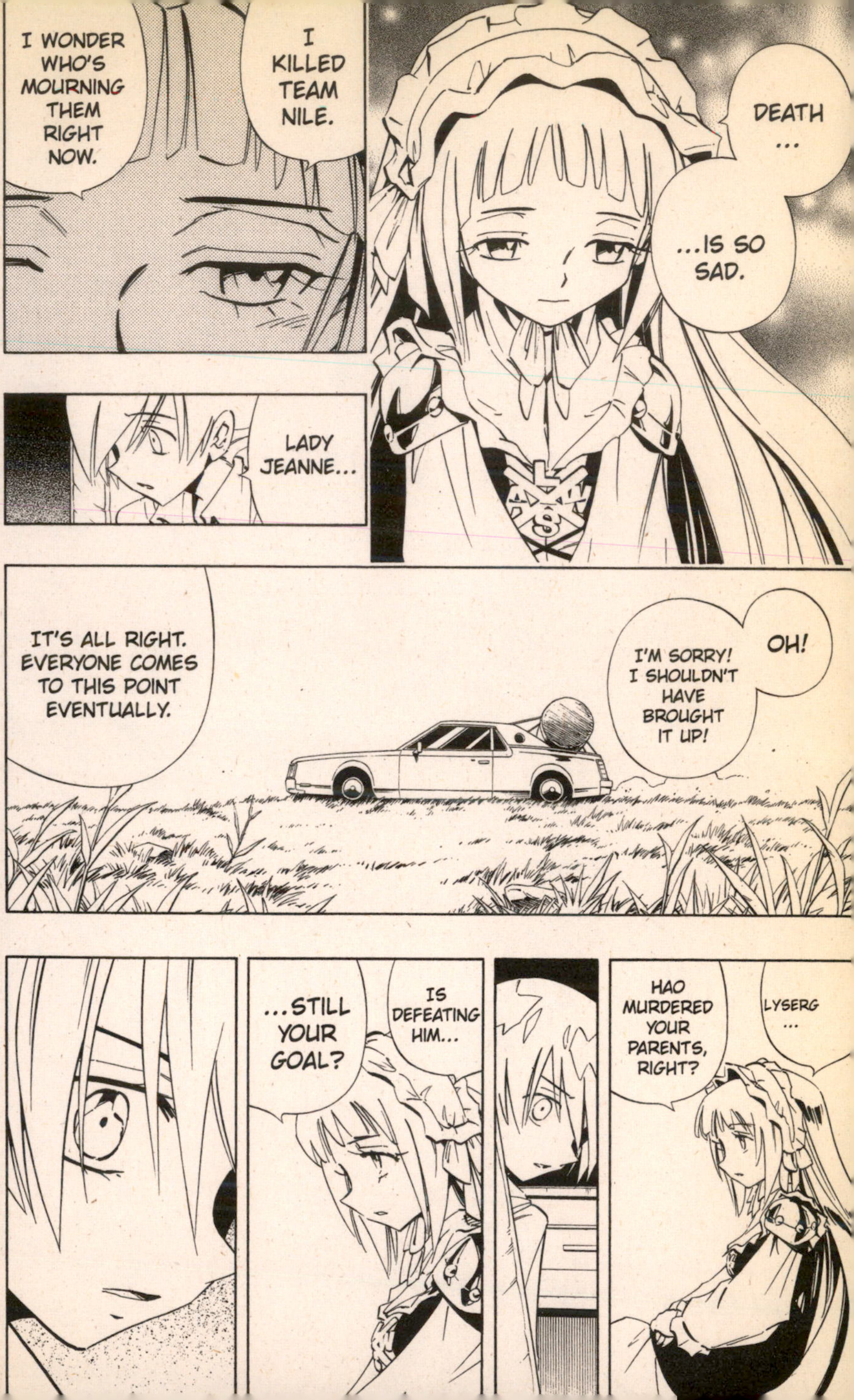
DEATH ...
...IS SO SAD.
I KILLED TEAM NILE.
I WONDER WHO'S MOURNING THEM RIGHT NOW.
LADY JEANNE...
OH!
I'M SORRY! I SHOULDN'T HAVE BROUGHT IT UP!
IT'S ALL RIGHT. EVERYONE COMES TO THIS POINT EVENTUALLY.
LYSERG ...
HAO MURDERED YOUR PARENTS, RIGHT?
IS DEFEATING HIM...
...STILL YOUR GOAL?

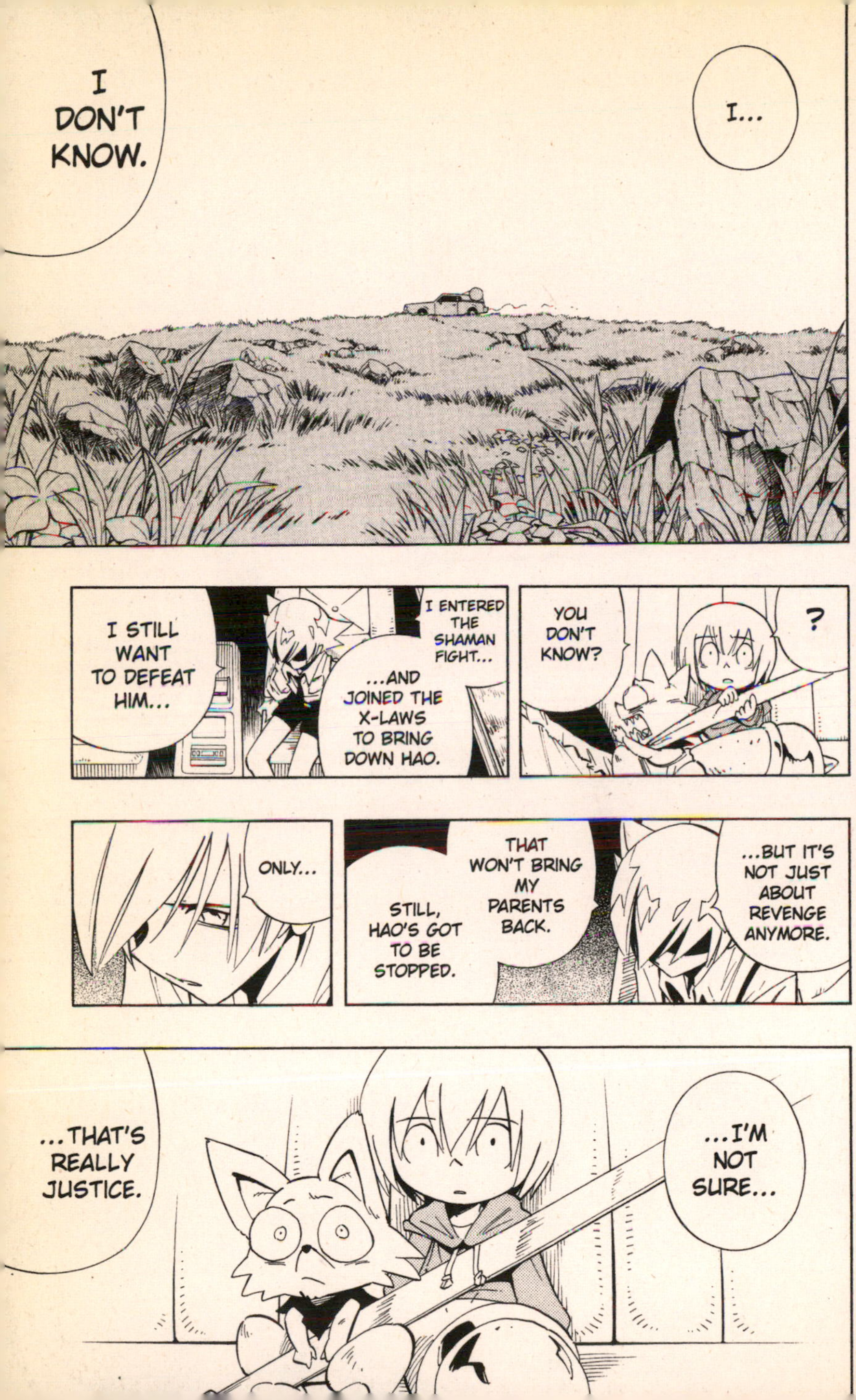
I...
I DON'T KNOW.
?
YOU DON'T KNOW?
I ENTERED THE SHAMAN FIGHT...
...AND JOINED THE X-LAWS TO BRING DOWN HAO.
I STILL WANT TO DEFEAT HIM...
...BUT IT'S NOT JUST ABOUT REVENGE ANYMORE.
THAT WON'T BRING MY PARENTS BACK.
STILL, HAO'S GOT TO BE STOPPED.
ONLY...
...I'M NOT SURE...
...THAT'S REALLY JUSTICE.

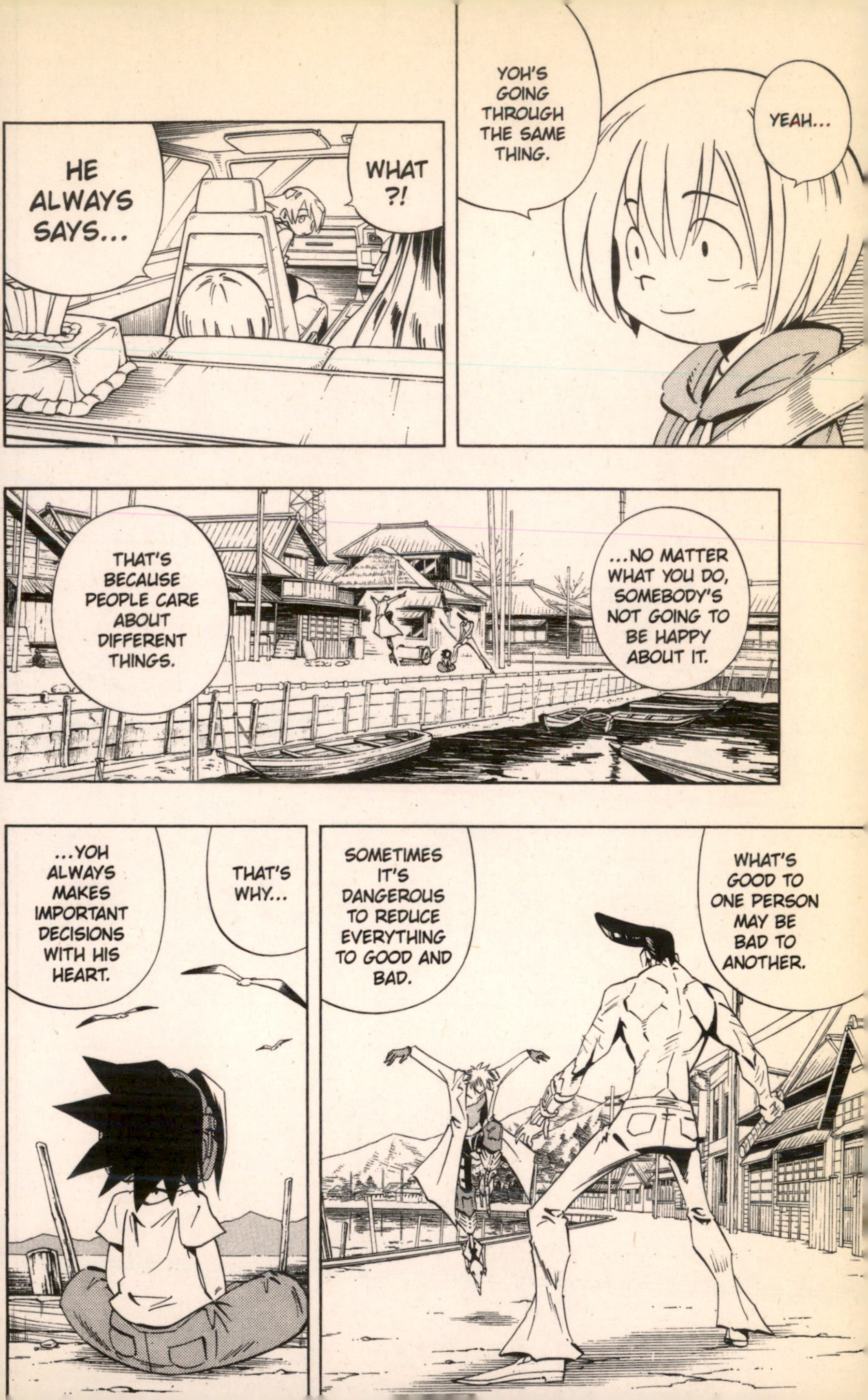
YEAH...
YOH'S GOING THROUGH THE SAME THING.
WHAT?!
HE ALWAYS SAYS...
...NO MATTER WHAT YOU DO, SOMEBODY'S NOT GOING TO BE HAPPY ABOUT IT.
THAT'S BECAUSE PEOPLE CARE ABOUT DIFFERENT THINGS.
WHAT'S GOOD TO ONE PERSON MAY BE BAD TO ANOTHER.
SOMETIMES IT'S DANGEROUS TO REDUCE EVERYTHING TO GOOD AND BAD.
THAT'S WHY...
...YOH ALWAYS MAKES IMPORTANT DECISIONS WITH HIS HEART.

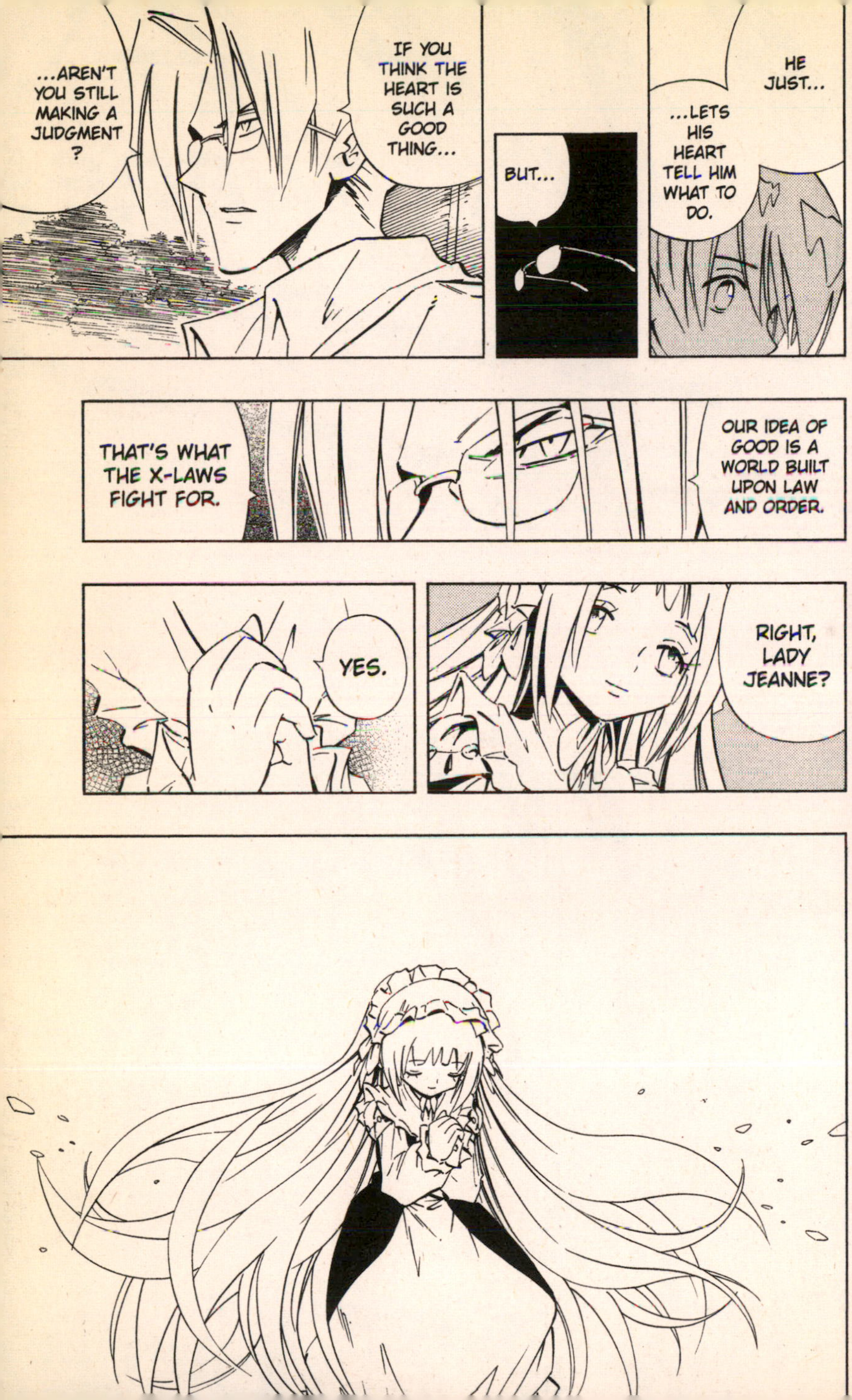
HE JUST...
...LETS HIS HEART TELL HIM WHAT TO DO.
BUT...
IF YOU THINK THE HEART IS SUCH A GOOD THING...
...AREN'T YOU STILL MAKING A JUDGMENT?
OUR IDEA OF GOOD IS A WORLD BUILT UPON LAW AND ORDER.
THAT'S WHAT THE X-LAWS FIGHT FOR.
RIGHT, LADY JEANNE?
YES.

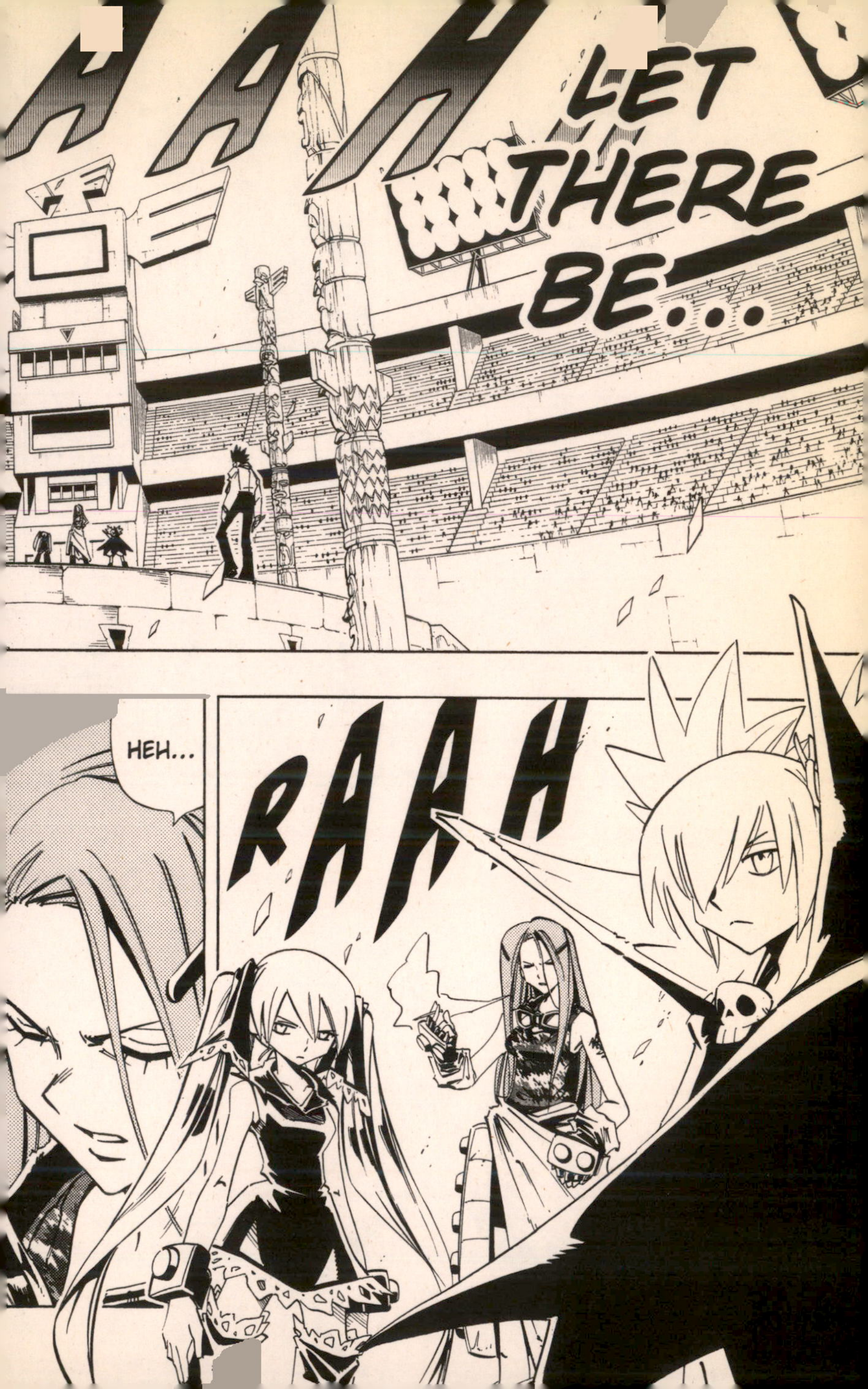
HAAH
LET THERE BE...
RAAH
HEH...

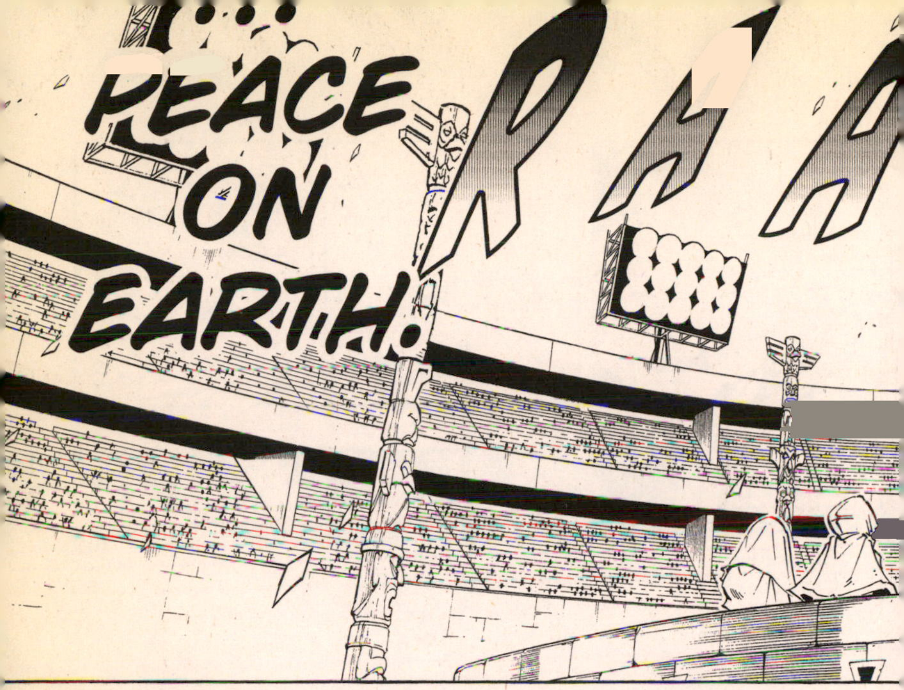
...PEACE ON EARTH!

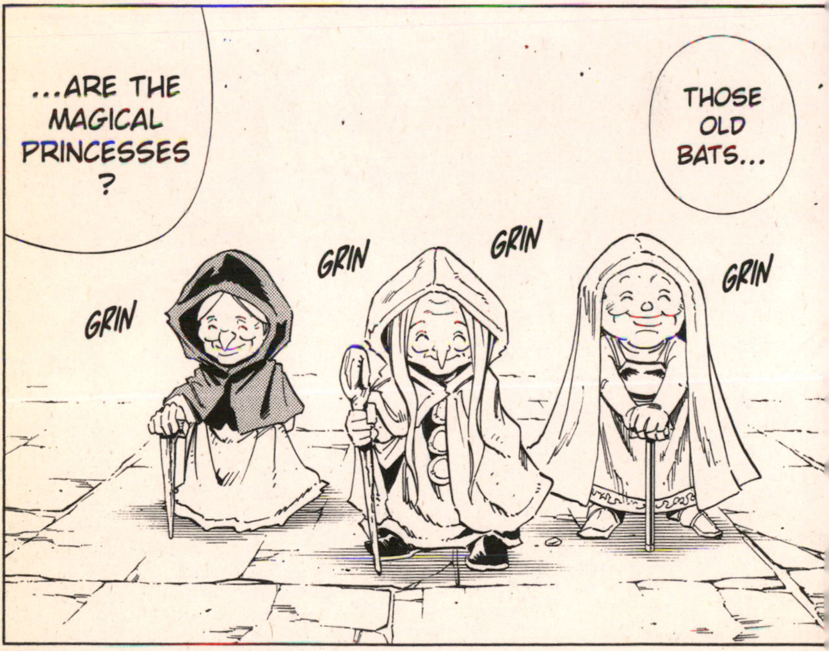
THOSE OLD BATS...
...ARE THE MAGICAL PRINCESSES?
GRIN
GRIN
GRIN
GRIN

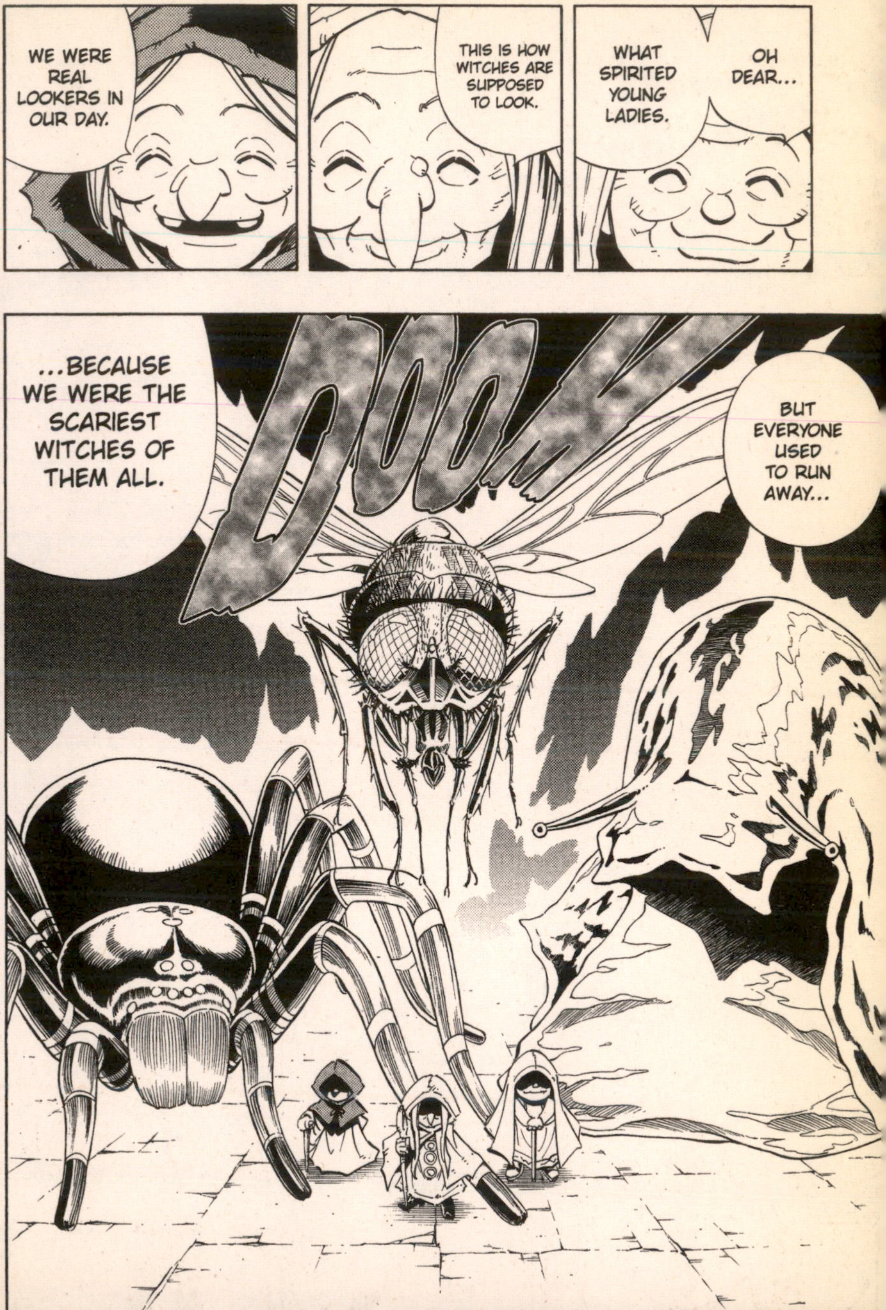
OH DEAR...
WHAT SPIRITED YOUNG LADIES.
THIS IS HOW WITCHES ARE SUPPOSED TO LOOK.
WE WERE REAL LOOKERS IN OUR DAY.
BUT EVERYONE USED TO RUN AWAY...
DOOM
...BECAUSE WE WERE THE SCARIEST WITCHES OF THEM ALL.

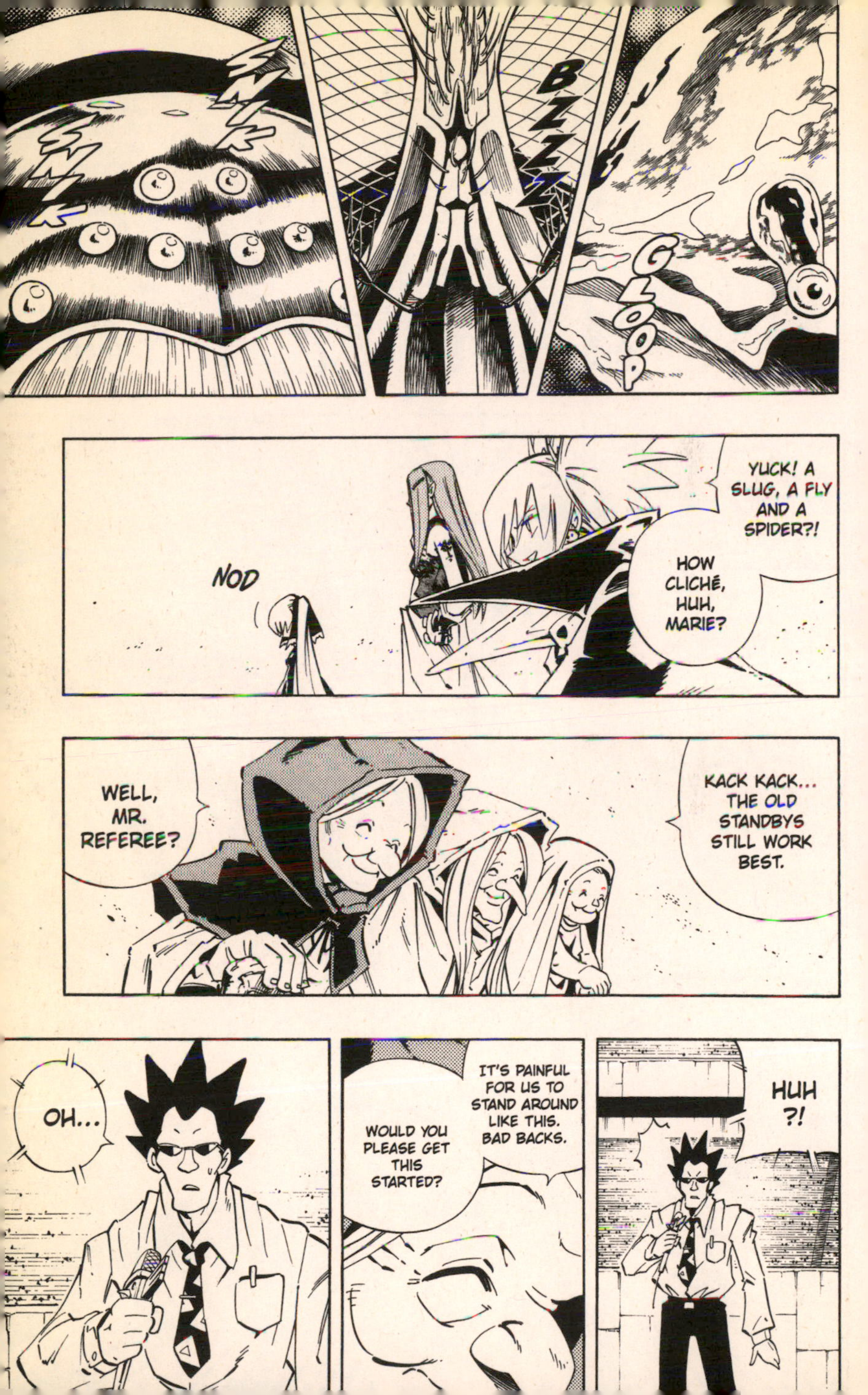
GLOOP
BZZZ
SNIK
SNIK
YUCK! A SLUG, A FLY AND A SPIDER?!
HOW CLICHÉ, HUH, MARIE?
NOD
KACK KACK... THE OLD STANDBYS STILL WORK BEST.
WELL, MR. REFEREE?
HUH ?!
IT'S PAINFUL FOR US TO STAND AROUND LIKE THIS. BAD BACKS.
WOULD YOU PLEASE GET THIS STARTED?
OH...

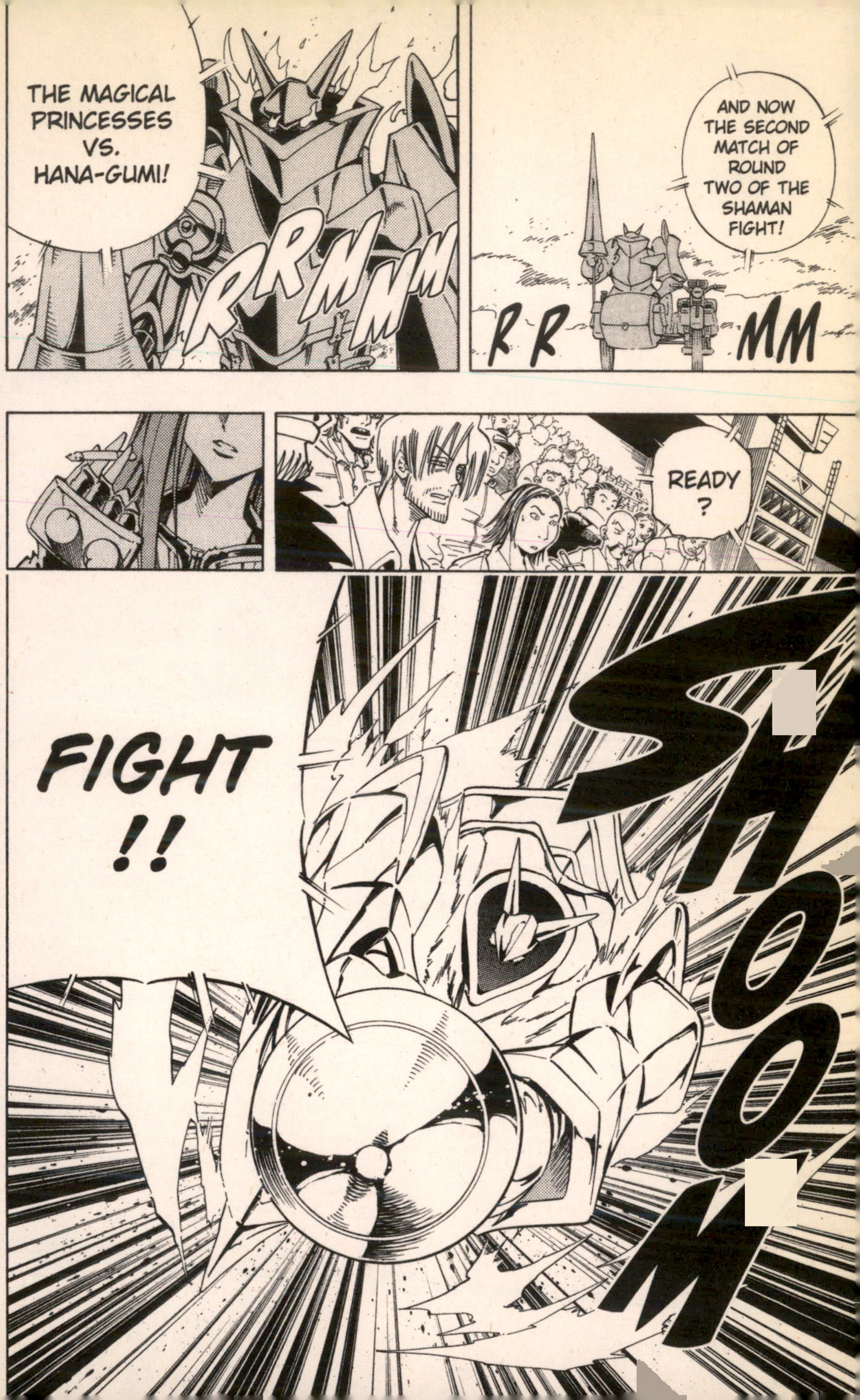
AND NOW THE SECOND MATCH OF ROUND TWO OF THE SHAMAN FIGHT!
RR MM
THE MAGICAL PRINCESSES VS. HANA-GUMI!
RRMMM
READY ?
SHOOM
FIGHT !!

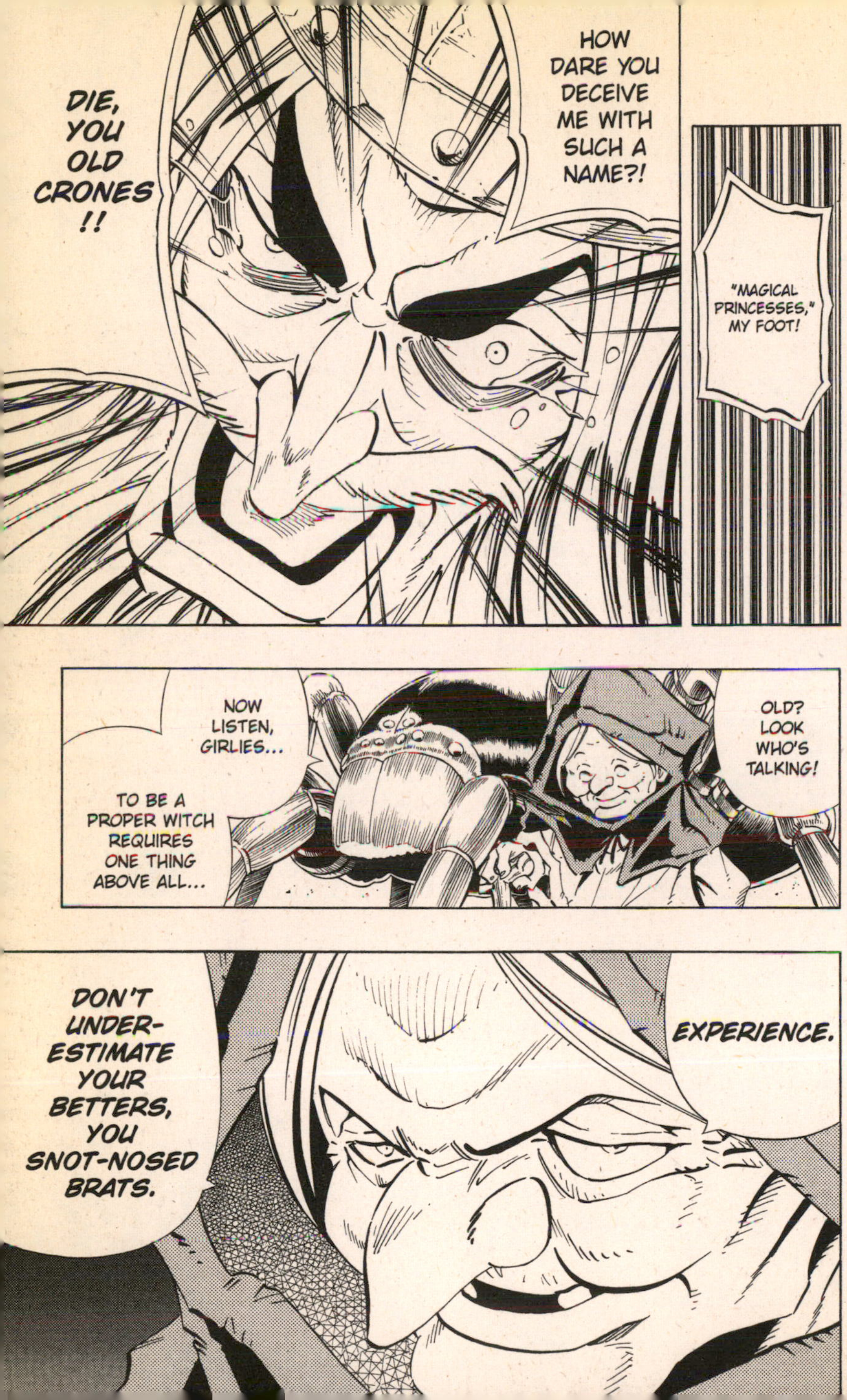
"MAGICAL PRINCESSES," MY FOOT!
HOW DARE YOU DECEIVE ME WITH SUCH A NAME?!
DIE, YOU OLD CRONES!!
OLD? LOOK WHO'S TALKING!
NOW LISTEN, GIRLIES...
TO BE A PROPER WITCH REQUIRES ONE THING ABOVE ALL...
EXPERIENCE.
DON'T UNDER-ESTIMATE YOUR BETTERS, YOU SNOT-NOSED BRATS.

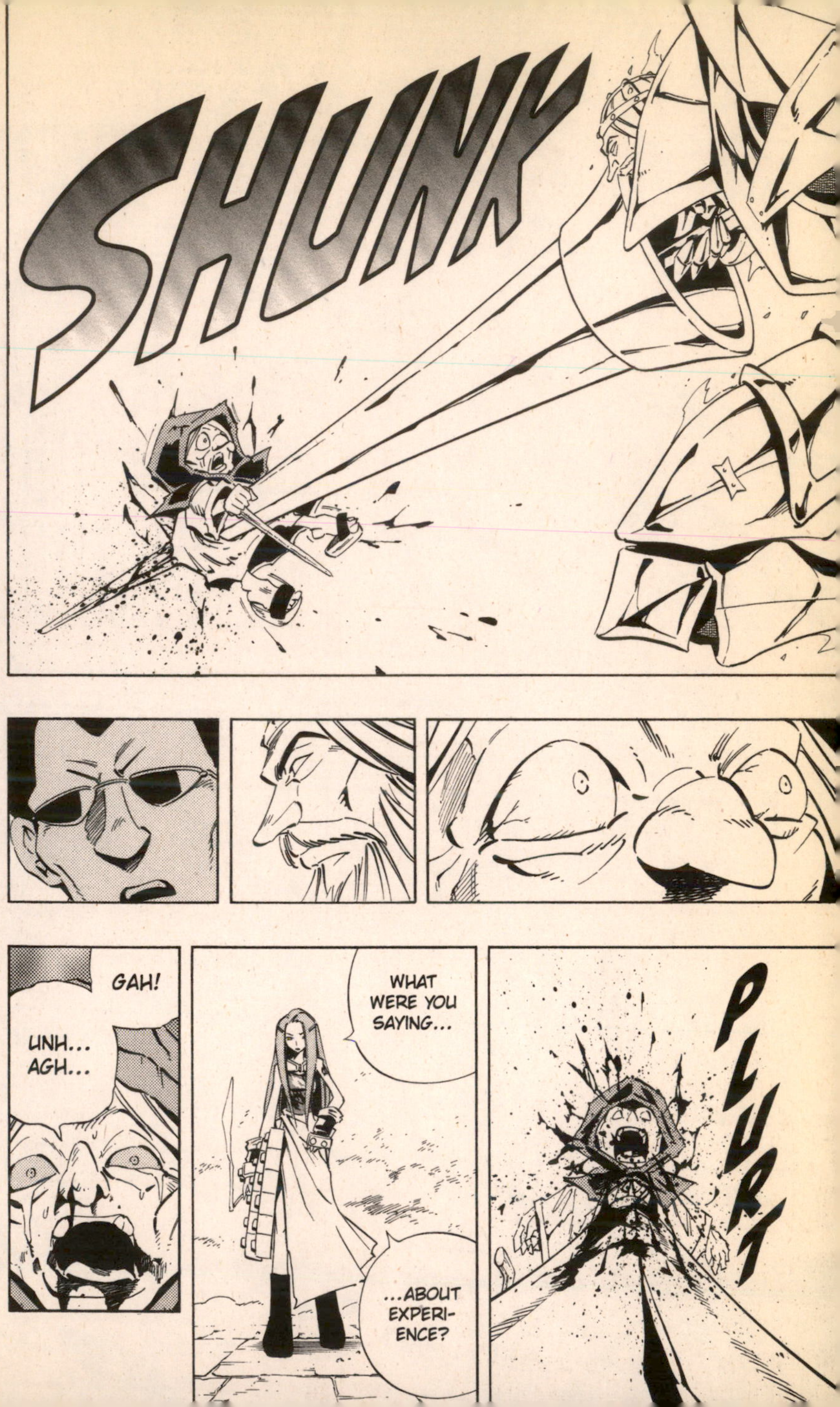
SHUNK
PLURT
WHAT WERE YOU SAYING...
...ABOUT EXPERIENCE?
GAH!
UNH... AGH...

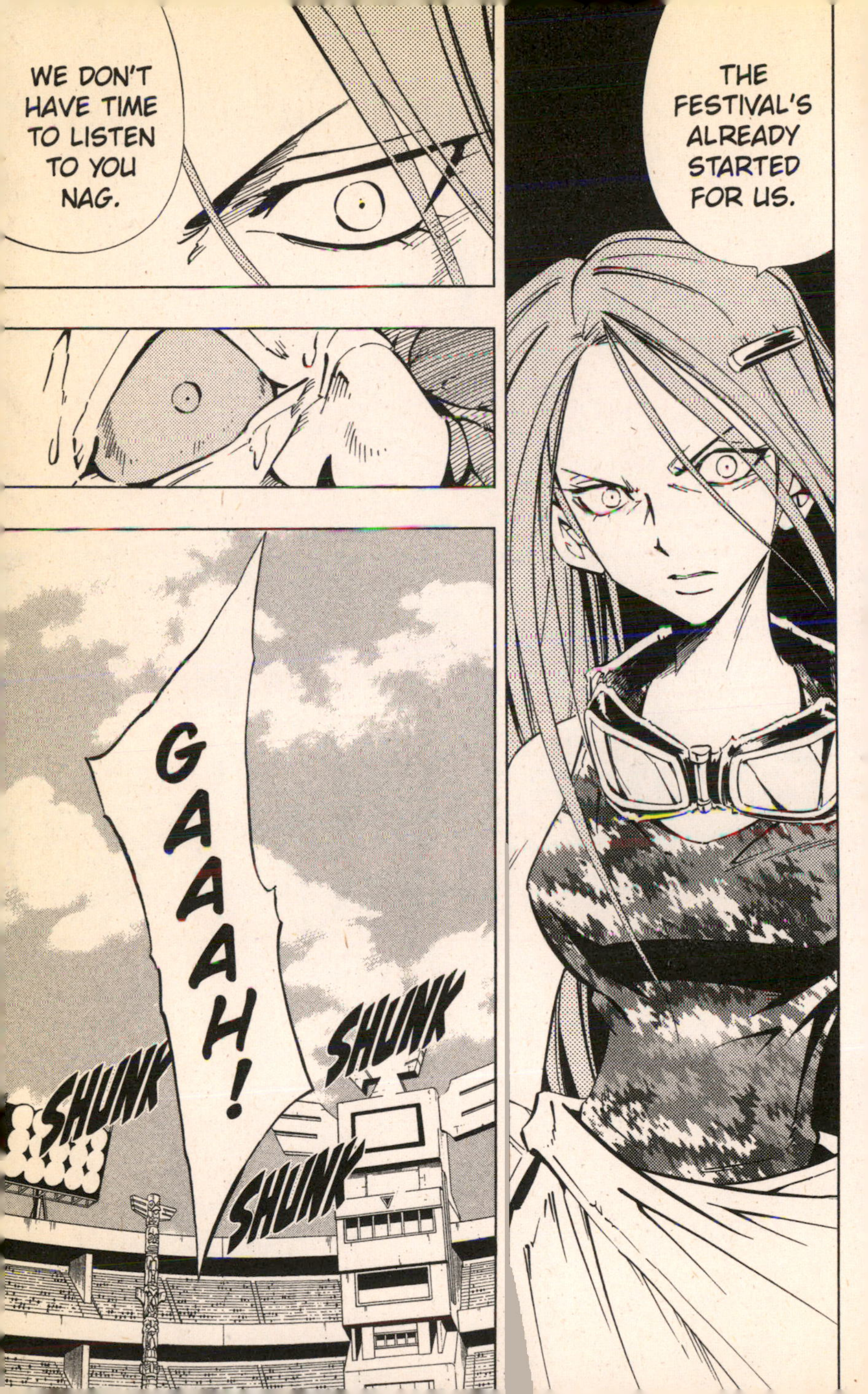
THE FESTIVAL'S ALREADY STARTED FOR US.
WE DON'T HAVE TIME TO LISTEN TO YOU NAG.
GAAAH!
SHUNK
SHUNK
SHUNK

SHAMAN KING CHARACTER FILE No.134

リルレッド
LITTLE RED

2001
(JAN)

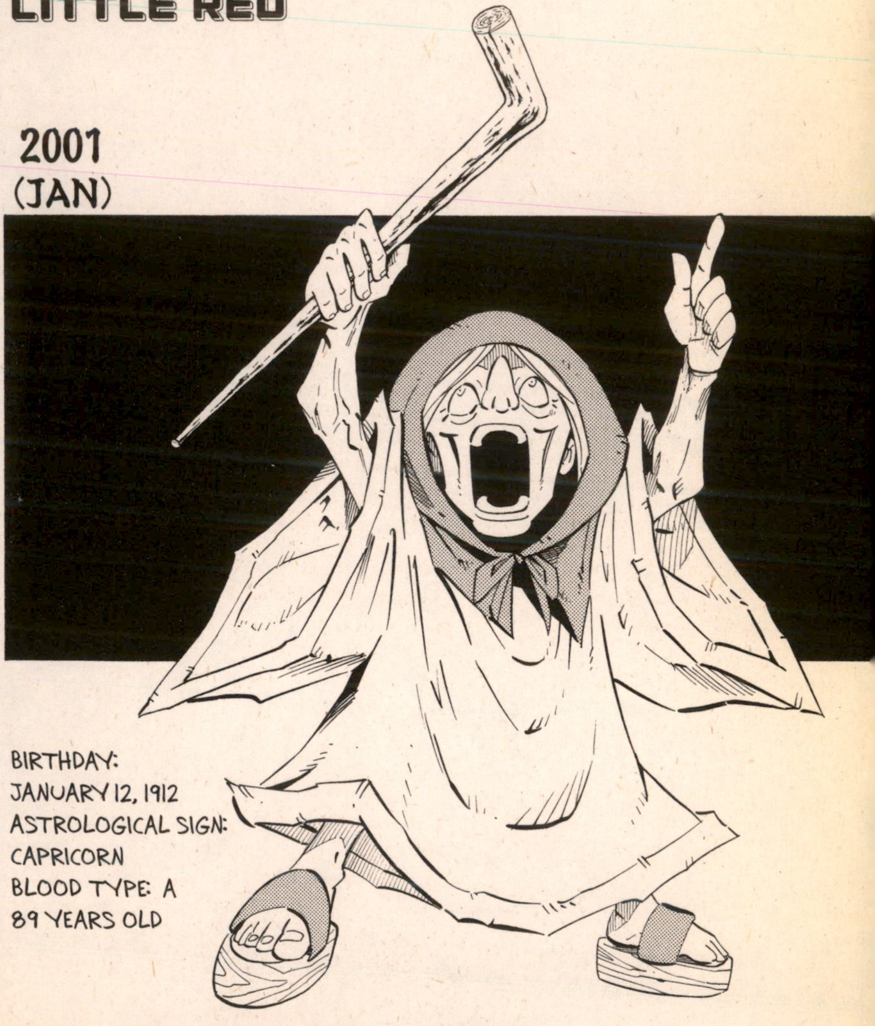

BIRTHDAY:
JANUARY 12, 1912
ASTROLOGICAL SIGN:
CAPRICORN
BLOOD TYPE: A
89 YEARS OLD

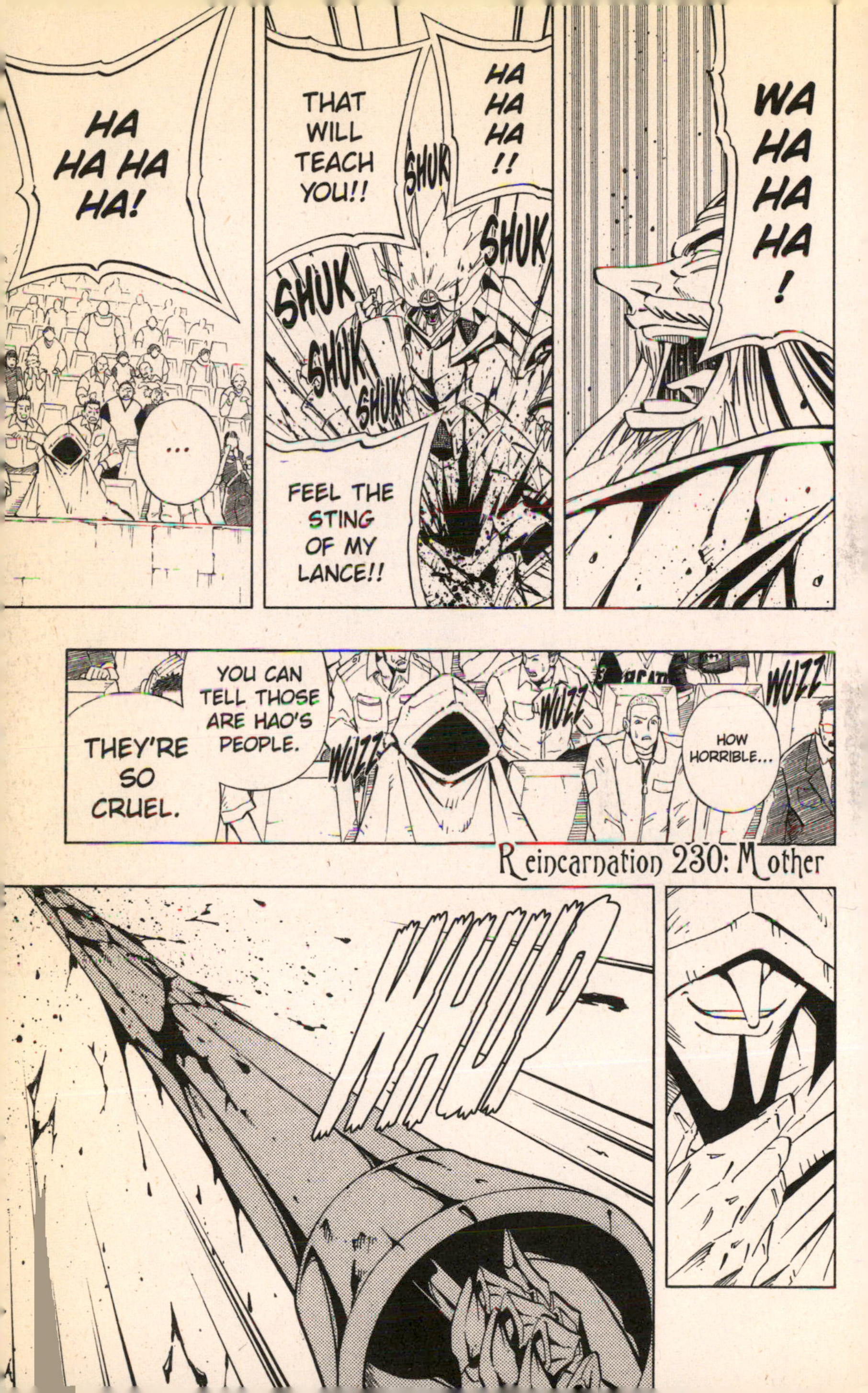
WA HA HA HA !
HA HA HA !!
SHUK
THAT WILL TEACH YOU!!
SHUK
SHUK
SHUK
SHUK
FEEL THE STING OF MY LANCE!!
HA HA HA HA!
...
WUZZ
HOW HORRIBLE...
WUZZ
WUZZ
YOU CAN TELL THOSE ARE HAO'S PEOPLE.
THEY'RE SO CRUEL.
Reincarnation 230: Mother
WHUP

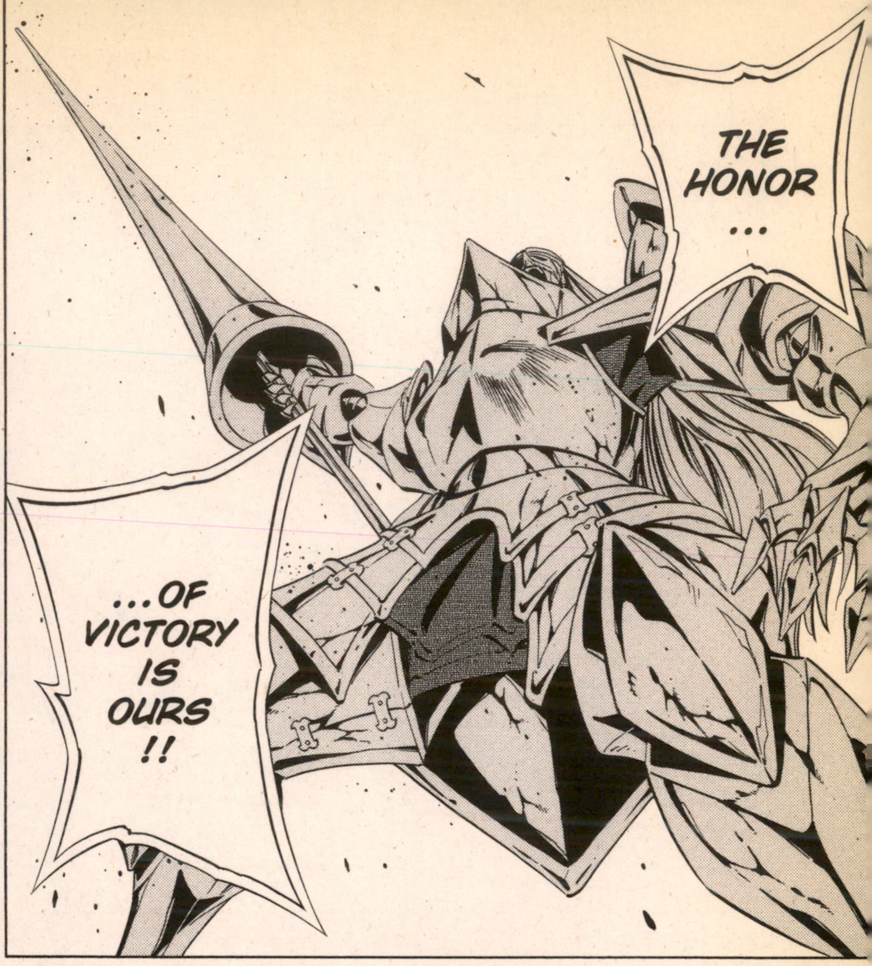
THE HONOR ...
...OF VICTORY IS OURS !!
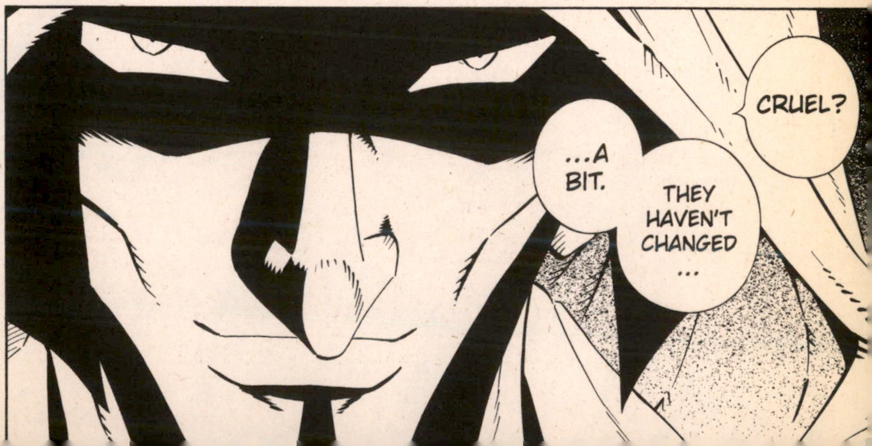
CRUEL?
...A BIT.
THEY HAVEN'T CHANGED ...

Reincarnation 230: Mother

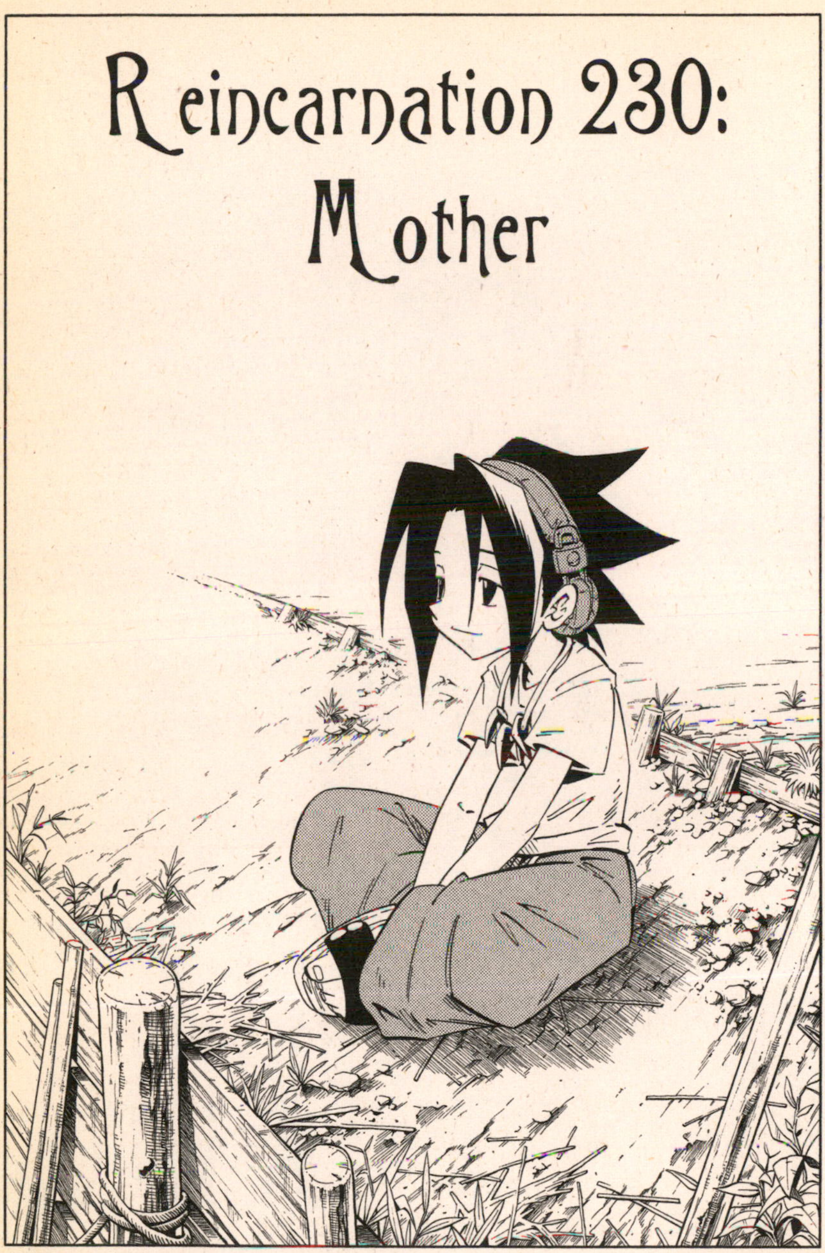

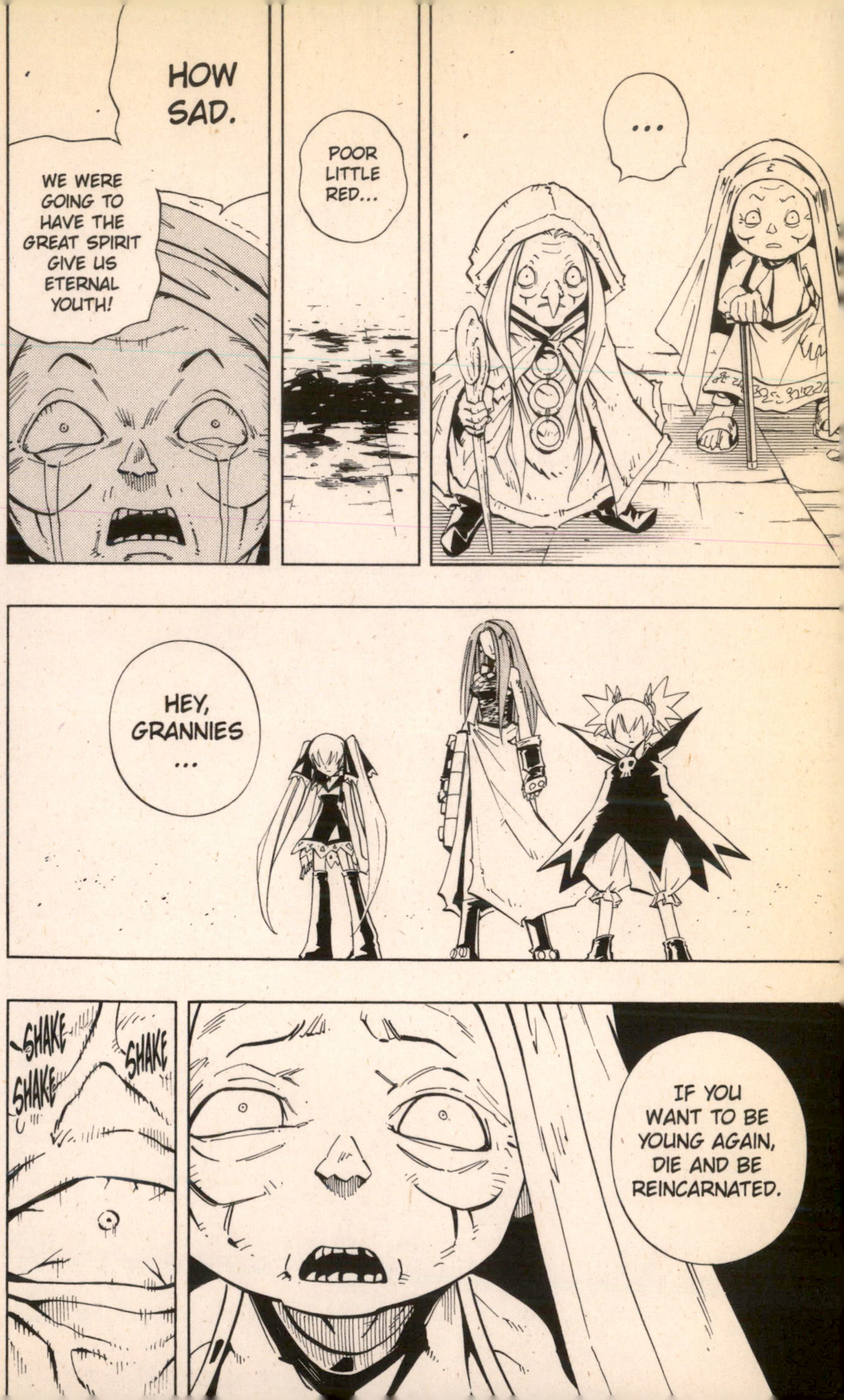
...
POOR LITTLE RED...
HOW SAD.
WE WERE GOING TO HAVE THE GREAT SPIRIT GIVE US ETERNAL YOUTH!
HEY, GRANNIES ...
IF YOU WANT TO BE YOUNG AGAIN, DIE AND BE REINCARNATED.
SHAKE
SHAKE
SHAKE

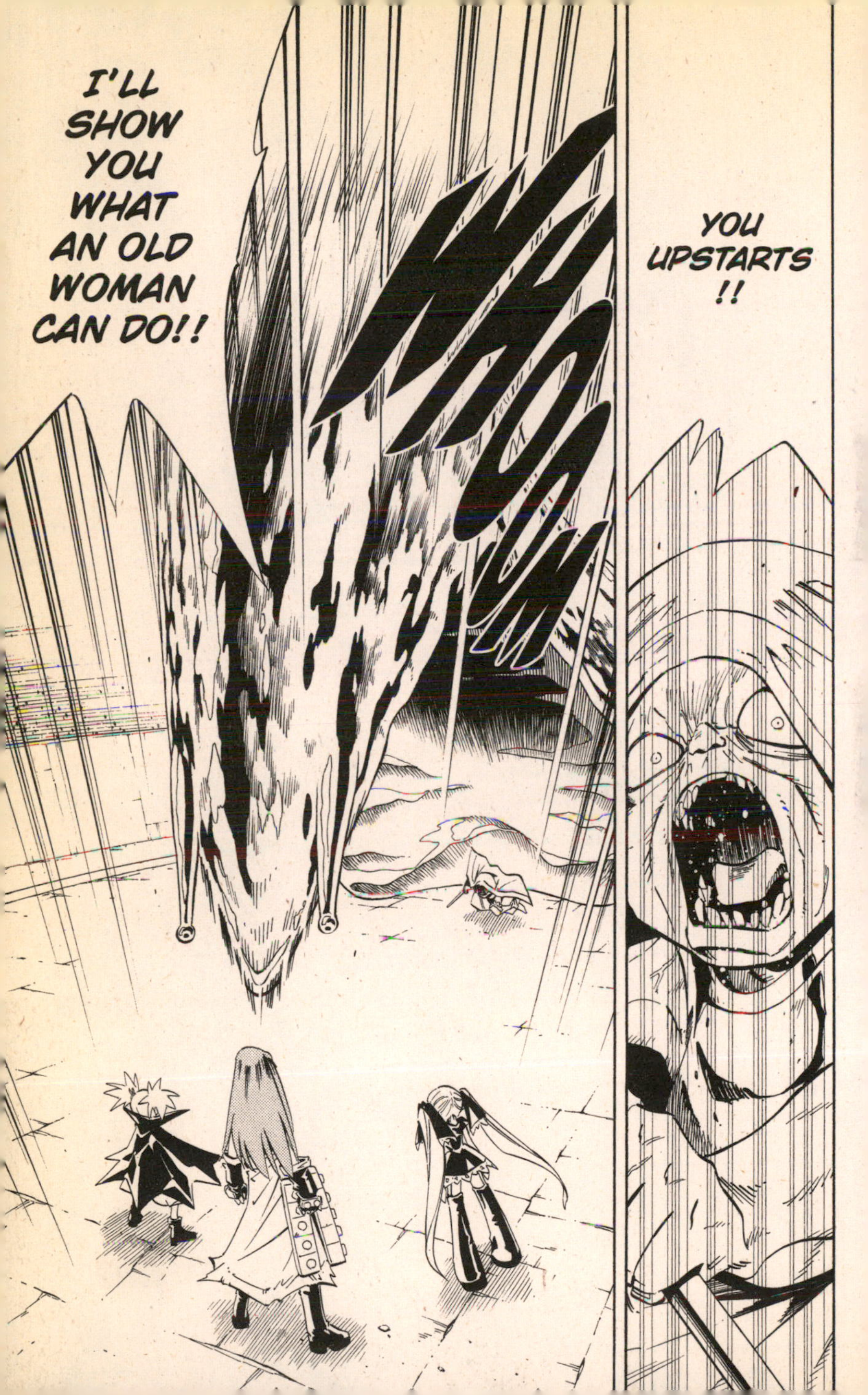
YOU UPSTARTS!!
I'LL SHOW YOU WHAT AN OLD WOMAN CAN DO!!

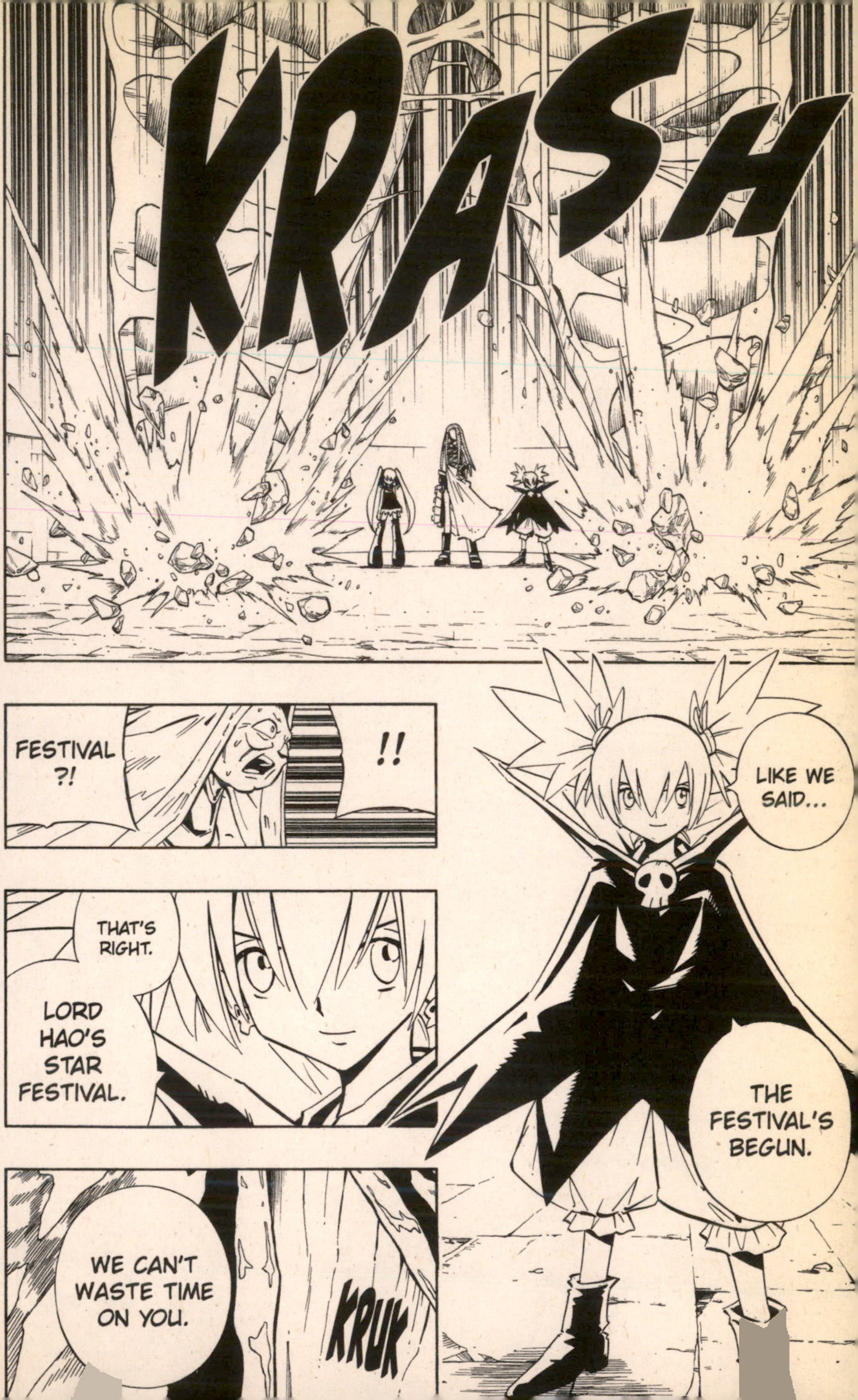
KRASH
LIKE WE SAID...
THE FESTIVAL'S BEGUN.
!!
FESTIVAL ?!
THAT'S RIGHT.
LORD HAO'S STAR FESTIVAL.
WE CAN'T WASTE TIME ON YOU.
KRUK

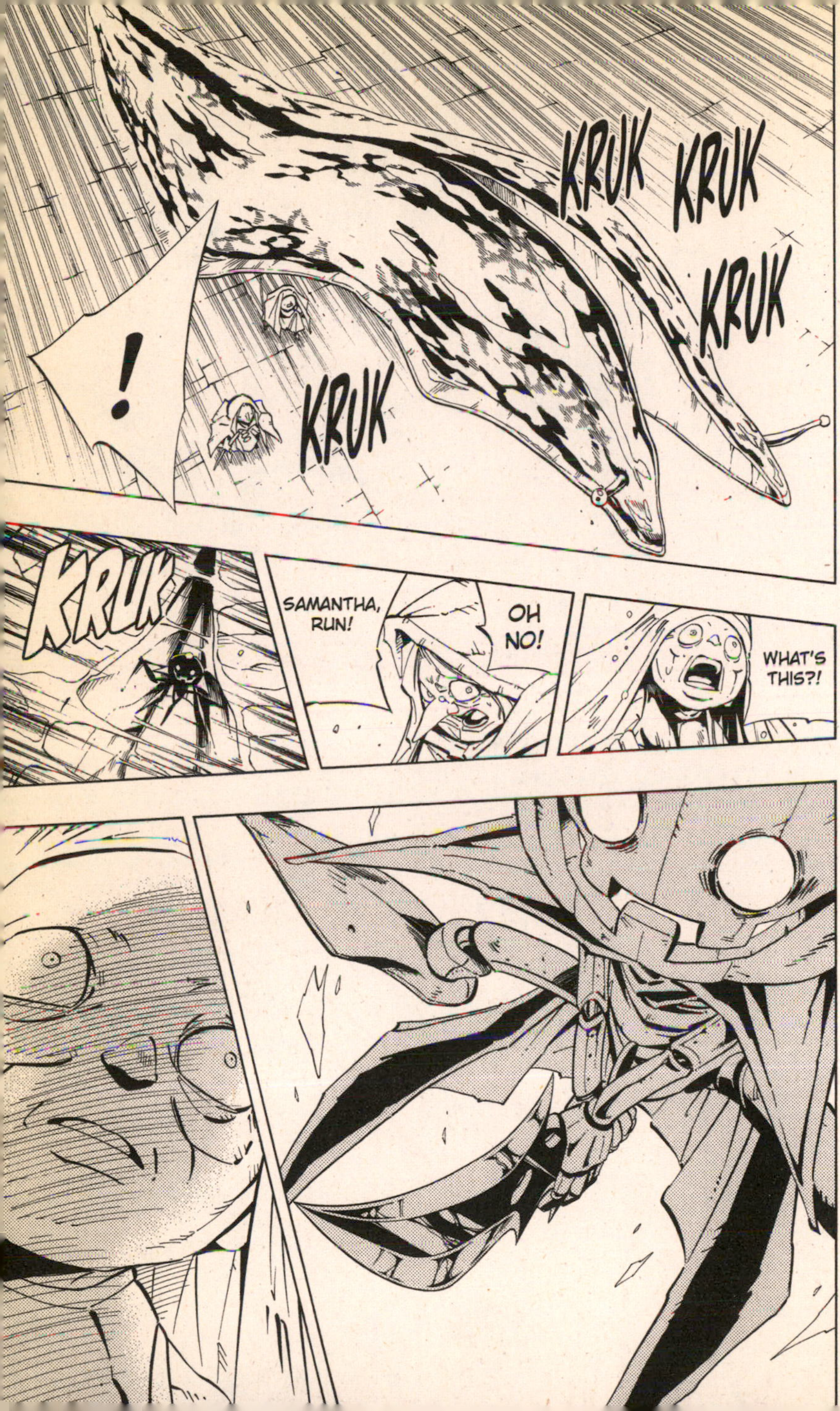
KRUK
KRUK
KRUK
KRUK
!
WHAT'S THIS?!
OH NO!
SAMANTHA, RUN!
KRUK

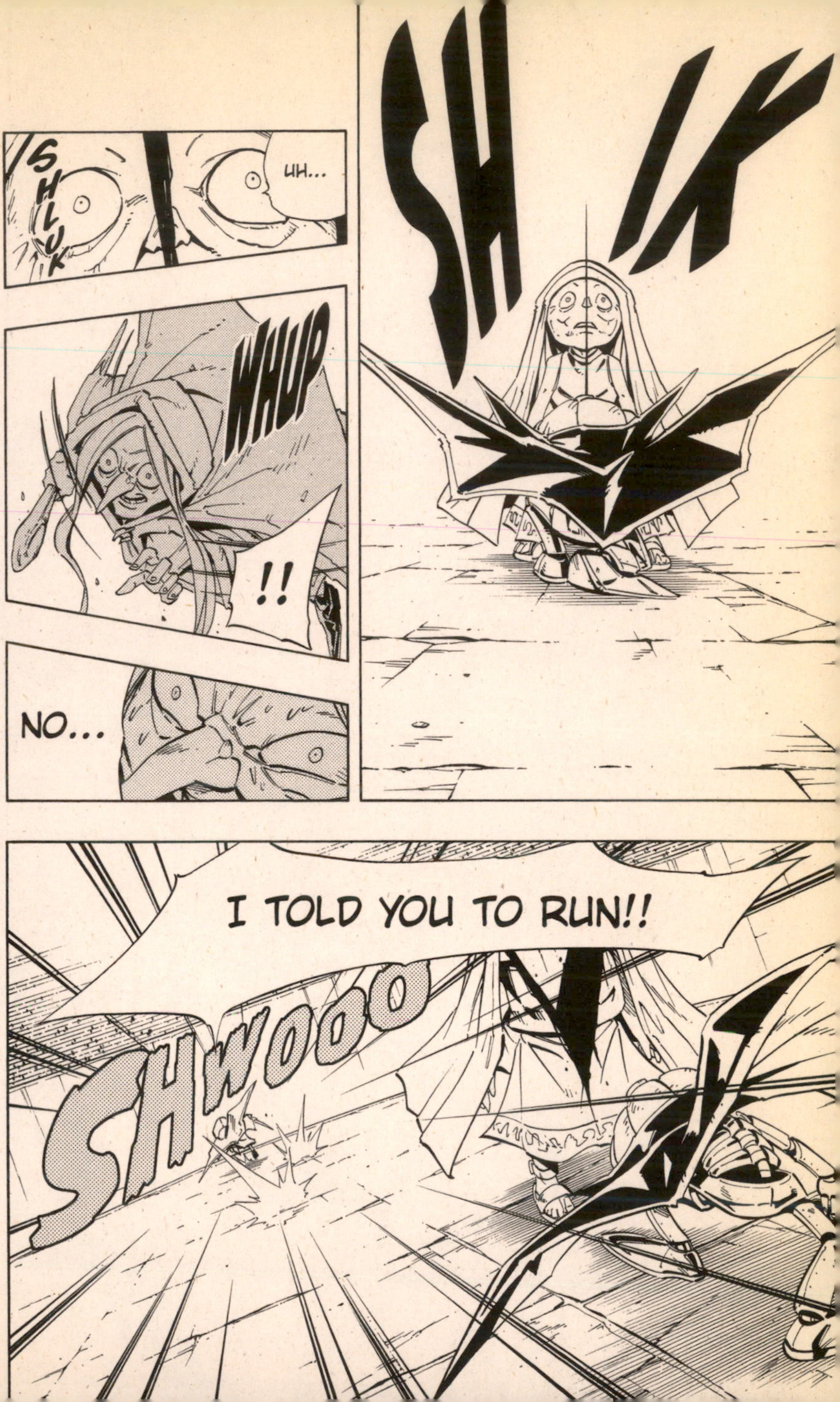
SHIK
UH...
SHLUK
WHUP
!!
NO...
I TOLD YOU TO RUN!!
SHWOOO

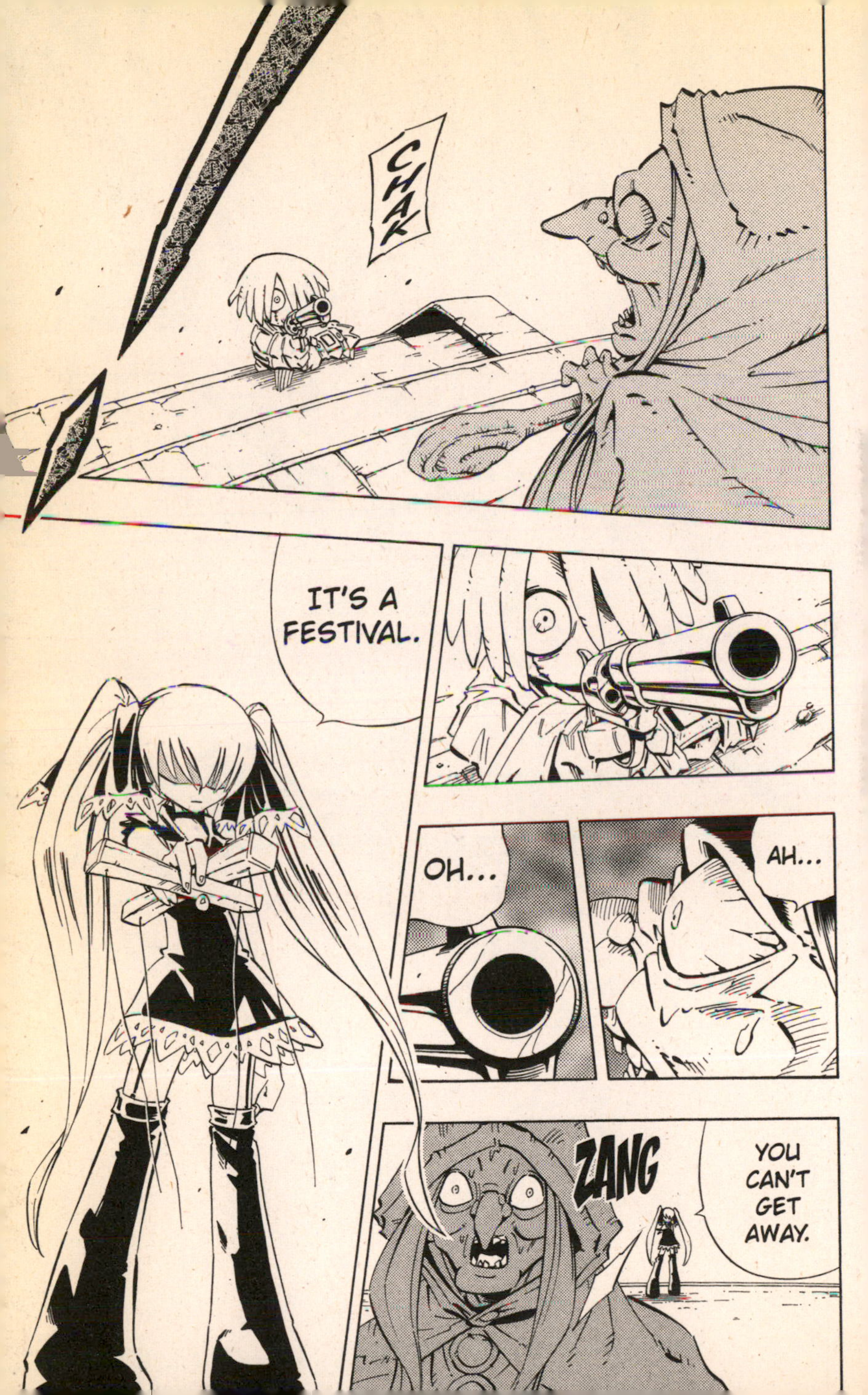
CHAK
AH...
OH...
ZANG
YOU CAN'T GET AWAY.
IT'S A FESTIVAL.

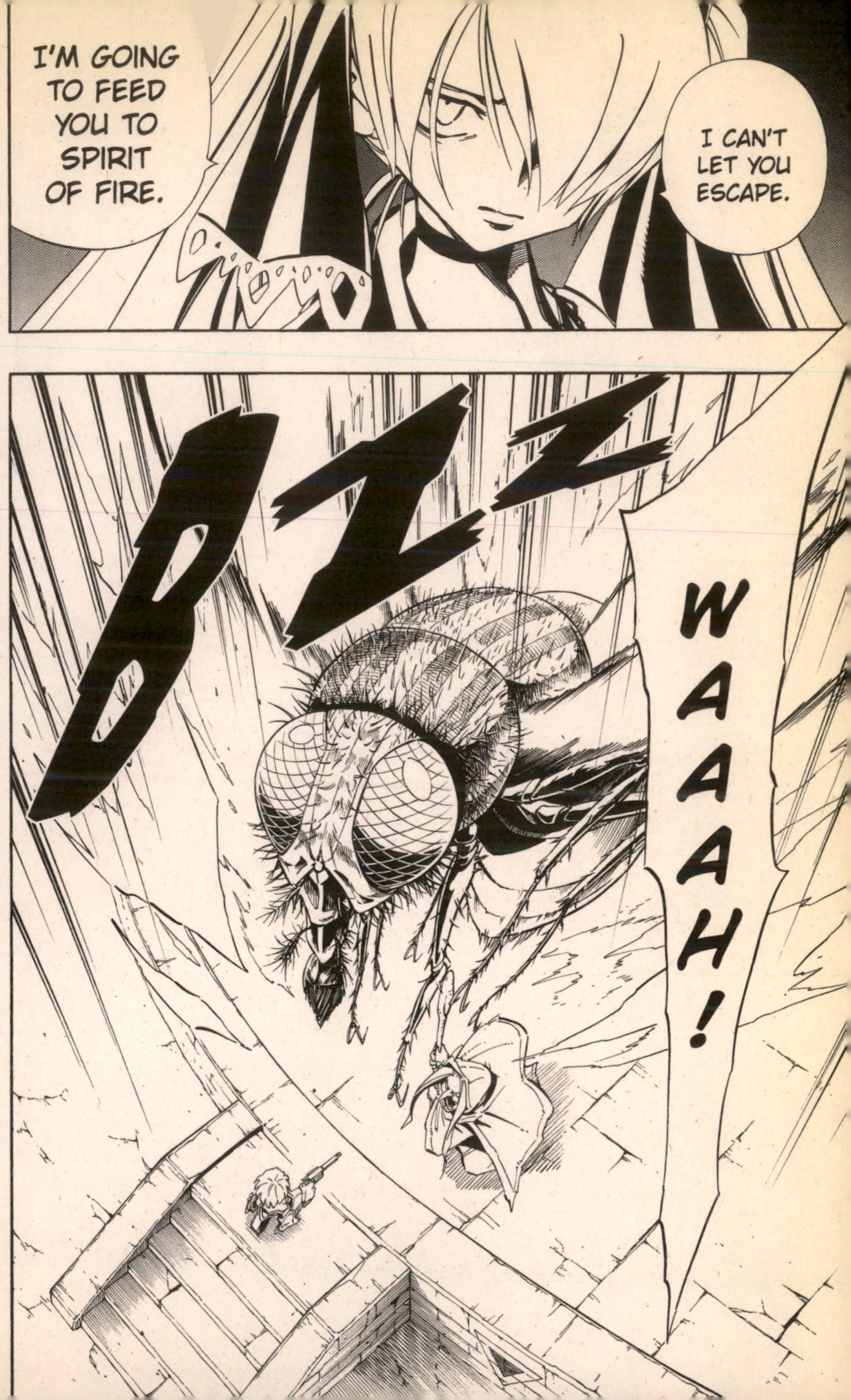
I CAN'T LET YOU ESCAPE.
I'M GOING TO FEED YOU TO SPIRIT OF FIRE.
WAAAAH!
BZZ

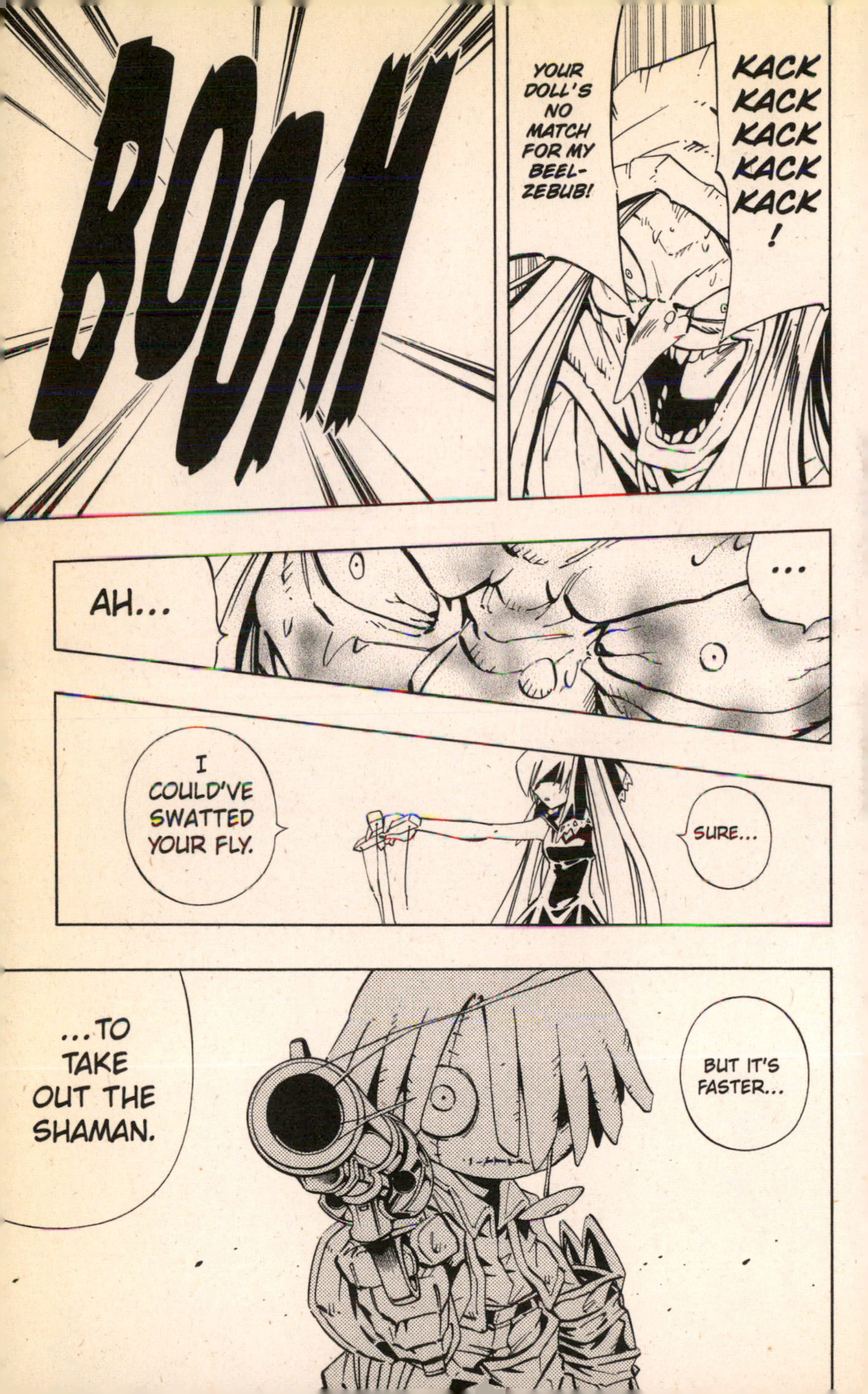
KACK KACK KACK KACK KACK!
YOUR DOLL'S NO MATCH FOR MY BEEL-ZEBUB!
BOOM
...
AH...
SURE...
I COULD'VE SWATTED YOUR FLY.
BUT IT'S FASTER...
...TO TAKE OUT THE SHAMAN.

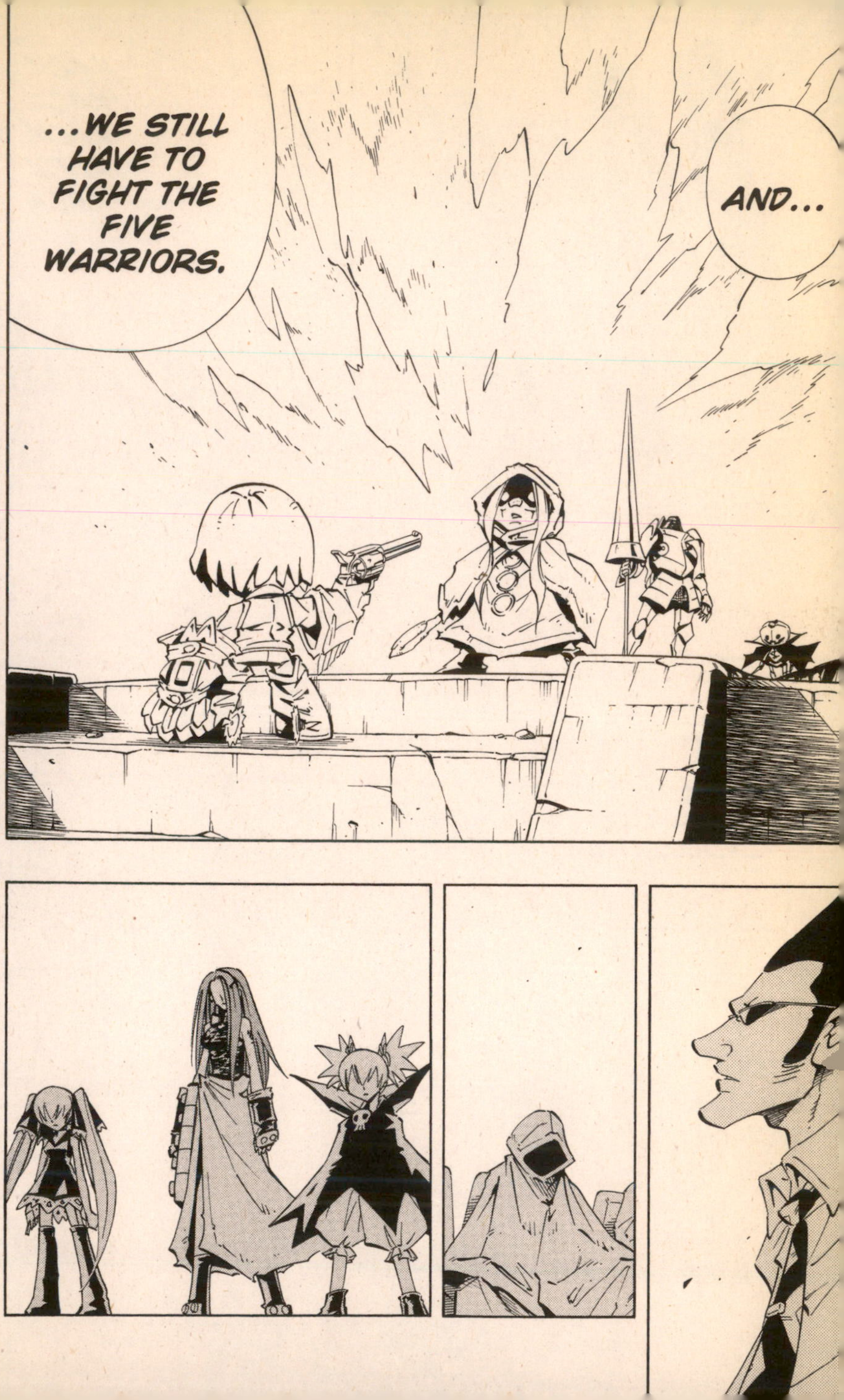
AND...
...WE STILL HAVE TO FIGHT THE FIVE WARRIORS.

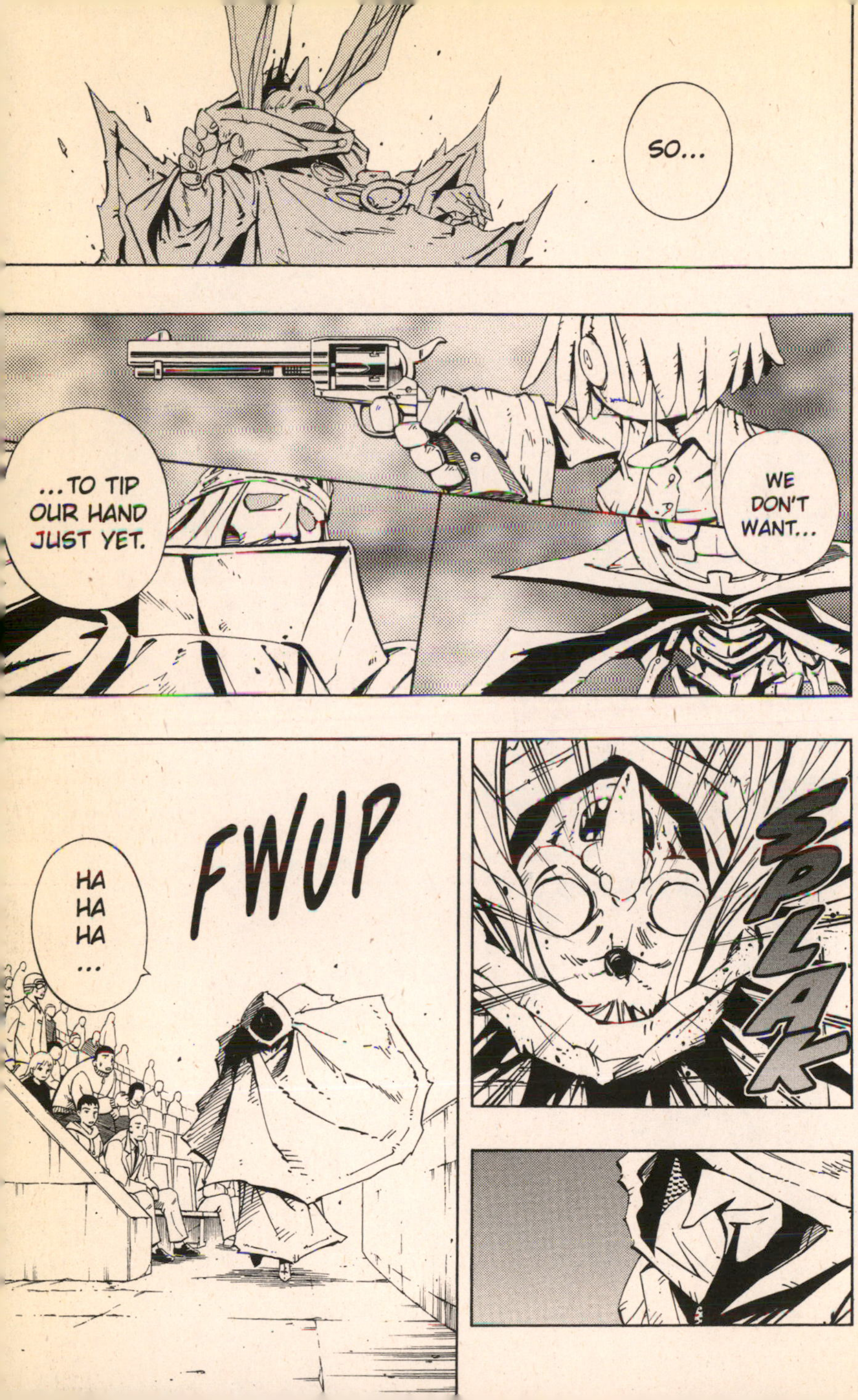
SO...
WE DON'T WANT...
...TO TIP OUR HAND JUST YET.
SPLAK
FWUP
HA HA HA ...

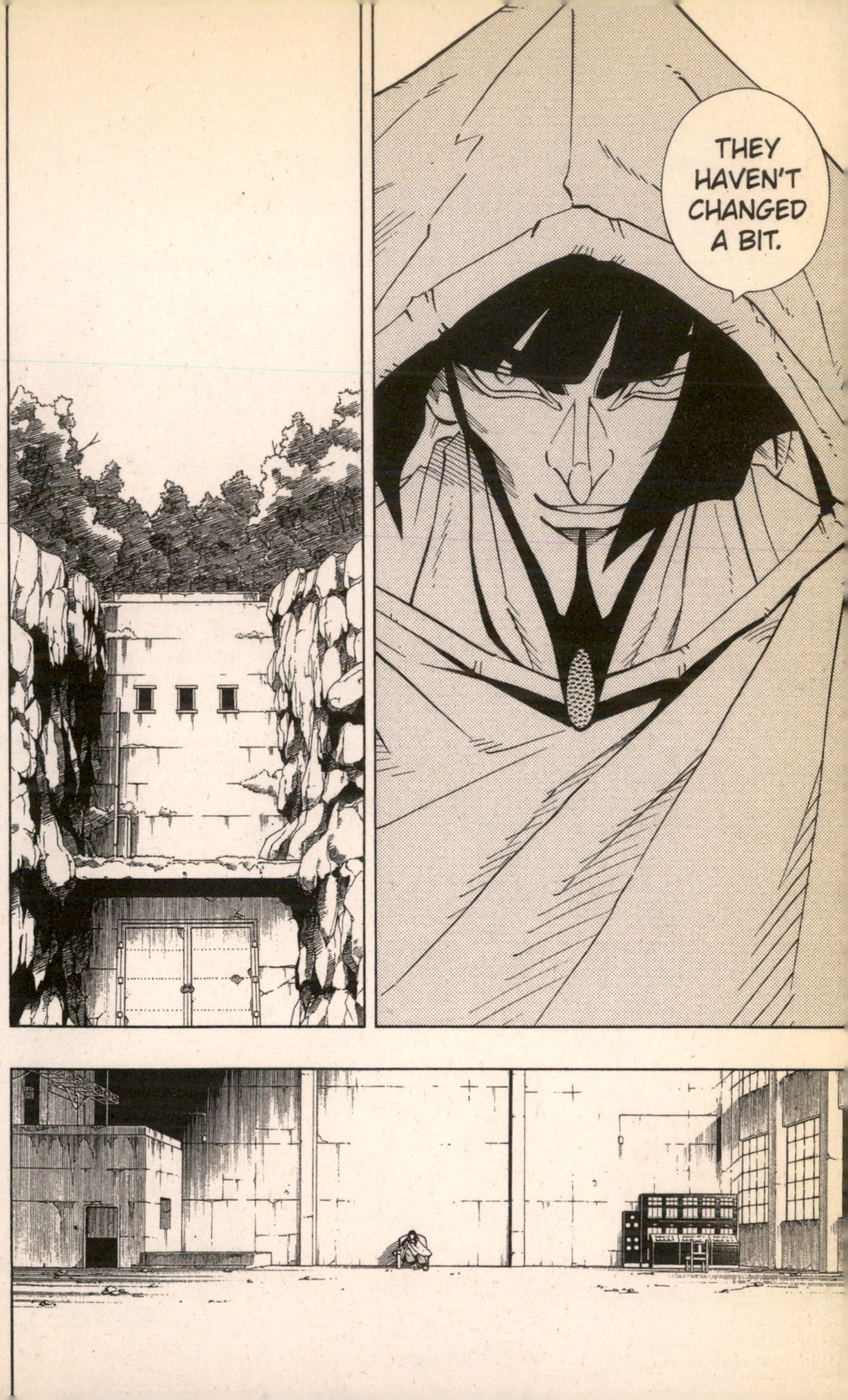
THEY HAVEN'T CHANGED A BIT.

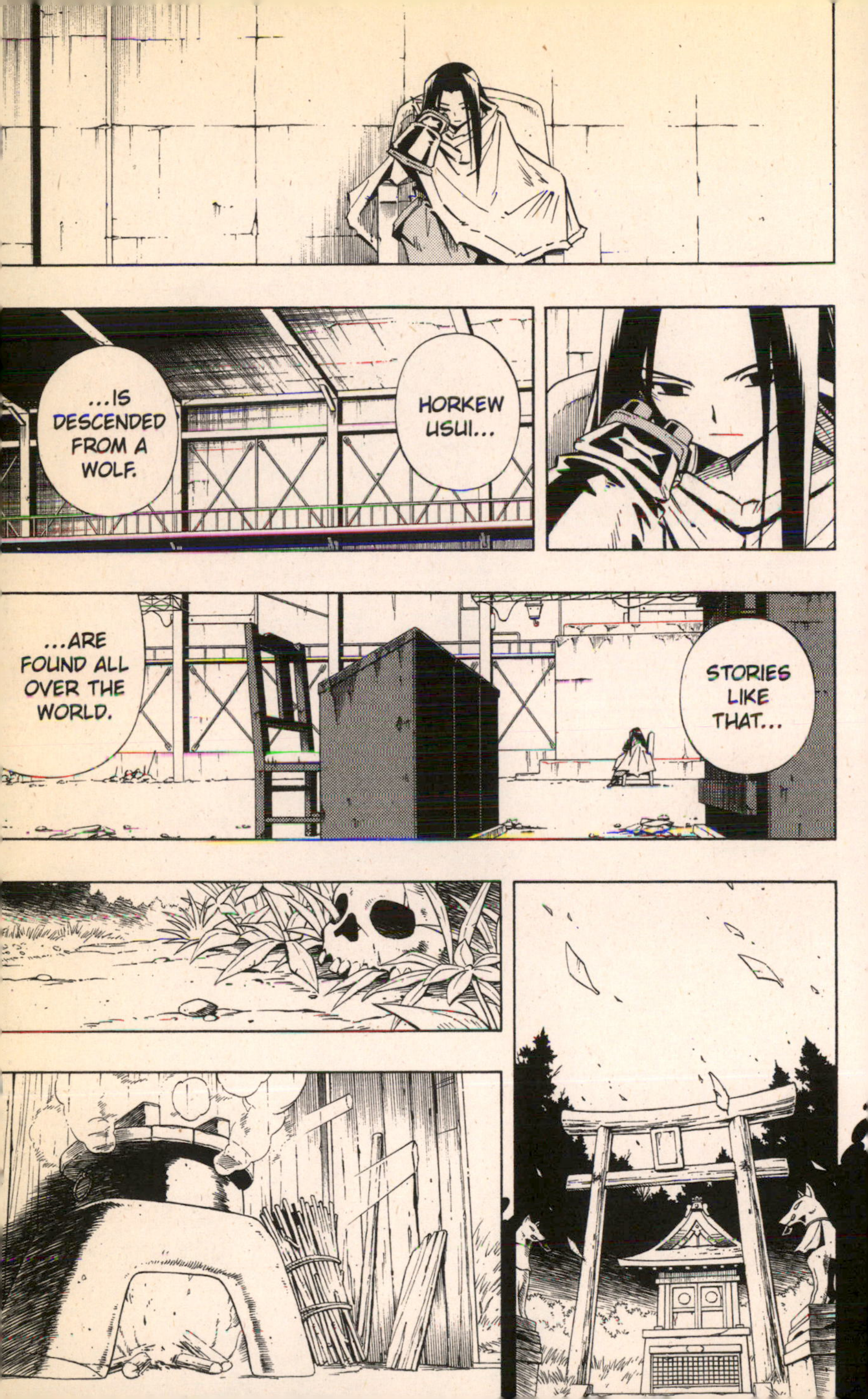
HORKEW USUI...
...IS DESCENDED FROM A WOLF.
STORIES LIKE THAT...
...ARE FOUND ALL OVER THE WORLD.

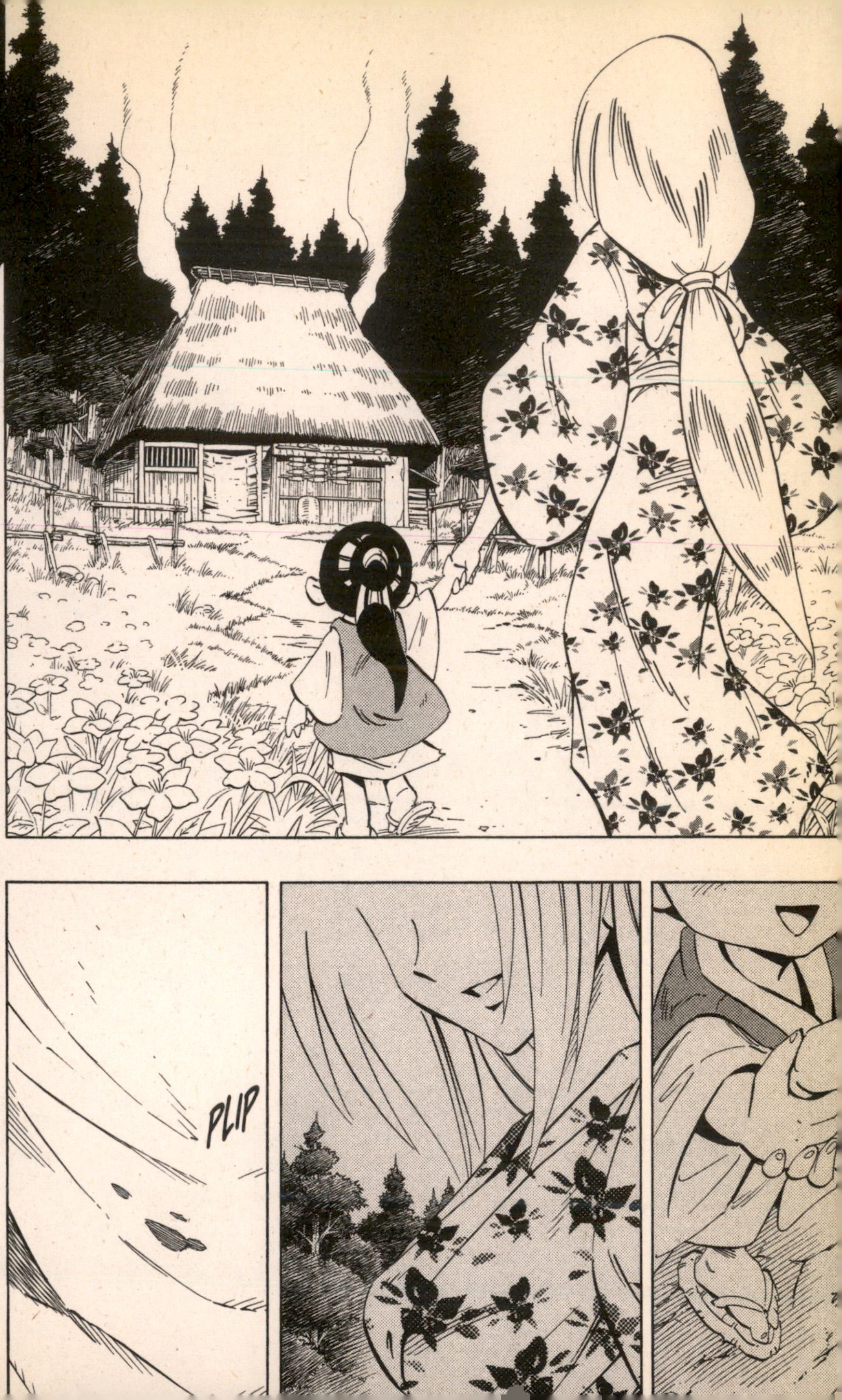
PLIP

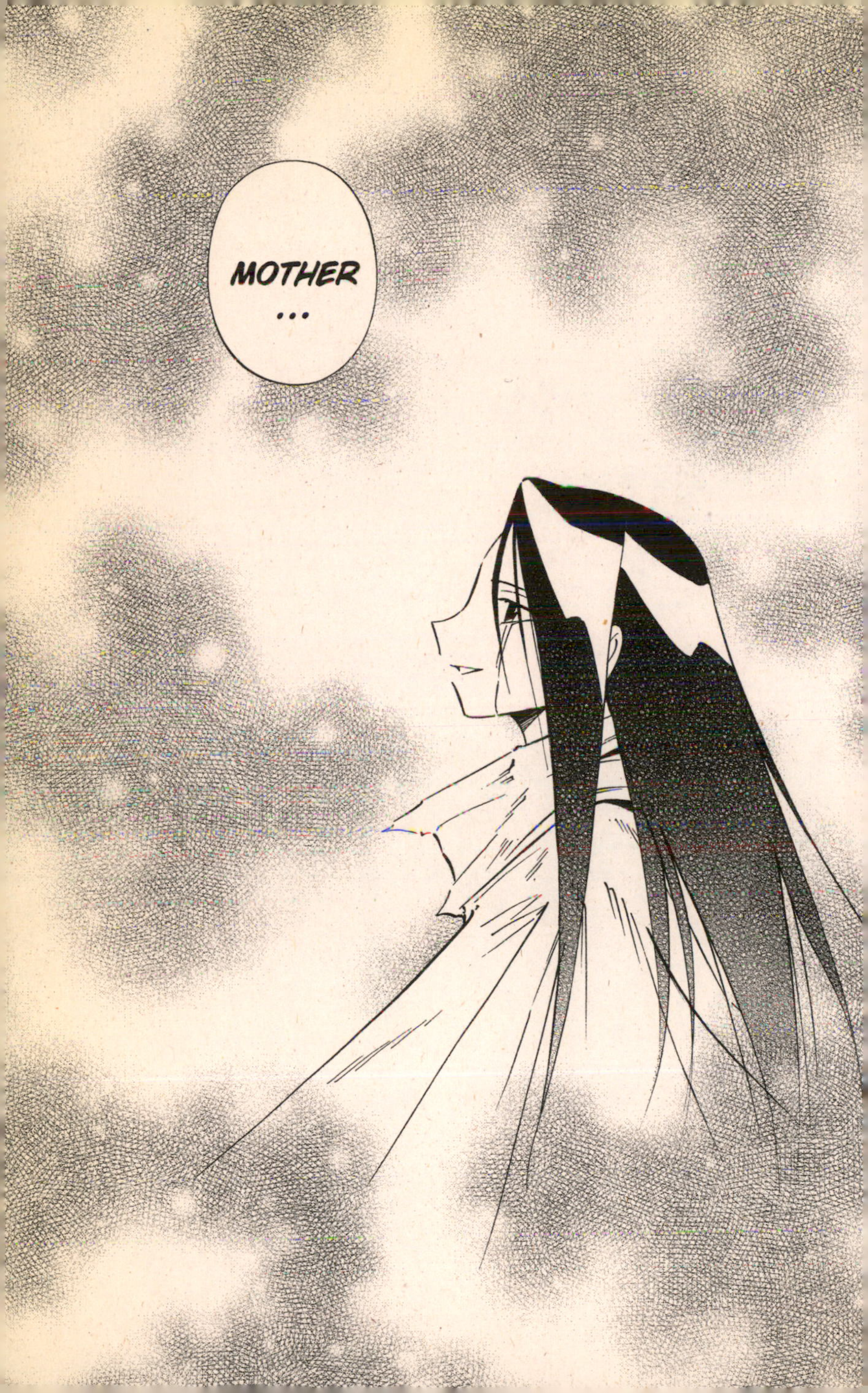
MOTHER ...

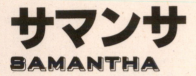

サマンサ
SAMANTHA

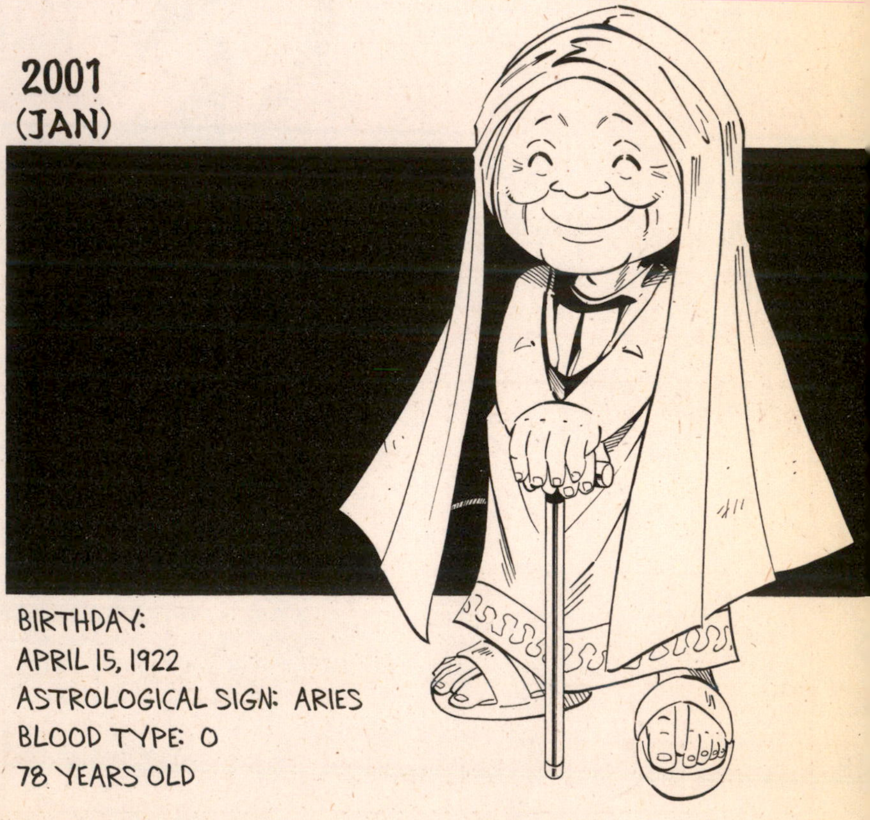
2001
(JAN)
BIRTHDAY:
APRIL 15, 1922
ASTROLOGICAL SIGN: ARIES
BLOOD TYPE: O
78 YEARS OLD

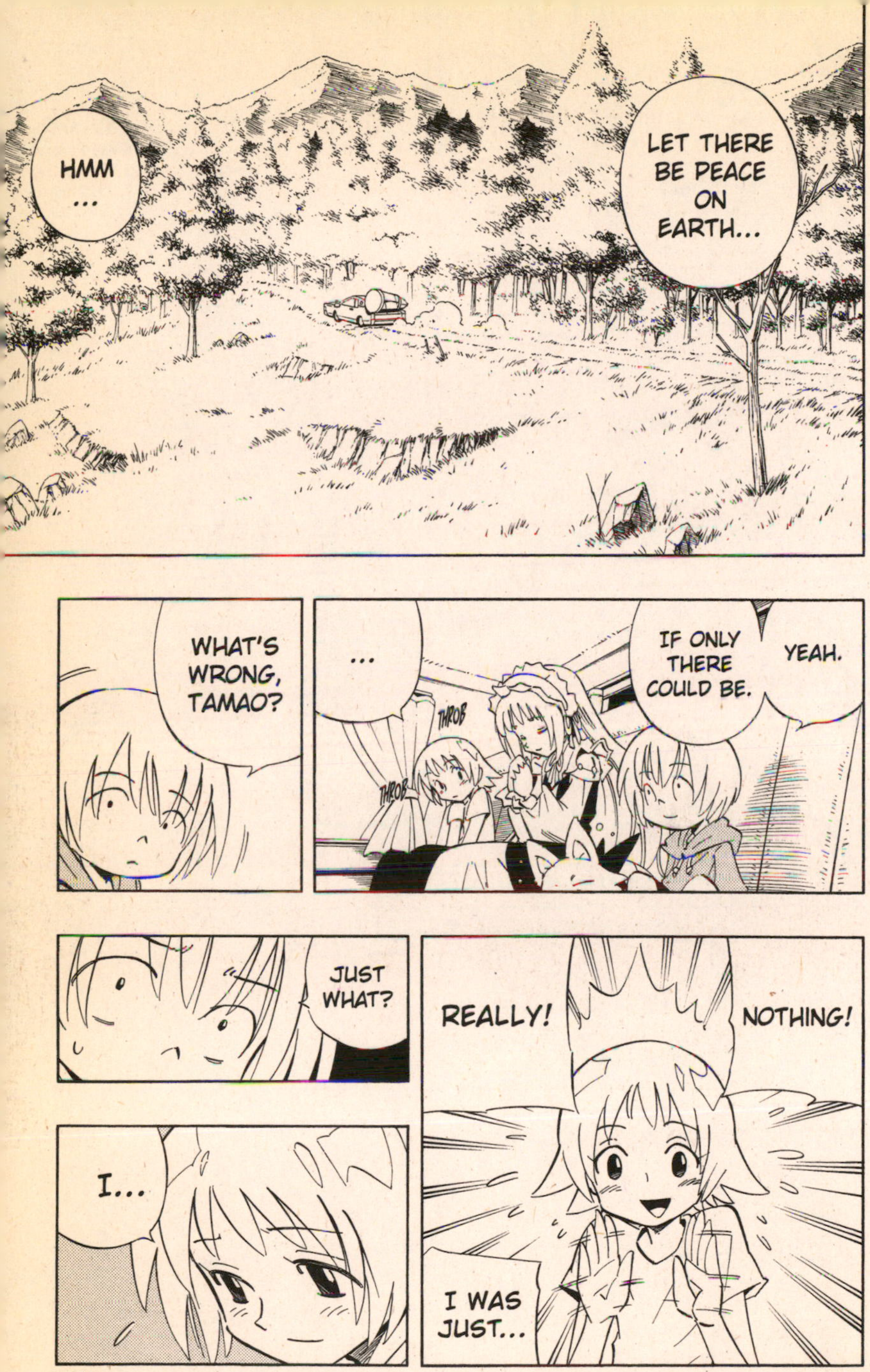
LET THERE BE PEACE ON EARTH...
HMM ...
YEAH.
IF ONLY THERE COULD BE.
...
THROB
THROB
WHAT'S WRONG, TAMAO?
NOTHING!
REALLY!
I WAS JUST...
JUST WHAT?
I...

Reincarnation 231: Countdown to Destruction

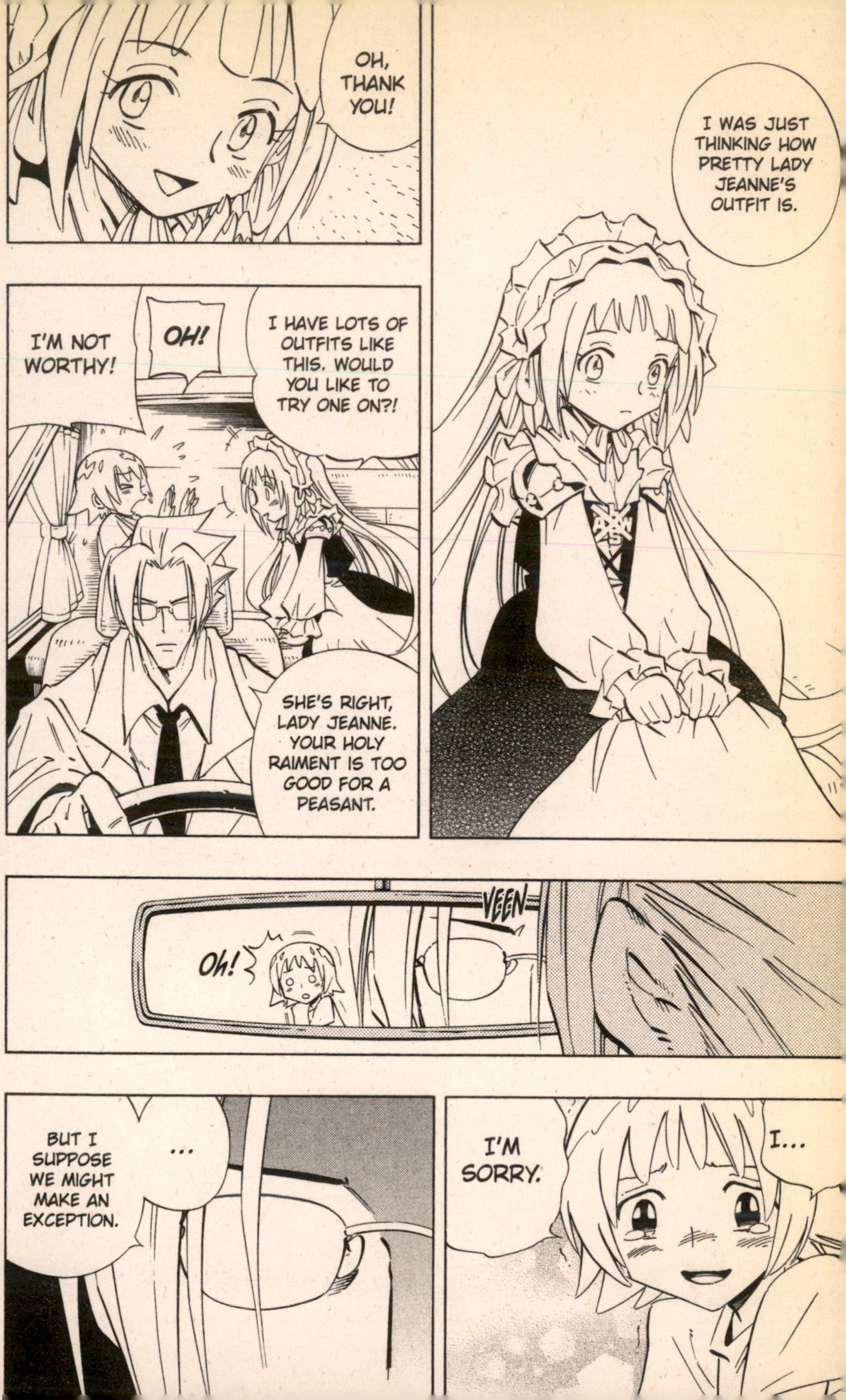

I WAS JUST THINKING HOW PRETTY LADY JEANNE'S OUTFIT IS.
OH, THANK YOU!
I HAVE LOTS OF OUTFITS LIKE THIS. WOULD YOU LIKE TO TRY ONE ON?!
OH!
I'M NOT WORTHY!
SHE'S RIGHT, LADY JEANNE. YOUR HOLY RAIMENT IS TOO GOOD FOR A PEASANT.
VEEN
Oh!
I...
I'M SORRY.
...
BUT I SUPPOSE WE MIGHT MAKE AN EXCEPTION.

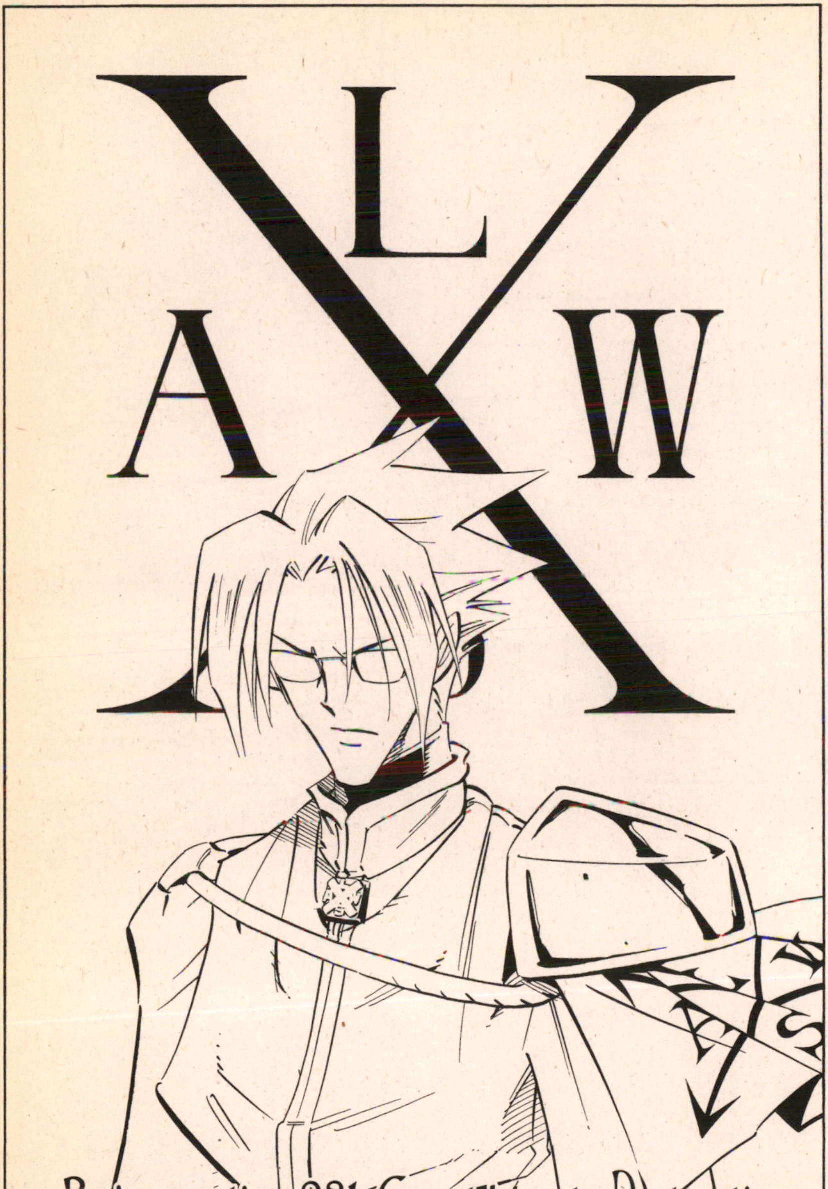
XLAW
Reincarnation 231: Countdown to Destruction

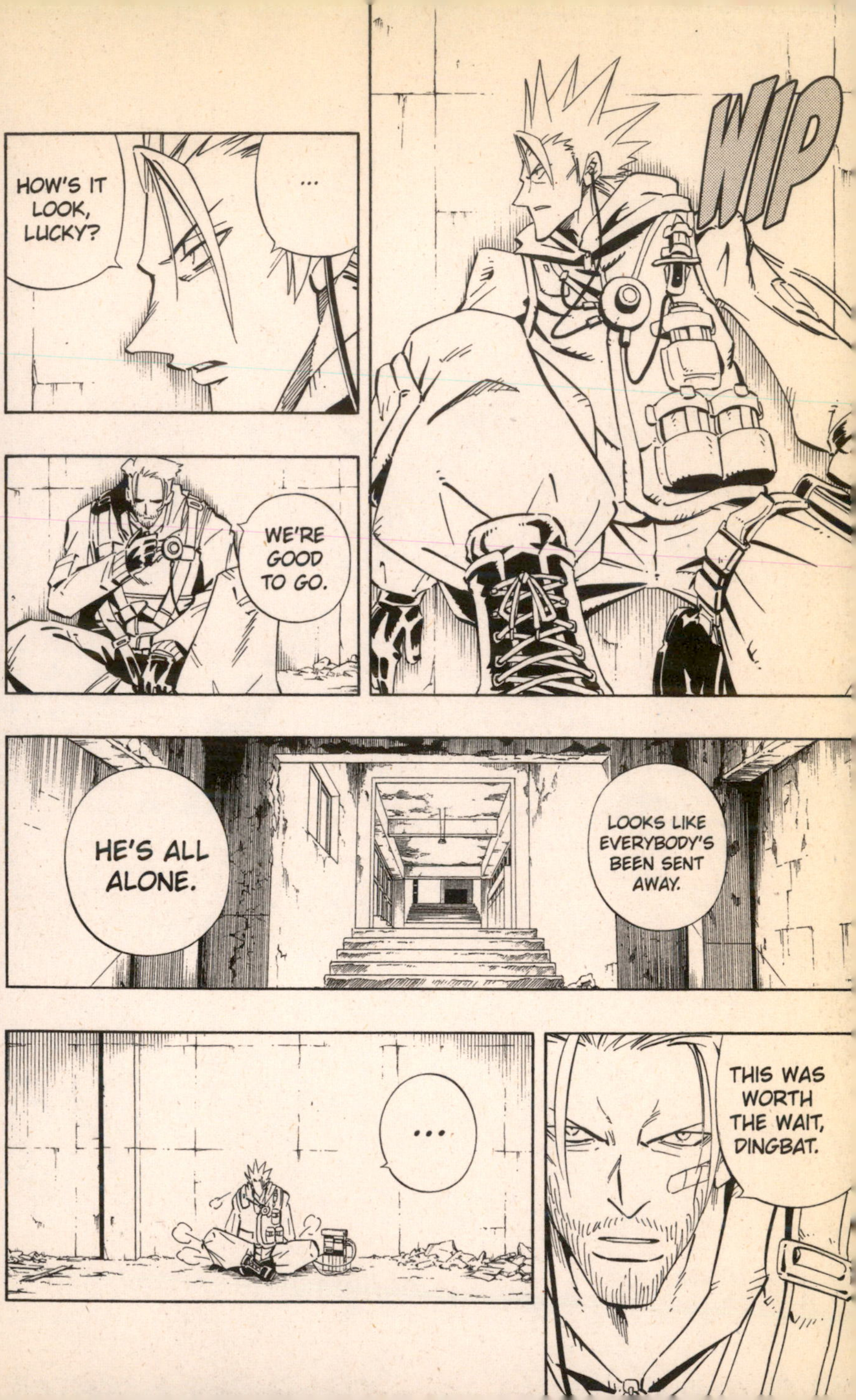
WIP
...
HOW'S IT LOOK, LUCKY?
WE'RE GOOD TO GO.
LOOKS LIKE EVERYBODY'S BEEN SENT AWAY.
HE'S ALL ALONE.
THIS WAS WORTH THE WAIT, DINGBAT.
...

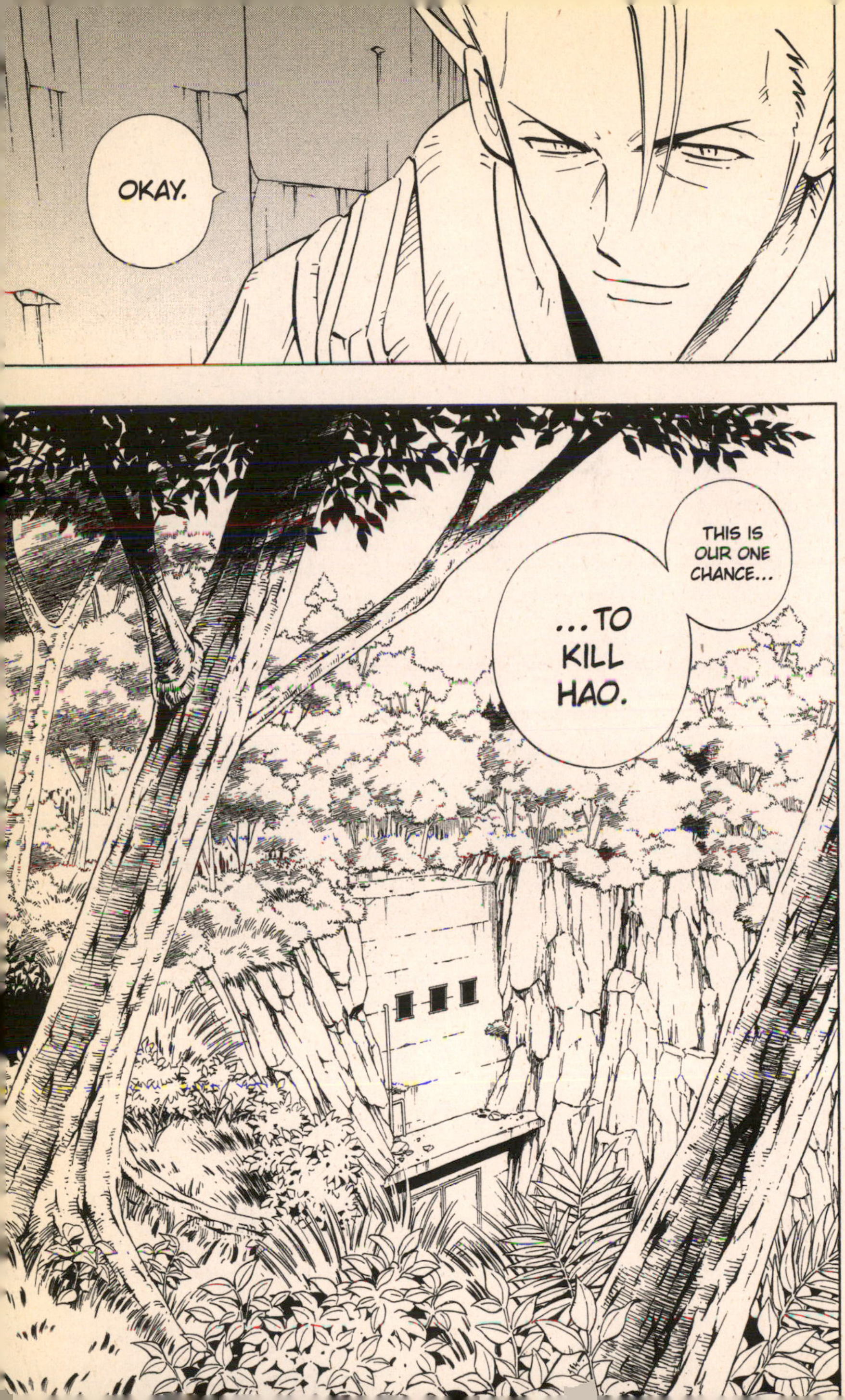
OKAY.
THIS IS OUR ONE CHANCE...
...TO KILL HAO.

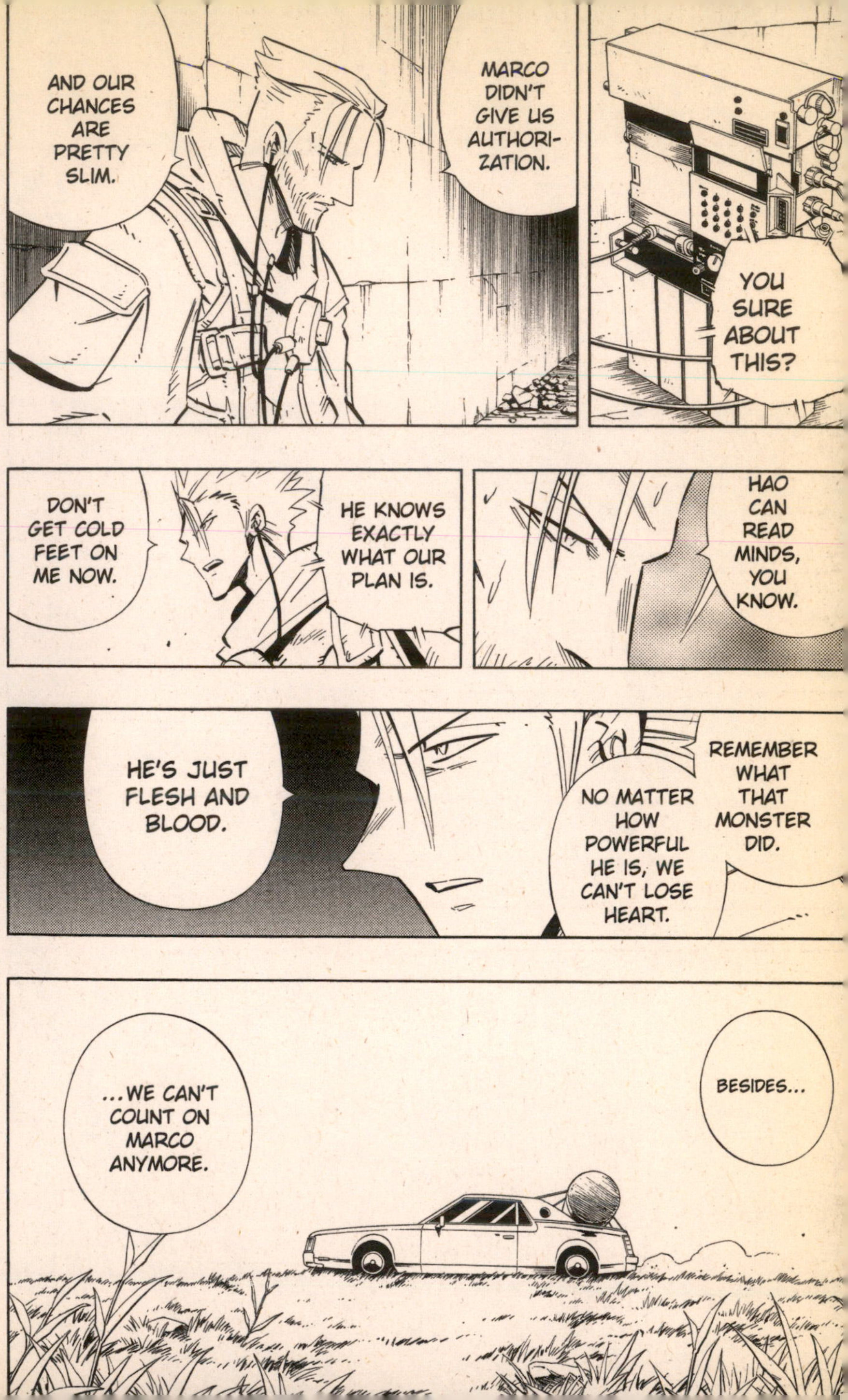
YOU SURE ABOUT THIS?
MARCO DIDN'T GIVE US AUTHORIZATION.
AND OUR CHANCES ARE PRETTY SLIM.
HAO CAN READ MINDS, YOU KNOW.
HE KNOWS EXACTLY WHAT OUR PLAN IS.
DON'T GET COLD FEET ON ME NOW.
REMEMBER WHAT THAT MONSTER DID.
NO MATTER HOW POWERFUL HE IS, WE CAN'T LOSE HEART.
HE'S JUST FLESH AND BLOOD.
BESIDES...
...WE CAN'T COUNT ON MARCO ANYMORE.

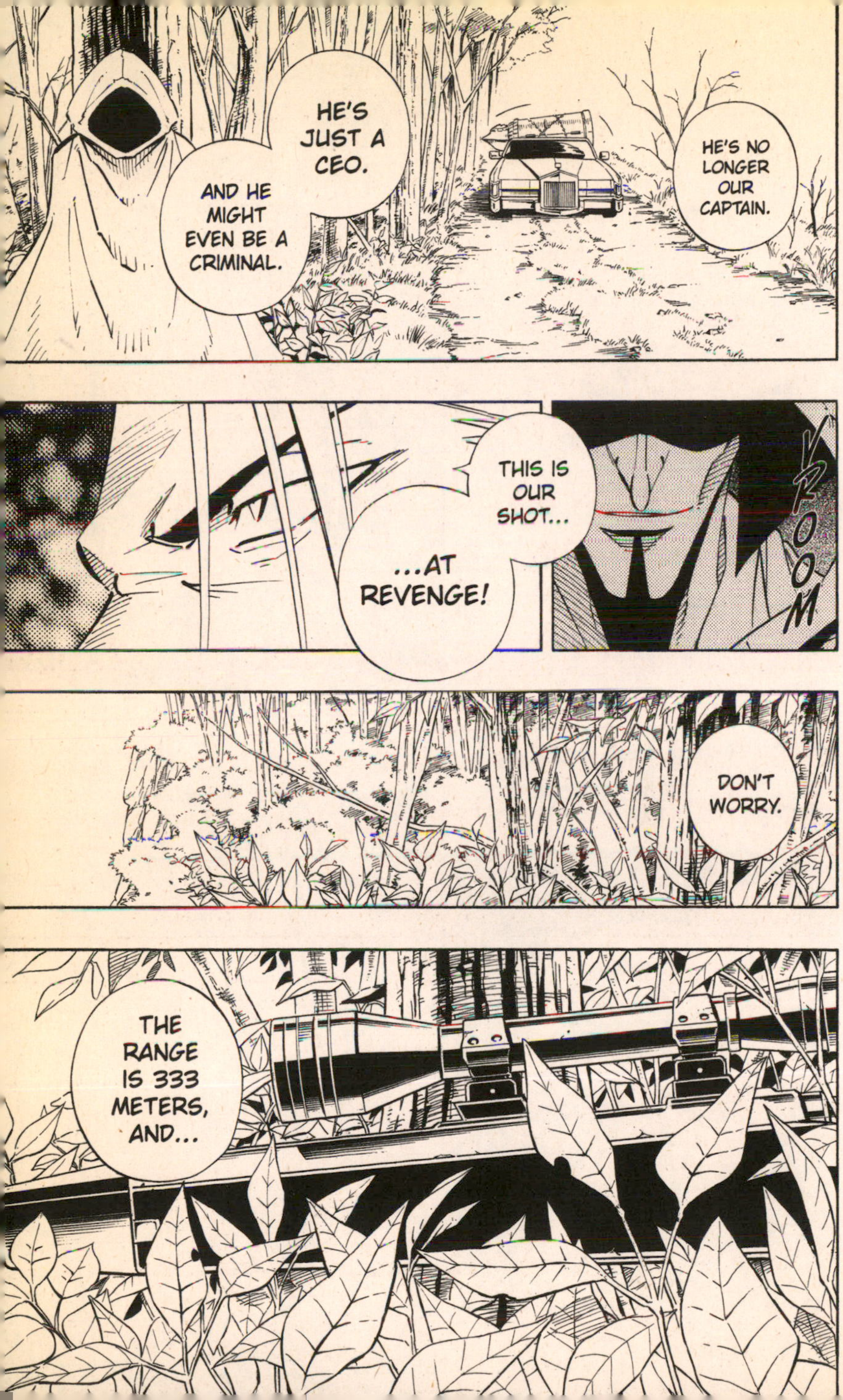
HE'S NO LONGER OUR CAPTAIN.
HE'S JUST A CEO.
AND HE MIGHT EVEN BE A CRIMINAL.
VROOM
THIS IS OUR SHOT...
...AT REVENGE!
DON'T WORRY.
THE RANGE IS 333 METERS, AND...

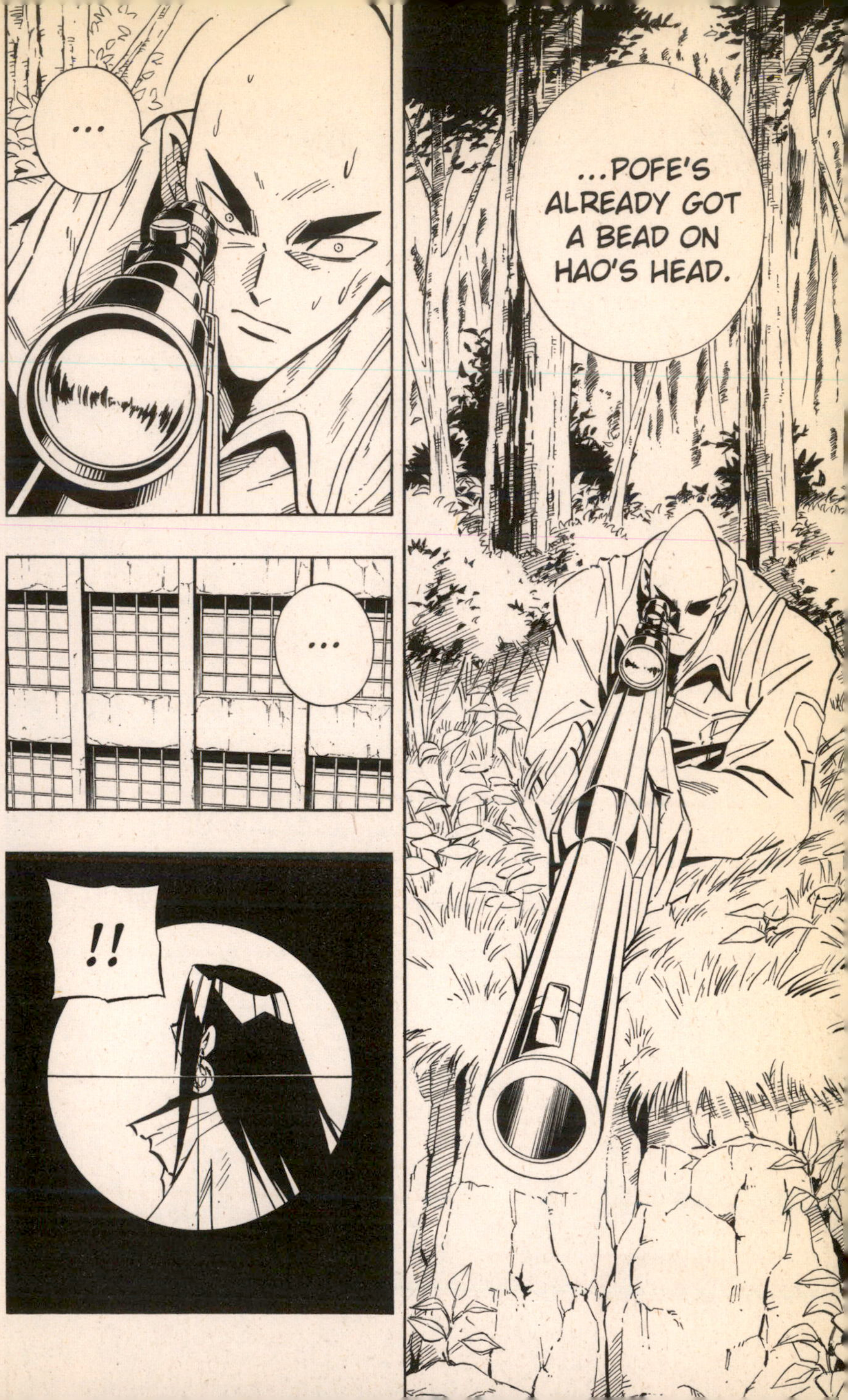
...POFE'S ALREADY GOT A BEAD ON HAO'S HEAD.
...
...
!!

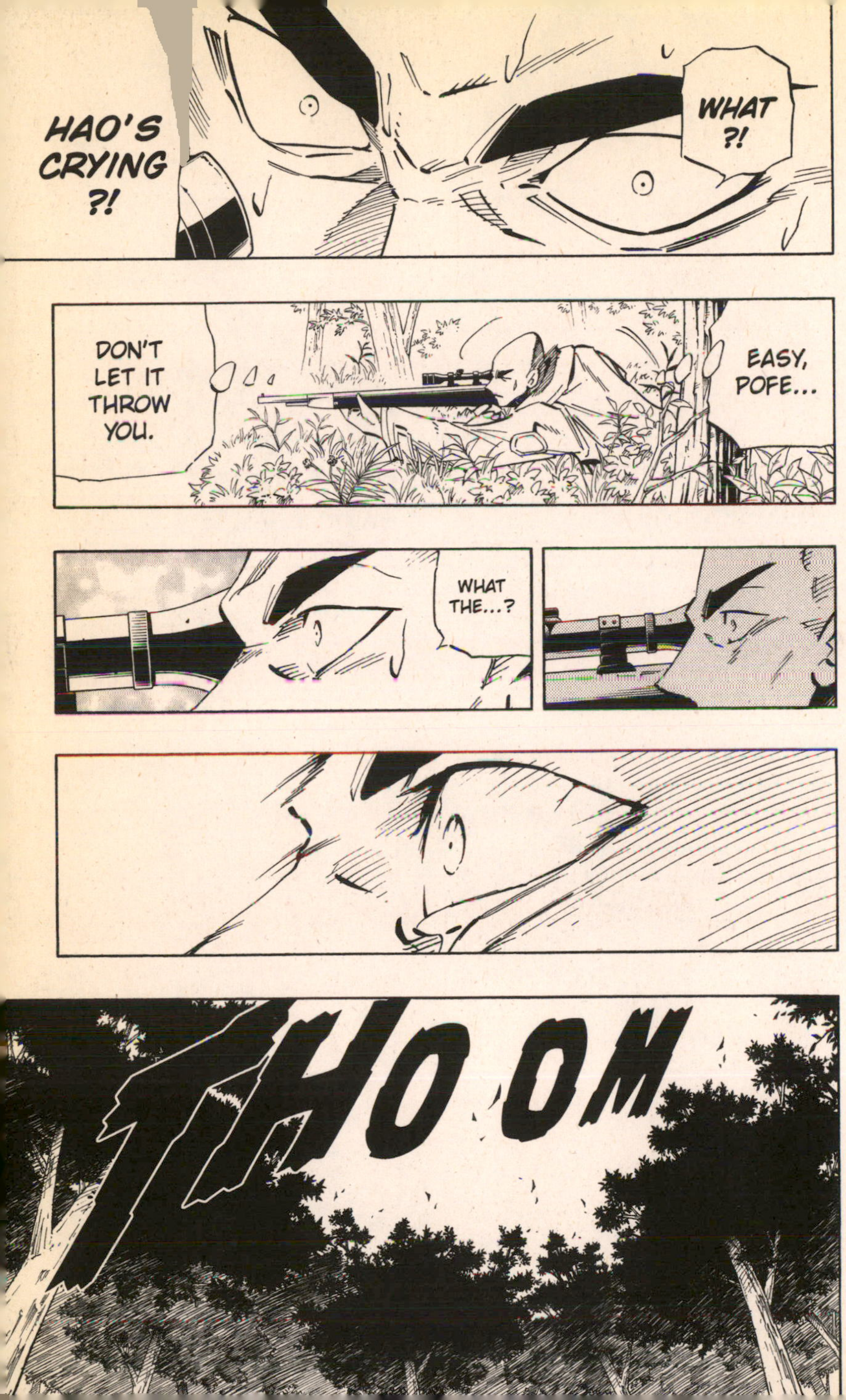
WHAT ?!
HAO'S CRYING ?!
EASY, POFE...
DON'T LET IT THROW YOU.
WHAT THE...?
THOOM

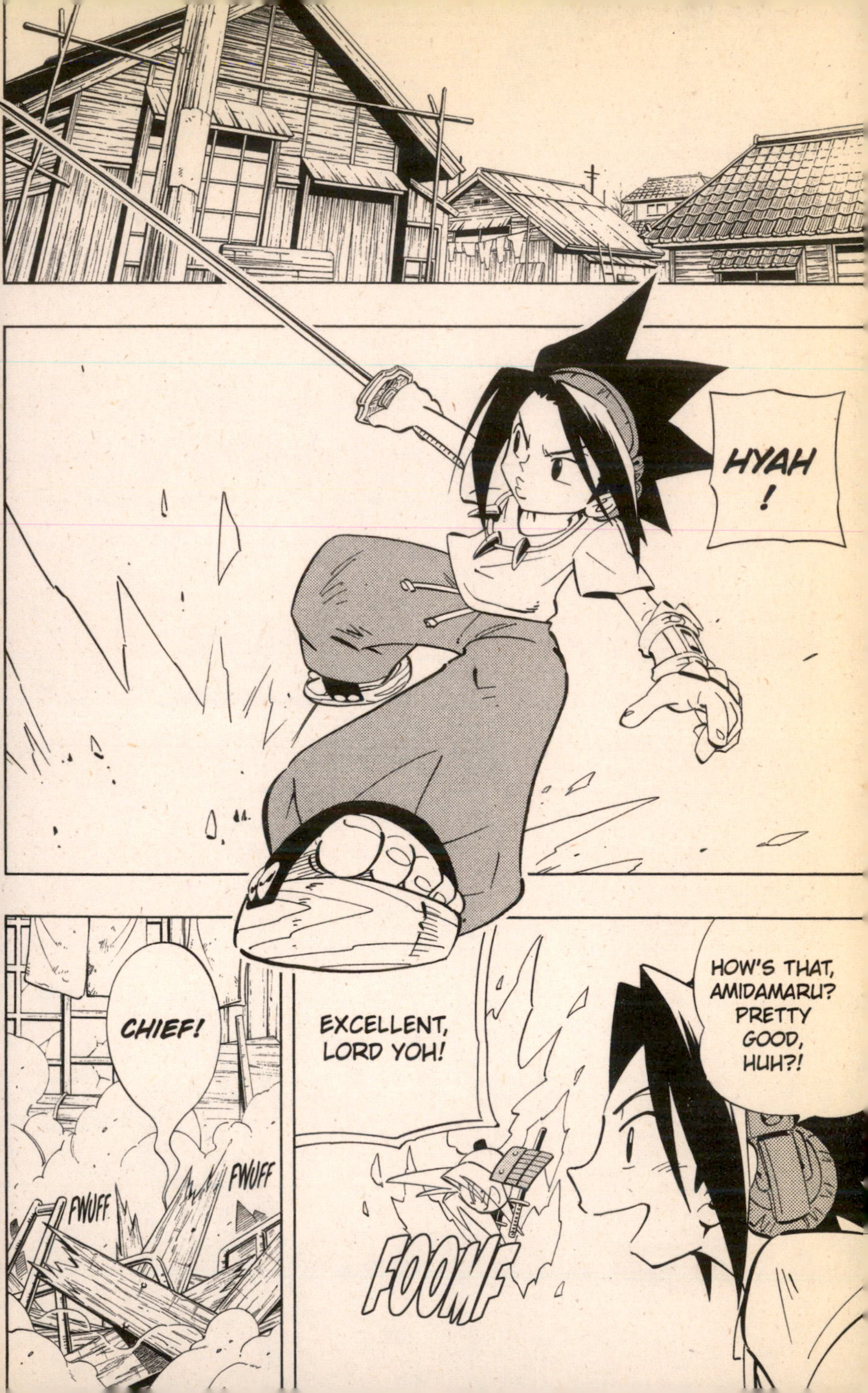
HYAH!
HOW'S THAT, AMIDAMARU? PRETTY GOOD, HUH?!
EXCELLENT, LORD YOH!
FOOMF
CHIEF!
FWUFF
FWUFF

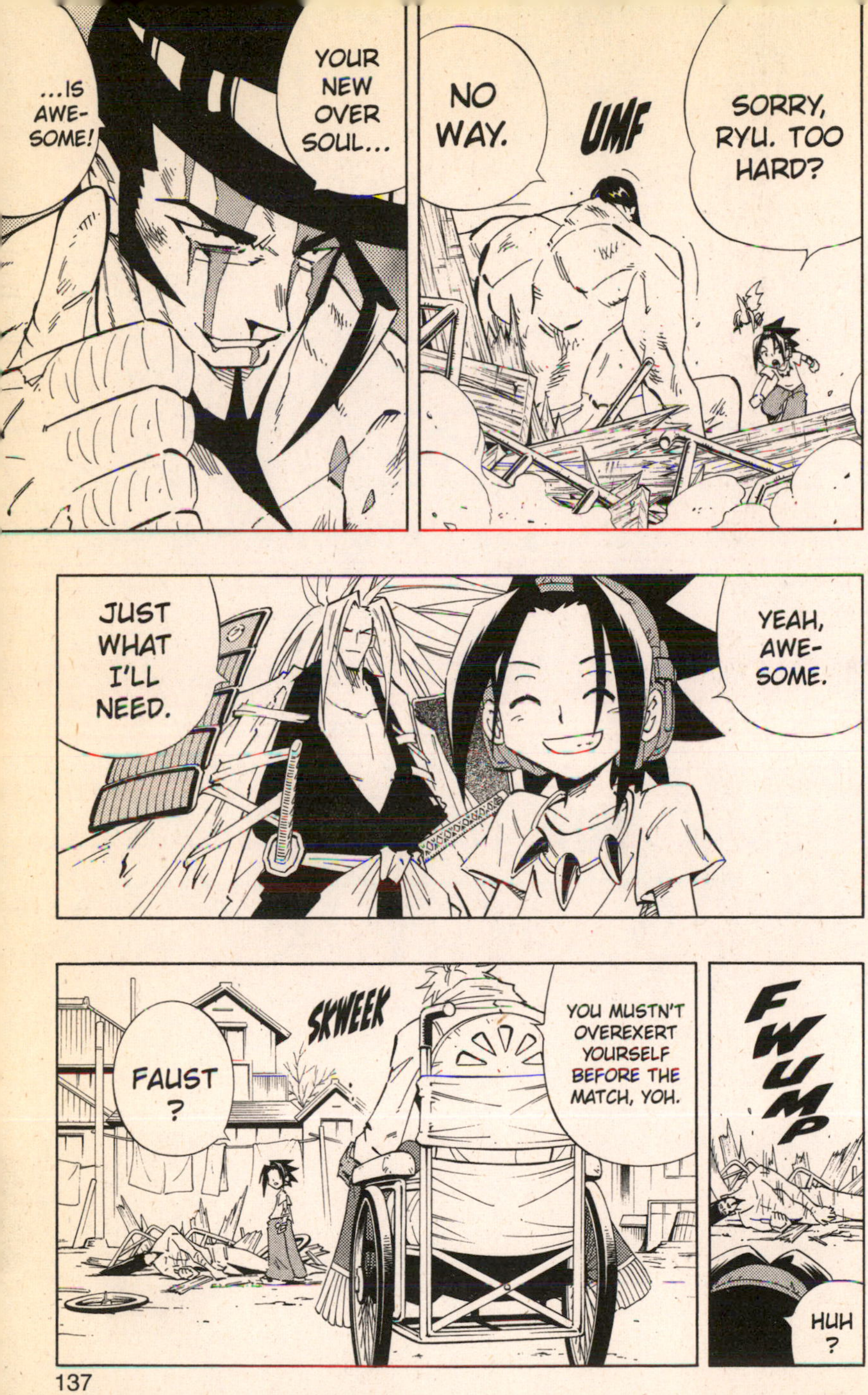
SORRY, RYU. TOO HARD?
UMF
NO WAY.
YOUR NEW OVER SOUL...
...IS AWE-SOME!
YEAH, AWE-SOME.
JUST WHAT I'LL NEED.
FWUMP
HUH?
YOU MUSTN'T OVEREXERT YOURSELF BEFORE THE MATCH, YOH.
SKWEEK
FAUST?

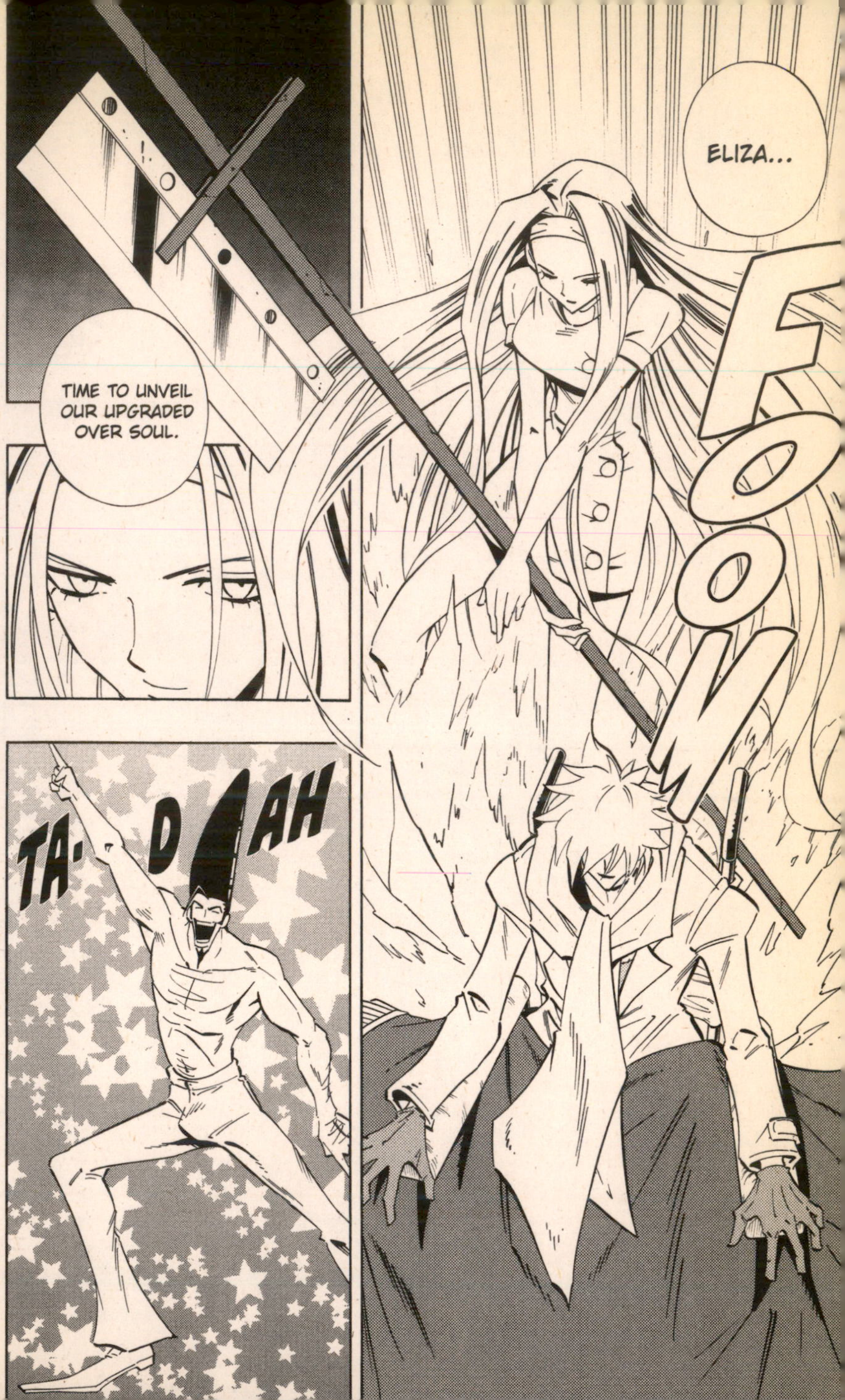
ELIZA...
FOOM
TIME TO UNVEIL OUR UPGRADED OVER SOUL.
TA-DAAH

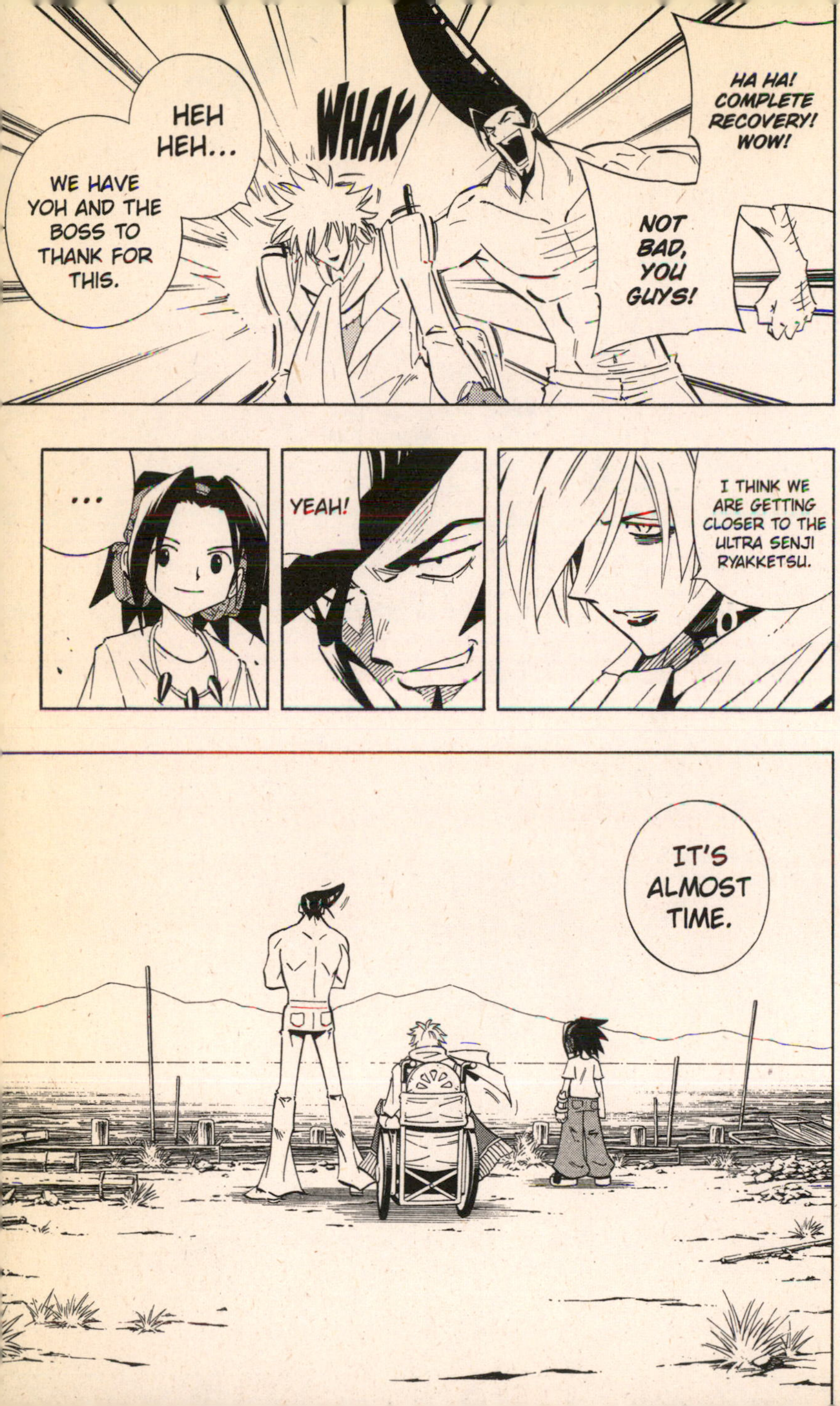
HA HA! COMPLETE RECOVERY! WOW!
NOT BAD, YOU GUYS!
WHAK
HEH HEH...
WE HAVE YOH AND THE BOSS TO THANK FOR THIS.
I THINK WE ARE GETTING CLOSER TO THE ULTRA SENJI RYAKKETSU.
YEAH!
...
IT'S ALMOST TIME.

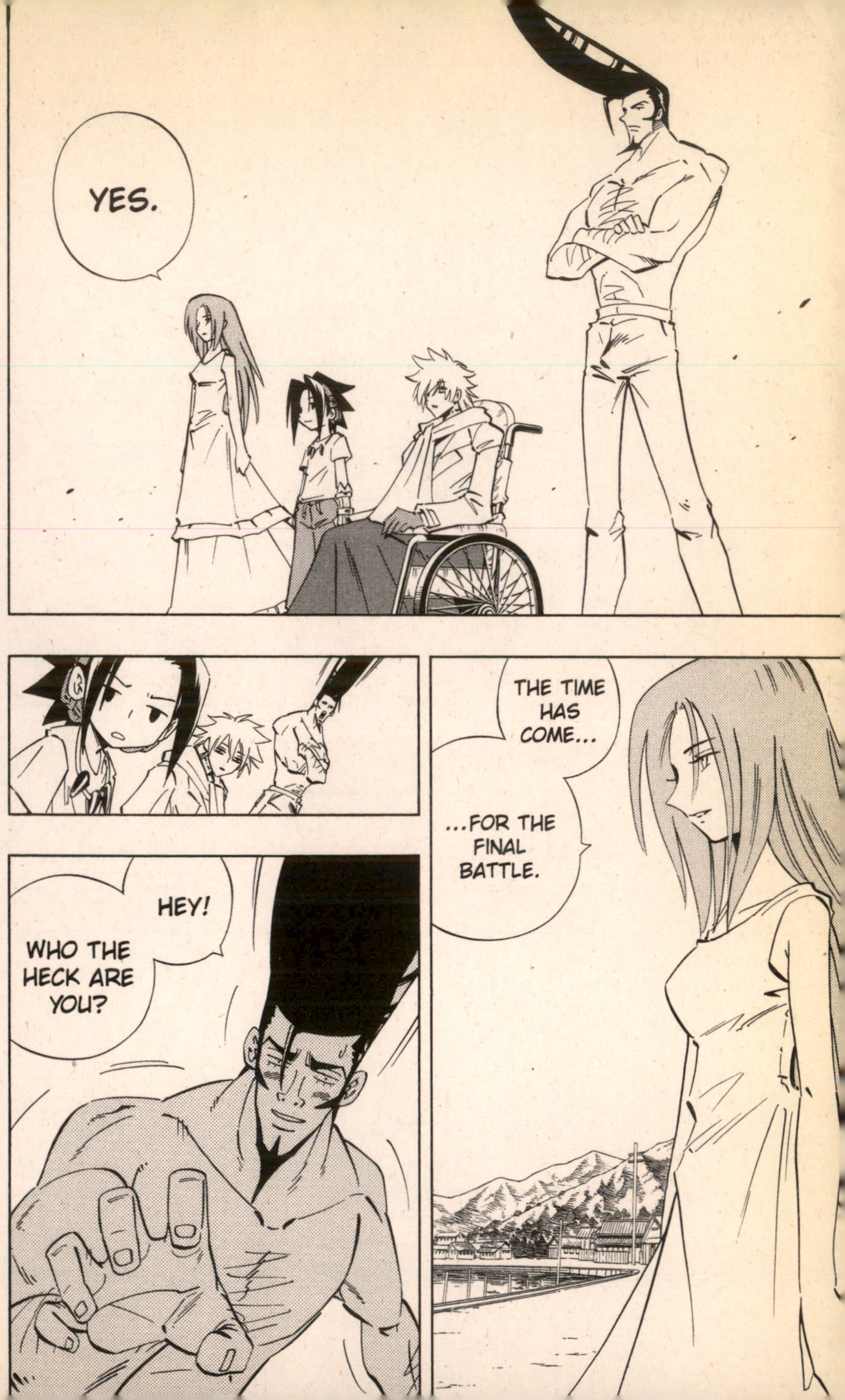
YES.
THE TIME HAS COME...
...FOR THE FINAL BATTLE.
HEY!
WHO THE HECK ARE YOU?

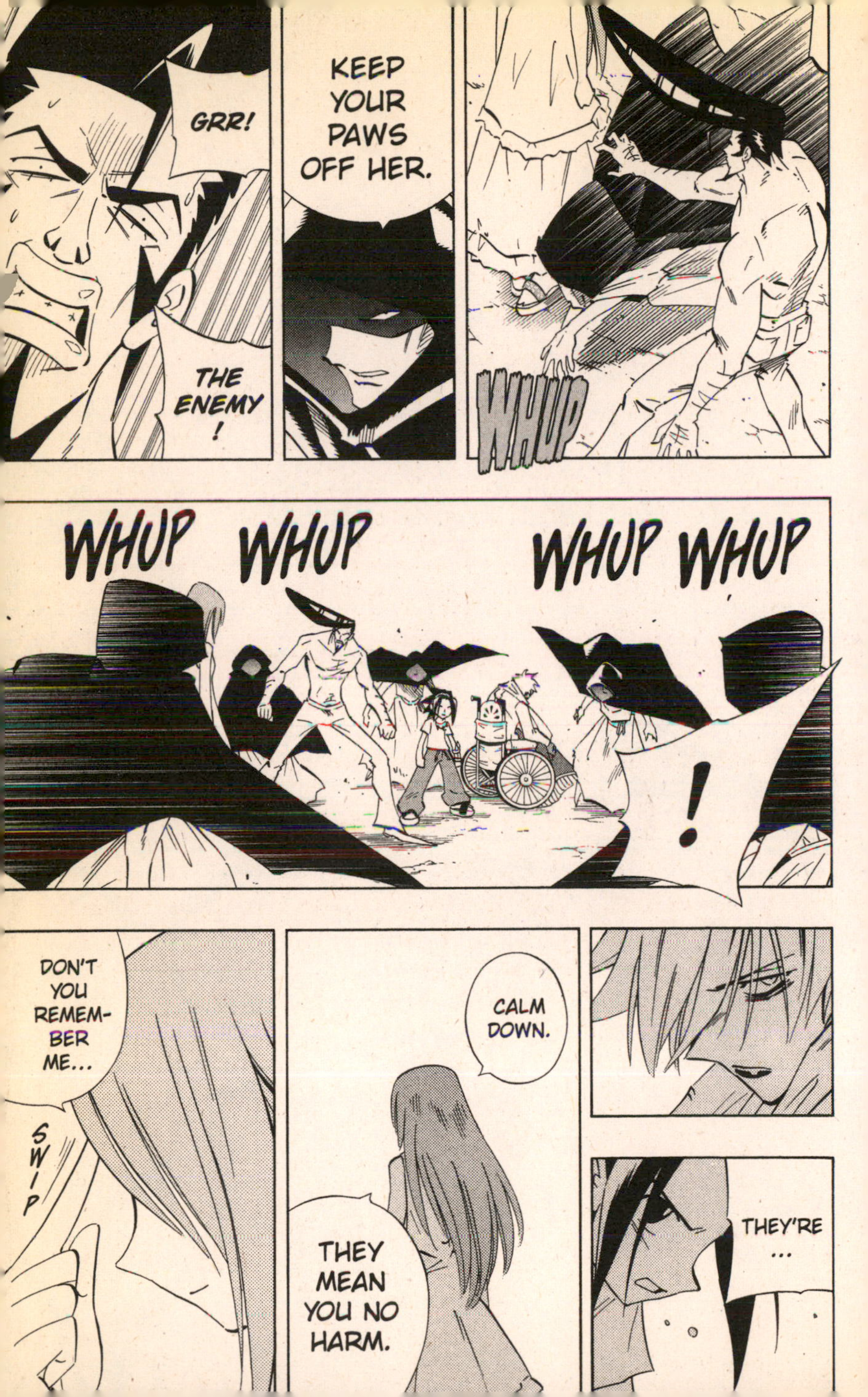
WHUP
KEEP YOUR PAWS OFF HER.
GRR!
THE ENEMY!
WHUP WHUP
WHUP WHUP
!
THEY'RE ...
CALM DOWN.
THEY MEAN YOU NO HARM.
DON'T YOU REMEMBER ME...
SWIP

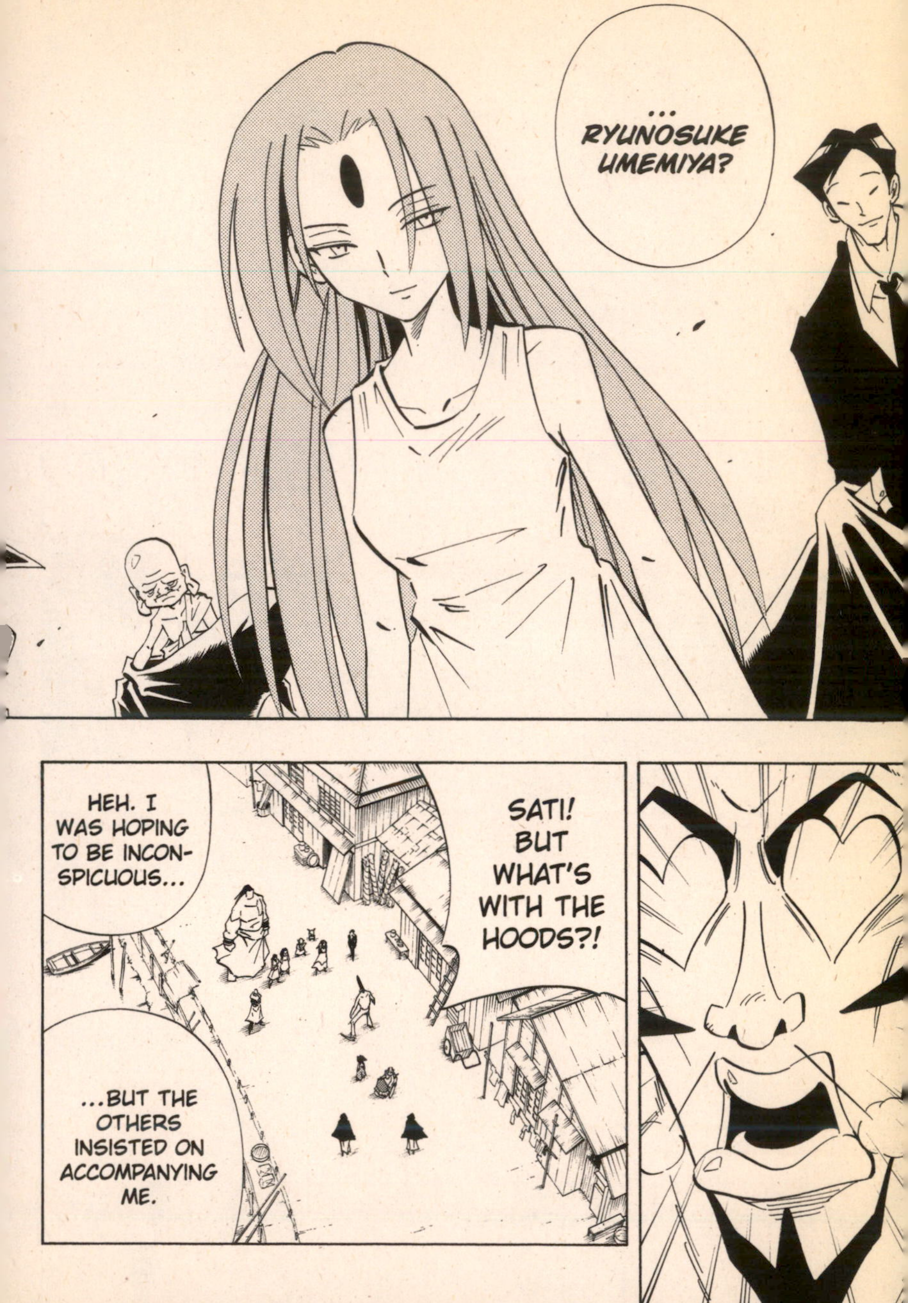
...
RYUNOSUKE UMEMIYA?
SATI! BUT WHAT'S WITH THE HOODS?!
HEH. I WAS HOPING TO BE INCON-SPICUOUS...
...BUT THE OTHERS INSISTED ON ACCOMPANYING ME.

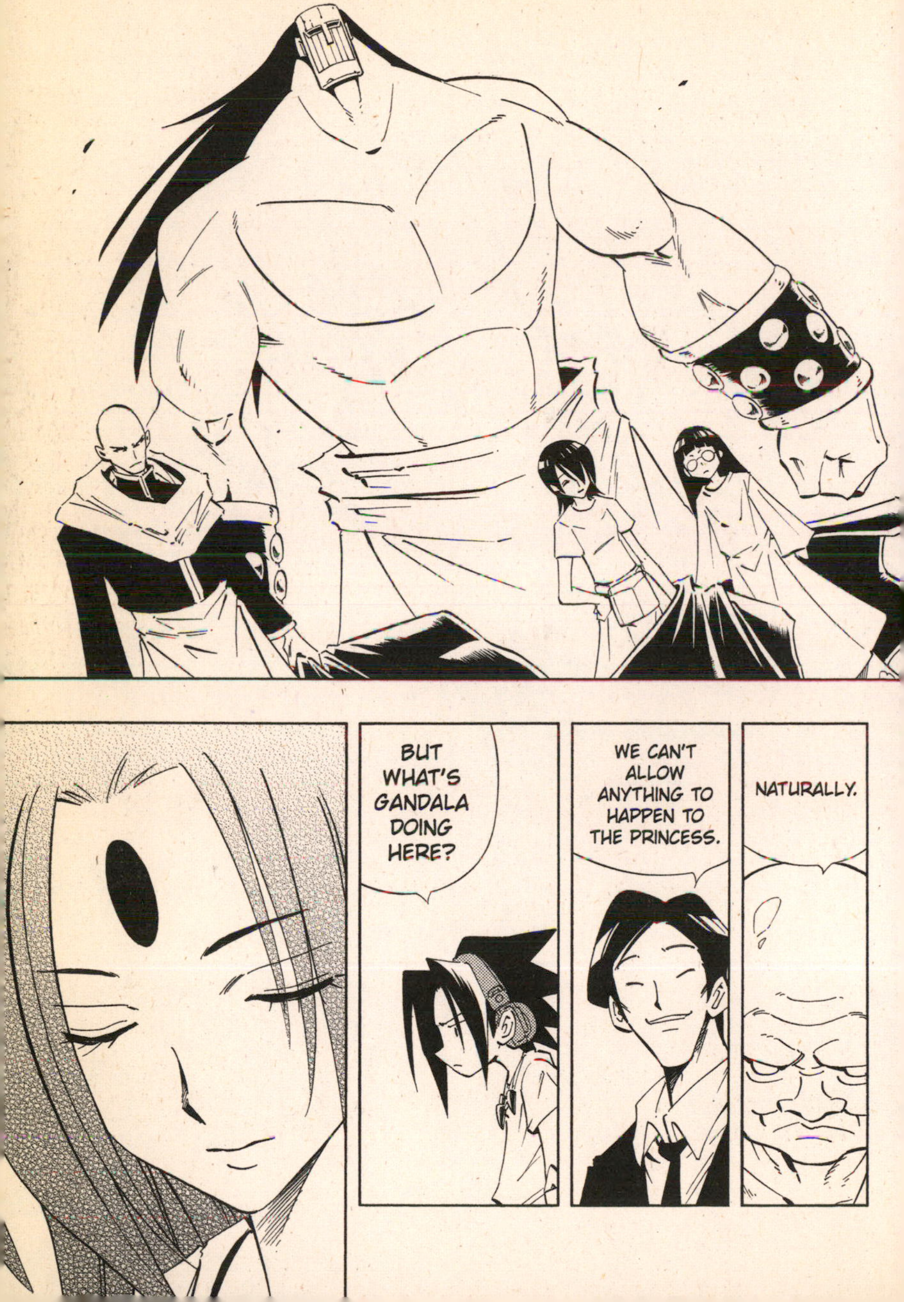
NATURALLY.
WE CAN'T ALLOW ANYTHING TO HAPPEN TO THE PRINCESS.
BUT WHAT'S GANDALA DOING HERE?

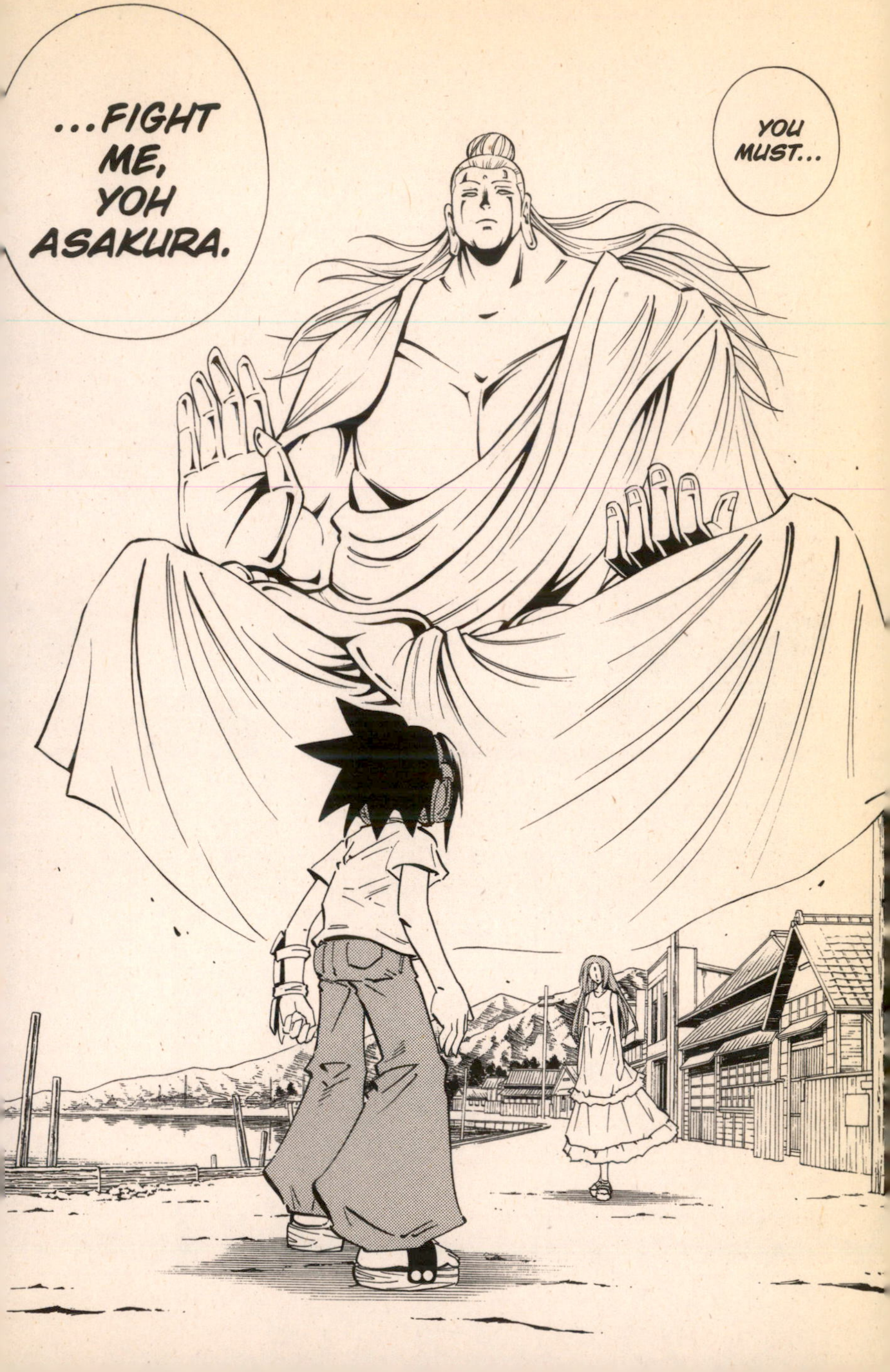
YOU MUST...
...FIGHT ME, YOH ASAKURA.

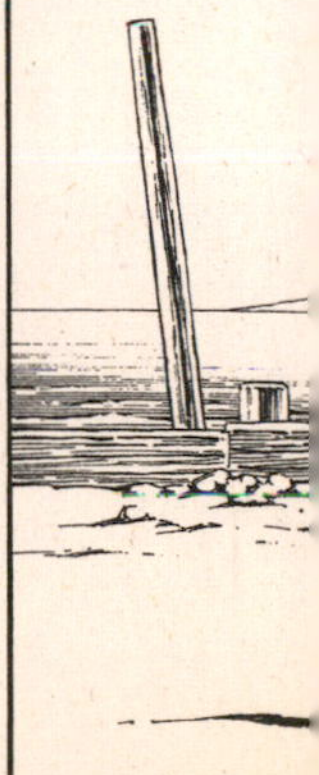

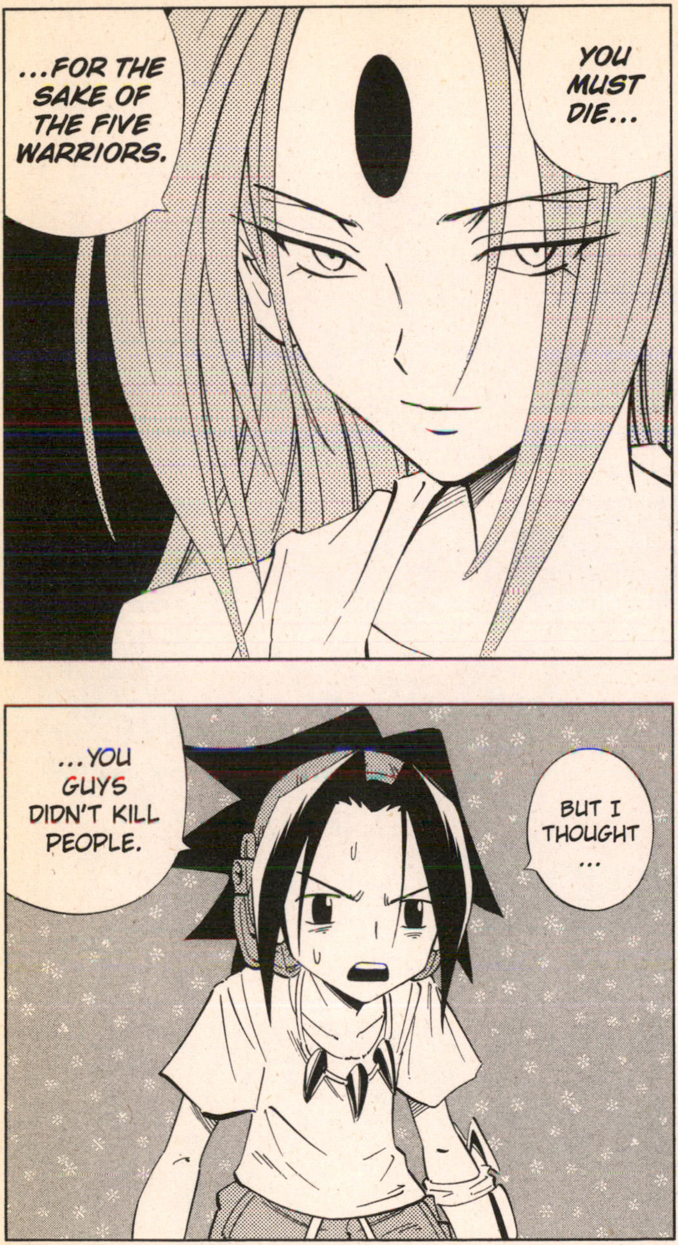
YOU MUST DIE...
...FOR THE SAKE OF THE FIVE WARRIORS.
BUT I THOUGHT ...
...YOU GUYS DIDN'T KILL PEOPLE.

SHAMAN KING CHARACTER FILE No.136

マーリン
MERLIN

2001
(JAN)

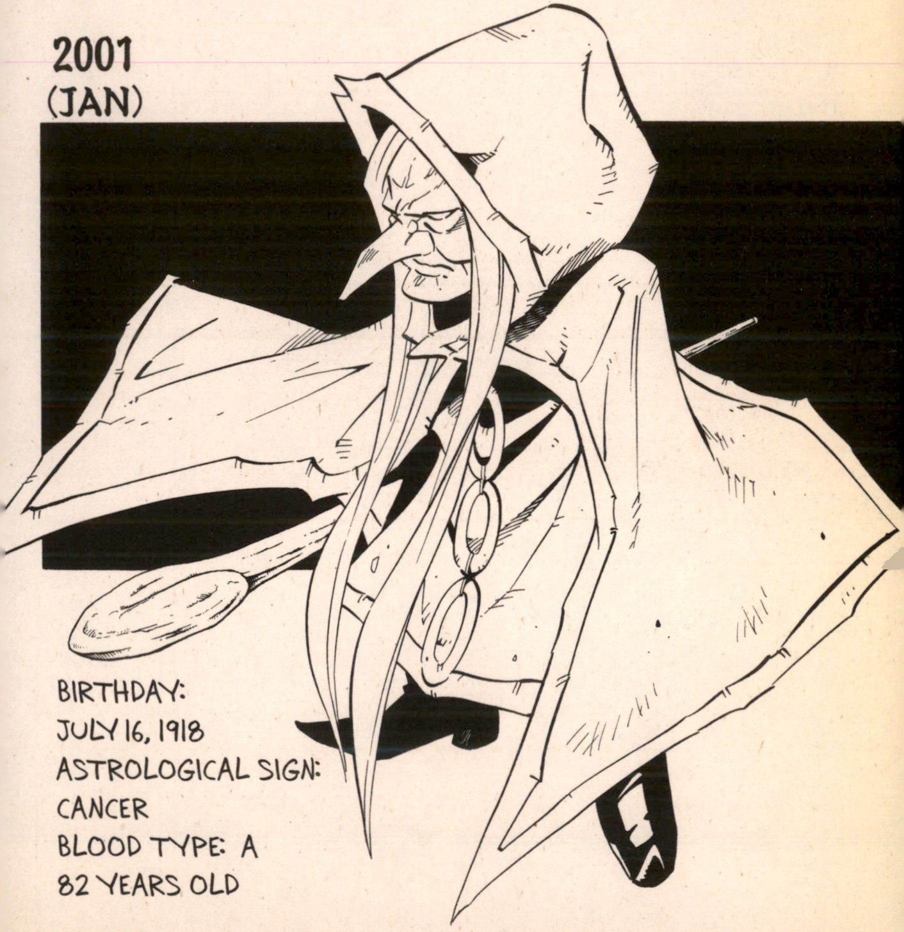

BIRTHDAY:
JULY 16, 1918
ASTROLOGICAL SIGN:
CANCER
BLOOD TYPE: A
82 YEARS OLD

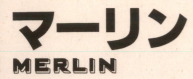

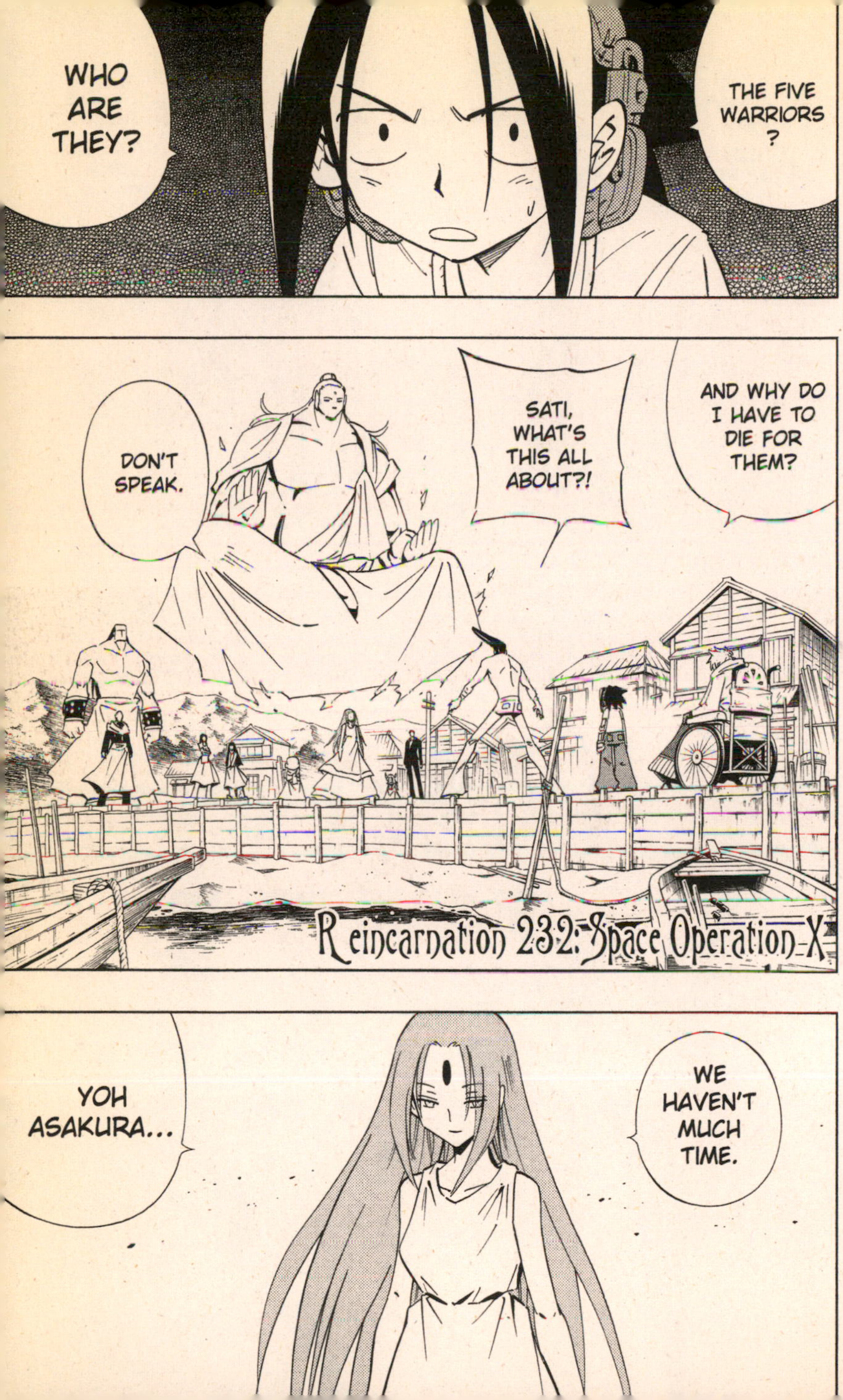
THE FIVE WARRIORS ?
WHO ARE THEY?
AND WHY DO I HAVE TO DIE FOR THEM?
SATI, WHAT'S THIS ALL ABOUT?!
DON'T SPEAK.
Reincarnation 232: Space Operation X
WE HAVEN'T MUCH TIME.
YOH ASAKURA...

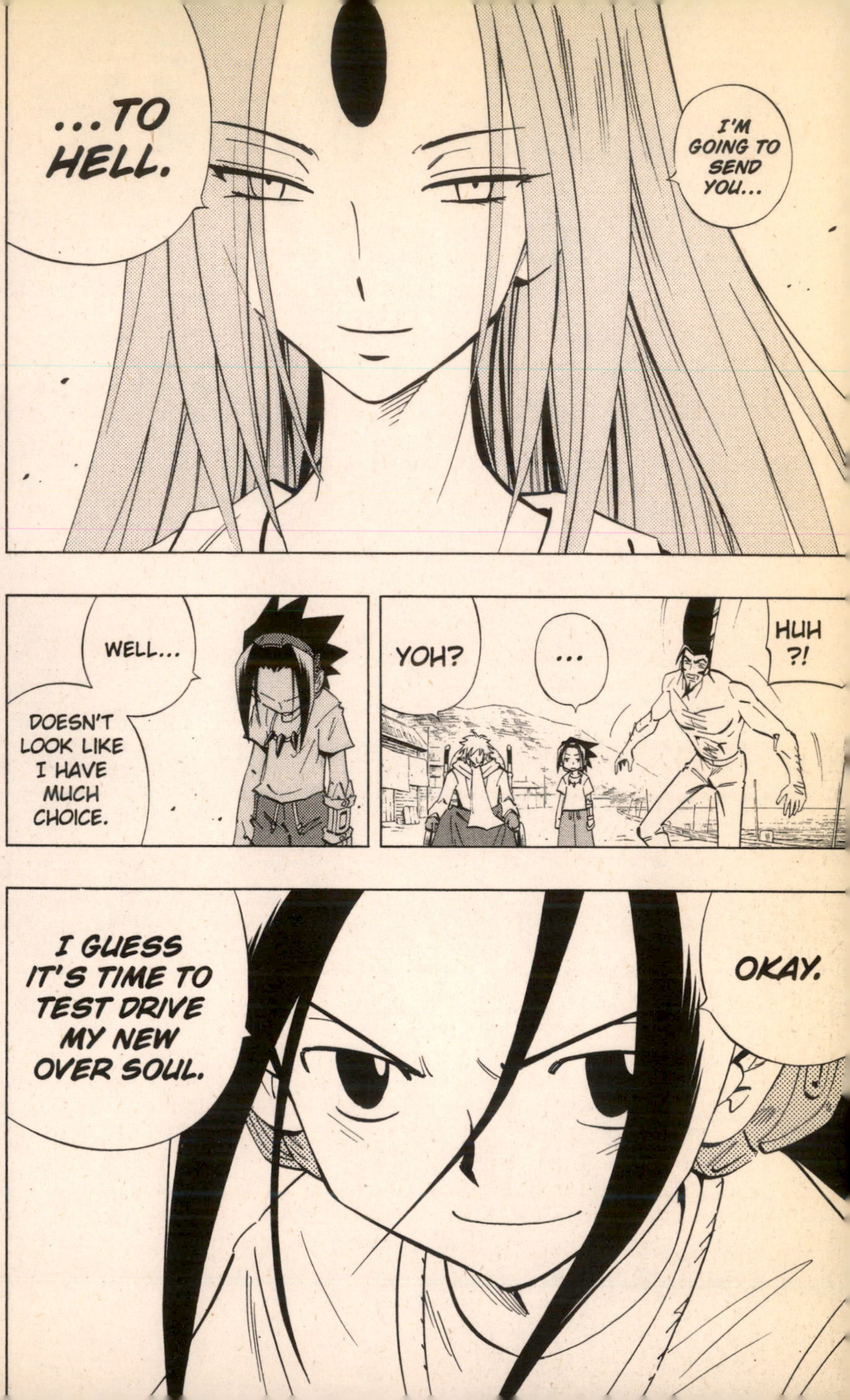
I'M GOING TO SEND YOU...
...TO HELL.
HUH ?!
...
YOH?
WELL...
DOESN'T LOOK LIKE I HAVE MUCH CHOICE.
OKAY.
I GUESS IT'S TIME TO TEST DRIVE MY NEW OVER SOUL.

Reincarnation 232: Space Operation X

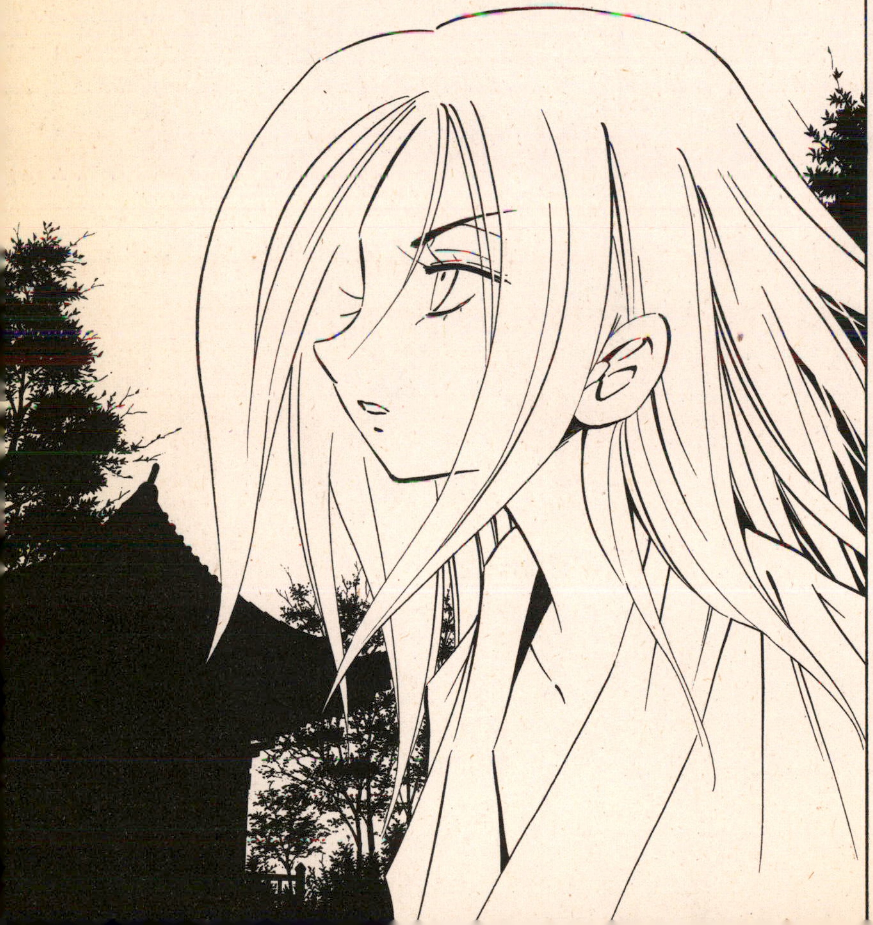

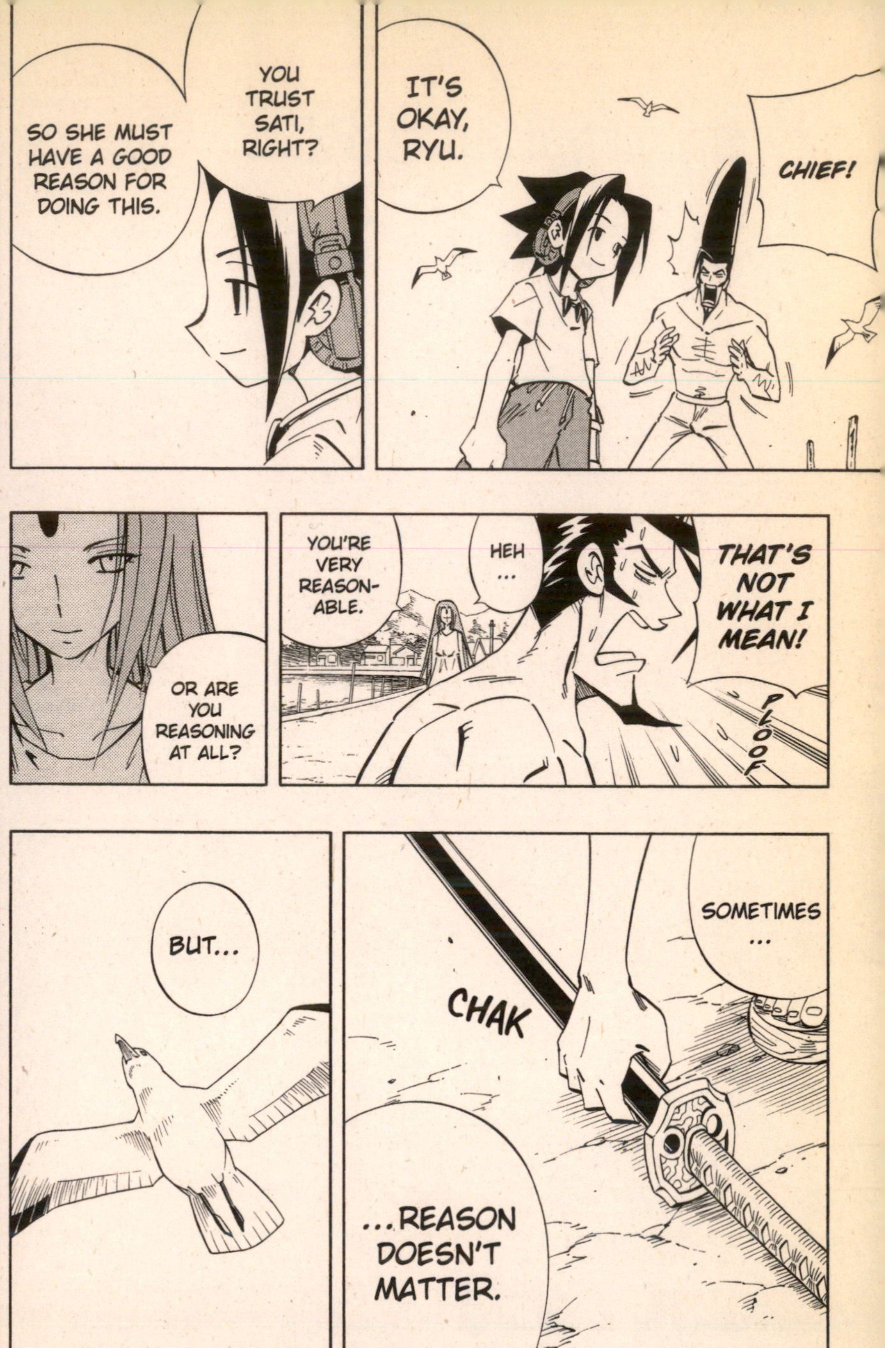
CHIEF!
IT'S OKAY, RYU.
YOU TRUST SATI, RIGHT?
SO SHE MUST HAVE A GOOD REASON FOR DOING THIS.
THAT'S NOT WHAT I MEAN!
HEH ...
YOU'RE VERY REASON-ABLE.
PLOOF
OR ARE YOU REASONING AT ALL?
SOMETIMES ...
CHAK
...REASON DOESN'T MATTER.
BUT...

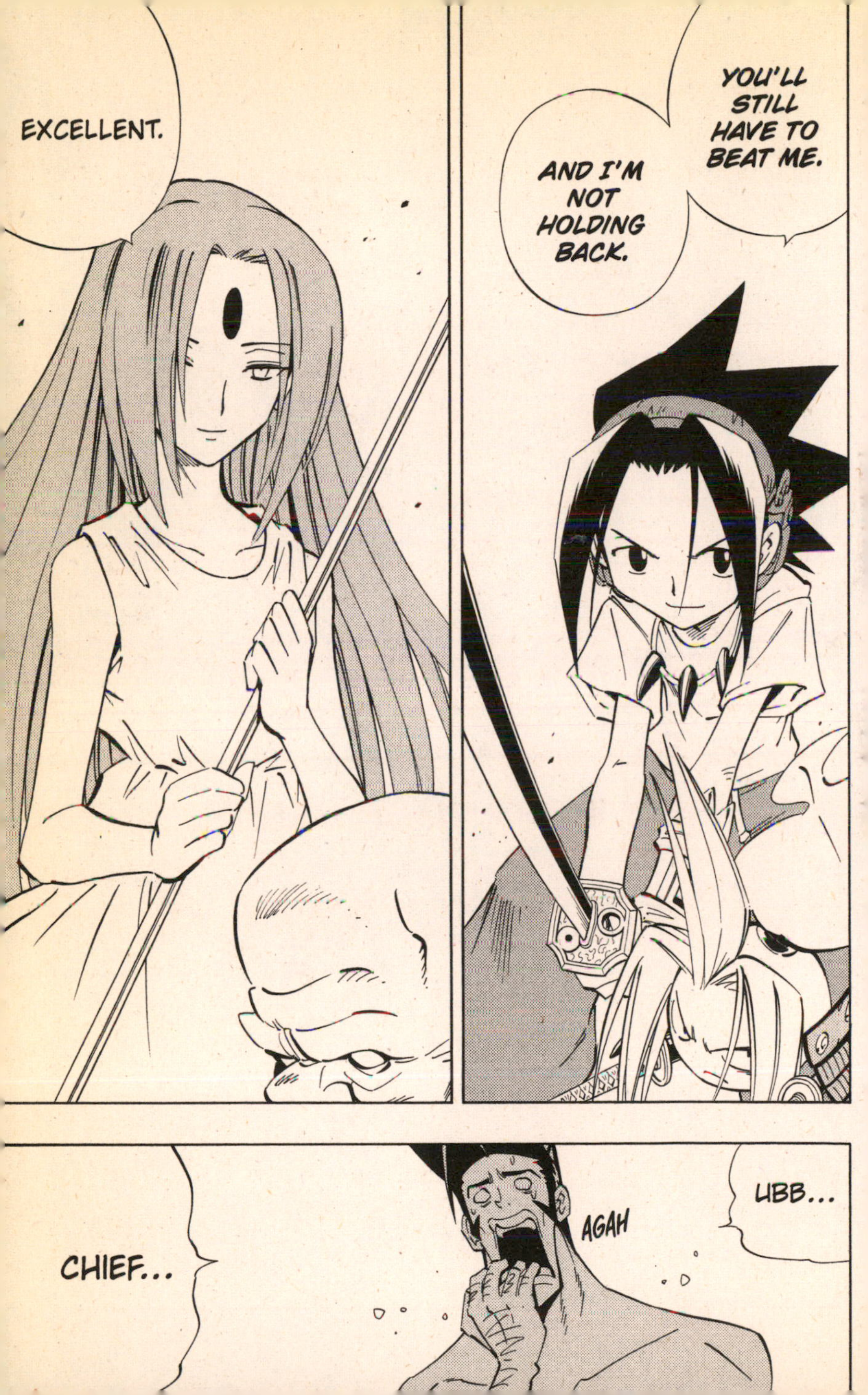
YOU'LL STILL HAVE TO BEAT ME.
AND I'M NOT HOLDING BACK.
EXCELLENT.
UBB...
AGAH
CHIEF...

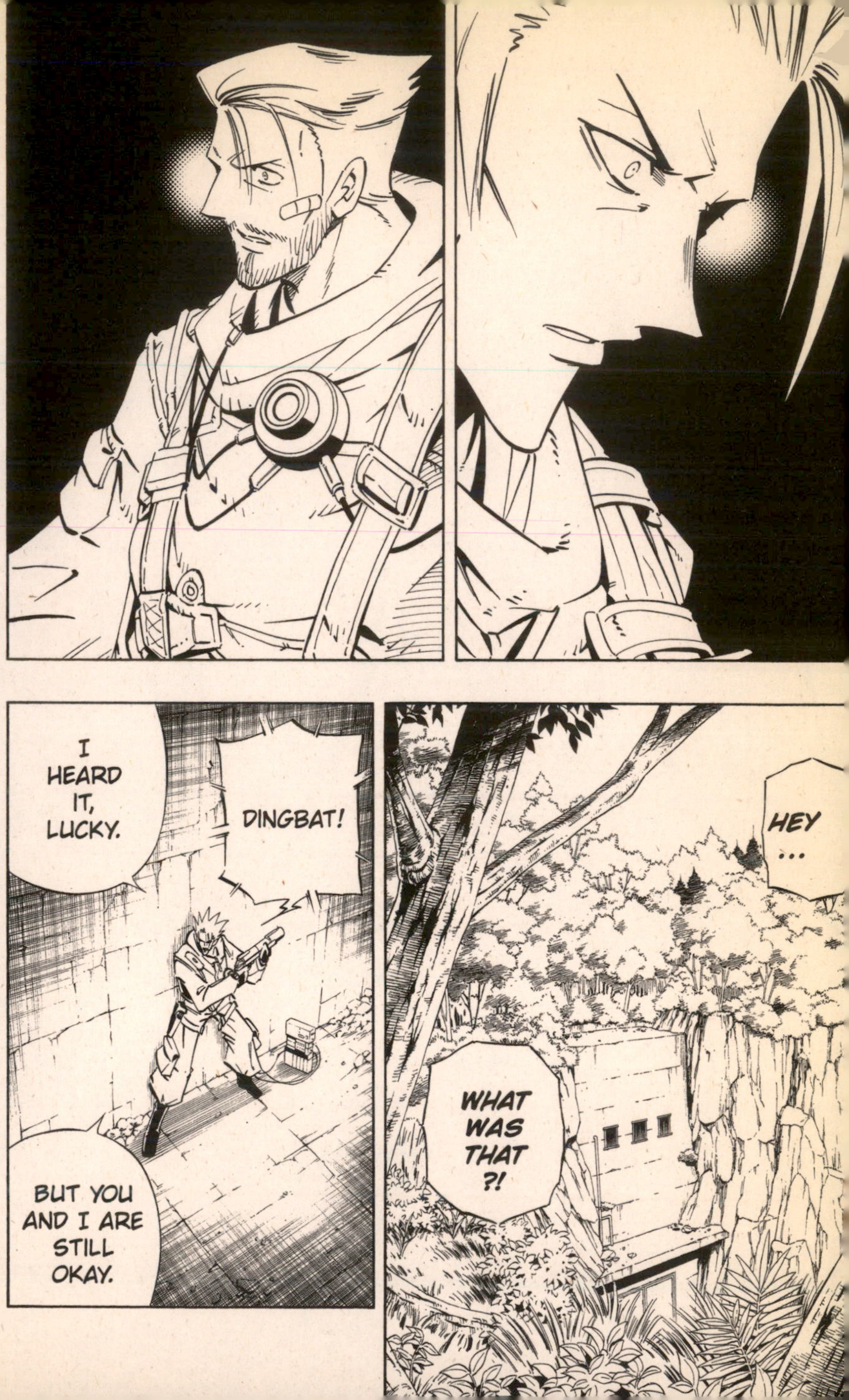
HEY ...
WHAT WAS THAT ?!
DINGBAT!
I HEARD IT, LUCKY.
BUT YOU AND I ARE STILL OKAY.

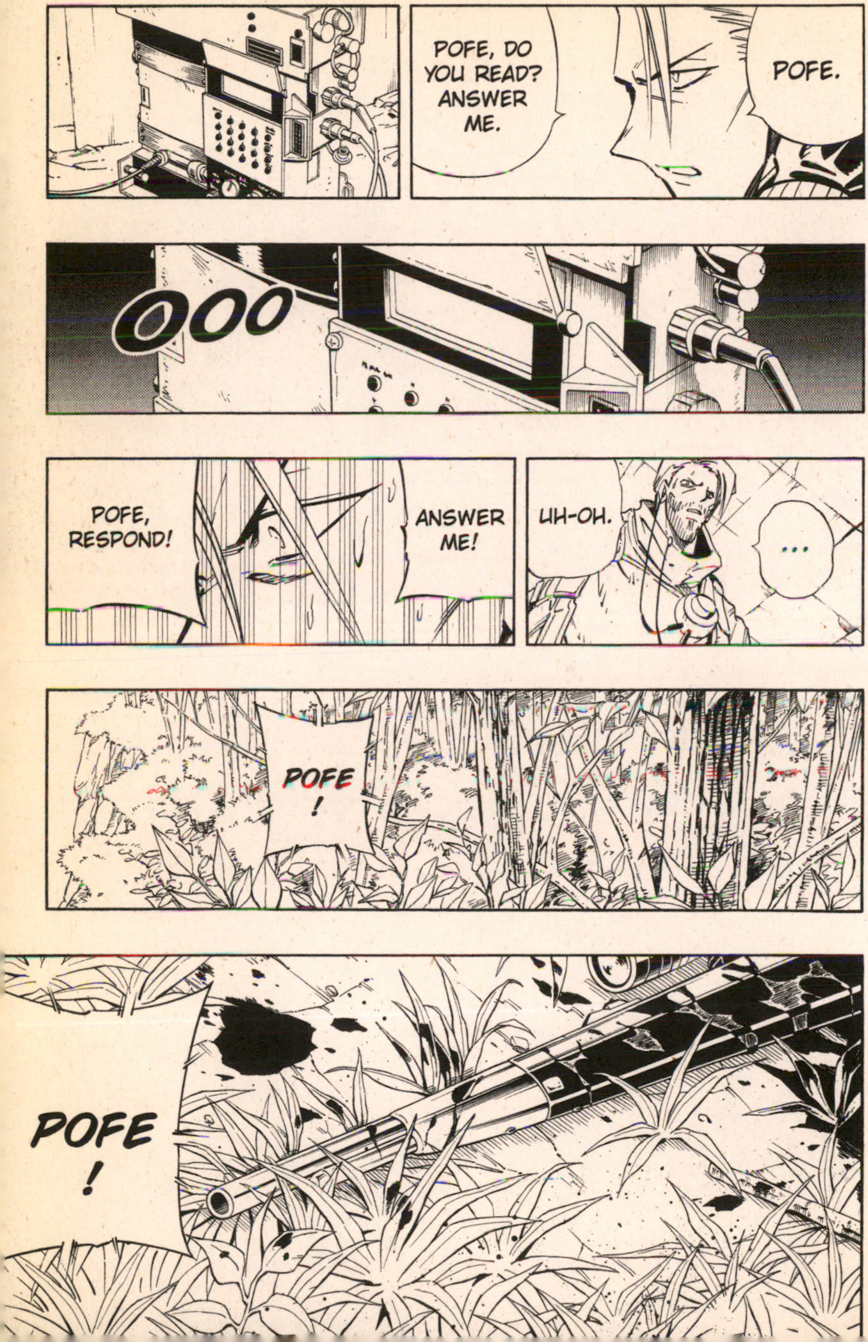
POFE.
POFE, DO YOU READ? ANSWER ME.
OOO
UH-OH.
...
ANSWER ME!
POFE, RESPOND!
POFE !
POFE !

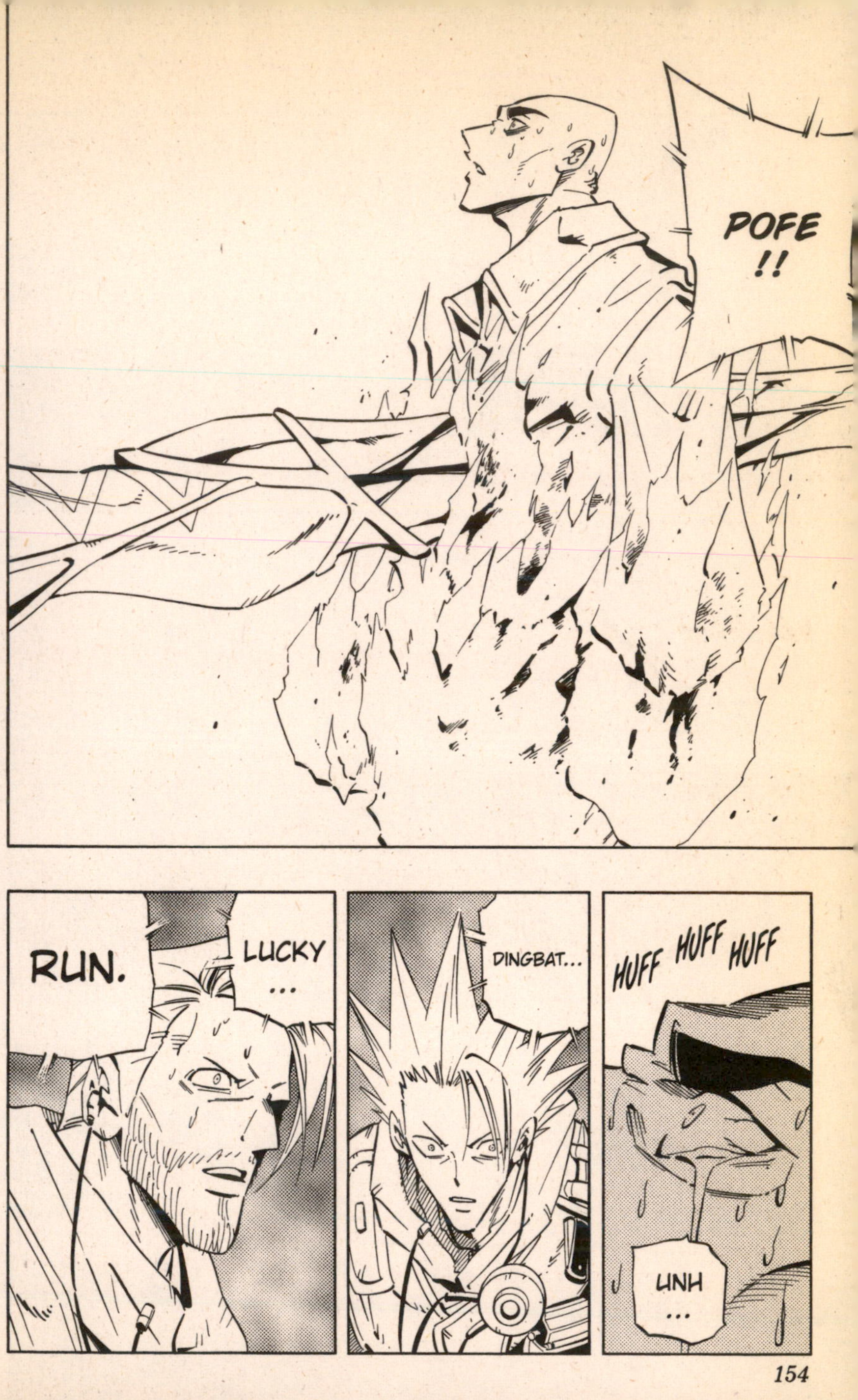
POFE !!
HUFF HUFF HUFF
UNH ...
DINGBAT...
LUCKY ...
RUN.

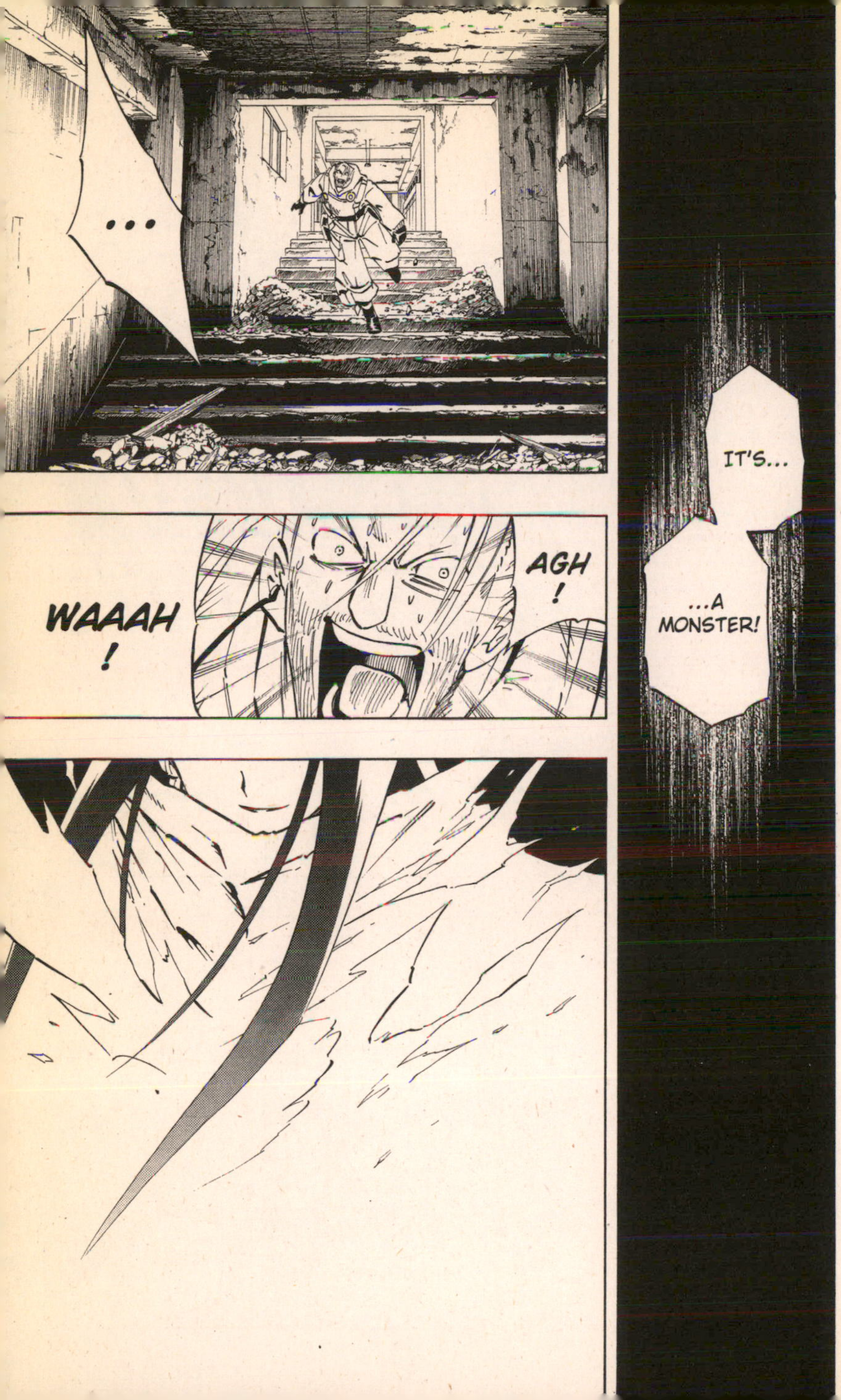
IT'S...
...A MONSTER!
...
AGH!
WAAAH!

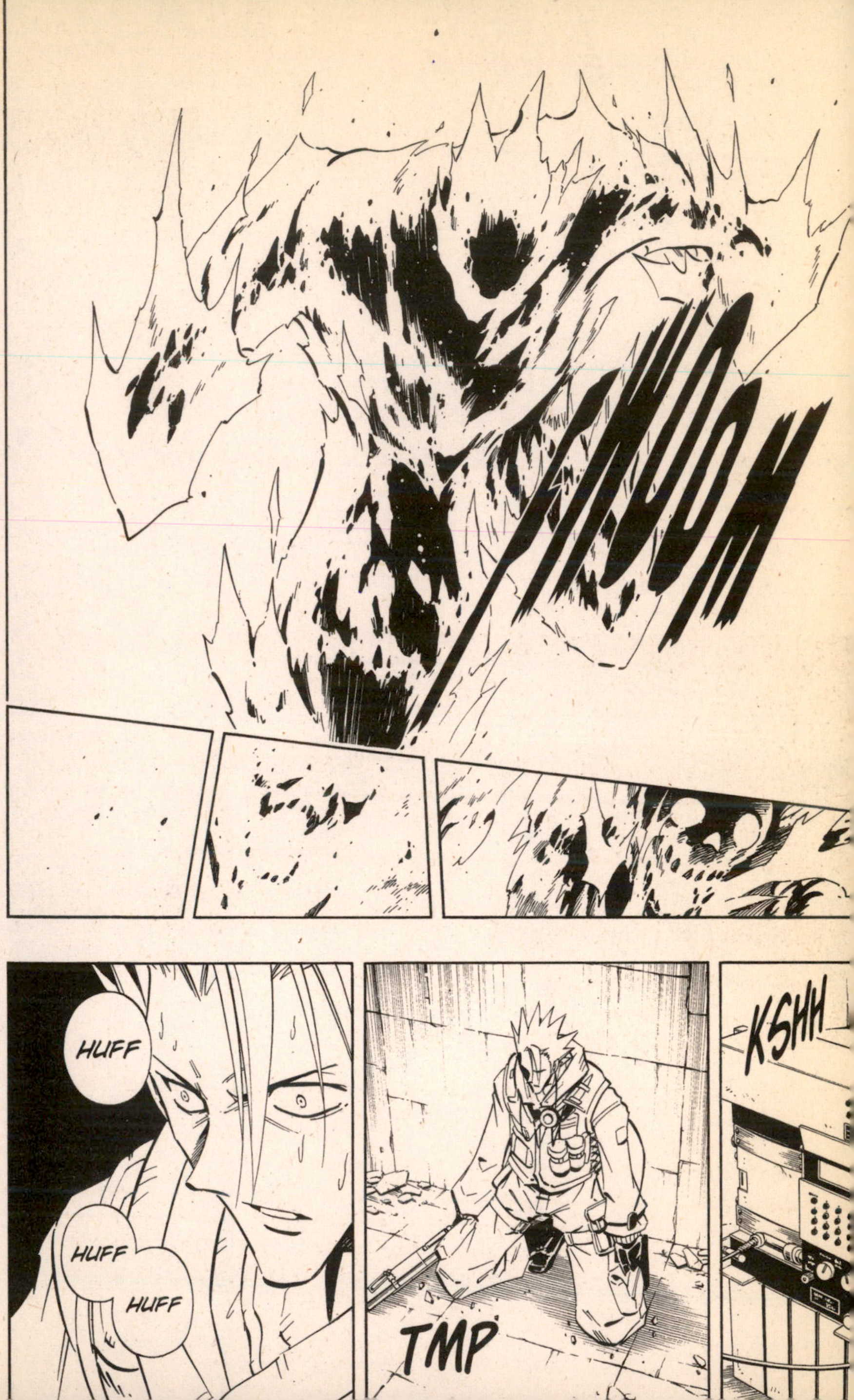
FWOOM
KSHH
TMP
HUFF
HUFF
HUFF

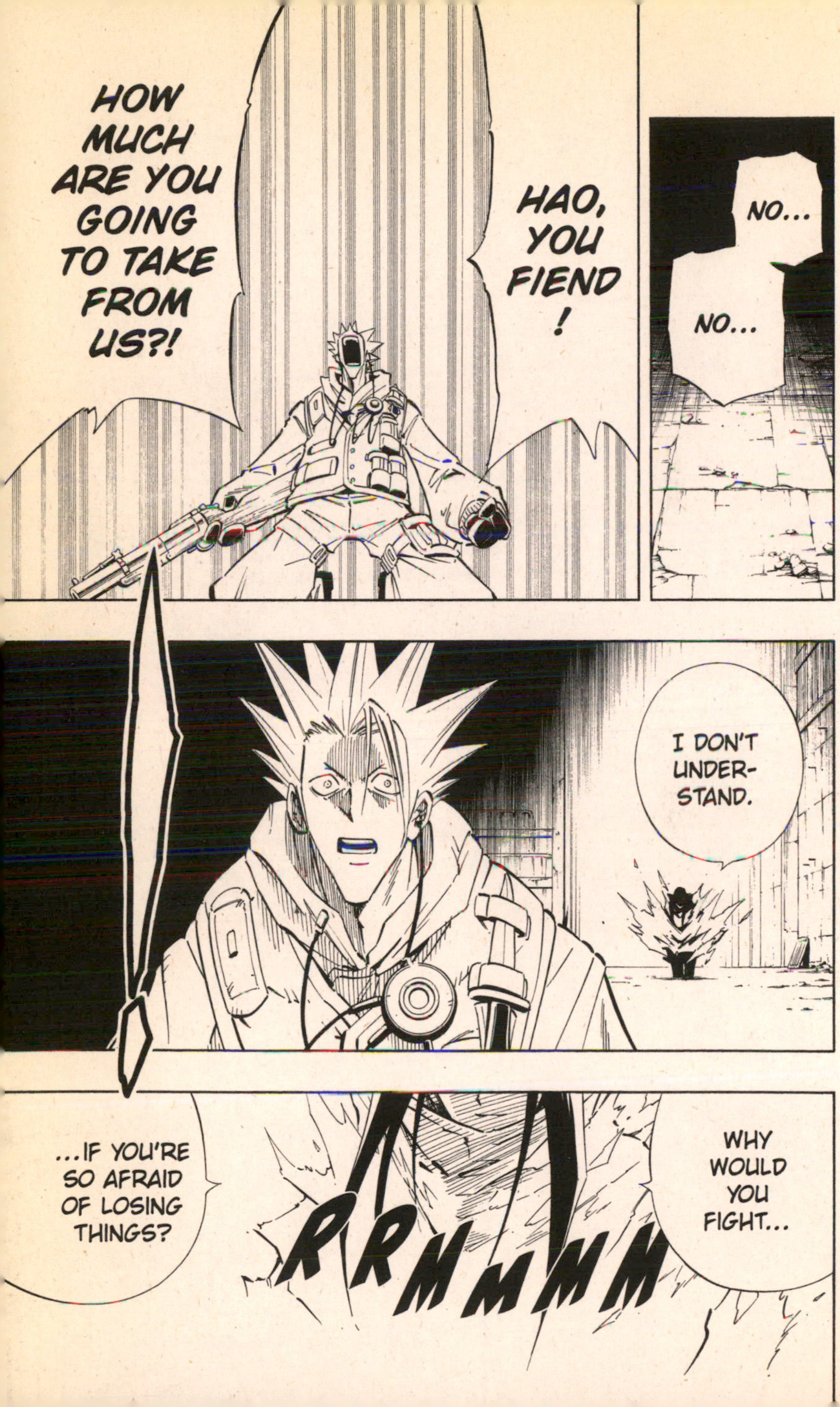
NO...
NO...
HAO, YOU FIEND!
HOW MUCH ARE YOU GOING TO TAKE FROM US?!
I DON'T UNDER-STAND.
WHY WOULD YOU FIGHT...
RRMMMMM
...IF YOU'RE SO AFRAID OF LOSING THINGS?

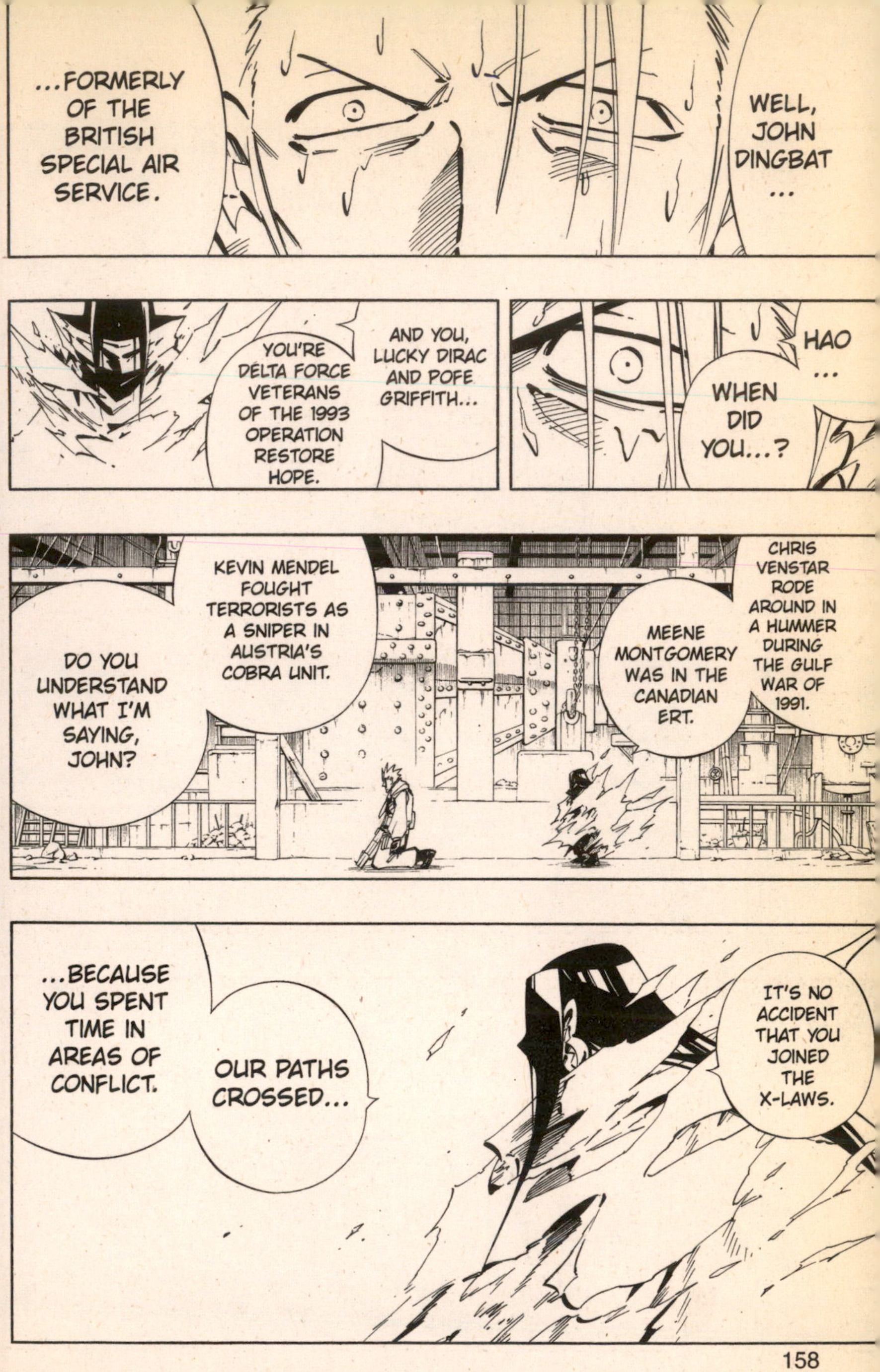
WELL, JOHN DINGBAT...
...FORMERLY OF THE BRITISH SPECIAL AIR SERVICE.
HAO...
WHEN DID YOU...?
AND YOU, LUCKY DIRAC AND POFE GRIFFITH...
YOU'RE DELTA FORCE VETERANS OF THE 1993 OPERATION RESTORE HOPE.
CHRIS VENSTAR RODE AROUND IN A HUMMER DURING THE GULF WAR OF 1991.
MEENE MONTGOMERY WAS IN THE CANADIAN ERT.
KEVIN MENDEL FOUGHT TERRORISTS AS A SNIPER IN AUSTRIA'S COBRA UNIT.
DO YOU UNDERSTAND WHAT I'M SAYING, JOHN?
IT'S NO ACCIDENT THAT YOU JOINED THE X-LAWS.
OUR PATHS CROSSED...
...BECAUSE YOU SPENT TIME IN AREAS OF CONFLICT.

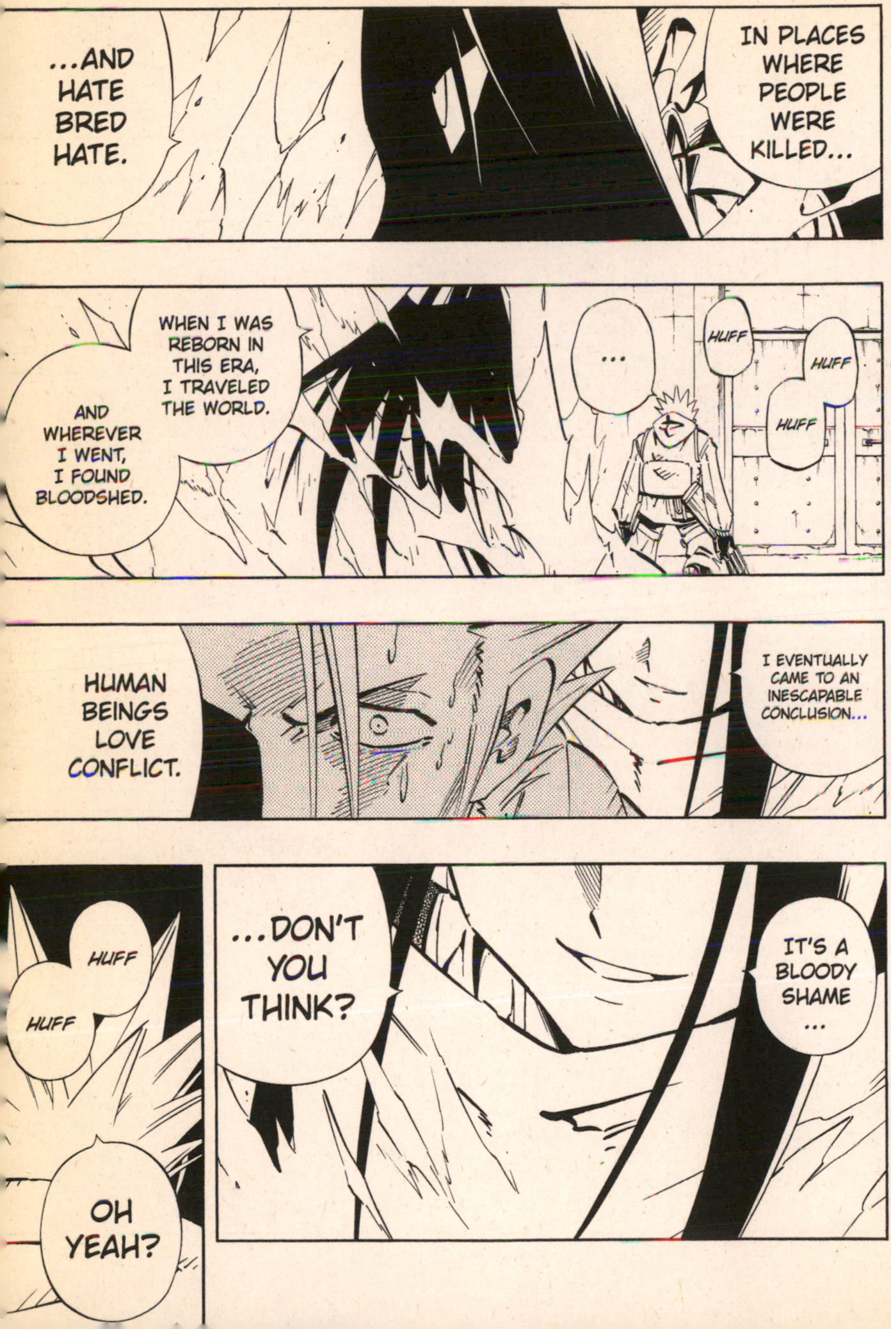
IN PLACES WHERE PEOPLE WERE KILLED...
...AND HATE BRED HATE.
HUFF
HUFF
HUFF
...
WHEN I WAS REBORN IN THIS ERA, I TRAVELED THE WORLD.
AND WHEREVER I WENT, I FOUND BLOODSHED.
I EVENTUALLY CAME TO AN INESCAPABLE CONCLUSION...
HUMAN BEINGS LOVE CONFLICT.
IT'S A BLOODY SHAME...
...DON'T YOU THINK?
HUFF
HUFF
OH YEAH?

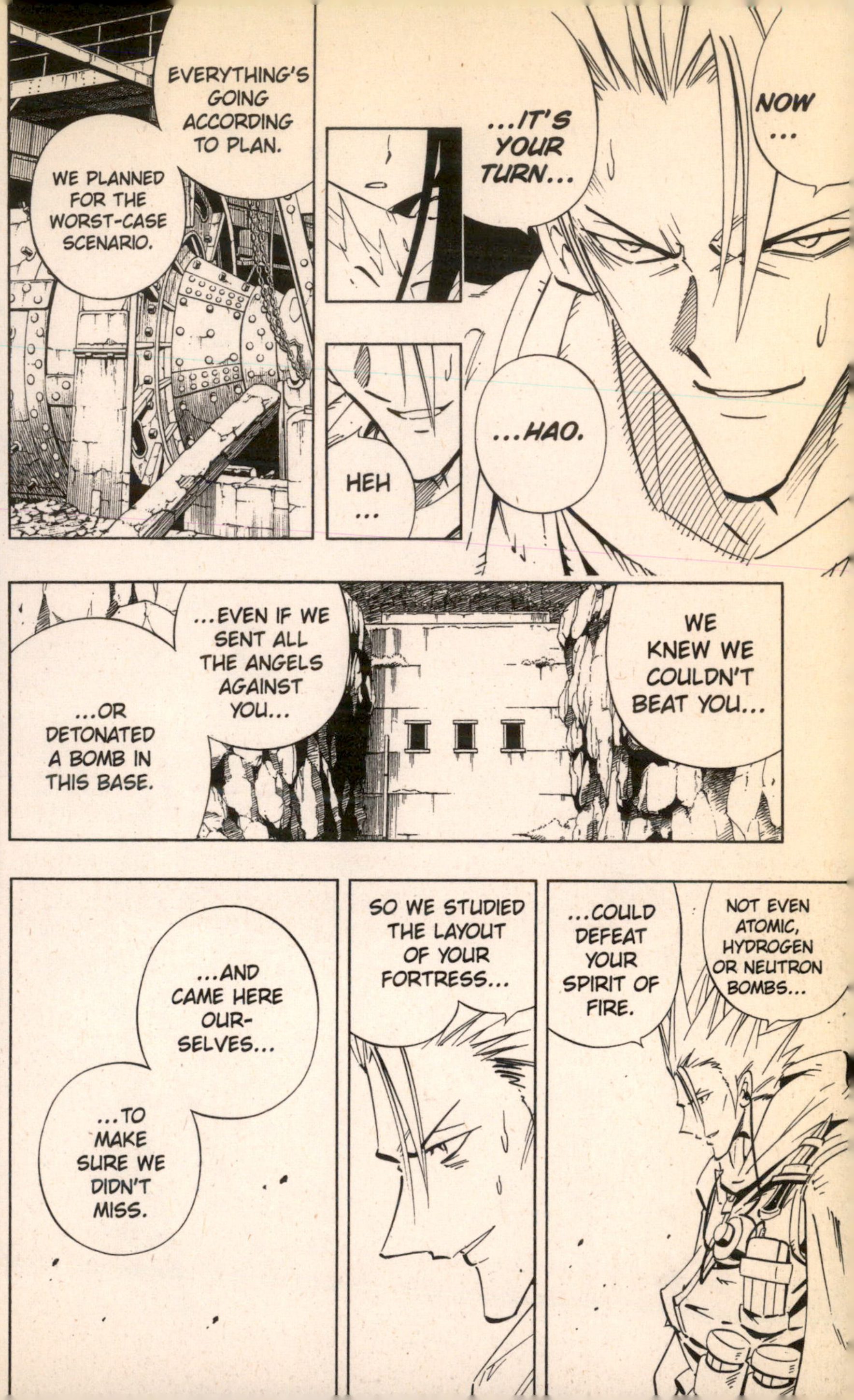
NOW...
...IT'S YOUR TURN...
...HAO.
HEH...
EVERYTHING'S GOING ACCORDING TO PLAN.
WE PLANNED FOR THE WORST-CASE SCENARIO.
WE KNEW WE COULDN'T BEAT YOU...
...EVEN IF WE SENT ALL THE ANGELS AGAINST YOU...
...OR DETONATED A BOMB IN THIS BASE.
NOT EVEN ATOMIC, HYDROGEN OR NEUTRON BOMBS...
...COULD DEFEAT YOUR SPIRIT OF FIRE.
SO WE STUDIED THE LAYOUT OF YOUR FORTRESS...
...AND CAME HERE OUR-SELVES...
...TO MAKE SURE WE DIDN'T MISS.

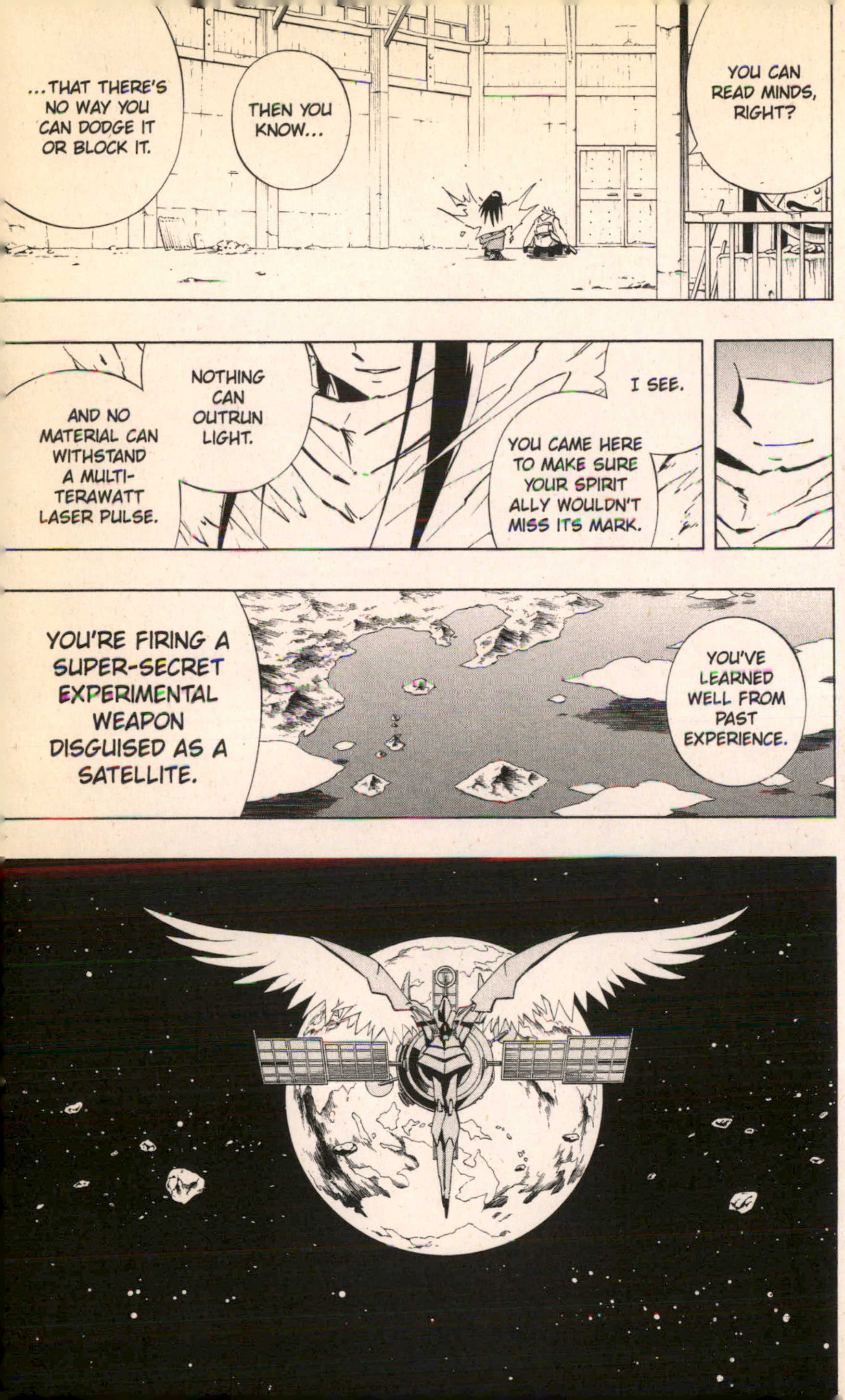
YOU CAN READ MINDS, RIGHT?
THEN YOU KNOW...
...THAT THERE'S NO WAY YOU CAN DODGE IT OR BLOCK IT.
I SEE.
YOU CAME HERE TO MAKE SURE YOUR SPIRIT ALLY WOULDN'T MISS ITS MARK.
NOTHING CAN OUTRUN LIGHT.
AND NO MATERIAL CAN WITHSTAND A MULTI-TERAWATT LASER PULSE.
YOU'VE LEARNED WELL FROM PAST EXPERIENCE.
YOU'RE FIRING A SUPER-SECRET EXPERIMENTAL WEAPON DISGUISED AS A SATELLITE.

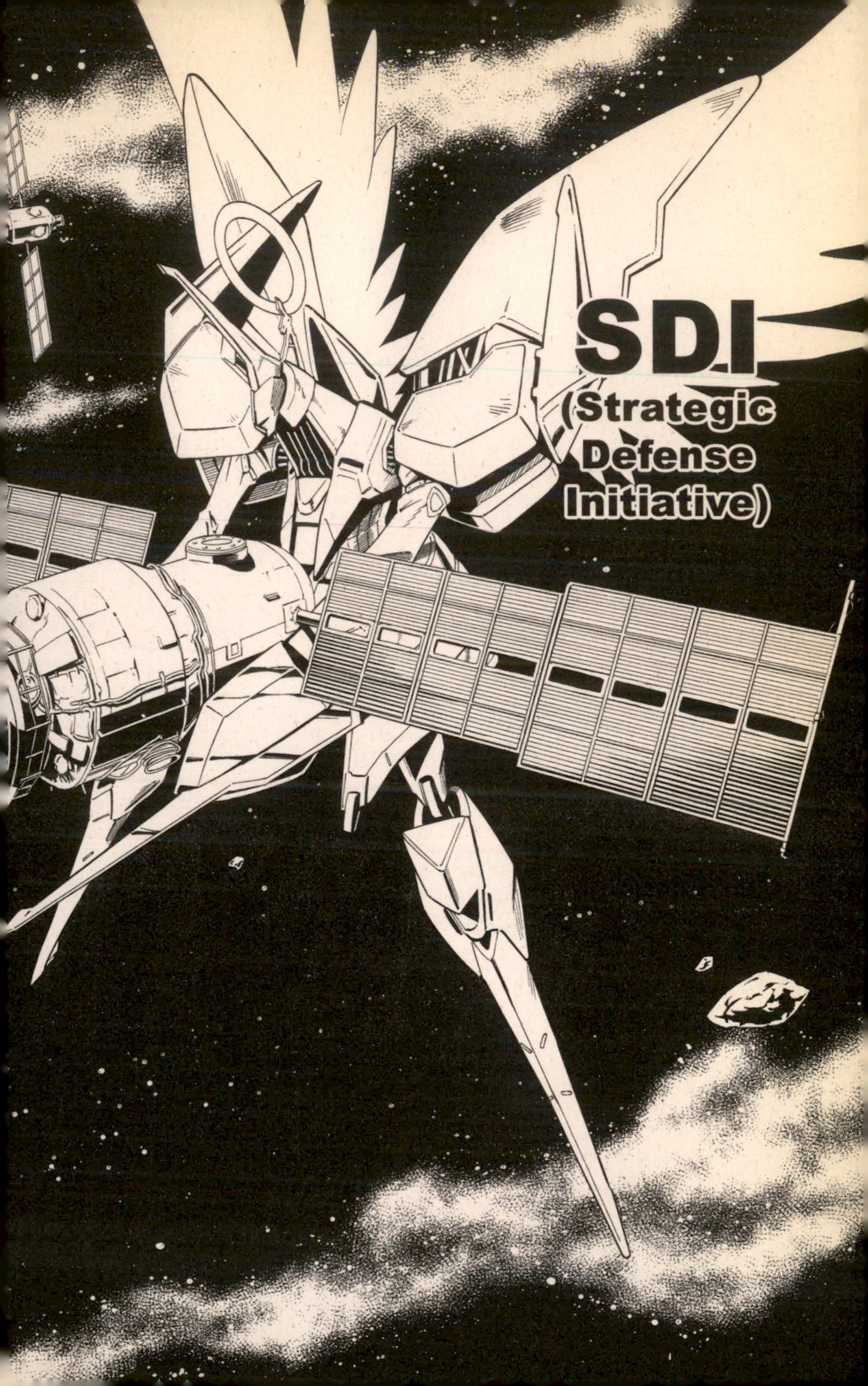
SDI
(Strategic Defense Initiative)

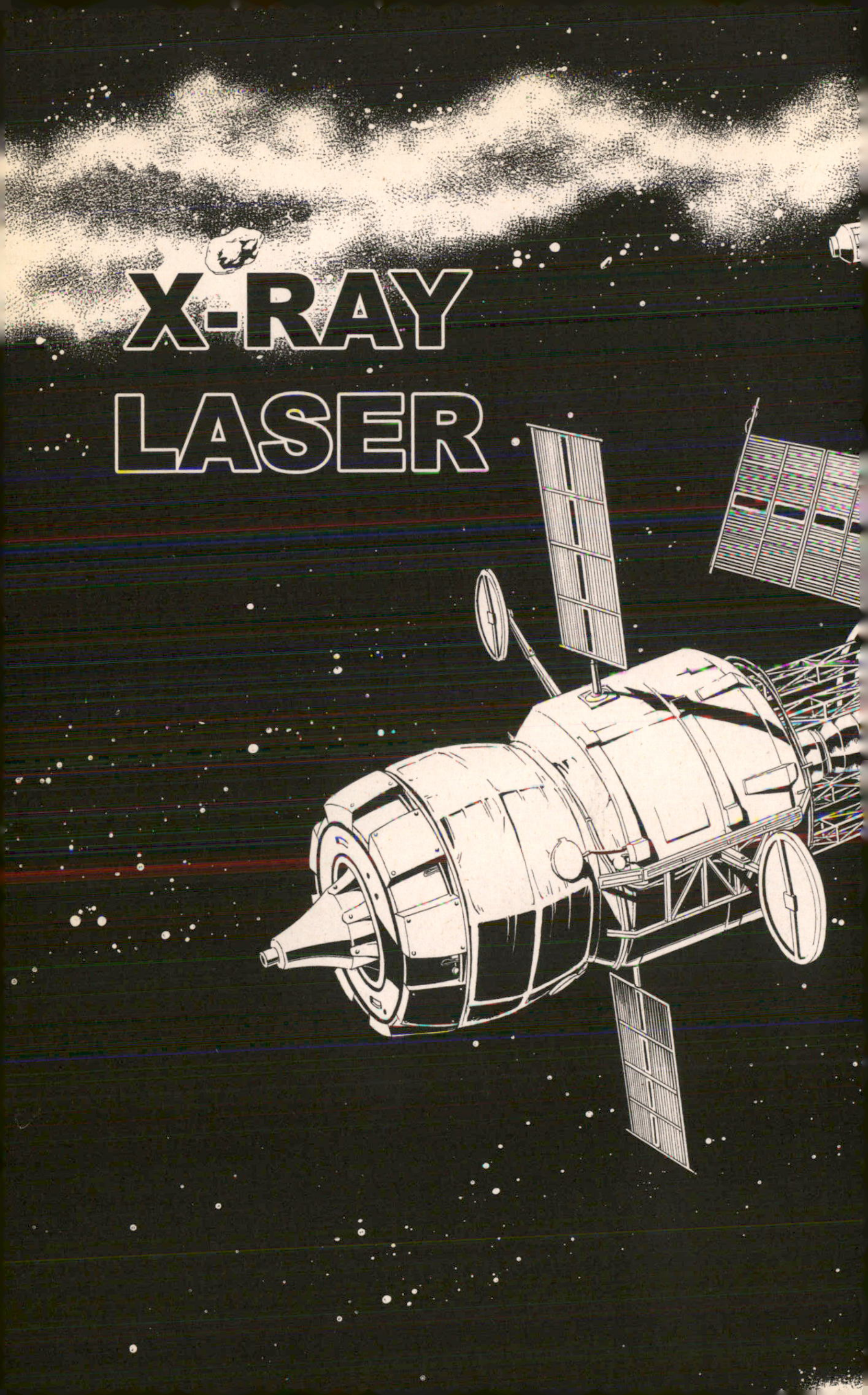
X-RAY
LASER

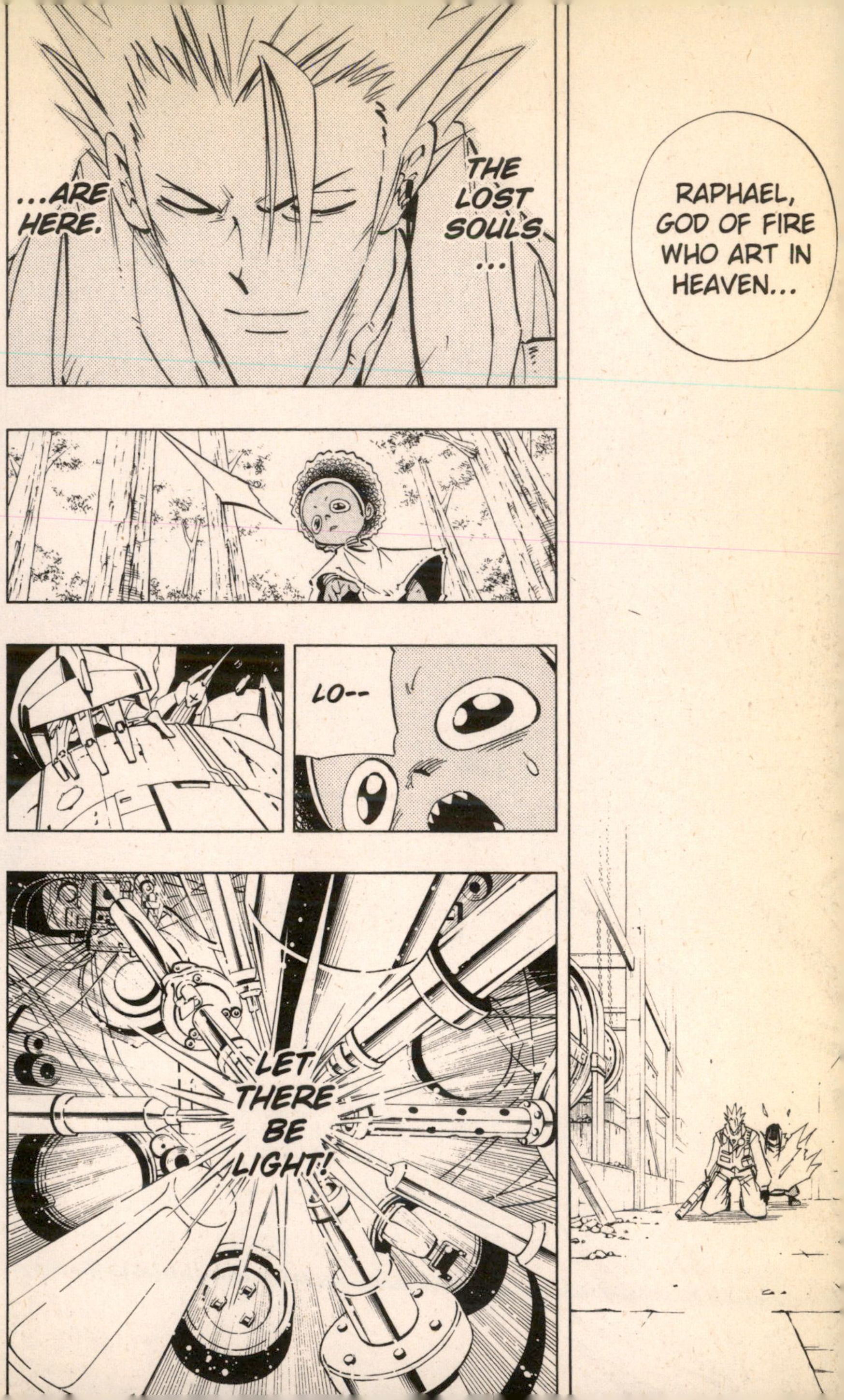
RAPHAEL, GOD OF FIRE WHO ART IN HEAVEN...
THE LOST SOULS...
...ARE HERE.
LO--
LET THERE BE LIGHT!

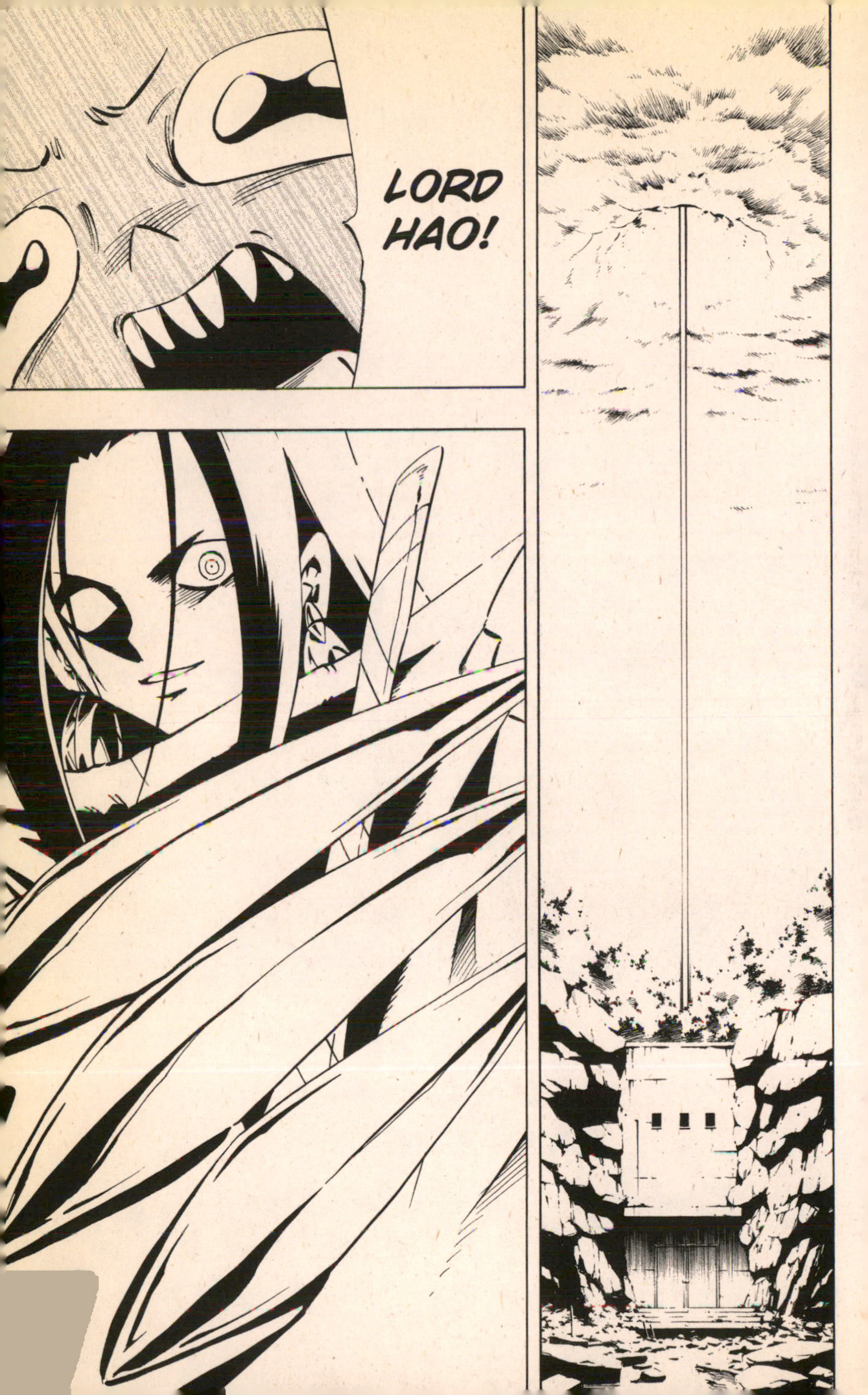
LORD HAO!

SHAMAN KING CHARACTER FILE No.137

2001 (JAN)

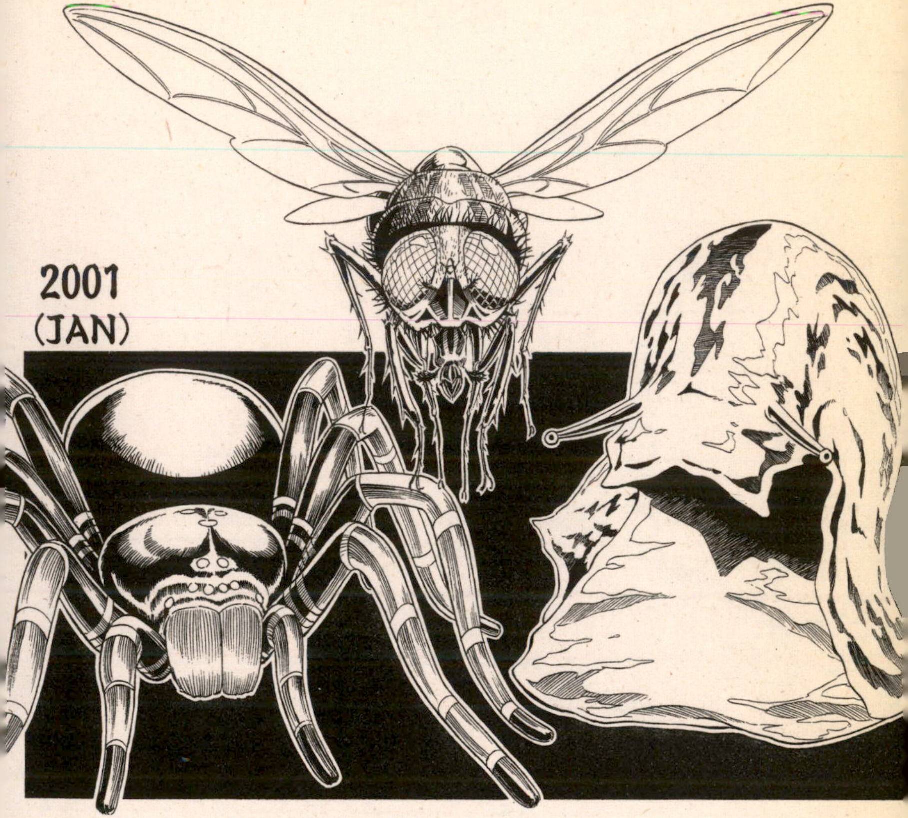

ベルゼバブ

BEELZEBUB

タラさん

MR. TARANTULA

ナメちゃん

SLUGGY

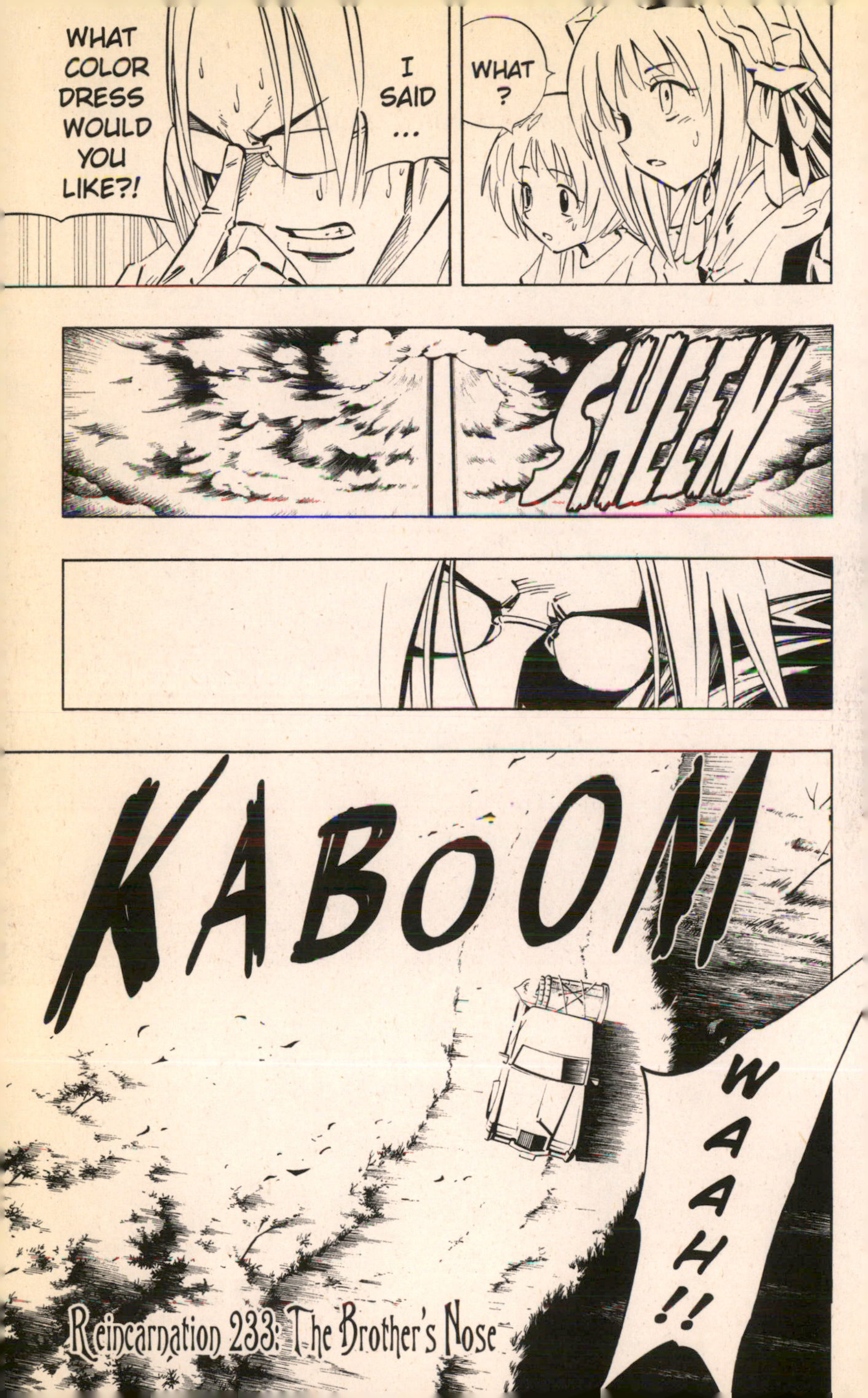
WHAT?
I SAID...
WHAT COLOR DRESS WOULD YOU LIKE?!
SHEEN
KABOOM
WAAH!!
Reincarnation 233: The Brother's Nose

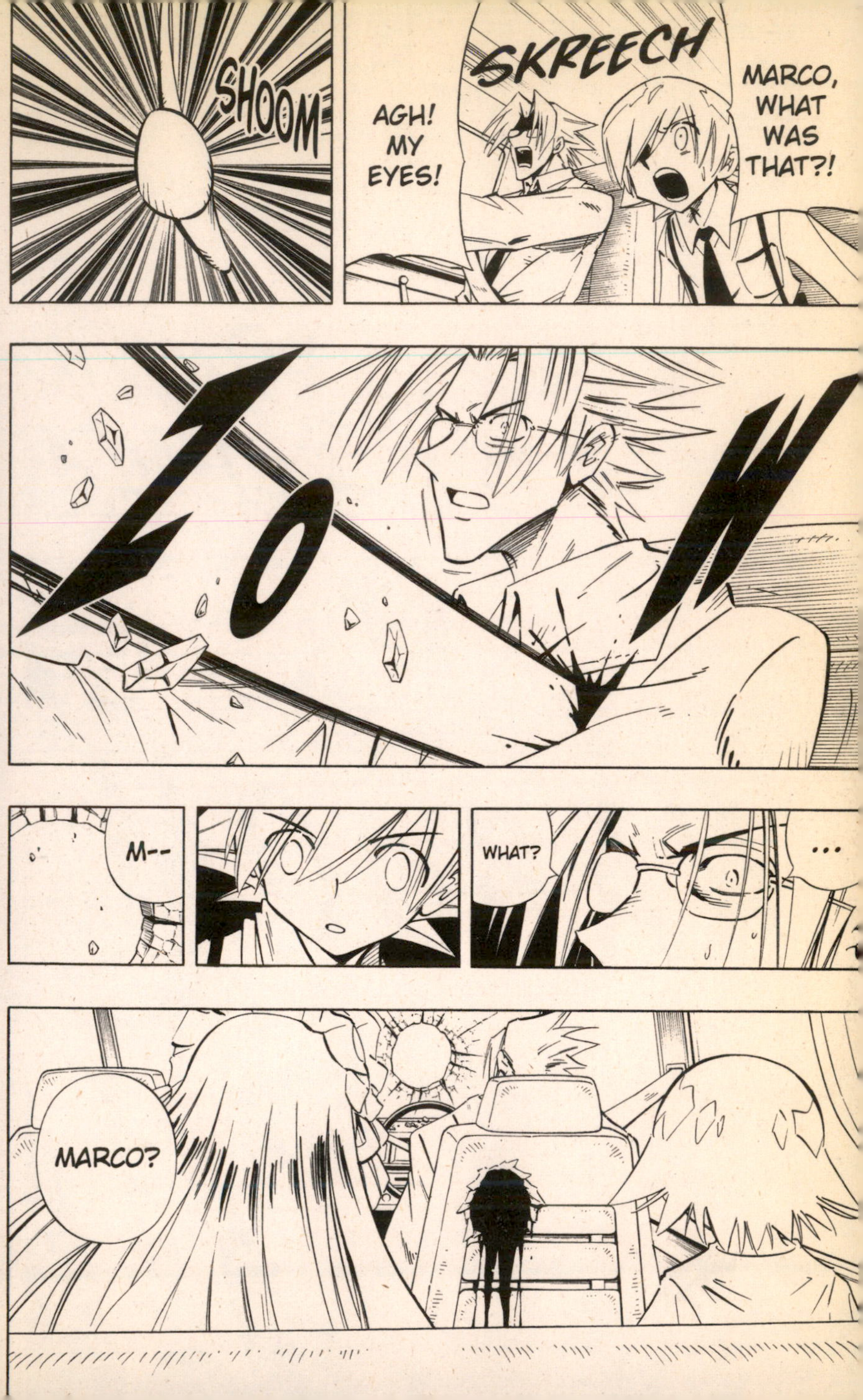

SKREECH
MARCO, WHAT WAS THAT?!
AGH! MY EYES!
SHOOM
...
WHAT?
M--
MARCO?

Reincarnation 233: The Brother's Nose

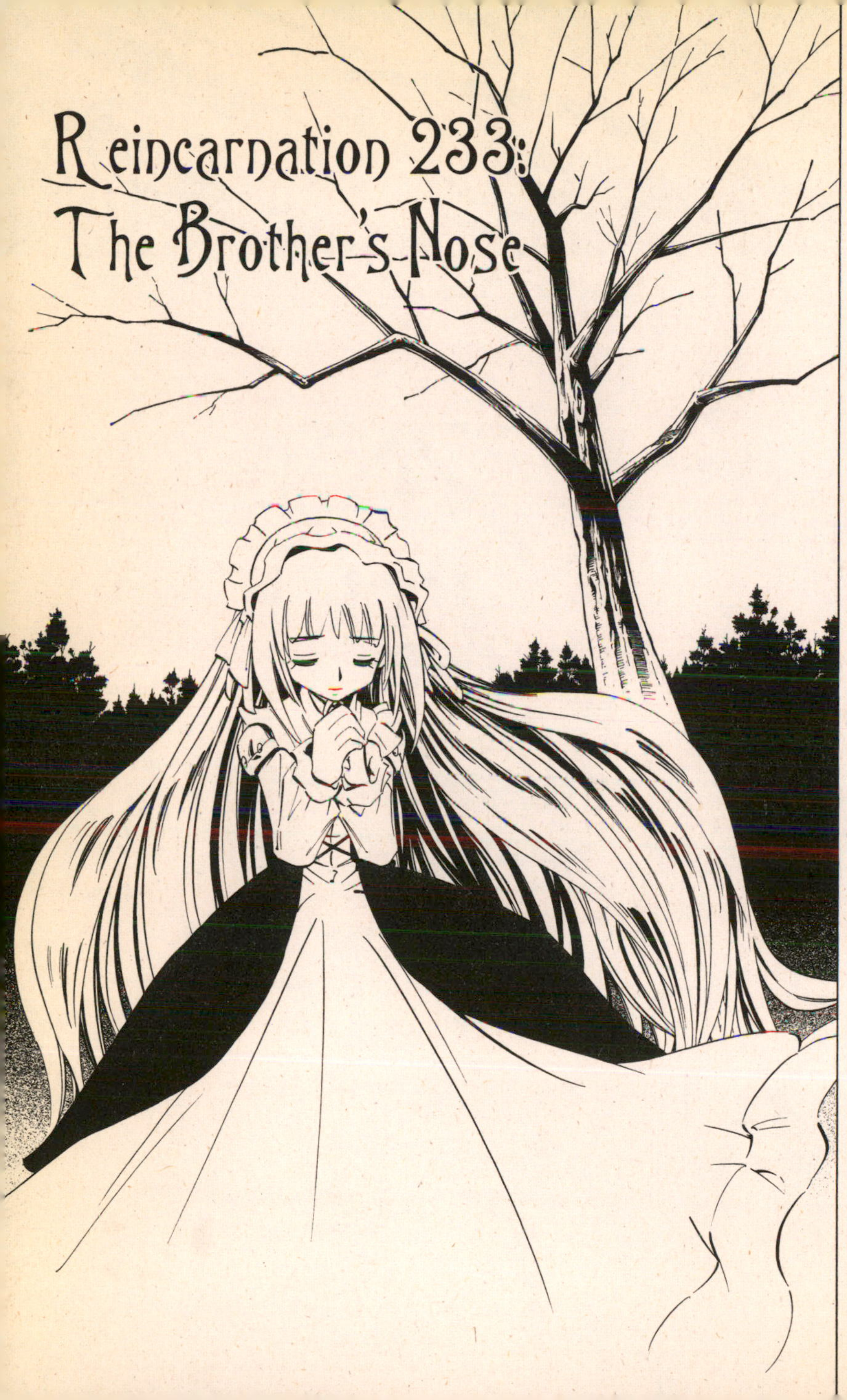

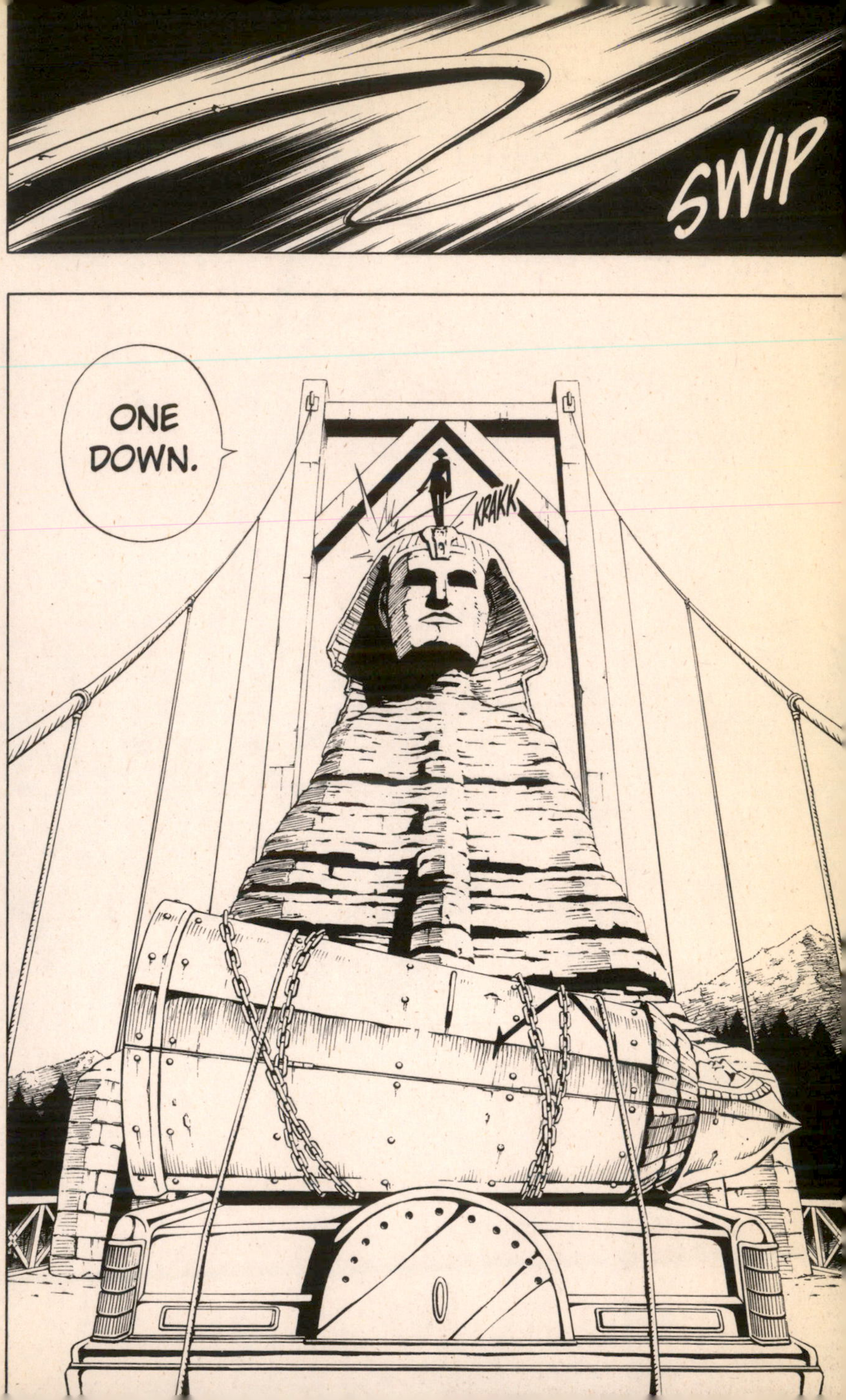
SWIP
ONE DOWN.
KRAKK

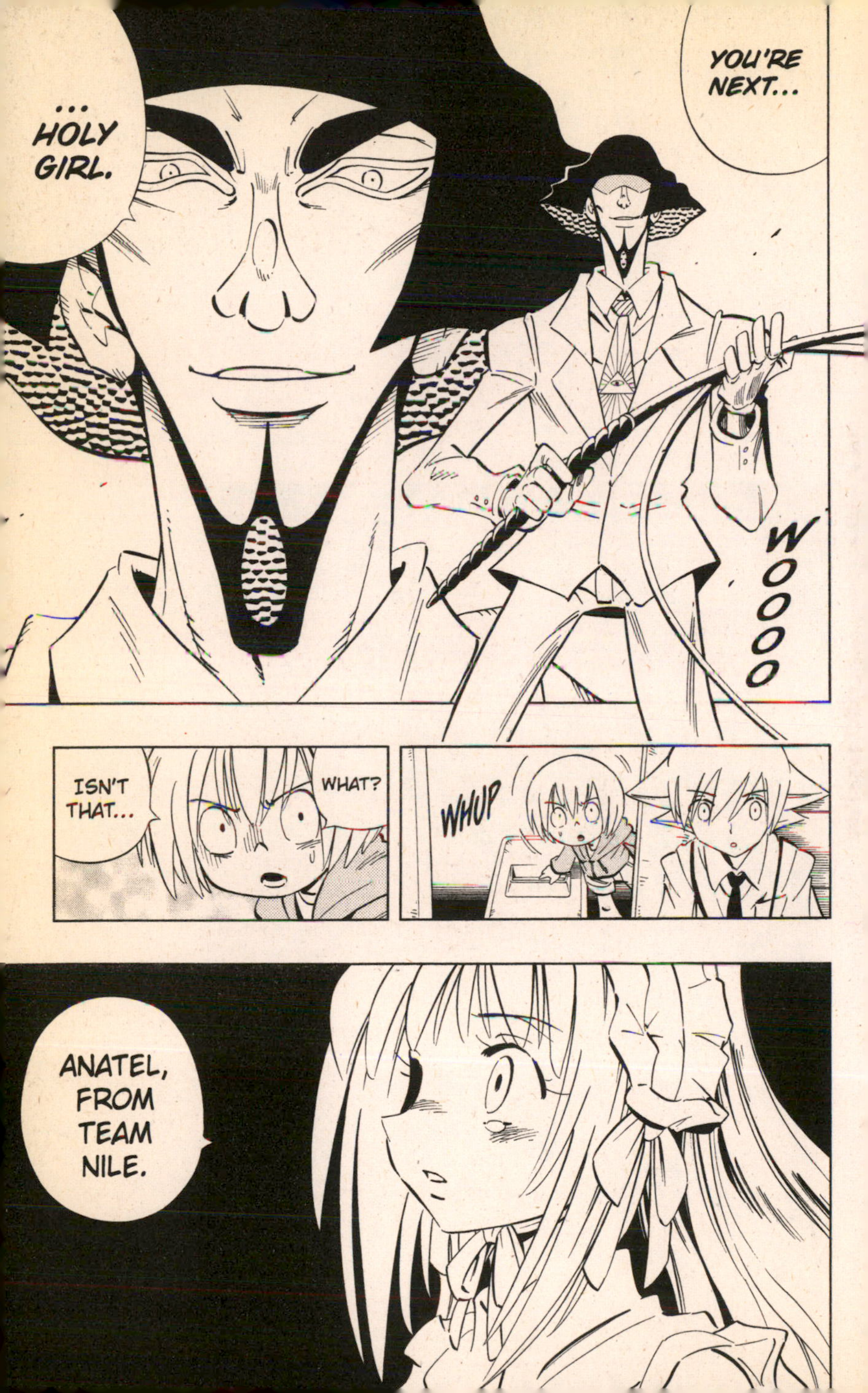
YOU'RE NEXT...
... HOLY GIRL.
WOOOOO
WHUP
WHAT?
ISN'T THAT...
ANATEL, FROM TEAM NILE.

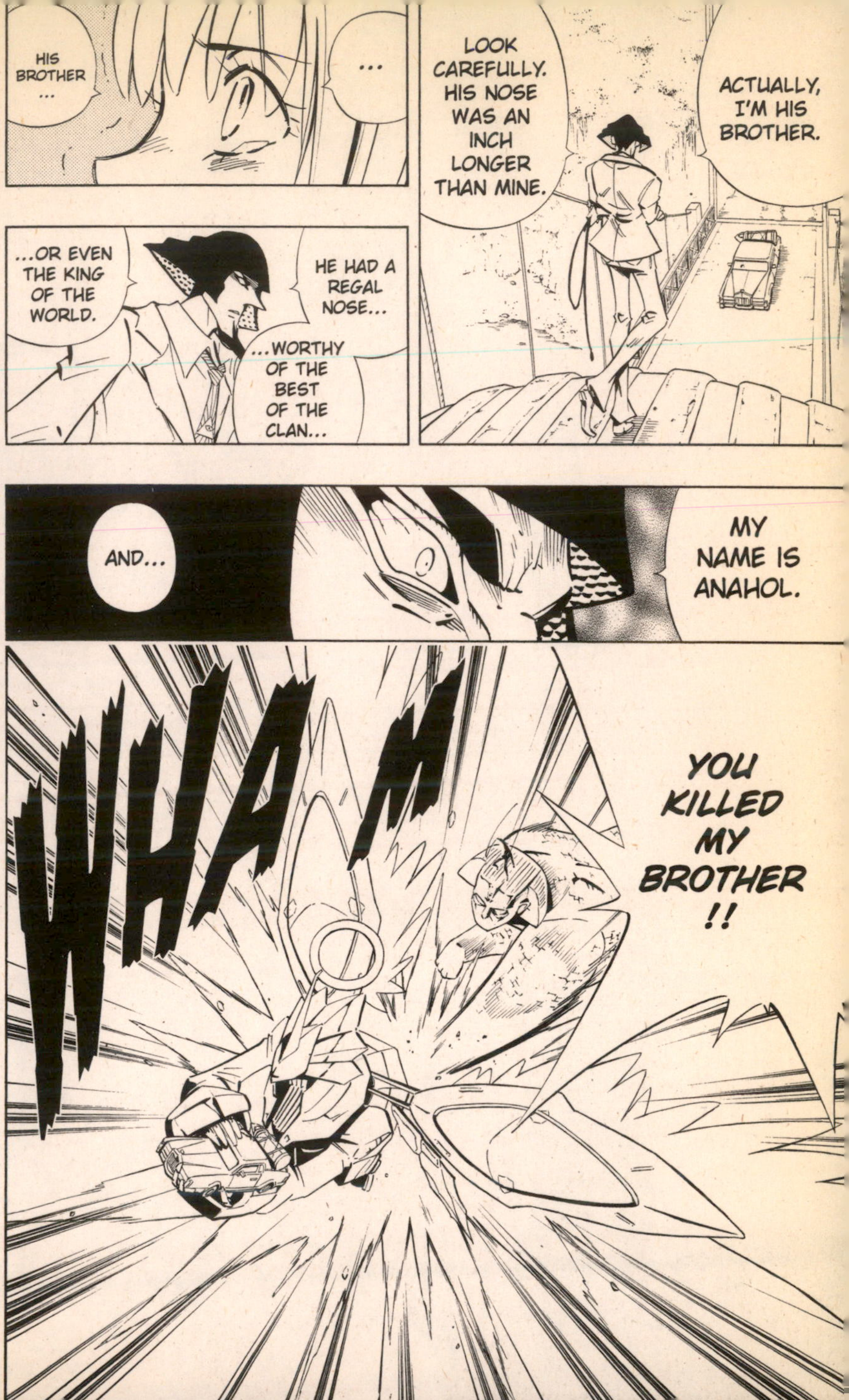
ACTUALLY, I'M HIS BROTHER.
LOOK CAREFULLY. HIS NOSE WAS AN INCH LONGER THAN MINE.
...
HIS BROTHER ...
HE HAD A REGAL NOSE...
...WORTHY OF THE BEST OF THE CLAN...
...OR EVEN THE KING OF THE WORLD.
MY NAME IS ANAHOL.
AND...
WHAM
YOU KILLED MY BROTHER !!

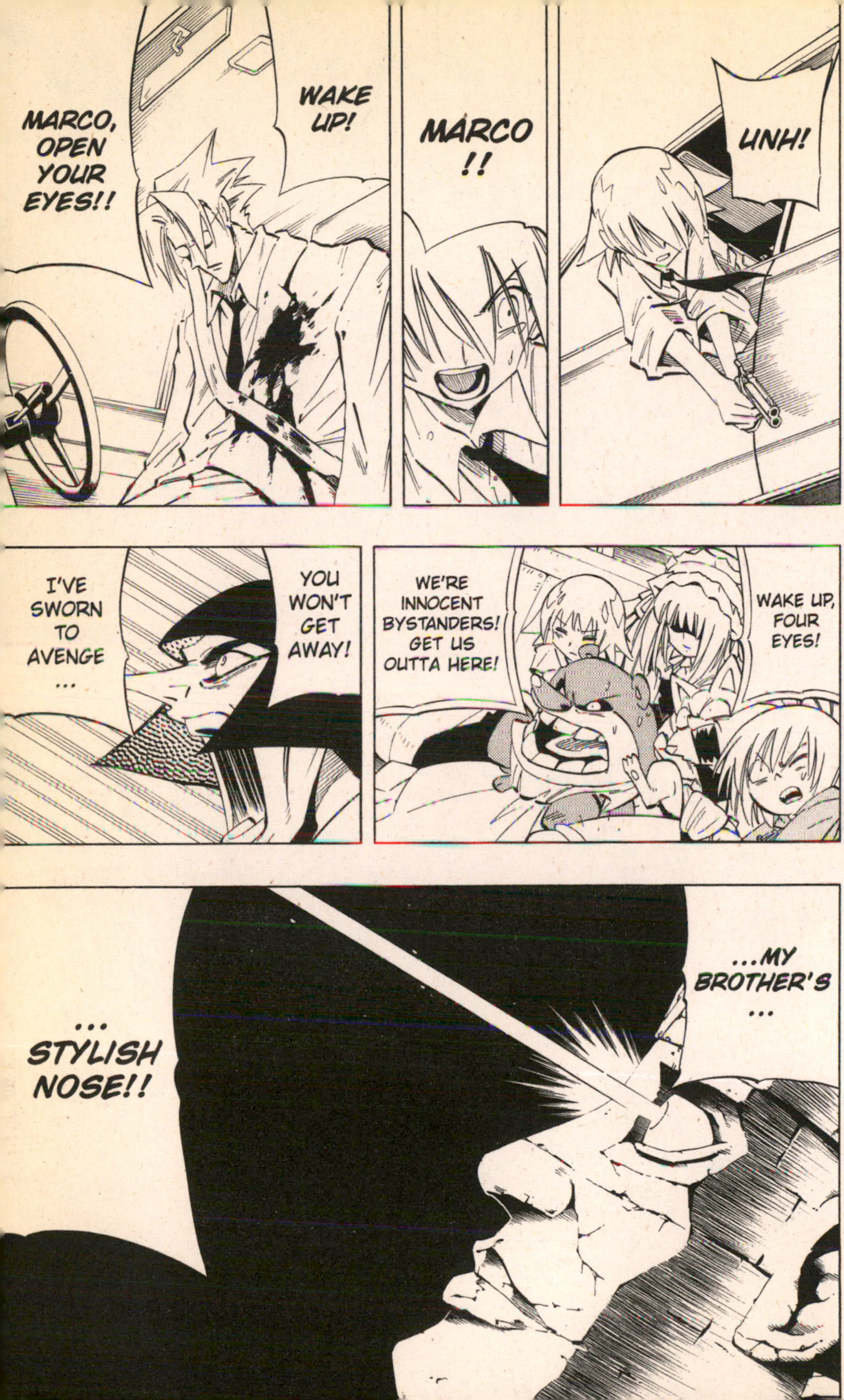
UNH!
MARCO !!
WAKE UP!
MARCO, OPEN YOUR EYES!!
WAKE UP, FOUR EYES!
WE'RE INNOCENT BYSTANDERS! GET US OUTTA HERE!
YOU WON'T GET AWAY!
I'VE SWORN TO AVENGE ...
...MY BROTHER'S ...
... STYLISH NOSE!!

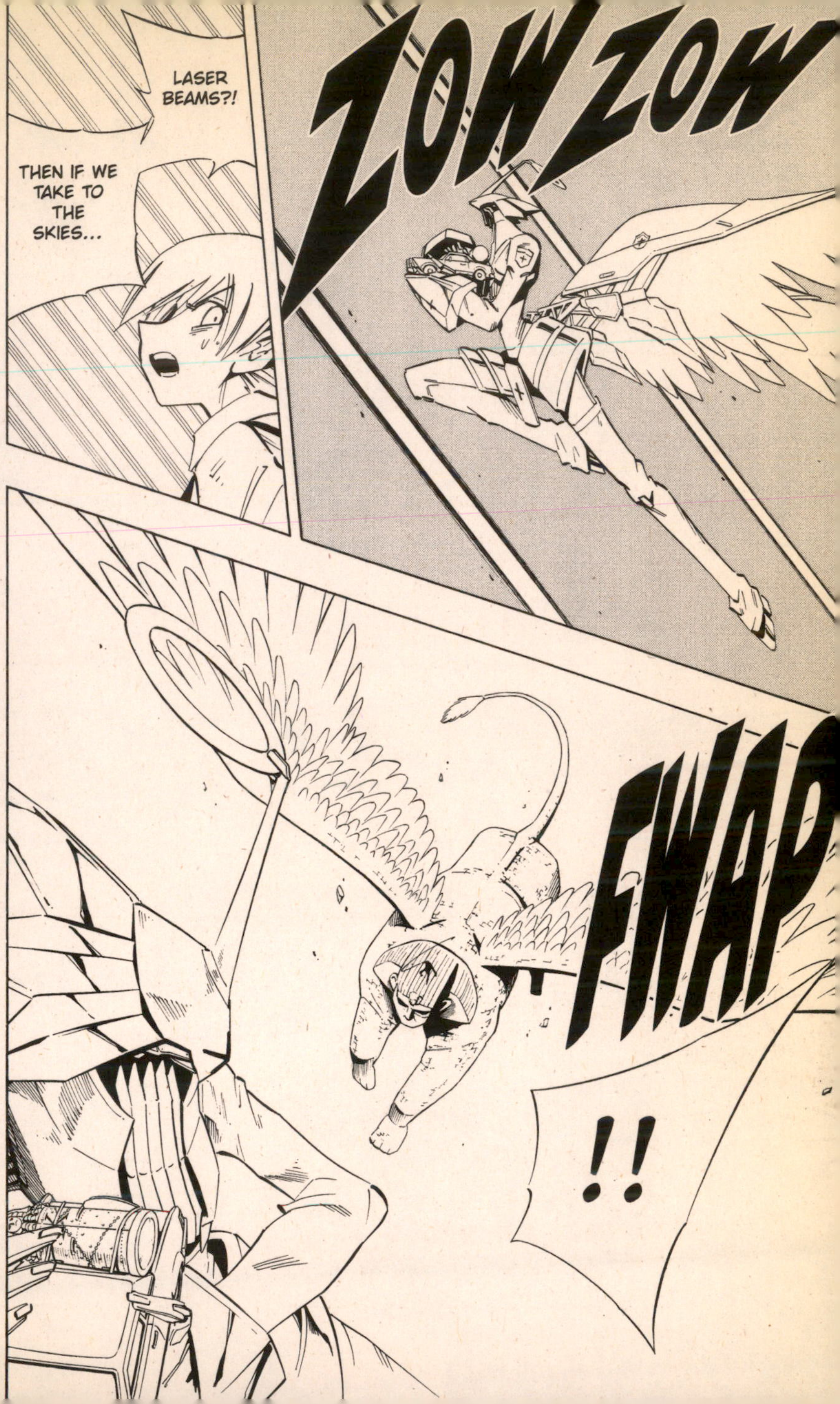
ZOW ZOW
LASER BEAMS?!
THEN IF WE TAKE TO THE SKIES...
FWAP
!!

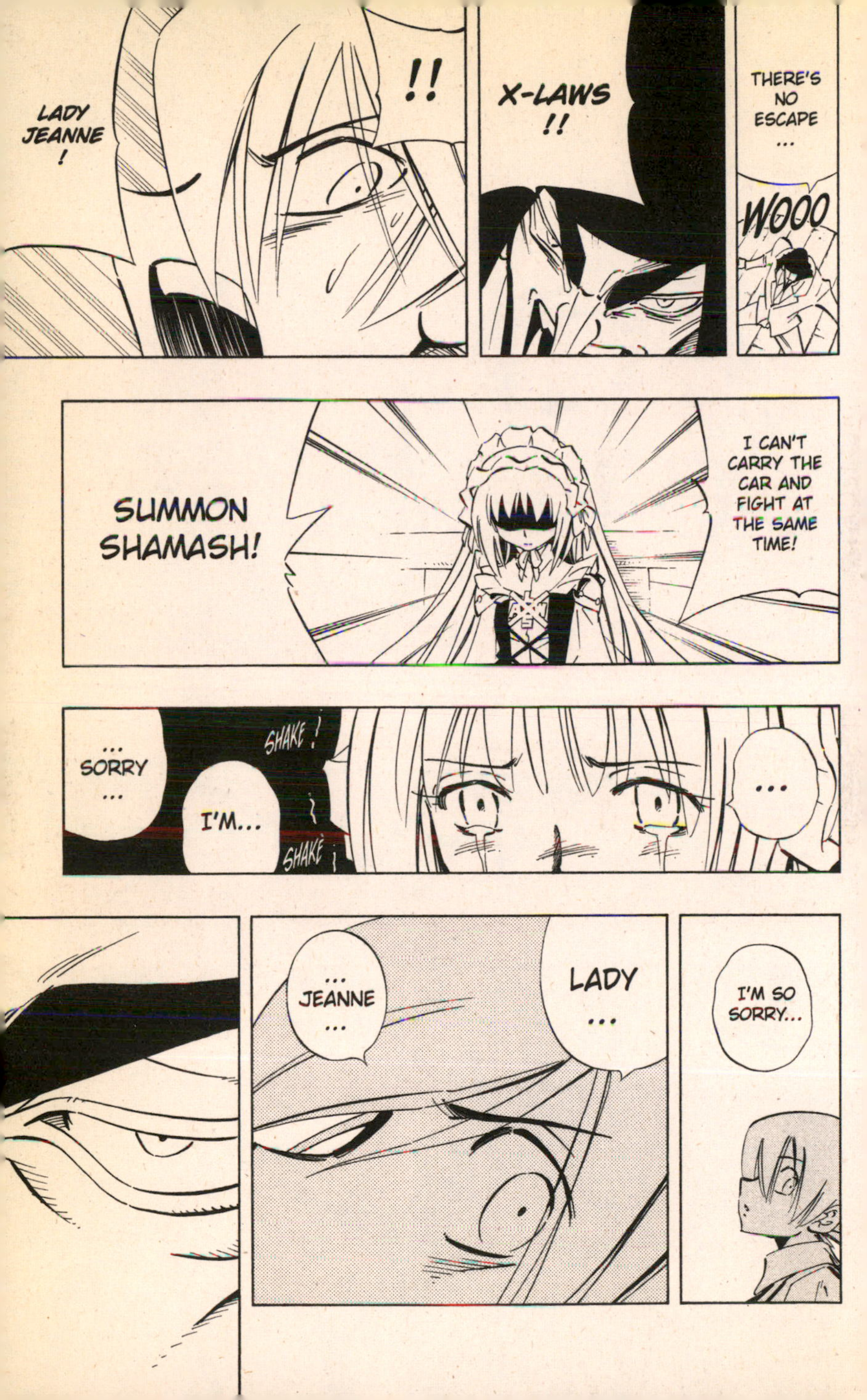
THERE'S NO ESCAPE ...
WOOO
X-LAWS !!
!!
LADY JEANNE !
I CAN'T CARRY THE CAR AND FIGHT AT THE SAME TIME!
SUMMON SHAMASH!
...
SHAKE !
SHAKE !
I'M...
... SORRY ...
I'M SO SORRY...
LADY ...
... JEANNE ...

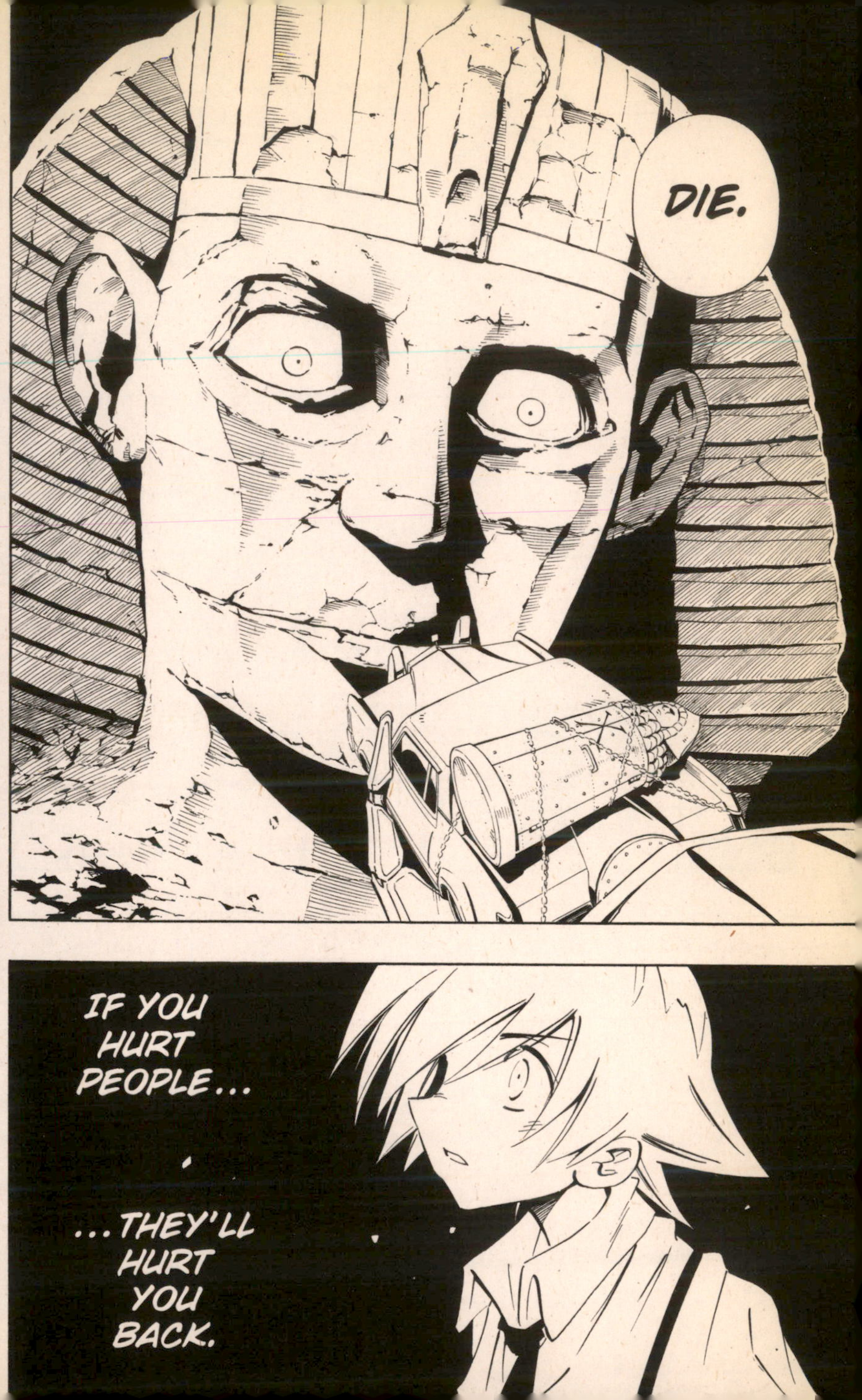
DIE.
IF YOU HURT PEOPLE...
...THEY'LL HURT YOU BACK.

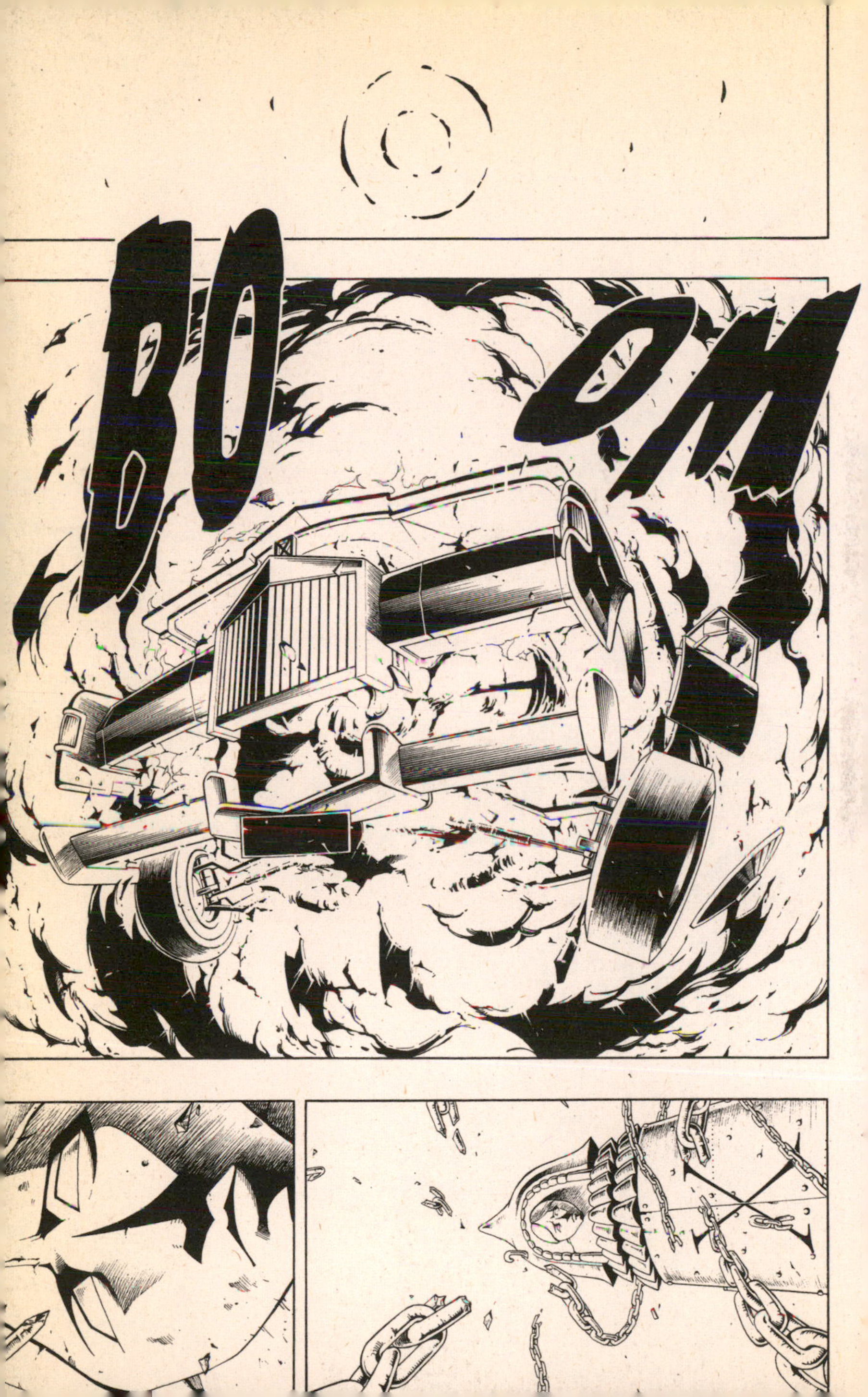
BOOM

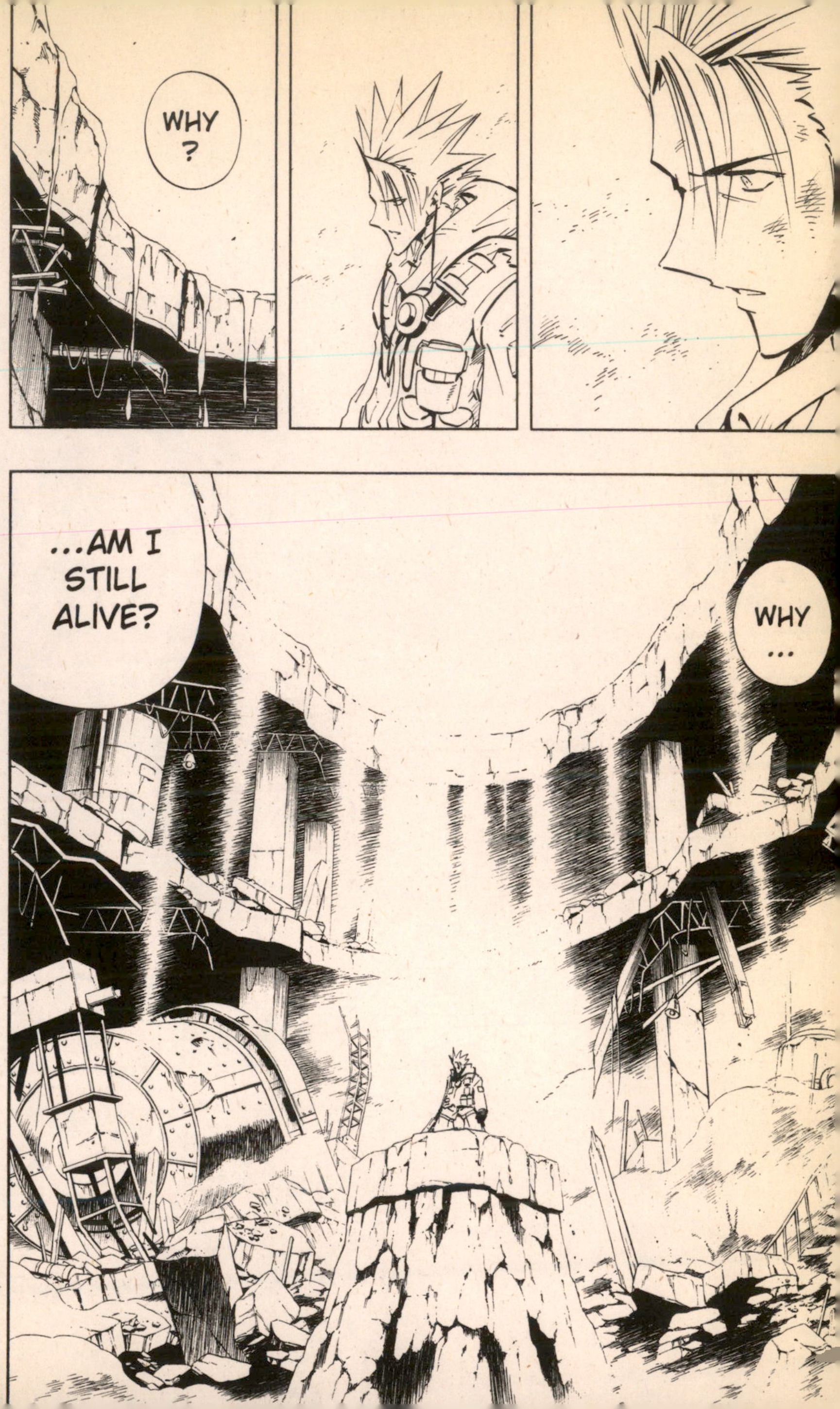
WHY ?
WHY ...
...AM I STILL ALIVE?

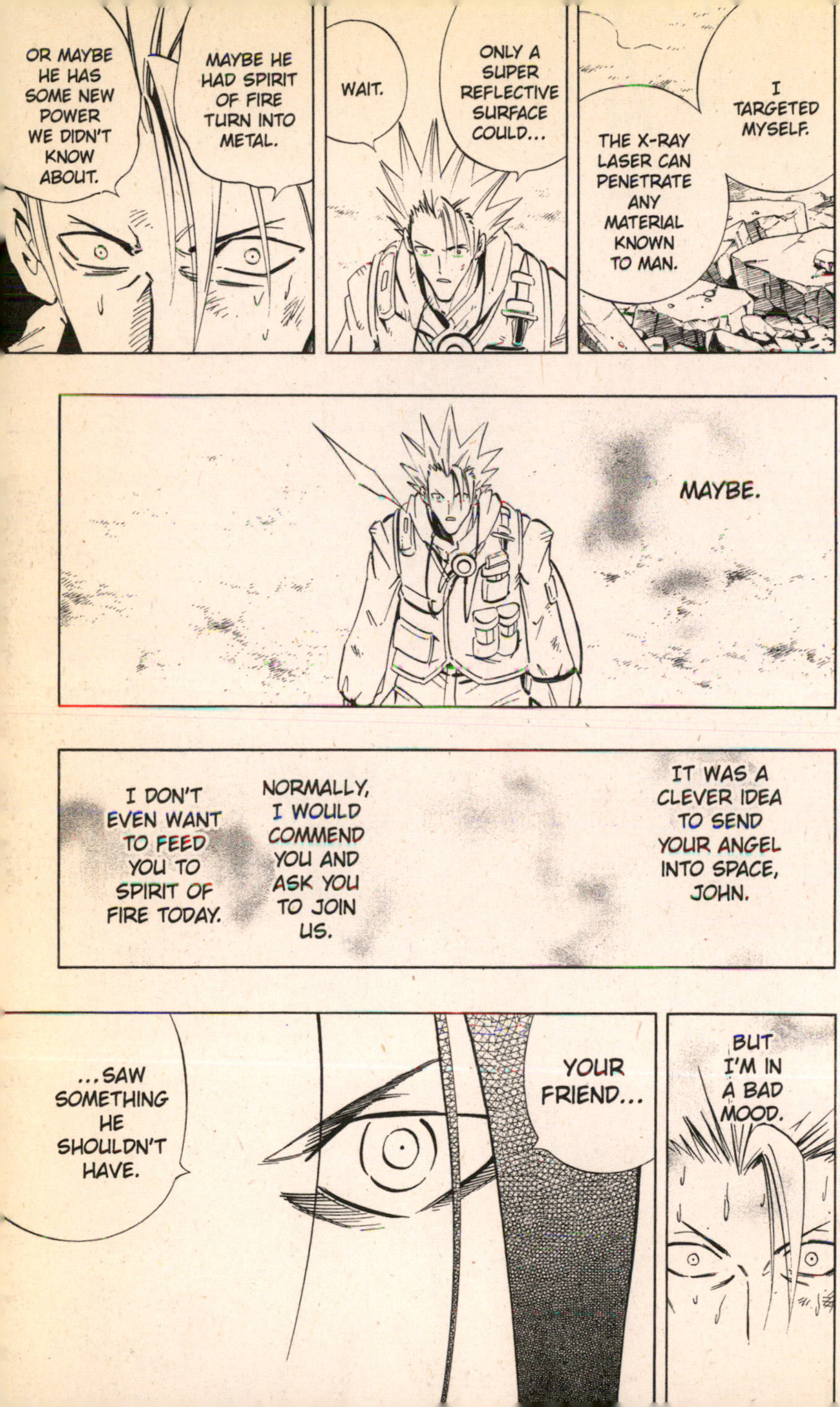
I TARGETED MYSELF.
THE X-RAY LASER CAN PENETRATE ANY MATERIAL KNOWN TO MAN.
ONLY A SUPER REFLECTIVE SURFACE COULD...
WAIT.
MAYBE HE HAD SPIRIT OF FIRE TURN INTO METAL.
OR MAYBE HE HAS SOME NEW POWER WE DIDN'T KNOW ABOUT.
MAYBE.
IT WAS A CLEVER IDEA TO SEND YOUR ANGEL INTO SPACE, JOHN.
NORMALLY, I WOULD COMMEND YOU AND ASK YOU TO JOIN US.
I DON'T EVEN WANT TO FEED YOU TO SPIRIT OF FIRE TODAY.
BUT I'M IN A BAD MOOD.
YOUR FRIEND...
...SAW SOMETHING HE SHOULDN'T HAVE.

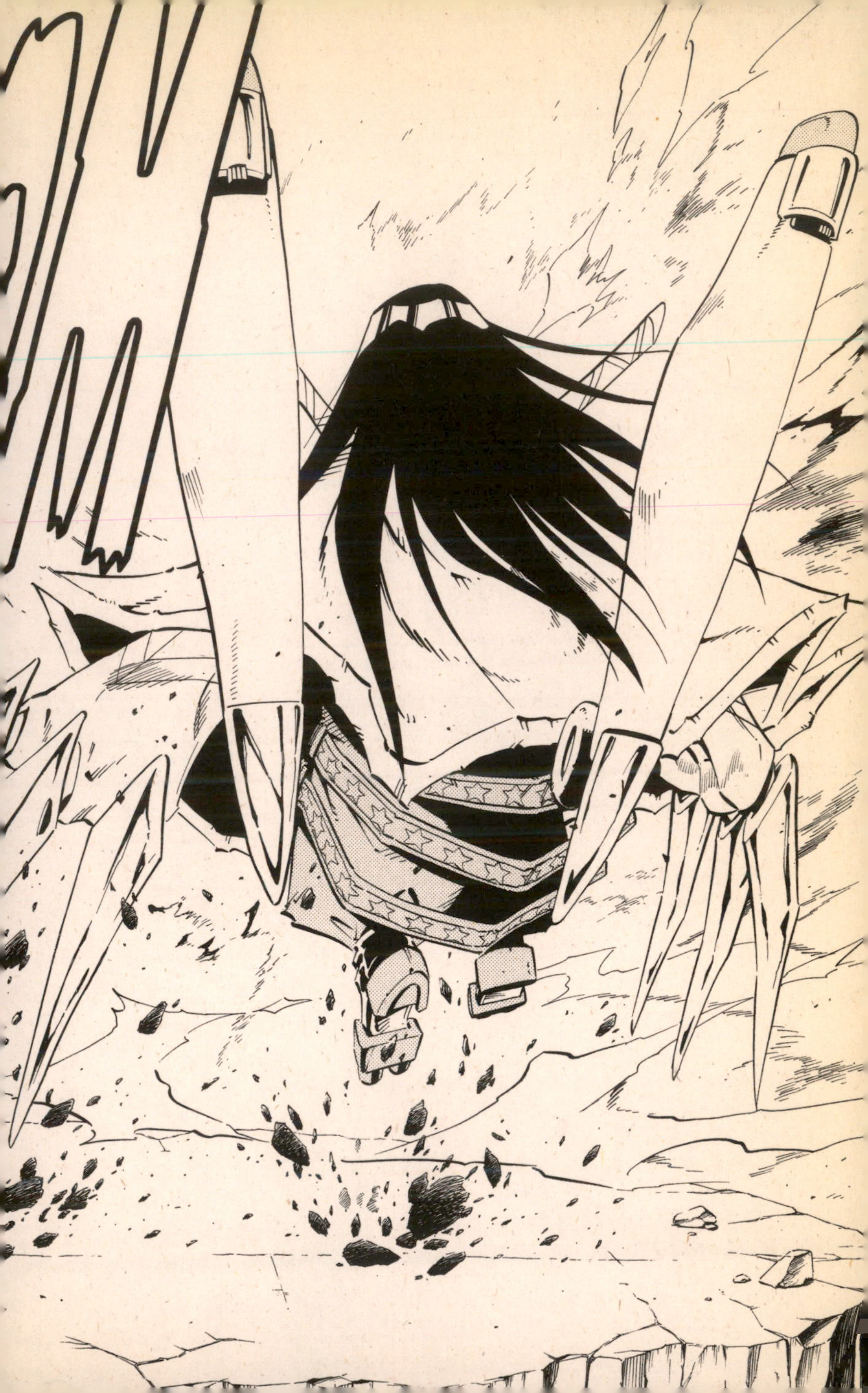

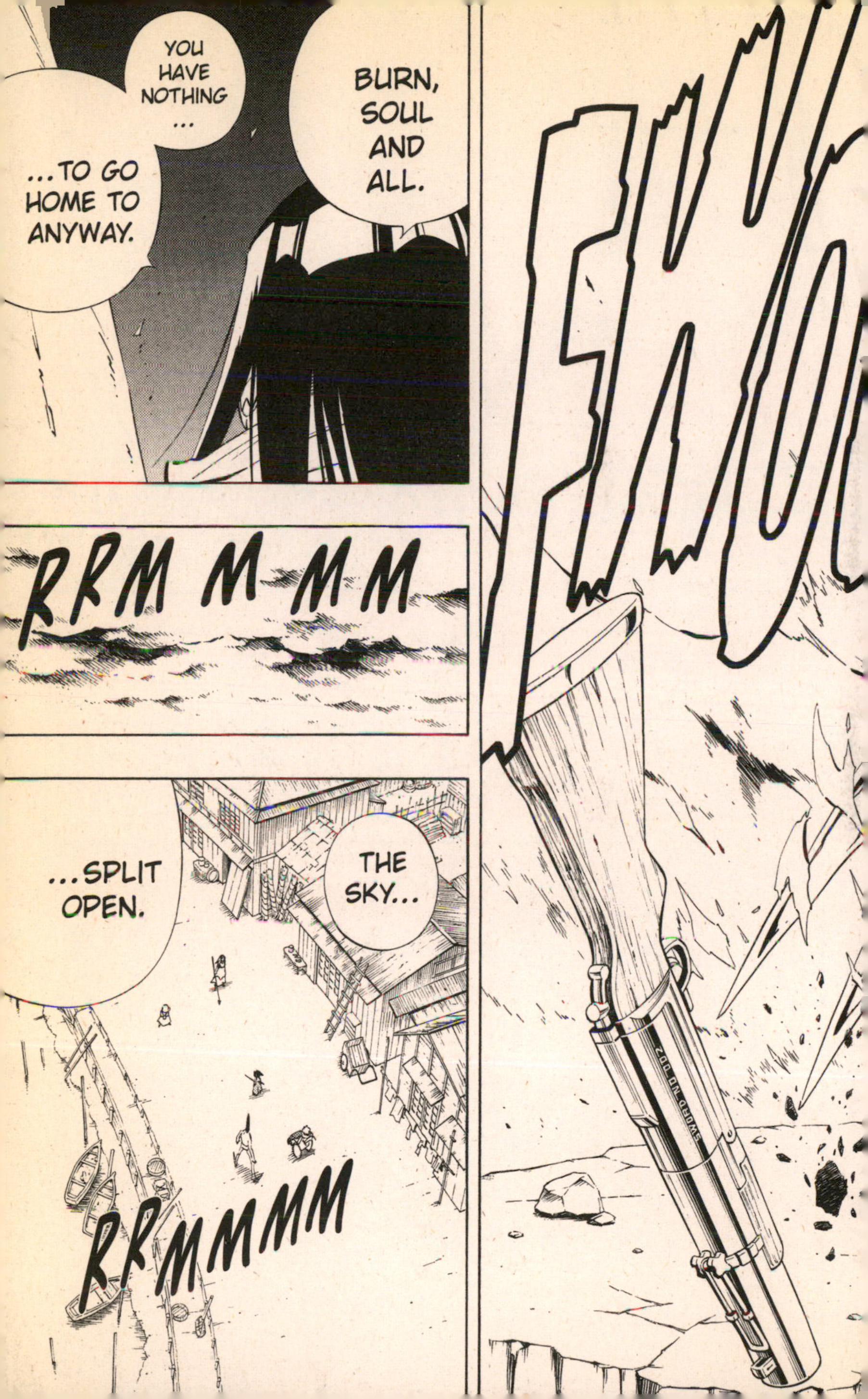
BURN, SOUL AND ALL.
YOU HAVE NOTHING ...
...TO GO HOME TO ANYWAY.
RRMMMMM
THE SKY...
...SPLIT OPEN.
RRMMMMM

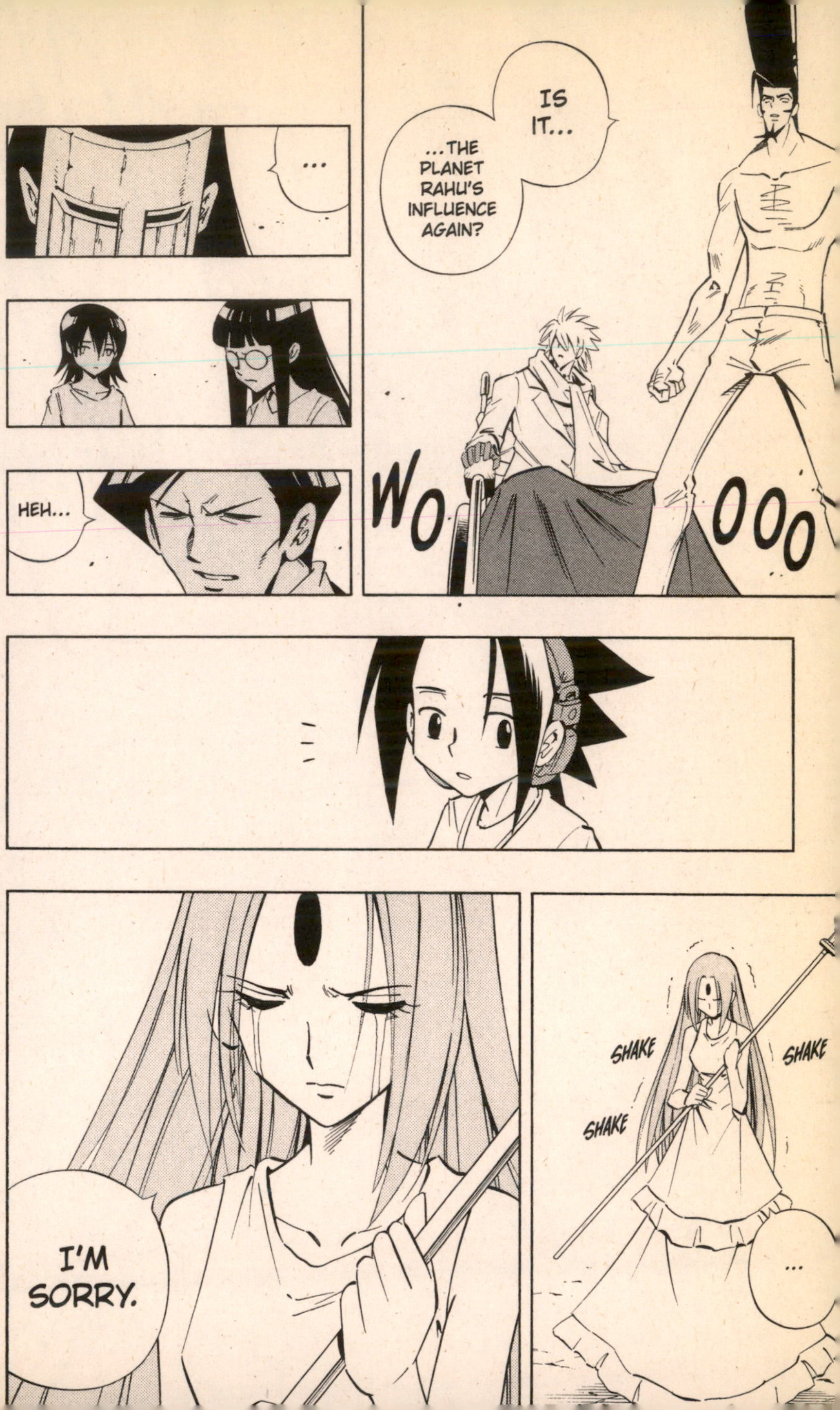
IS IT...
...THE PLANET RAHU'S INFLUENCE AGAIN?
WOOOO
...
HEH...
SHAKE
SHAKE
SHAKE
...
I'M SORRY.

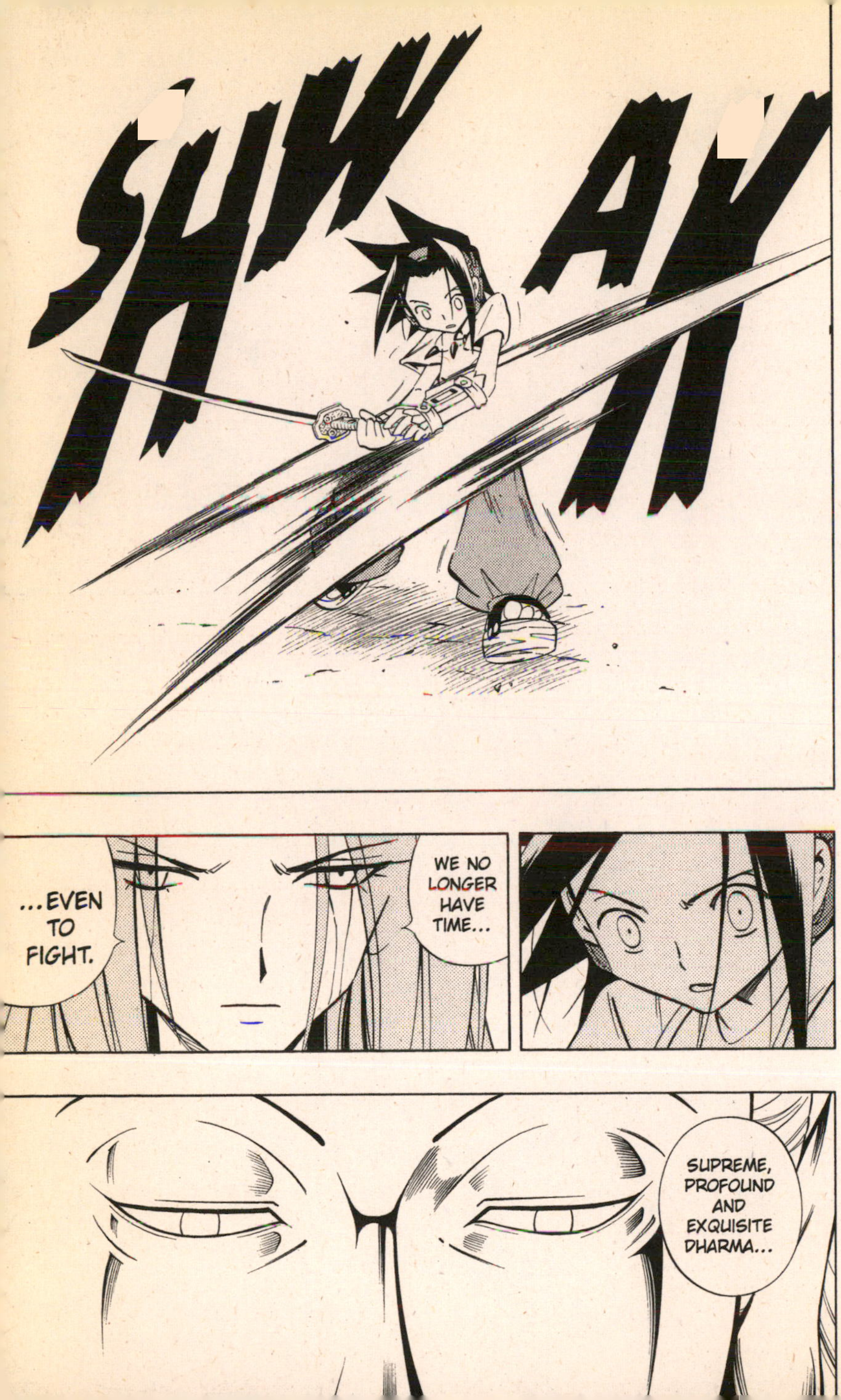
SHWAY
WE NO LONGER HAVE TIME...
...EVEN TO FIGHT.
SUPREME, PROFOUND AND EXQUISITE DHARMA...

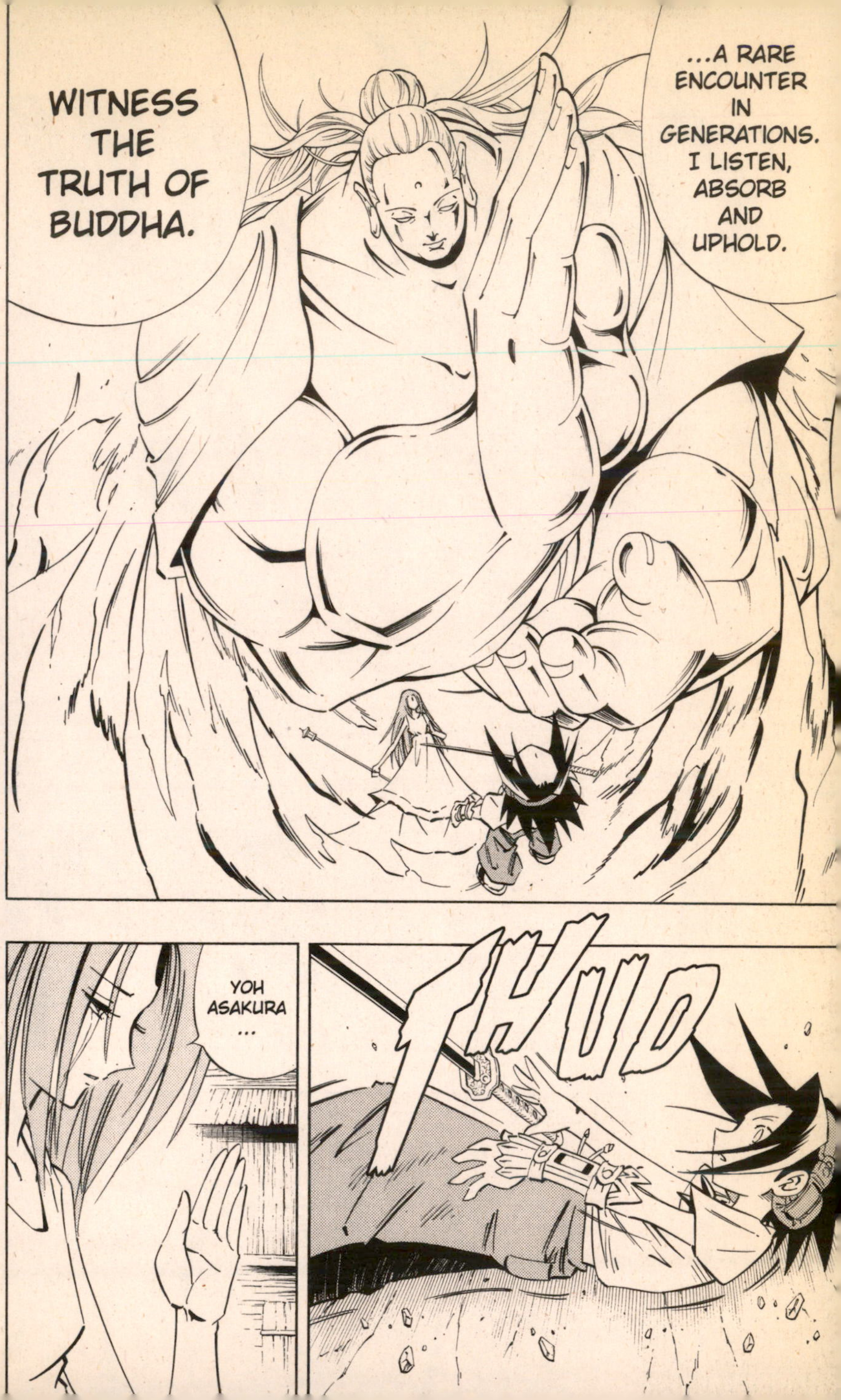
...A RARE ENCOUNTER IN GENERATIONS. I LISTEN, ABSORB AND UPHOLD.
WITNESS THE TRUTH OF BUDDHA.
THUD
YOH ASAKURA ...

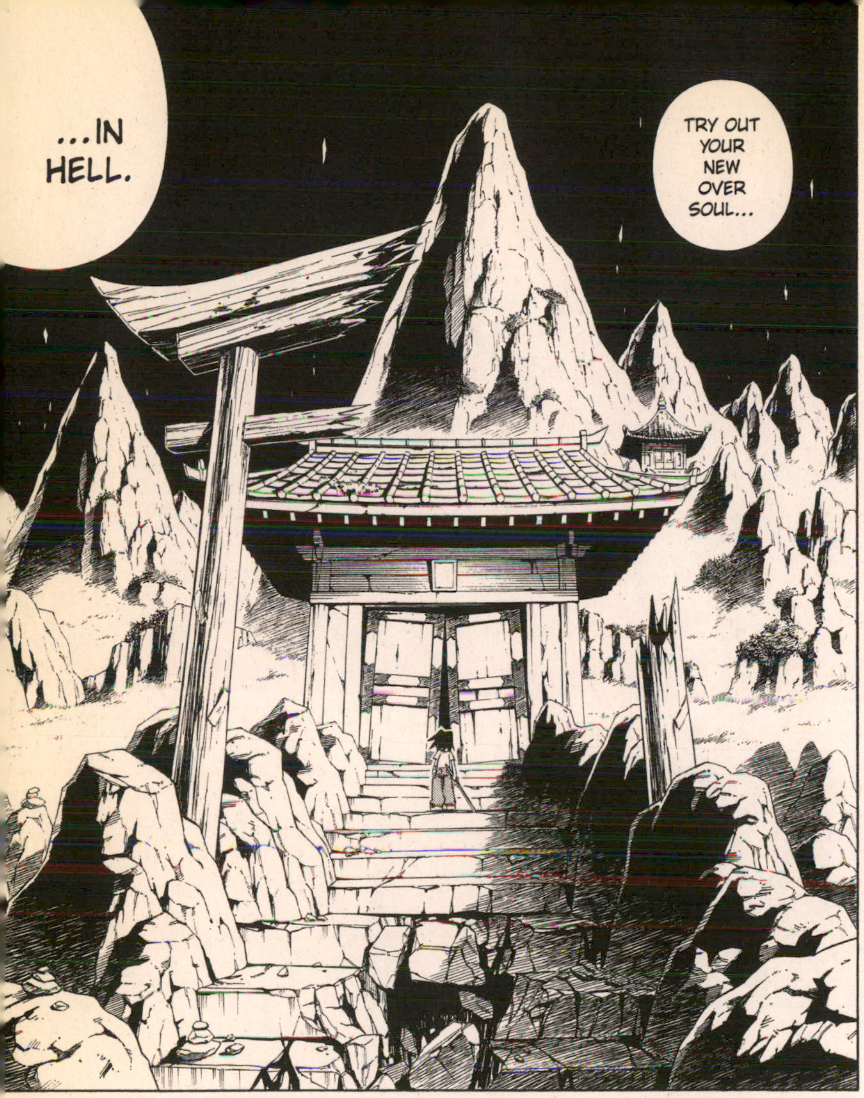
TRY OUT YOUR NEW OVER SOUL...
...IN HELL.

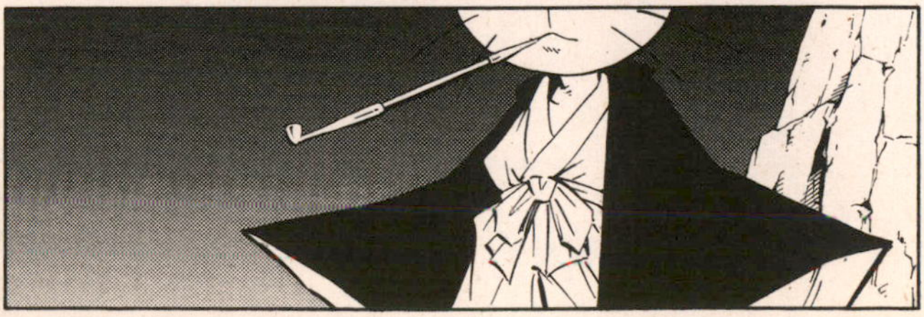

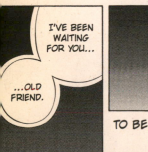

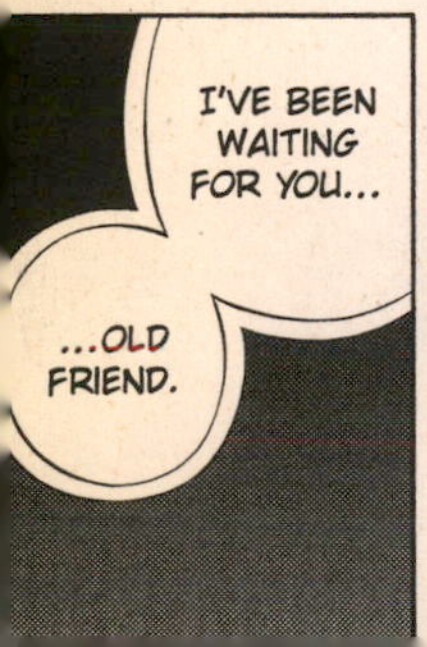
I'VE BEEN WAITING FOR YOU...
...OLD FRIEND.

TO BE CONTINUED!!

SHAMAN KING CHARACTER FILE No.138

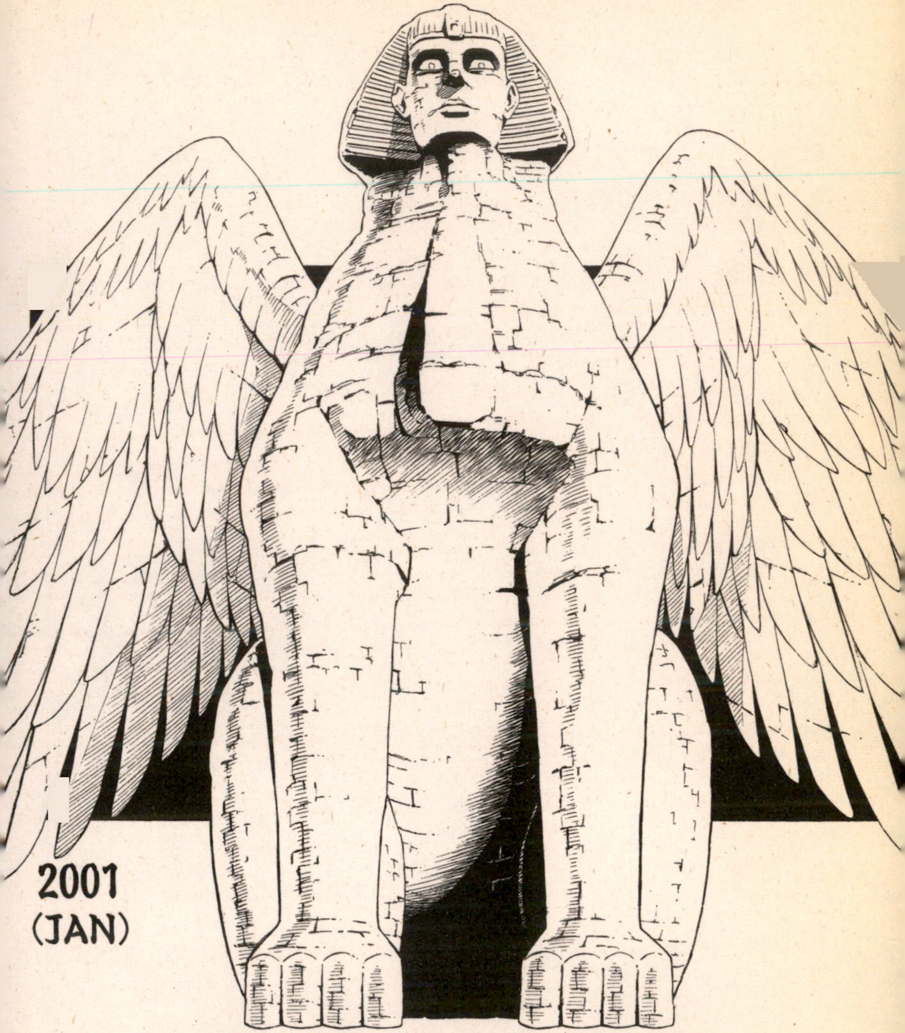

2001
(JAN)

スフィンクス

SPHINX

SHAMAN KING CHARACTER FILE No.139

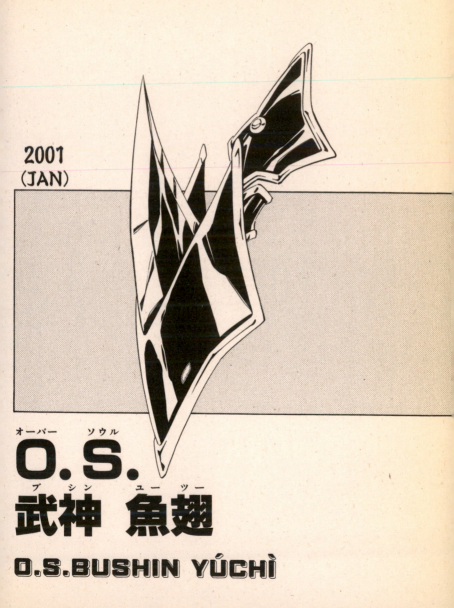

2001
(JAN)

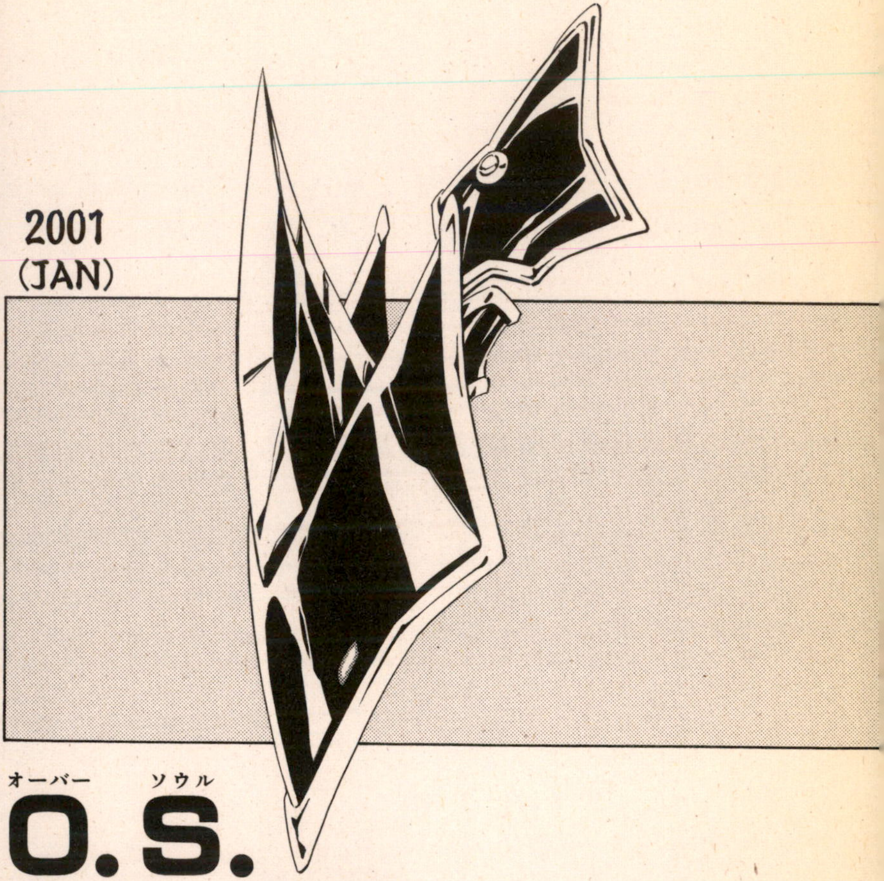

オーバーソウル
O.S.
ブシン ユーツー
武神 魚翅

O.S.BUSHIN YÚCHÌ

SHAMAN KING ITEM FILE No.77

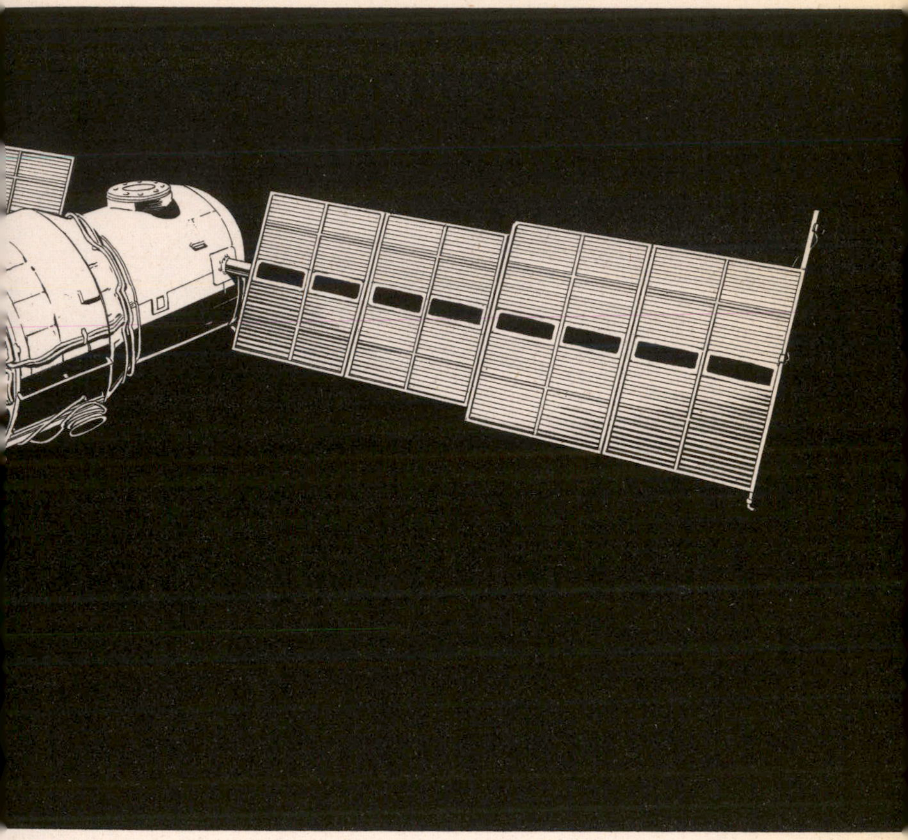

2001
(JAN)

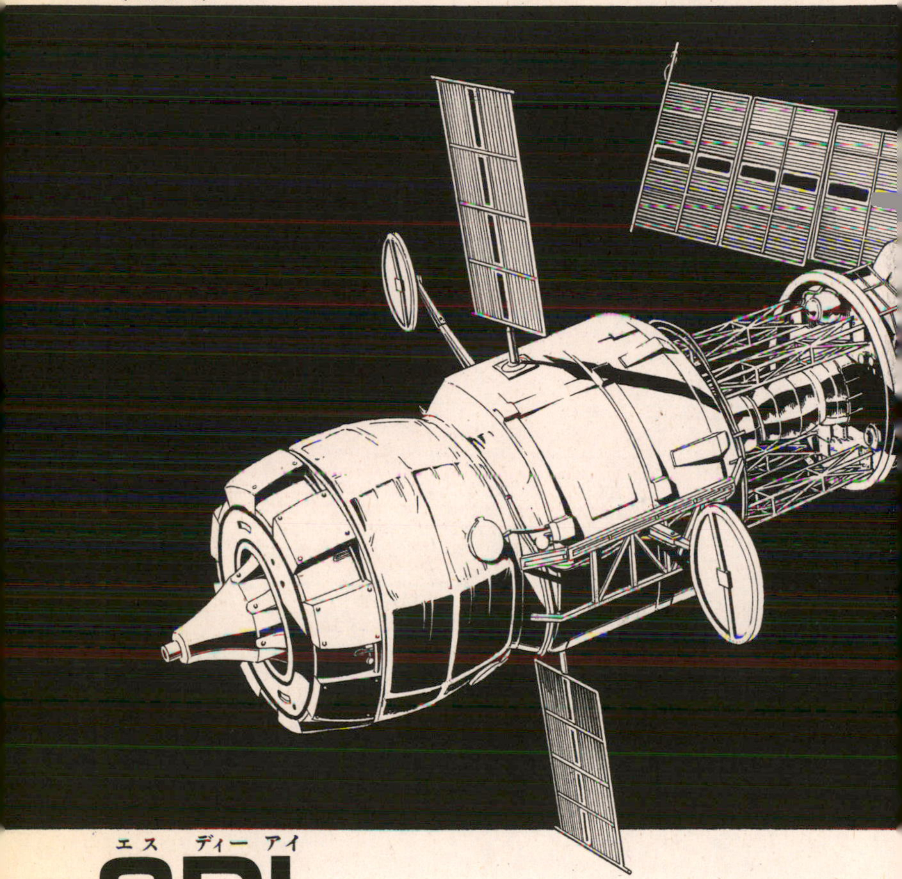

エス ディー アイ
SDI

エックス せん
X線レーザー

SDI X-RAY LASER

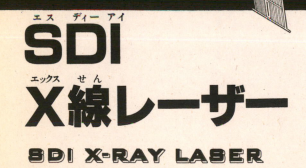

IN THE NEXT VOLUME...

Yoh is stuck in the first round of Hell... a place where murderers are condemned to kill each other for eternity! Armed with his new Over Soul, he faces a battery of opponents driven mad by their circumstances. Yoh quickly discovers that Hell ain't a good place to be.

AVAILABLE MARCH 2010!

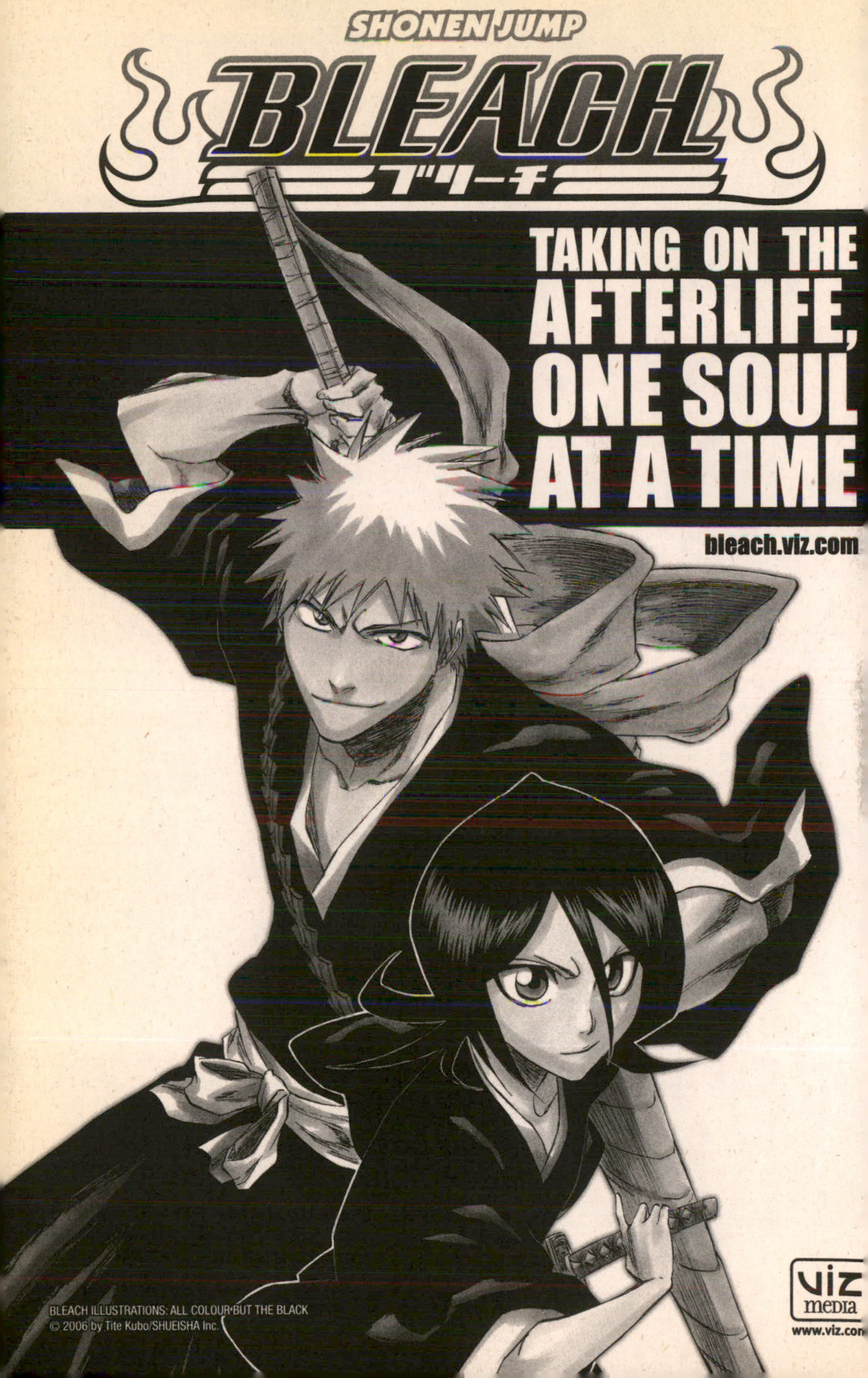
SHONEN JUMP
BLEACH
ブリーチ
TAKING ON THE AFTERLIFE, ONE SOUL AT A TIME
bleach.viz.com
BLEACH ILLUSTRATIONS: ALL COLOUR BUT THE BLACK
© 2006 by Tite Kubo/SHUEISHA Inc.
viz media
www.viz.com

SEE INTO THE SOUL
OF *BLEACH*
WITH THE MANGA, PROFILES, AND ART BOOKS

BLEACH © 2001 by Tite Kubo/SHUEISHA Inc.
BLEACH OFFICIAL CHARACTER BOOK SOULs. © 2005 by Tite Kubo/SHUEISHA Inc.
BLEACH ILLUSTRATIONS: ALL COLOUR BUT THE BLACK © 2006 by Tite Kubo/SHUEISHA Inc.

RATED
T
FOR
TEEN
ratings.viz.com

viz
media

www.viz.com

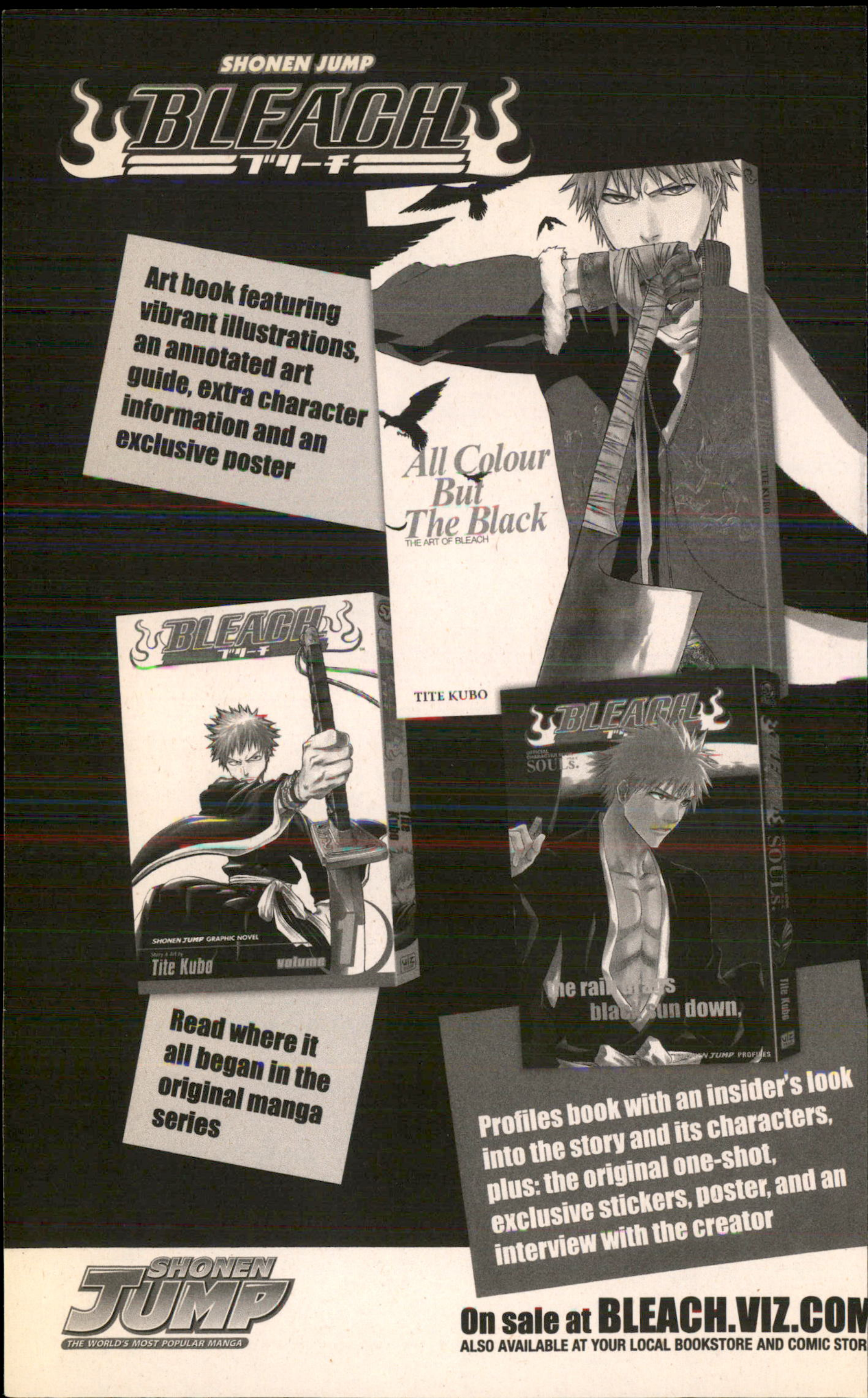

SHONEN JUMP

BLEACH
ブリーチ

Art book featuring vibrant illustrations, an annotated art guide, extra character information and an exclusive poster

All Colour But The Black
THE ART OF BLEACH

TITE KUBO

Read where it all began in the original manga series

SHONEN JUMP GRAPHIC NOVEL
Story & Art by
Tite Kubo
volume

BLEACH
SOULS.

ne rain erases
black sun down.

SHONEN JUMP PROFILES

Tite Kubo

Profiles book with an insider's look into the story and its characters, plus: the original one-shot, exclusive stickers, poster, and an interview with the creator

SHONEN JUMP
THE WORLD'S MOST POPULAR MANGA

On sale at BLEACH.VIZ.COM
ALSO AVAILABLE AT YOUR LOCAL BOOKSTORE AND COMIC STOR

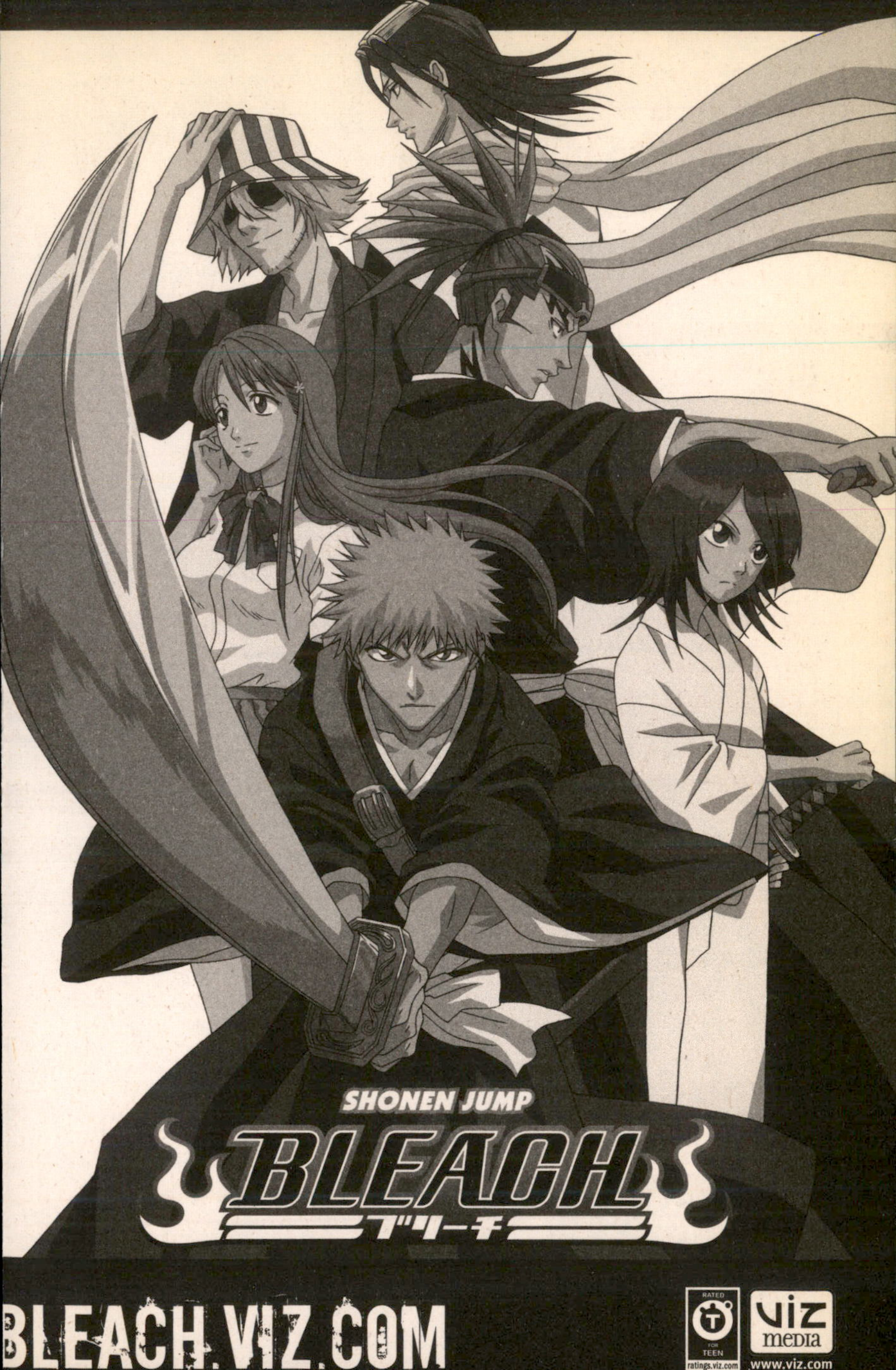
SHONEN JUMP
BLEACH
ブリーチ
BLEACH.VIZ.COM
RATED
T
FOR TEEN
ratings.viz.com
viz media
www.viz.com

JOURNEY TO THE SOUL SOCIETY WITH THE ANIME

GET AN ENTIRE TV SEASON IN ONE COLLECTIBLE DVD BOX SET

ORIGINAL AND UNCUT EPISODES NOW ON DVD

ANIME ALSO AVAILABLE FOR DOWNLOAD FIND OUT MORE AT bleach.viz.com

SHONEN JUMP
BLEACH
MEMORIES OF NOBODY
THE MOVIE

CAN THE SOUL REAPERS SAVE TWO WORLDS FROM TOTAL ANNIHILATION? FIND OUT IN THE FIRST FULL-LENGTH FEATURE FILM!

SHONEN JUMP
HOME VIDEO

© Tite Kubo/Shueisha, TV TOKYO, dentsu, Pierrot
© Tite Kubo/Shueisha, TV TOKYO, dentsu, Pierrot
© Tite Kubo/Shueisha, TV TOKYO, dentsu, Pierrot © BMP 2006

Tell us what you think about SHONEN JUMP manga!

Our survey is now available online.
Go to: www.SHONENJUMP.com/mangasurvey

Help us make our product offering better!

THE REAL ACTION
STARTS IN...

THE WORLD'S MOST POPULAR MANGA
www.shonenjump.com

ADVANCED

BLEACH © 2001 by Tite Kubo/SHUEISHA Inc. NARUTO © 1999 by Masashi Kishimoto/SHUEISHA Inc.
DEATH NOTE © 2003 by Tsugumi Ohba, Takeshi Obata/SHUEISHA Inc. ONE PIECE © 1997 by Eiichiro Oda/SHUEISHA Inc.

SHONEN JUMP
THE WORLD'S MOST POPULAR MANGA

350+

pages of the coolest manga available in the U.S., PLUS anime news, and info on video & card games, toys AND more!

50% OFF the cover price!
That's like getting 6 issues

FREE!

12 HUGE issues for ONLY $29.95*

3 EASY WAYS TO SUBCRIBE
1 Send in a subscription order form
2 Log on to: www.shonenjump.com
3 Call 1-800-541-7919

www.viz.com

* Canada price: $41.95 USD, including GST, HST, and QST. US/CAN orders only. Allow 6-8 weeks for deliver

ONE PIECE © 1997 by Eiichiro Oda/SHUEISHA Inc. BLEACH © 2001 by Tite Kubo/SHUEISHA Inc.
NARUTO © 1999 by Masashi Kishimoto/SHUEISHA Inc.

SAVE 50% OFF
THE COVER PRICE!

IT'S LIKE GETTING 6 ISSUES
FREE!

OVER 350+ PAGES PER ISSUE

SHONEN JUMP
THE WORLD'S MOST POPULAR MANGA

This monthly magazine contains 7 of the coolest manga available in the U.S., PLUS anime news, and info about video & card games, toys AND more!

❏ **I want 12 HUGE issues of SHONEN JUMP for only $29.95*!**

NAME _____

ADDRESS _____

CITY/STATE/ZIP _____

EMAIL ADDRESS _____ DATE OF BIRTH _____

❏ YES, send me via email information, advertising, offers, and promotions related to VIZ Media, SHONEN JUMP, and/or their business partners.

❏ **CHECK ENCLOSED** (payable to SHONEN JUMP)   ❏ **BILL ME LATER**

CREDIT CARD: ❏ **Visa** ❏ **Mastercard**

ACCOUNT NUMBER _____ EXP. DATE _____

SIGNATURE _____

CLIP & MAIL TO:
SHONEN JUMP Subscriptions Service Dept.
P.O. Box 515
Mount Morris, IL 61054-0515

P9GNC1

* Canada price: $41.95 USD, including GST, HST, and QST. US/CAN orders only. Allow 6-8 weeks for delivery.
ONE PIECE © 1997 by Eiichiro Oda/SHUEISHA Inc. BLEACH © 2001 by Tite Kubo/SHUEISHA Inc.
NARUTO © 1999 by Masashi Kishimoto/SHUEISHA Inc.

ratings.viz.com   www.viz.com